Enterprise Architectures
and Digital Administration
Planning, Design and Assessment

Enterprise Architectures
and Digital Administration
Planning, Design and Assessment

Ambrose Goikoetxea

Mondragon University, Euskadi

World Scientific

NEW JERSEY · LONDON · SINGAPORE · BEIJING · SHANGHAI · HONG KONG · TAIPEI · CHENNAI

Published by

World Scientific Publishing Co. Pte. Ltd.

5 Toh Tuck Link, Singapore 596224

USA office: 27 Warren Street, Suite 401-402, Hackensack, NJ 07601

UK office: 57 Shelton Street, Covent Garden, London WC2H 9HE

British Library Cataloguing-in-Publication Data
A catalogue record for this book is available from the British Library.

ENTERPRISE ARCHITECTURES AND DIGITAL ADMINISTRATION
Planning, Design and Assessment

ISBN-13 978-981-270-027-8
ISBN-10 981-270-027-7
ISBN-13 978-981-270-028-5 (pbk)
ISBN-10 981-270-028-5 (pbk)

Printed in Singapore.

To Aloña who shares in my dreams, with love and passion

To my parents, Eusebio and Teresa, who had the courage to go West.

To my sister and brother, Esperanza and Xabier, who shared in the hardships and ecstasy of that long road West.

To my children, Miguel and Charley, who understood I had to write this book and gave me of their patience and encouragement generously.

To my teacher and friend, Lucien Duckstein, who showed me the way.

To our students at Mondragon University who inspire us with their questions, quest for life, and the belief of a Free Euskadi one day.

Acknowledgements

A great deal of effort has gone into the writing of this book over the last five years. I would like to thank the many engineers, computer scientists, and managers at Lockheed Martin, MITRE Corporation, Statcom, CSC, the US IRS organization, US Army Corps of Engineers, and Mondragon University with whom I have had the opportunity to work in many architecture and engineering projects, learning from them, sharing in the planning the harsh realities of schedules and budgets, and the joy of delivering those systems to the customer, sometimes even on a timely basis. Special thanks to my day-to-day colleagues at MITRE Corporation: Charles Hone, Gwendolyn Humphries, Vance Kauzlarich, Mimi Hailegiorghis, Kathy Lum, Carlos Gonzalez, Glenda Hayes, Paula Hagan, Kathie Sowell, John A. Anderson, Terry Boschert, Ann Reedy, Michael J. Schrank, Andy Reho, Dalton Graham, Charles Yokley and many more. Without doubt this book owes greatly to contract folks and EA planners that work in the trenches developing the new Enterprise Architectures in the Federal Sector, including Tim Smith, Walter Bohon, Gene Z. Stakhiv, Julian Chang, Mark Gregory, Michael F. Spiotta, Roger Reider, Rich Smolen, Greg Todd (specially), Glen Milner, Mark St. Jean, Grace Chapa, and so many more who shared their insight with me on the drawing board, in the design reviews, and by the coffee machines. To Lucien Duckstein, my dissertation director at the University of Arizona and friend who gave me the tools, lighted the way, and would pick me up the times I fell down. To students, fellow teachers, and directors at Mondragon University, in particular Osane Lizarralde, Urtzi Markiegi, Jesus Lizarraga, Xabier Elkorobarrutia, Alberto Izaguirre, Iñaki Lakarra, Jose Mari Aizega, Javier Retegui, Juani Igartua, Txema Perez, Xabier

Sagarna, and Javier Mendiluce for the opportunity to work together in the tailoring of these architectures to needs in the small and large corporations that make up the Mondragon Cooperativas Corporation (MCC). Thanks to Arantzazu Viteri for her skills, patience, and care in the formatting of the chapters in this book. Very special thanks to Niklas Lagerblad and Lou Varveris of Telelogic Inc. (www.telelogic.com) for allowing us to feature a special edition of the System Architect (SA) software in CD format, and to Craig Allan of Sparx Systems (www.sparxsystems.com) for allowing us to feature a special edition of the Enterprise Architect (EA) software in CD format in our book for the benefit of our readers and EA builders. Finally, but not last, many thanks to my editor, Steven Patt, for taking this project under his arm, guiding the effort in the shop, for lending his experience and skills, and for believing with me that this book and project could be done.

Preface

This book is about Enterprise Architectures (EA), how to plan them, how to design them, and how to assess their capabilities in a team effort. It also presents a list of the new Technologies of Information and Communication (TICs), their main characteristics, their utilization in Digital Administration, and how they fit within the larger framework of Enterprise Arcuitectures. An Enterprise Architecture is a business-and-engineering data repository and a roadmap, and both are used today by Federal Agencies, organizations in the Department of Defense (DoD), and corporations in the private sector in order to conduct their day-to-day businesses in a timely and cost effective manner.

This book reflects on the contributions of many individuals and organizations in those major EA-user communities and proceeds to highlight some of the steps involved in the planning, design, and assessment of these enterprise architectures. These steps, as we shall see, include the formulation of a statement of vision or mission by the owners of a current architecture that is to be modernized or one to be created, the translation of that statement into a set of system requirements, the development of a set of views or layers of "architectural knowledge" (e.g., a Business Process Architectural View, a Business Systems Architectural View, a Data Architectural View, an Applications Architectural View, and a Technology Architectural View), guidelines for organizational change, the design of sub-systems within those layers, the building of performance capabilities into the overall system, and a set of procedures for the operation and maintenance of such an enterprise architecture.

I wanted to write this book to share skills and experience with my students, the future architects and builders of EAs. The didactic approach and content in this book borrows from the author's own work and experience in several organizations in the last 20 years in the USA,

Europe, and Latin America, while benefiting greatly from the many leading-edge contributions and experiences of dedicated engineers, computer scientists, and program managers in those organizations and countries. The summers of 1979 and 1980 as a NASA-ASEE Research Fellow at the Jet Propulsion Laboratory of the California Institute of Technology (Cal-Tech) allowed me the opportunity to begin to appreciate simplicity and purpose in engineering system design while observing the complexity of resource allocation and funding mechanisms in Government. It was however during my years of tenure with the U.S. Army Corps of Engineers at Ft. Belvoir, Virginia (Resident Scholar, 1980–1985) that concepts in "trade-off analysis" and "cost efficiency" captured my curiosity and became part of my box of tools and way of looking at and evaluating alternative designs on a given project.

The Corps' "incremental approach" to learning from the design, construction, and fielding of a sub-system first, followed by the gathering of lessons learned before proceeding to the next, larger, more complex sub-system also became part of that tool box and mind set. Still, it took a few more years before I began to assess and appreciate the challenges and importance of enginering design and organizational change (OC), one working with the other, as a crucial collaborative effort in the design of large-scale business and engineering systems such as the Strategic Defense Initiative Program, otherwise known as the "Star Wars" program (NAVY-ASEE Research Fellow, Naval Research Laboratory, Washington, D.C., summers of 1988 and 1989). Other work experience also related to ways and means to mitigate risks in the engineering and management of data-centric space programs (NASA-ASEE Research Fellow at the Goddard Space Flight Center, Greenbelt, Maryland).

Later, it was gratifying to be able to translate these real-world experiences into case studies and examples in the classroom and to note that undergraduate and graduate students related well to those examples in terms of their own work and experience (Adjunct Professor, School of Business, George Washington University, 1990–Present; Research Associate Professor, School of Engineering, George Mason University, 1983–1990; and Research Associate Professor, School of Engineering, George Washington University, 1980–1983).

A pattern began to emerge in my approach to learning and doing things. I would be teaching for 4–5 years, next I would go back to industry to design and build systems with a team of people for 4–5 years, again go back to teaching for another 4–5 years, and so forth. At times the cycles could be shorter. From 1997 to 1999 as lead performance engineer in the Global Transportation Network (GTN) program at Lockheed Martin, Manassas, Virginia, I was given the task of putting together the first Capacity and Performance Group in that organization. This task gave me the experience in that often underestimated yet crucial engineering function, capacity and performance engineering, that I would carry with me as I joined the MITRE Corporation in McLean, Virginia in 1999 to work in the planning, design, building, and assessment of large enterprise architectures. As a government designated federally funded research and development center (FFRDC), MITRE has major contractual agreements with many Federal Agencies (Internal Revenue Services (IRS), Home Security Agency, other) and government agencies in the armed services (Air Force, Army, Navy, other) to provide engineering oversight in the modernization of their respective enterprise architectures.

It was during those 5 years at MITRE that I had the opportunity to work with and learn from many EA architects and engineers in the validation and verification (V&V) of EA sistem requirements, the design of sub-systems in the various engineering teams (e.g., business systems team, applications arquitecture team, the infrastructure and technology team, the organizational team (OC), the performance engineering team, and so on), the testing of software code, prototype development, and the testing of the overall system for capacity and performance capabilities. There were many challenges to meet in enterprise architectures to be modernized or created from scratch. I had the opportunity to work with brilliant EA planners and engineers in many of the organizations involved: MITRE Corporation, the Federal Agencies (e.g., Internal Revenue Service, US. Treasury, others), Armed Services (e.g., US Army, US Air Force, others), universities, and the Contractor community (e.g., Computer Sciences Corporation). These were all individuals that not only had formal training in multiple disciplines, years of experience in many projects, and upmost dedication, but were also great communicators. Great communicators, I say it again. Each one would do its homework first, and when their time came they were able to stand in front of a room filled with either 4–6 or 40–60 other profesionals and convey knowledge, insight, and self-assurance. They were able to convey a vision of things to would come with the new enterprise architecture being proposed at the time. Engineering, business processes, and communication. Success of the EA work to be done depends greatly in the ability of planners, engineers, and would-be users of the new architecture to do well these three things.

The Technical Exchange Management (TEM) series at MITRE. While many objetives of the MITRE oversight function were met with each new EA to design and build, many of us felt that there was room for improvement and so, encouraged by management, we designed and produced six one-day conferences in 2003 and 2004. We had carte blanche to propose and address any EA topic and we all had a ball in the process. Soon we had a group of 15–25 EA architects from all the engineering and management departments within MITRE and together we identified areas where EA work (i.e., planning, design, business modeling, testing, performance, EA compliance, other) was involved to identify issues, invite speakers, organize each TEM, and gather comments and lessons learned from each of the speakers, as these papers were presented in an auditorium and broadcasted to 12 MITRE centers in the USA and Europe. With each TEM, comments and lessons learned were communicated to management. Well, success came about much faster than many of us in the organizing committees had anticipated and, as it happened, the change came about torrentially and swiftly. Before the 2003–2004 TEM series had concluded over 8 departments within MITRE were significantly re-organized in terms of engineering and business responsibilities, peoples, skills sets, and corporate commitment to be received. Notably, the business modeling and performance engineering functions that many of us had advocated during those 5 years were promoted to the "top of the list" by management executives. MITRE had changed for the better, for the benefit of the EA community, many of us felt.

From 1994 to 2004 many enterprise architecture efforts had been funded, and while their completion was well underway in several agencies (Government Sector) and corporations (Private Sector) there was increased awareness of the need to assess the value of these large-scale engineering and business efforts. By 2004, "EA value assessment" had become the new thing to do. The Office of Management and Budget (OMB), for example, had began to publish four large volumes of "reference models" to inquire into the business and engineering value of the EAs and to promote the use of indicators to measure such value. The EA community and the taxpayers both felt it was time to find out whether all those millions of taxpayer dollars spent in EA work during the last 10 years were going to produce the goods promised or whether "mid-course" corrective action would have to take place. The mood of the EA community and a nation had begun to change and to reconsider things. I, too, felt it was time for me to go back to academia and share with others this experience.

This time, however, I felt it was time for me to share this engineering and business experience in EA work with folks in the "old country", Euskadi, the Basque Country. So I joined the Computer Sciences Department at the Mondragon University in February 2004. In the USA we had learned to do EAs and soon enough digital and Web-based services would be all over the landscape. And what about Europe? Are towns, cities, and countries in Europe also experiencing this interest in enterprise architectures and digital services, and if so where, how, who is paying the bills, and are the taxpayers getting the goods? Over the next 5 years I hope to find out and share my answers to this questions.

Acronyms

ACC	Architecture Coordination Council
ADM	Architectural Development Method
ADL	Architectural Development Languages
ADS	Architecture Description Standards
AMC	Army Materiel Command
API	Application Program Interface
AQT	Acceptance Quality Testing
AWG	Architecture Working Group
BR	Business rules
BRM	Business Reference Model
CALRE	Council of Legislative Regions in the European Union
CCA	Clinger-Cohen Act
C4ISR	Command, Control, Communications, Computers, Intelligence, Surveillance, and Reconnaisance
CIO	Chief Information Officer
CJCS	Chairman Joint Chiefs of Staff
COE	Common Operating Environment
CORBA	Common Object Request Broker Architecture
COTS	Customer off-the-shelf
CPIC	Capital Planning and Investment Control Process
CRM	Customer Relationship Management
CI	Configuration Item
CINC	Commander in Chief
CIOC	Chief Information Officer Council
CEO	Chief Executive Officer
CIO	Chief Information Officer
CRM	Customer Relationship Management
CPE	Current Processing Environment

CPU	Central Processing Unit
DA	Digital Administration
DB	Data Base
DBMS	Database Management System
DDL	Data Definition Language
DISA	Defense Information Systrems Agency
DR	Disaster Recovery
DRM	Data and Information Reference Model
DOD	Department of Defense
EA	Enterprise Architecture
EAF	Enterprise Architecture Framework
EAMM	Enterprise Architecture Maturity Model
EAP	Enterprise Architecture Planning
EPCM	Enterprise-wide Performance and Capacity Engineering Model
ESM	Analysis Management
FFRDC	Federally Funded Research and Development Center
FPI	*Formacion Profesional Integral*
GAO	General Accounting Office
GCCS	Global Command and Control System
GCSS	Global Combat Support System
GERAM	Generalized Enterprise Reference Architecture and Methodology
HCI	Human Computer Interface
IBM	International Business Machines
ICT	Information and Communication Technology
IEA	Institute for Enterprise Architectures
IAF	Integrated Architecture Framework
IFIP	International Federation for Information Processing
I&RTS	Integration and Runtime Specification
I/O	Input/Output
IROR	Internal Rate of Return
ISO	International Standards Organization
ISSP	Information Systems Strategic Plan
IEEE	Institute of Electrical and Electronic Engineers
JCS	Joint Chiefs of Staff

LAN	Local Area Network
MCC	Mondragon Cooperativa Corporacion
MCDM	Multiple Criteria Decision Making
MIPS	Millions of instructions per second
NPV	Net Present Value
OC	Organizational Change
ODP	Open Distributed Processing
OMB	Office of Management and Budget, USA
OMG	Open Management Group
P&C	Performance and Capacity
PMO	Program Management Office
PRM	Performance Reference Model
RAM	Random Access Memory
RFP	Request for Proposal
RM-ODP	Reference Model for Open Distributed Processing
ROM	
EPO	Recovery Point Objective
RTO	Recovery Time Objective
SAT	System Acceptance Testing
SENA	*Servicio Nacional de Aprendizaje*
SEO	Systems Engineering Office
SIB	Standards Information Base
SPRI	Sociedad para la Promocion y Renovación Industrial
SIPRNET	Secret Internet Protocol Router Network
SIT	System Integration Testing
SQL	Sequential Query Language
SRM	Service Reference Model
SYR	System Requirements
TAFIM	Technical Architecture Framework for Information Management
TCP/IP	Transport Control Protocol/Internet Protocol
TIC	Technologies of Information and Communication
TOGAF	The Open Group Architectural Framework
TOR	**Terms of Reference**
TRM	Technical Reference Model
UML	Unified Modelling Language
USTRANSCOM	US Transportation Command
WAN	Wide Area Network

Contents

Chapter 1

Introduction

1.1. A New Era of Enterprise Architecture (EA) Planning

The decade and era of Enterprise Architectures (EA) is just beginning and already architects and engineers in industry and business sectors, Department of Defense (DoD) and the Federal Agencies are becoming painfully aware of the variety and magnitude of challenges in the design and assessment of these architectures. Enterprise architectures are characterized by large-scale, legacy-rich, business-process-driven, organizationally intensive, and geographically distributed systems that must meet a vast array of functional and performance requirements while observing significant build time and funding constraints. The problem is often exacerbated by the existence of multiple legacy sub-systems that perform critical functions on a round-the-clock, continuous basis (i.e., 24x7) and cannot be simply "turned off" and replaced with new architecture components weeks or months later. Also, in the last 3–5 years the General Accounting Office (GAO), the Office of Management and Budget (OMB) and other overseeing organizations are providing recommendations and guidelines for the use of business processes, business systems, and system performance measurements that must be identified and defined at the outset of the design effort. Some existing EA frameworks, although rich in text and graphical representation, lack in formal representation, with little or no theoretical basis, thus potentially limiting their applicability and usefulness across domains.

Business, industry, and government publications show a clear and marked trend towards both business and technical solutions that address the entire enterprise, not just a part of it. In fact, these business process and business systems drive these architecture design efforts, it is now recognized. The Internal Revenue Services (IRS), US Customs, Virginia's Veterans' Affairs and other Federal and state agencies are currently involved in enterprise-level architecture planning, design, and implementation efforts. There are a myriad of challenges to the tasks of defining, designing, and assessing architectures:

- Architectures of large-scale systems are often functionally complex, their design evolves over long time frames (years), and are difficult to assess due to changing requirements, complex business processes, large number of distributed systems, emerging new technologies and business paradigms.
- It is not crystal-clear today how to best proceed with the identification, representation, and measurement of critical EA components, including business processes, business systems, data model, and infrastructure.
- A major challenge facing the design and assessment of architectures of very-large systems today is the gathering and documentation of architectural concepts across multiple domains, the limited availability of modeling and simulation tools, as well as the presentation and publication of agreed-upon design principles in the enterprise architecture community.
- Business process models (e.g., boxes and arrows), component/COTS evaluation frameworks (e.g., checklists), business systems models (e.g., hierarchical trees), etc. all use different structural representations. Presentations, workshops, and inter-team participation then essentially provide a "unifying model" that generally is able to combine value across of those structurally different models.

1.2. What is an Enterprise Architecture?

An Enterprise Architecture (EA) is a set of business and engineering artifacts, including text and graphical documentation, that describes and guide the operation of an enterprise-wide system, including instructions for its life cycle operation, management, evolution, and maintenance. Specific content of these artifacts can include a vision or mission statement, a set of system requirements, a Business Process Architectural View, a Business Systems Architectural View, a Data

Architectural View, an Applications Architectural View, and a Technology Architectural View.

1.3. What is an Enterprise Architecture Framework?

An Enterprise Architecture (EA) framework is a business and engineering recipe (i.e., a blueprint, a set of instructions, a specification) for the construction of an Enterprise Architecture (EA).

Although this field is still evolving, there are already a number of definitions of EA in the published literature. "...there are three architectures: a data architecture, an applications architecture, and a technology architecture. Architectures in this context are like blueprints, drawings, or models ...", Spewak (1992). "An enterprise ... as a business association, consisting of a recognized set of interacting business functions, able to operate as an independent, stand-alone entity. There are enterprises within enterprises. For instance, a business unit within the overall corporate entity may be considered an enterprise as long as it could be operated independently..." T. Finneran (2001). The Catalyst methodology of Computer Sciences Corporation (CSC 2005) proposes eight model views to build EAs: a Business Model View, a System Engineering Model View, a Business Process Model View, an Organization Model View, a Location Model View, an Application Model View, a Data Model View, and a Technology Model View. Still earlier Zachman (1987) is among the pioneers of EA work who has described the EA framework as a "simple, logical structure of descriptive representations for identifying models that are the basis for designing the enterprise and for building the enterprise's systems".

In Circular A-130, the Office of Management and Budget (OMB) has defined an EA as "the explicit description and documentation of the current and desired relationships among business and management processes and information technology. It describes the 'current architecture' and 'target architecture' to include the rules and standards and systems life cycle information to optimize and maintain the environment which the agency wishes to create and maintain by managing its IT portfolio..." In the creation of an EA, Circular A-130 adds, agencies must identify and document:

(i) Business Processes - Agencies must identify the work performed to support its mission, vision and performance goals. Agencies must also document change agents, such as legislation or new technologies that will drive changes in the EA.

(ii) Information Flow and Relationships - Agencies must analyze the information utilized by the agency in its business processes, identifying the information used and the movement of the information. These information flows indicate where the information is needed and how the information is shared to support mission functions.

(iii) Applications - Agencies must identify, define, and organize the activities that capture, manipulate, and manage the business information to support business processes. The EA also describes the logical dependencies and relationships among business activities.

(iv) Data Descriptions and Relationships - Agencies must identify how data is created, maintained, accessed, and used. At a high level, agencies must define the data and describe the relationships among data elements used in the agency's information systems.

(v) Technology Infrastructure - Agencies must describe and identify the functional characteristics, capabilities, and interconnections of the hardware, software, and telecommunications.

Essentially, then, Circular A-130 requires five views or collections of definitions and component relationships in the creation of EAs and their documentation.

1.4. What is EA Planning?

Enterprise Architecture Planning (EAP) is the set of business and engineering methods, procedures, and activities that are applied to an Enterprise Architecture Framework for purposes of translating a "vision and strategy" into a set of system requirements and a set of architectural views leading to the construction, operation, and maintenance of an Enterprise Architecture (EA).

1.5. Who is Doing EA Planning Today?

Many organizations in business, industry, and government are pursuing enterprise information architecture (EA) planning, design, and implementation activities today while several universities are already conducting related research and incorporating EA courses in their undergraduate and graduate programs:

Government Organizations and Corporations:

- Office of Management and Budget (OMB)
- U.S. Customs
- Internal Revenue Services (IRS)
- U.S. Army Corps of Engineers
- Department of Veterans Affairs (VA),
  www.fcw.com/fcw/articles/2002/0610/mgt-va-06-10-02.asp
- The MITRE Corporation

Universities:

- California State University at Los Angeles
- The George Washington University
- Universidad Autonoma of Mexico City (UNAM)
- University of Mondragón, Euskadi
- University of the Basque Country (UPV), Euskadi

Conferences:

- Enterprise Architecture in Federal Government (Telelogic Inc. foremerly Popkin Inc.), www.telelogic.com
- Enterprise Architecture Conference (EAC), www.government.popkin.com/events/events.htm

1.6. Why Organizations Are Doing EA Planning?

Economic efficiency in the implementation of business processes and systems is one reason Federal agencies are building enterprise information architectures. The Department of Veterans Affairs (VA), for example, has been actively involved in EA planning. "One of VA's most essential yet challenging undertakings has been developing and implementing an enterprise architecture to guide the department's IT efforts. An enterprise architecture – a blueprint for systematically and completely defining an organization's current (baseline) operational and technology environment and a roadmap toward the desired (target) state – is an essential tool for effectively and efficiently engineering business processes and implementing their supporting systems and helping them evolve. Office of Management and Budget (OBM) guidelines (OBM Circular A-130) require VA and other federal agencies to develop and implement enterprise architectures to provide a framework or maintaining existing and planned IT" (GAO-02-703, June 2002).

1.7. The Zachman Architectural Framework

The notion of looking at an architecture from several vantage points has been in the literature for a number of years already, but it was Zachman (1987) who probably best succeeded in conveying that notion with his concept and graphical representation of multiple views, as depicted on Figure 1.

The seven columns in this matrix organize architecture information into the categories of Data, Function, Network, People, Time, and Motivation. The five rows in this matrix organize architecture information into the categories of Planners's View, Owner's View, Designer's View, Bulder's View, and Subcontractor's View.

1.8. Multiple Architectural Views

As stated earlier, Spewak (1992) proposes three architectural views, while Zachman (1987) proposes 7 categories of data, and the CSC Catalyst methodology for the enterprise life cycle (ELC 2005) makes use of 8 architectural views. My own work and experience in EA planning, design, implementation, assessment, and deployment, coupled with the insight reported in those three earlier works, leads me to propose the use of these five *architectural views*:

- Business Process Architectural View
- Business Systems Architectural View
- Data Architectural View
- Applications Architectural View
- Technologies Architectural View

In my opinion, these five architectural views allow for adequate and sufficient variety of architectural representation (i.e., business processes, business systems, data model, etc.), a manageable set of business and engineering activities by the EA owners and team of contractors, cost efficiency in the application of guiding business and engineering design principles to multiple EA projects, and the potential for realistic EA completion, testing, and deployment over a 3–5 year time frame. The reader is reminded, however, to become familiar with each set of views prescribed by a customer, e.g., an Agency, Department of Defense (DoD) organization, or corporation.

1.9. Objectives of this Book

Specific objective of this book are as follows:

- To define an Enterprise Architecture (EA) in terms of its basic components, their interrelationships, an initial vision that will guide the articulation of a set of requirements, a set of business processes, and a set of engineering instructions for the implementation of these components into a working architecture in a production environment;
- To identify and briefly describe major Enterprise Architecture Frameworks in the Federal Agencies, Department of Defense, and the private sector;
- To add structure and mathematical rigor to the engineering phases of Enterprise Architecture representation, planning, design, and measurement;
- To identify and select a "central core" of Enterprise Architecture components, to develop a set of concepts and basis for interrelationships among these components (EA Representation), and to develop a set of Metrics that cut across multiple architectural views that can be used to conduct Attribute Tradeoff Analysis (EA Measurement);
- To provide step-by-step procedures in the construction of the five proposed architectural views: Business Process Architectural View, Business Systems Architectural View, Data Architectural View, Applications Architectural View, and Technologies Infrastructure Architectural View;

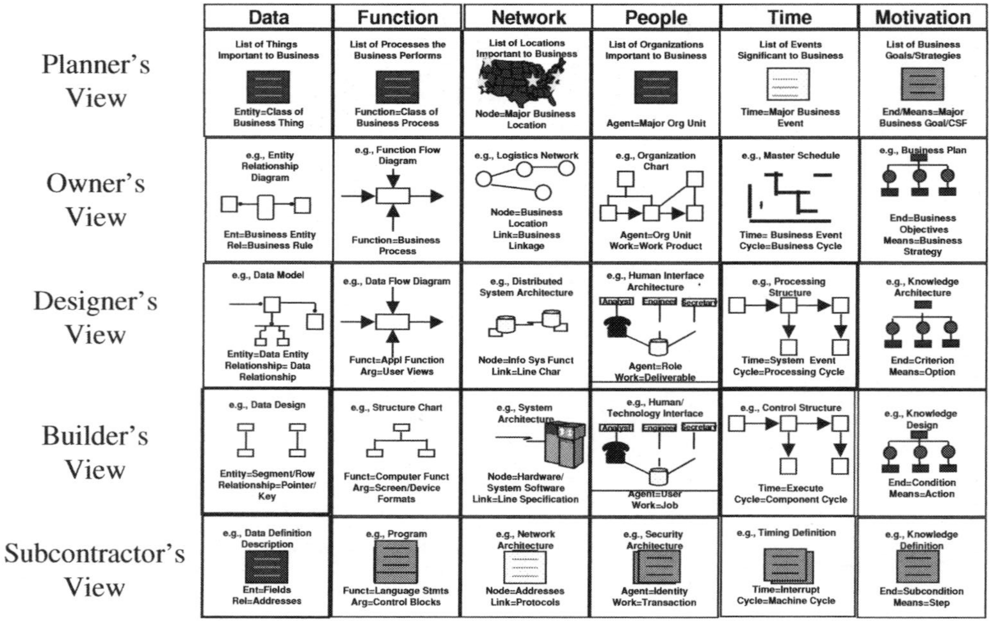

Figure 1. Zachman's Matrix of Architectural Views (Zachman 1987)

- To encourage and promote the creation and adoption of EA-related courses, training programs, and workshops in colleges and universities, both undergraduate and graduate programs; and
- To make these concepts and procedures available to business modelers, architecture designers, engineers, architecture owners, and designers of EA toolsets in the vendor community to help expedite the many activities involved in the design of modern, web-based enterprise information architectures.

1.10. EA Vision and Concept

How does an organization go about the business of modernizing its enterprise architecture? Is a "vision" or plan truly needed to gather the many resources required and the many activities that will be carried out in the months and possibly years that it takes to build an enterprise architecture? And should the "vision provider" be the owner of the future enterprise architecture, or can it be made up of consortium, a group if you will of enterprise owners, architects, engineers, decision makers? Well, yes, it makes both business and engineering sense to begin with an idea, vision, or high-level plan that lists the 5-10 major attributes of the future architecture, including a desire to modify and improve existing business practices in the current organization, to bring in and adopt new technologies, to increase market penetration, and to possibly re-structure the human side of the existing architecture through changes in its decision-making processes, its organizational structure, and the geographical distribution of components of the new enterprise architecture across departments, divisions, service centers, geographical regions, if applicable.

1.11. EA Representation

By EA representation I mean the application and use of concepts, notation, methods, step-by-step procedures, and tools already developed and available in several areas of discipline, including business, engineering, economics, and decision making. Already there are in the market today very fine works that address the basics of enterprise architecture planning (Spewak 1992, Zachman 1987). These works, however, although rich in text that describes those concepts and step-by-step procedures, they lack design detail and the mathematical representation that offer the potential for uncovering and capturing additional insight into the development of business processes, business systems, the adoption of new technologies, and the trade-offs involved, in my opinion.

1.12. EA Design Teams and Work Products

Once the vision or plan has been formulated, the architectural effort can proceed to the creation of the various *business and engineering teams* that will be responsible for the implementation of that vision into a set of *work products*. Generally, an enterprise engineering organization will be made up several teams:

- Business Processes Team
- Business Systems Team
- Enterprise Standards Team
- Data Model Team
- Systems Engineering Team
- Infrastructure team

The Business Processes Team is responsible for translating the Vision and Strategy document (i.e., work product) into a set of business processes that describe the day-to-day business of the enterprise, e.g., preparing and submitting an order electronically to a vendor to replenish an inventory item, gathering information on the demographics of a particular region to support marketing goals, and applying payments to a customer account in the enterprise database; typically, there may be 100–200 business processes and each one will be represented in text form with 2–3 flowcharts that show the decomposition of a business process into 4–6 *business activities*. A Business Process Team is often made up of 4–8 people and their business modeling activity will produce the Business Processes Work Product.

In turn, the *Business Systems Team* will receive the Business Processes work product and use it as a basis to modify and extend the existing set of logical business systems into the new set of logical enterprise business systems. These business systems will provide the business services needed by the various business processes, so that typically one business process will require business services provided by several business systems in a one-to-may working relationship; for example, the business process "Apply payment to customer account in the database" will require the existence and application of the business services "Receive electronic payment", "Authenticate sender of payment against existing database account", "Apply payment against account balance", "Update database account", and "Send receipt to customer via FAX". Again, the Business Systems Team will often be made up of 3–6 individuals with basic skills in business modeling, systems engineering, network services, and possibly database design. This is a particularly difficult and challenging endeavor as the members of this team must not only create a long list of appropriate business systems that will enable the enterprise architecture to carry out the many business processes already identified, and do so with a desired set of existing and new business and engineering frameworks, i.e., web-based processing if called for in the Vision and Strategy document, a relational or object-oriented database management system, encryption of messaging, other options. The work product of this team is a list of 200–300 business systems complete with business definitions, their representation in *a business system hierarchical tree* with appropriate interface definition and content. A substantial undertaking, indeed.

1.13. EA Measurement

How do the owner of the enterprise (i.e., the Customer) and the builder of the enterprise (i.e., the Contractor) know that the design and building of the enterprise architecture is progressing in effective and efficient ways? Measurement and assessment are essential. One way is to have each of the work products that document the evolution of the EA undergo a review and assessment process. Essential to this measurement process are two things: (a) scale of measurement, and (b) measurement criteria.

Nominal Scale: This is the most basic scale of measurement and it is used to differentiate one thing or object from another, e.g., personal names such Peter, Helen, or Iñaki; telephone numbers; architectural components such as portal, web server, and database; etc.

Ordinal Scale: This scale can be used to convey the relative merit, importance, or preference of one object (e.g., attribute, objective, plan, component) over another object. There is no meaningful numerical value assigned to the various objects being measured according to this scale.

Accordingly, we may opt for a scale that reads "Very Poor", "Poor", "Fair", "Good", "Very Good" and "Excellent" to assess the reliability of a Web server, for example. When using this scale with regards to the attribute RELIABILITY we can only say that server brand A with an assessment of "Very Good" is preferred to server brand B with an assessment of "Good", but we cannot say by how much. The intensity of preferences cannot be quantified in ordinal scales.

Ranking of objects also makes use of ordinal scales. A method can be said to rank-order a set of architectures or architectural components:

Architecture	A	D	C	B
Evaluation	Very Good	Good	Poor	Very Poor
Ranking	1	2	3	4

So that Architecture A is preferred to Architecture D, Architecture D is preferred to Architecture C, and so on. In this manner one would also say that "Architecture A out-ranks Architecture D", "Architecture D out-ranks Architecture B" and so on.

Cardinal Scale: This scale assigns numerical values to the objects being measured so that addition, subtraction, and multiplication are meaningful operations. Differences between values, for example, convey precise meaning about the intensity of a preference. Assignment of weights to attributes by a planner or decision maker is often performed on a cardinal scale, and the meaning of this scale should be communicated to the decision maker. Furthermore, cardinal scales can be of two types: *Interval* and *Ratio* scales.

Interval scale: This scale has an arbitrary "zero point" or reference point to allow addition, subtraction, and multiplication by a constant to yield meaningful results. The planner may want to use a scale for attribute weight assessment with values from 0 to 10, for example, but other ranges also apply:

Attribute	Weight
Reliability	8
Interoperability	6
License Terms	10
Standards Compliance	3
Performance	5
Security	5
Cost	6

In this example the planner INTEROPERABILITY was assigned a weight value of 6 and STANDARDS COMPLIANCE was assigned a weight value of 3. Thus, in this case the planner perceived the attribute INTEROPERABILITY to be twice as important as attribute STANDARDS COMPLIANCE and assigned weight values accordingly. The Celsius temperature scale is another example where the "zero point" was arbitrarily but conveniently taken to be the freezing point of water.

Ratio scale: This scale requires the adoption of a non-arbitrary "zero point". The Kelvin temperature scale is a good example of a scale with a non-arbitrary, absolute zero point, 0.0 degrees Kelvin. In fact, the lowest temperature that could be measured is 0.0 degrees Kelvin. Ratios of individual scale values have true meaning:

Architecture	A	B	C	D
Performance (Queries/Second)	15	8	10	20

We note that if the ratio scale for measurement is applied to the attribute PERFORMANCE (queries/second), then for D/C the ratio 20/10 = 2.0 means that "20" is to be 2.0 times as large as "10". Questions in a survey or questionnaire also generally make use of a ratio scale. Ratio scales, therefore, are said to be ratio-preserving scales with a non-arbitrary anchor point of zero.

1.14. Multiple Criteria

So once a determination is made about the type of measurement scale to use in EA assessment, how does one choose attributes (i.e., criteria, factors, dimensions) for EA assessment? By now the EA community has accumulated experience on categories of criteria and questions to ask in the assessment of alternative architectures as presented in Chapter 16, EA Evaluation and Assessment.

1.15. How this Book is Organized

The contents of this book are organized into 20 Chapters, 2 Appendices, and 1 CD-ROM as depicted in Figure 2.

- *Chapter 1, Introduction*: This chapter presents definitions for an Enterprise Architecture (EA), Enterprise Architecture Planning (EAP), gives credit to and brings to the attention of the reader earlier work by J. Zachman, S.H. Spewak, the Computer Sciences Corporation (Catalyst methodology), and MITRE Corporation, addresses the need for EA Vision and Strategy, and presents one list of criteria for architecture assessment.
- *Chapter 2, Motivation and Impetus for Enterprise Architectures:* This chapter discusses de origins of EAs in the Department of Defense (DoD) and its symbiotic relationship with agencies in the Government Sector and corporations in the Private Sector.
- *Chapter 3, The Business Process Architectural View*: It introduces the reader to the sequence of concepts and planning activities leading to the creation of a set of business processes and activities that reflect the vision of the owners of the enterprise architecture.
- *Chapter 4, The Business Systems Architectural View*: It guides the reader through the definition of the business systems and business services that are needed to implement and support each of the business processes and activities listed in Chapter 3.
- *Chapter 5, The Data Architectural View*: This chapter addresses data flows across components of the enterprise architecture, their storage, retrieval, and management within a data model and database management system (DBMS).
- *Chapter 6, The Applications Architectural View*: It introduces the reader to the basics of a software application architecture that houses the various categories of software components that implement the business services listed in Chapter 4. Applications reside within logical business systems and make possible the business services needed to carry out the business processes of the enterprise.
- *Chapter 7, The Unified Modeling Language in EA Design:* Software development is a crucial necessity in the process of planning, designing, and building enterprise architectures. This chapter discusses salient features of the Unified Modeling Language (UML), its use in the representation of the software design (Applications Architectural View), and essential role in the effective communication among the various design teams that must work together to make the EA happen. Use Case Diagrams,

Activity Diagrams, Diagram of Classes, and Sequence Diagrams are produced by the Enterprise Architect UML tool (by Sparx Systems) to illustrate the use of UML in EA design.

- *Chapter 8, The Technology Architectural View*: It discusses salient features of the hardware components that will house the applications. Salient hardware components include web-based portals, web application servers, security firewalls, transaction processors, database management systems, data warehouses, and tools for system management and decision support.
- *Chapter 9, Distributed Database Design with Multiple Criteria:* Enterprise architectures are data intensive by nature and design. In this chapter I review the pros and cons of multiple, geographically distributed small data stores versus a single data store; selection of data elements across multiple databases; strategies and rationale for database segmentation; and multiple criteria optimization techniques in distributed database planning and design.
- *Chapter 10, System Capacity and Performance:* This chapter highlights the importance of the enterprise architecture meeting both the functional and non-functional (i.e., performance) requirements. Organizations are learning the hard way the importance of having a system capacity and performance plan early in the EA program.
- *Chapter 11, Disaster Recovery Strategies in EA:* This chapter reflect s on real-life experience in the planning, design, and assessment of the disaster recovery (DR) component of EAs today (e.g., Air Force's Global Transportation System, IRS Modernization, US Customs, other). DR capability is "a must" in EA work, both from an economic and functional standpoint – Federal and DoD EA are mandated to have DR capability.
- *Chapter 12, An Overview of the TOGAF Architecture:* This chapter presents basic principles and main development elements of the Open Group's Architectural Framework (TOGAF), including the Standards Information Base (SIB), Technical Reference Model (TRF), and the steps in the Architectural Development Method (ADM). An example of a manufacturer and distributor of confection goods is borrowed (Perks and Beveridge 2003) to illustrate each of the seven phases of ADM.

- *Chapter 13, An Overview of the C4ISR (DoD) Architecture:* A large body of organizations in the Department of Defense (Dod) have developed principles, guidelines, data repositories, and Web sites for EA planning, design, building, and application in mission-critical environments. This chapter presents highlights of selected EA resources in DoD and their representation and management in highly useful tools such as System Architect (by Telelogic Inc.). Lessons learned on how to save time and money following successful strategies while avoiding costly pitfalls when meeting C4ISR requirements.

- *Chapter 14, The SENA Enterprise Architecture:* This chapter presents an illustrative example in the design of an enterprise architecture for the *Servicio Nacional de Aprendizaje* (SENA) in Bogotá, Colombia, made up of 114 vocational centers distributed throughout this county. Beginning with a set of system requirements, the design is detailed across the 5 architectural views.

- *Chapter 15, Multiple Criteria for EA Selection and Tailoring:* A variety of Enterprise Architecture (EA) frameworks are emerging today in response to an array of needs in organizations in the Federal Agency, Department of Defense (DoD), and the Private Sector. These needs reflect a rich mosaic of institutional settings, congressional mandates, capital availability for public investment, timeframe, complexity of business processes involve, system processing and performance requirements, stakeholders composition, and system release strategies, to mention a few. To a significant extent, the decision on which EA framework to select will impact the ability to plan for, design, and deliver a successful system to the customer on a timely and cost efficient manner.

- *Chapter 16, EA Evaluation and Assessment:* Enterprise Architectures need to be evaluated at several points in time in the life cycle in order to understand how well the planning, design, and implementation of the EA are proceeding, i.e., how well EA work is progressing against a set of goals and scheduled targets. This chapter presents examples of evaluation factors, including highlights of the set of EA indicators used by the General Accounting Office (GAO) to evaluate and classify EAs of 93 government agencies.

- *Chapter 17, Digital Administration:* This chapter presents a framework for the study of new the technologies involved in the recent phenomena of e-Government, e-Business, e-Learning, e-Democracy, e-Commerce, and other enterprises. Almost every business activity wants to have the letter *e* as a prefix to that business activity as if to communicate a new approach to doing business with implied economic and technological advantage. If so, why, where, when to do it, when not to do *e-Something*, what are the business and economic advantages, the costs, what does this paradigm mean about efficiency, how does it relate to the new technologies of information and communication (TICs), how does it relate to enterprise architectures (EA), who is doing it, and who is paying for it? These are some of the questions addressed in this chapter.

- *Chapter 18, Lessons Learned:* There are many challenges to the planning, building, and implementing of enterprise architectures today. We have learned that there are some things to do in a certain manner and that there are other things not to do and the reasons why. Reasons why EA work may not progress under time and budget constraints can include: Resources needed to support multiple, parallel activities are not in place; release strategy tried to release big chunks of functionality that required long time intervals (e.g., 2–3 years), lack of adequate integration among program components; lack of control points/gating; lack of performance planning, others.

- *Chapter 19, EA Implementation Strategies*: Because an enterprise architecture is a major engineering and organizational undertaking, it becomes necessary to "break it" into smaller pieces that are subsequently constituted as "projects" to be built by a community of contractors. Although the current state-of-the-art does make use of experience and sound engineering practices, there is not a well-defined, repeatable, and efficient basis or rationale for architectural decomposition and allocation to projects. This chapter takes the reader through a sequence of steps intended to allocate business systems into groups so that each group can later be constituted into an EA project. In the process, an Enterprise Systems Engineering Board (ESEB) plays a significant and crucial role in guiding planning, design, and implementation efforts within each project and the interfaces required.

- *Chapter 20, A Mathematical Framework for EAs:* This chapter introduces a new mathematical foundation of concepts, notation, and analytical artifacts for the representation, design, and measurement of enterprise architectures. For the first time in the literature, this chapter presents a unifying perspective of the five architectural views: Business Process Architectural View, Business Systems Architectural View, Data Architectural View, Applications Architectural View, and the Technology Architectural View. Ultimately, the goal of this framework is to improve communication among the various design teams and to achieve economic efficiency in the design and construction of enterprise architectures.

- *Appendix A:* CD ROM of *System Architect (SA)*, student version, the leading tool in the market today for representation, storage, management, and report generation of data across the 5 EA architectural views, courtesy of Telelogic Inc., www.telelogic.com (Formerly Popkin Inc.). Also, CD ROM of *the Enterprise Architect (EA) UML Tool,* a leading tool for UML representation of software design in EA work today, courtesy of Sparx Systems, www.sparxsystems.com, to assist both the instructor and the students with exercises and the design of software systems in the Applications Architectural View.

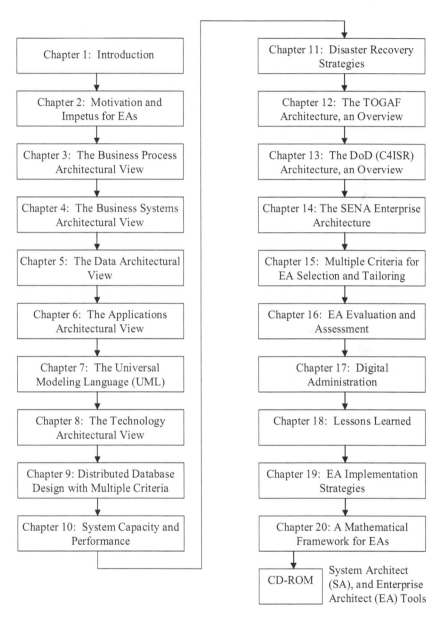

Figure 2. Flow of Chapters in this Book

Chapter 2

Motivation and Impetus for Enterprise Architectures: Government, Federal, and Commercial Sectors

2.1. Introduction

Motivation and impetus for the Enterprise Architecture Frameworks (EAF) in the USA is to be found in three most significant sectors: Federal Agency Sector, Department of Defense (DoD), and the Private Sector, as depicted in Figure 1.

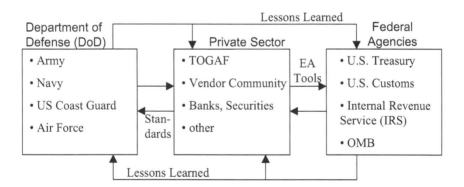

Figure 1. EA Synergism Among Federal Agencies, DoD, and Private Sector

Over the last 10-15 years organizations in the Federal Agencies and the Department of Defense have published guidelines and mandates for the design, construction, assessment, maintenance, and streamlining of enterprise architectures. Organizations in the Private Sector (e.g., university and industry committees at national and international levels) on the other hand have gathered, studied, approved, and recommended technology-based guidelines and procedures (i.e., standards); small and large commercial organizations have also produced tools that aim to support enterprise architecture projects (e.g., Telelogic's System Architect, IBM's Erwin data modeling tool, Spark Systems's Enterprise Architect tool for UML representation, Rational Rose's software modeling and XML browser, other). It is in this triage of sectors that the synergism, promotion, and application of enterprise architectures (EA) is to be found today.

2.2. Organization of this Chapter

This chapter lists some of the benefits of building enterprise architectures (EA), it traces the beginnings of EA planning to the Clinger Cohen Act of 1996, the Office of Management and Budget (OMB) Circular A-130, and the Federal Enterprise Architecture Framework (FEAF) of 1999. "Work Products" are identified and described as the bodies of knowledge that make up the enterprise architecture frameworks (EAF), truly substantive, even monumental at times, volumes of text and graphics that document how an EA is supposed to be put together, how parts relate to each other across various architectural views, and how projects and subsystems will be fielded and deployed according to a multi-year schedule. Next, a very brief introduction of the DoD (C4ISR) and TOGAF frameworks and the Office of Management of the Budget (OMB) reference models, followed by a last section of exercises.

2.3. Benefits of an Enterprise Architecture

There are a variety of benefits to be derived from the planning, design, construction, operation, and maintenance of an enterprise architecture (EA):

- Achievement of economies of scale by providing services that can be shared across the entire enterprise (i.e., the organization).
- Improvement of consistency, accuracy, and timeliness of information technology (IT)-managed resources.
- Capture and dissemination of elements in the vision and mission of the organization for effective investment planning and decision-making.

> **Enterprise**
> An organization supporting a defined business scope and mission. An enterprise is composed of intedependent resources (e.g., people, organizations, capital, and technologies). These resources must coordinate their functions and share information in support of a common mission.
> *Source*: Adapted from TEAF

- A basis of enterprise knowledge in areas of architecture requirements, business processes, vision and strategy for the future, data bases, the architecture of software applications, and an infrastructure of local area networks upon which rational decisions can be made regarding the implementation of the new technologies of information and communication (TICs); without the prior implementation of an enterprise architecture the implementation of the TICs will likely render very limited results; and
- Use of the EA by business planners and owners for purposes of strategic planning, coordination of operations across the organization, business process engineering, introduction of automation processes, reallocation of resources, modernization of legacy systems, assessment of new proposed technologies from the vendor community, and managing and priority setting of IT investments.

2.4. EA Development in the Federal Agencies

The direction and impetus for the planning, development, fielding, and operation of enterprise architectures derives from Federal legislation and guidance in the USA, including the Clinger Cohen Act of 1996, the Office of Management and Budget (OMB) Circular A-130, and the Federal Enterprise Architecture Framework (FEAF) of 1999, as depicted in Figure 2.

More recently, the Office of Budget and Management (OMB) has proposed four "reference models": Business, Service Component, Technical Reference Model, and Performance Reference Model (OMB, 12 June 2003).

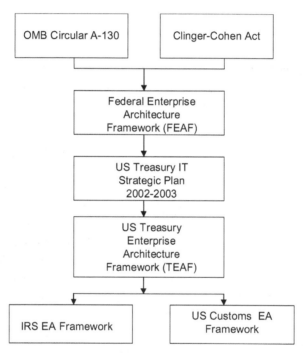

Figure 2. Enterprise Architecture Framework Development in the Federal Sector

2.5. Clinger-Cohen Act of 1996

Recognizing the importance of information technology for effective government, in 1996 Congress enacted the Information Technology Management Reform Act and the Federal Acquisition Reform Act, which together these two acts are known as the Clinger-Cohen Act of 1996. This act directs Federal agencies to link IT investments (Information Technology, also known as Technologies of Information and Communication, TICs, in Europe) to agency accomplishments by:

- Requiring that agency heads establish a process to select, manage and control their IT investments.
- Providing for relief from cumbersome processes that add little value, but significant cost to the acquisition of information technologies.
- Allowing DoD to focus on the appropriate use and management of information technology resources.
- Reducing the amount of time an information technology acquisition takes by reducing the number and frequency of protests "while moving the Department in the direction of the use of sound acquisition strategies".
- Providing a framework for performance measurement and capital planning titled "Performance-Based Management: Eight Steps to Develop and Use Information Technology Performance Measures Effectively", which is based on lessons learned from Federal and State governments as well as private industry.

> **Enterprise Architecture (EA)**
> A strategic information asset base which defines the agency's mission and business activities supporting the mission, the information necessary for agency operations, the technologies needed to support the operations, organizational needs, and transitional strategies to implement business and technology changes. An enterprise architecture is an integrated model or representation.
> *Source*: Adapted from FEAF version 1.1

The term "agency" here means any executive department, military department, government research center, or other establishment in the executive branch of the Federal government, as well as regulatory agencies. Within the Executive Office of the President, the term includes only OMB and the Office of Administration.

2.6. OMB Circular A-130

This circular directs Federal Agencies to conduct their information management planning in specific ways. Agencies will:

(a) Consider, at each stage of the information life cycle, the effects of decisions and actions on other stages of the life cycle, particularly those concerning information dissemination;

> **Framework**
> A logical structure for classifying and organizing complex information, including a set of guidelines for the construcion of an Enterprise Arcuitecture (EA)
> *Source*: FEAF version 1.1

(b) Consider the effects of their actions on members of the public and ensure consultation with the public as appropriate;

(c) Consider the effects of their actions on State and local governments and ensure consultation with those governments as appropriate;

(d) Seek to satisfy new information needs through interagency or intergovernmental sharing of information, or through commercial sources, where appropriate, before creating or collecting new information;

(e) Integrate planning for information systems with plans for resource allocation and use, including budgeting, acquisition, and use of information technology;

(f) Train personnel in skills appropriate to management of information;

(g) Protect government information commensurate with the risk and magnitude of harm that could result from the loss, misuse, or unauthorized access to or modification of such information;

(h) Use voluntary standards and Federal Information Processing Standards where appropriate or required;

(i) Consider the effects of their actions on the privacy rights of individuals, and ensure that appropriate legal and technical safeguards are implemented.

With reference to the definition and purpose of enterprise architectures, the Circular is also specific:

> An EA is the explicit description and documentation of the current and desired relationships among business and management processes and information technology. It describes the "current architecture" ("As-is") and "target architecture" ("To-be") to include the rules and standards and systems life cycle information to optimize and maintain the environment which the agency wishes to create and maintain by managing its IT portfolio. The EA must also provide a strategy that will enable the agency to support its current state and also act as the roadmap for transition to its target environment. These transition processes will include an agency's capital planning and investment control processes, agency EA planning processes, and agency systems life cycle methodologies... Agencies must implement the EA consistent with following principles:
>
> (i) Develop information systems that facilitate interoperability, application portability, and scalability of electronic applications across networks of heterogeneous hardware, software, and telecommunications platforms;
>
> (ii) Meet information technology needs through cost effective intra-agency and interagency sharing, before acquiring new information technology resources; and
>
> (iii) Establish a level of security for all information systems that is commensurate to the risk and magnitude of the harm resulting from the loss, misuse, unauthorized access to, or

modification of the information stored or flowing through these systems.

With regards to the creation and maintenance of the EA, the Circular states (verbatim, next six paragraphs):

(1) As part of the EA effort, agencies must use or create an Enterprise Architecture Framework. The Framework must document linkages between mission needs, information content, and information technology capabilities. The Framework must also guide both strategic and operational IRM planning.

(2) Business Processes - Agencies must identify the work performed to support its mission, vision and performance goals. Agencies must also document change agents, such as legislation or new technologies that will drive changes in the EA.

(3) Information Flow and Relationships - Agencies must analyze the information utilized by the agency in its business processes, identifying the information used and the movement of the information. These information flows indicate where the information is needed and how the information is shared to support mission functions.

(4) Applications - Agencies must identify, define, and organize the activities that capture, manipulate, and manage the business information to support business processes. The EA also describes the logical dependencies and relationships among business activities.

(5) Data Descriptions and Relationships - Agencies must identify how data is created, maintained, accessed, and used. At a high level, agencies must define the data and describe the relationships among data elements used in the agency's information systems; and

(6) Technology Infrastructure - Agencies must describe and identify the functional characteristics, capabilities, and interconnections of the hardware, software, and telecommunications.

2.7. Federal Enterprise Architecture Framework (FEAF) of 1999

Established by the Chief Information Officers (CIO) Council 1n 1999, The Federal Enterprise Architecture Framework (FEAF) promotes shared development for common Federal processes, interoperability, and sharing of information among the Federal agencies and other Governmental entities, in response to the Clinger-Cohen Act of 1996. To that end, the Framework consists of various approaches, models, and definitions for communicating the overall organization and relationships of architecture components required for developing and maintaining a Federal Enterprise Architecture. There are four levels of increasing detail. The fourth level provides detail of a framework that is based on a tailored version of the Zachman framework (Zachman, 1987). This master framework then serves as an "umbrella" set of guidelines for the development of EA frameworks by and within the various individual agencies, as discussed next.

2.8. US Treasury Enterprise Architecture Framework (TEAF)

Among the various Departments in the US Government, the Department of the Treasury is one of several leading organizations in the promotion of a Treasury enterprise architecture framework (TEAF) in response to the FEAF and the Treasury IT Strategic 2000-2003 Plan. Goals of the TEAF include:

- To guide the Treasury Bureaus and offices in meeting and satisfying federal requirements, including those stated in the Clinger-Cohen Act and OMB Circular A-130.
- To provide guidance in the development, maintenance, and general use of EAs as an integral part of normal business planning and management activities.
- To highlight the value-added benefits of establishing and maintaining an Enterprise Architecture (EA), and
- To encourage Bureaus and Offices to evolve and share best practices across business and engineering activities in the enterprise.

2.9. Enterprise Architecture Framework (EAF)

A framework is a logical structure for classifying and organizing complex information (FEAF version 1.1). An enterprise architecture framework is then a logical structure for classifying and organizing information on the software, hardware, and procedural composition of an enterprise architecture, including information on how the various architectural components relate to each other (i.e., metadata) in response to the desire to meet a set of system requirements. To manage complexity, the information needed to develop the EA is gathered into several compartments so as to be able to use it independently or subsequently in separate projects. Specifically, the TEAF is organized into four views (Functional View, Information view, Organizational View, and Infrastructure View), four perspectives (EA Planner, Owner, Designer, and Builder), and multiple work products, as depicted in Figure 3. Additionally, the TEAF provides direction and guidance in the construction of an EA by organizing the work products into three groups: EA Direction group, EA Description group, and EA Accomplishment group, to be prepared in that order.

2.10. Technical Architecture Framework for Information Management (TAFIM)

Moving now to our description of EA work in the Department of Defense (DoD), by 1990 it had already become apparent to many armed services that military systems and architectures were becoming increasingly complex and that the need existed to help guide the design, implementation, operation, management, and evolution of these systems. Accordingly, in 1994 DoD created the Technical Architecture Framework for Information Management (TAFIM) in order to provide guidance for the evolution of DoD technical that meet specific mission requirements while providing for multiple desired system characteristics such as interoperability, portability, and scalability.

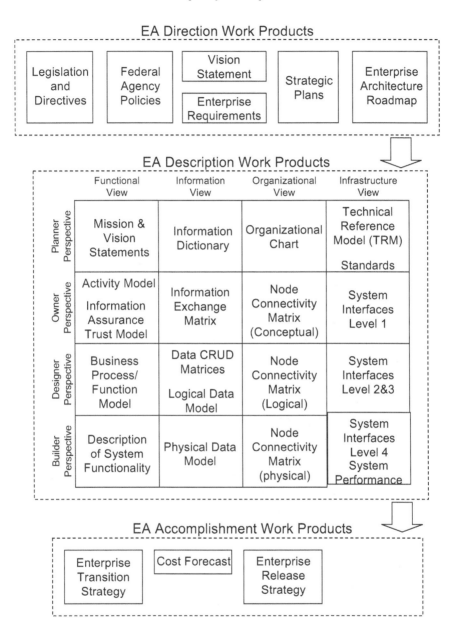

Figure 3. Resource and Work Products for EA Direction, Description, and Accomplishment (*Source*: Adapted from TEAF vs. 1.1)

Accordingly, the TAFIM consisted of multiple bodies of information and guidance:

- A *Technical Reference Model (TRM)* to provide a conceptual model for information system services and their interfaces in the architecture. See Chapter 4 for a detailed description of the TRM.
- *Architecture Concepts and Guidance Design* with concepts and guidance for the design and integration of architectural components.
- A *DoD Standards-Based Architecture Planning Guide* for the translation of functional requirements into business services, standards, components, configuration of these components, their phasing, and the acquisition of products and services to implement them.
- A *DoD Goal Security Architecture (DGSA)* that addressed security requirements derived from mission statements and threat descriptions.
- An *Adopted Information Technology Standards (AITS)* intended to guide DoD acquisition and the migration of legacy systems while supporting multiple TAFIM objectives such as interoperability, reduced life-cycle costs, and security.
- A *DoD Human Computer Interface (HCI) Style Guide* which provided a common framework and set of concepts in HCI design and implementation.

The TAFIM did serve well the armed services community from 1998 until 7 January 2000 when it was cancelled by Architecture Coordinating Council (ACC) in response to a shifting in the strategic direction of all architectural efforts in DoD caused by challenges in its implementation (Perks and Beveridge, 2003), including:

- Time in years required to build a TAFIM architecture can be so great, 3-5 years, that the architecture would be obsolete from the very beginning;
- Considerable IT and business modeling expertise required, thus often times the final product was difficult for business oriented professionals to follow and understand;

- No specific method was offered to the general public to build TAFIM-like architectures.

The TRM portion of TAFIM, however, was deemed relevant to existing needs in DoD and allowed to continue as a guiding document. See Chapter 4, The Business Systems Architectural View for a description of the Technical Reference Model (TRM).

2.11. Command, Control, Communications, Computers, Intelligence, Surveillance, and Reconnaissance (C4ISR) Architecture Framework

In October 1995 the Deputy Secretary of Defense directed that a DoD-wide effort be conducted "to define and develop better means and processes for ensuring that C4I capabilities meet the needs of war fighters", such as military aircraft, ships, and tank units. Towards that end, an integration task force (ITF) was formed under the direction of the Assistant Secretary of Defense for C4ISR consisting of representatives from the Joint Chiefs of Staff, the military Services, and DoD agencies. This ITF eventually emerged with a set of recommendations for the definition of an architectural framework that features three related architecture types or views:

- Operational View
- Systems View, and
- Technical View

Finally, on February 23, 1998 the tri-chairs of the Architecture Coordination Council (ACC) established the C4ISR architecture framework as a critical element of that change in strategic direction for all architectural efforts in DoD. Accordingly, the C4ISR framework provides rules, guidance, and work product descriptions to guide the development of interoperable, scalable, and cost-effective military systems across Joint and combined organizational boundaries. It is worth noting that while this framework provides direction on how to describe architectures, it does not provide guidance in how to design or implement architectures, or how to develop and acquire systems.

By June 1996 the C4ISR framework had steadily gained acceptance and support within many of DoD Services, and on 23 February 1998 the Office of the Secretary of Defense mandated the C4ISR as the EA framework to use across all Services. See Chapter 13 for a presentation of salient features of the C4ISR framework.

2.12. The Open Group's Architectural Framework (TOGAF)

Individuals and organizations in the Private Sector have also played a significant role in the creation and promotion of EA frameworks and their application to enterprise needs. The Open Group's Architectural Framework (TOGAF), for example, an open-source framework that embodies significant intellectual property and experience in architectural development.

> *A technical Architecture:* A capability, a discipline, and an approach used to define, apply, and maintain the technology environment within the organization. It embodies the life cycle for defining the organization's technical strategy, setting and adopting technical standards, and maintaining the technology environment through changes in both business and technology. It can be thought of as the technical equivalent of the business strategy (i.e., the future shape of business given a current environment) (Perks and Beveridge, 2003).

See Chapter 12 for a description of salient features of TOGAF, including the Standards Information Base (SIB), TOGAF's Technical Reference Model (TRF), and the Architectural Development Method (ADM).

2.13. OMB Reference Models

The Federal Enterprise Architecture (FEA) story is still in the making, and most likely will continue for the balance of this decade. On 12 June 2003 the Office of Management and the Budget (OMB) rolled out the latest FEA version, including a draft of a Business Reference Model

(BRM), a Service Component Model (SRM), and a Technical Reference Model (TRM). As of this date, OMB is working closely with federal agencies to extend these three models and add still two more models: a Performance Reference Model (PRM), and a Data and Information Reference Model (DRM), as shown on Figure 4.

The feeling among some EA-users in the Federal agencies reflects a frustration with lack of common measures of business and operational performance. "These models will enable better alignment of IT and the business of government. OMB and agency officials will use them to improve agency performance, increase intergovernmental collaboration and reduce costs for the taxpayer, furthering the goals of the President's Management Agenda and making government services more citizen centered", according to Mark Forman, OMB's Administrator for E-Gov and IT (Executive Office 2003). It is a bit early to tell yet, but likely the OMB Reference Models will significantly impact the direction, applicability, and assessment of EA frameworks in the Federal Agencies. See Hagan (2003) or a detailed presentation of the structural content of these models and their intended use in the Federal Agencies.

2.14. Conclusion

Enterprise Architecture (EA) frameworks are seen today by many decision makers in the Federal agencies, the Department of Defense (DoD), and some corporations in the private sector as the answer to very real needs in IT investment and enterprise resource management. Salient features of major EA frameworks were presented in this chapter, including FEAF, TEAF, TAFIM, TOGAF, and C4ISR/DoD, as well as a glimpse at OMB's forthcoming reference models. The writing is in the wall: EA frameworks are here to stay, for the foreseeable future, anyway, and these represent the vehicles that government, and to a significant extent individuals and organizations in the business and industrial communities, will use to address those IT investment and management challenges.

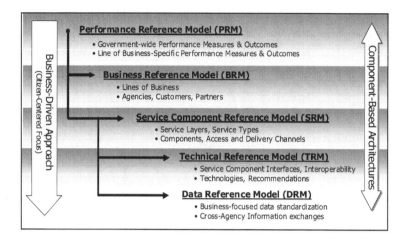

Figure 4. OMB Reference Models (*Source*: FEA-PMO Using the Business and Performance Reference Models to Help Improve Citizen Services, by Norman Lorentz, Oct 7-8, 2002)

2.15. Exercises

E2.1 Select a Federal Agency, conduct a search of the Web/Internet, and provide a narrative of each of the following components of its Enterprise Architecture (EA) framework:

(a) Vision/Mission Statement
(b) Organizational chart
(c) Business Processes; types of services this Agency provides
(d) High-level view of its technical architecture (if available)
(e) Technical reference model

Also, discuss briefly how the "architecture-to-be" for this agency is intended to be different, better, or more efficient than the "architecture-as-is", i.e., the present EA.

E2.2 How are the OMB Reference Models intended to complement the existing mandate and functionality of the FEAF? Conduct a search of the Web and prepare a 1-2 page critique.

E2.3 Who are the promoters of TOGAF today? Research this topic and prepare a briefing that address the following:

    (f) Constituency of the Open Group, i.e., general description of individuals, university organizations, URL, business and industry organizations

    (g) Cite one application of TOGAF in the private sector, e.g., title of paper or report, name of journal or organization, and half page discussion of this application

    (h) An update of TOGAF today, sponsors, demand for its use in the private sector

E2.4 Identify and list three forthcoming USA Conferences or Workshops that feature EA papers, and include a listing of paper topics with applications in the Federal Agencies, DoD, and corporations, if available.

E2.5 Identify and list three forthcoming International Conferences or Workshops that feature EA papers, and include a listing of paper topics with applications in the Federal Agencies, DoD, and corporations, if available.

E2.6 Identify a list of colleges and universities in the USA that offer courses or workshops in EA planning, design, and/or assessment. List course titles and description, if available.

E2.7 Homeland Security Enterprise Architgecture. Search the Web and prepare a 1-2 page briefing on why this architecture got started, how its design and implementation is progressing, views for and against this public investment.

Chapter 3

The Business Processes Architectural View

Vision and Strategy
Business Processes Architectural View
System Requirements Development
Business Systems Architectural View
Data Architectural View
Applications Architectural View
Technology Architectural View

3.1. What is a Business Process?

The *business activities* to be carried out by an organization constitute the main reason for the creation, operation, funding, maintenance, and growth of an enterprise architecture. In the case of a banking organization these activities include processing incoming check deposits, posting money amounts to the appropriate individual or corporate accounts, computing interest, managing loans to businesses, and conducting internal balance and control procedures at the end of each business cycle (i.e., daily, weekly, other) to mention a few. In the case of an airline, business activities include processing phone calls, computer, letter, and e-mail queries from travel agencies requesting flight information, processing seat reservations, maintaining an extensive database on air carrier flight departure and arrival times, origin and destination airports across a network of domestic and international cities, flight ticket prices, accruing debits and credits to individual and corporate customer accounts and, again, conducting accounting balance-and-control procedures at the end of a business cycle.

Next, sequences of similar business activities are grouped into *business processes*. In this manner, the business architect proceeds to identify and define individual business activities that make up the various business processes such as processing requests for information on flight availability, processing airline flight reservation requests, marketing of travel services, payroll, human resources services for its own employees, etc. Accordingly, a large set of business activities is decomposed and arranged into subsets of manageable business processes.

> *A business process is a grouping of 5-10 business activities that share in business affinity and that are carried out in a pre-determined sequence for purposes of accomplishing a significant business operation or goal.*

The Business Processes Design Team is responsible for translating the Vision and Strategy document (i.e., work product) into a set of business processes that describe the day-to-day business of the enterprise, e.g., preparing and submitting an order electronically to a vendor to replenish an inventory item, gathering information on the demographics of a particular region to support marketing goals, and applying payments to a customer account in the enterprise database; typically, there may be 100-200 business processes and each one will be represented in text form with 2-3 flowcharts that show the decomposition of a business process into 4-6 *business activities*. A Business Process Team is often made up of 4-8 people and their business modeling activity will produce the Business Processes Work Product.

3.2. How this Chapter is Organized

We need an example of a substantial business and engineering organization that is in the process of modernizing its operations worldwide in order to illustrate the many steps involved in the modernization of its legacy systems or the creation of new enterprise information architecture. The example created here is that of the **Global Airline Services Inc.**, a fictitious worldwide airline organization, referred to hereafter as Global Airlines. Global Airlines has been in existence and doing business in the international community for the 15 years, let us say, and it is now in the process of modernizing its architecture. This example will allow us to represent the business processes that are the bread-and-butter business activities of Global Services, including the Airline Ticket Sales, the Enterprise Database, and the financial business processes. We will make use of a "context diagram" to present a high-level corporate view and high-level view of the "to-be" enterprise architecture (i.e., architecture representation).

Next, this chapter takes us through a listing of the Business Process Principles, the Business Process Constraints, and the Business Process Assumptions that will guide the evolution of the current architecture of Global Services into a modernized, up-to-date, highly efficient enterprise architecture design over the next say five years.

Typically, software design representation includes Logical Business Process Design, specifically the design of Process Threads (TPs), Elementary Business Processes (EBPs), and System Business Services (SBSs). These are the artifacts that engineers and business designers utilize to break down the complex functionality of the design into smaller, do-able, and manageable design components that "functional" personnel, programmers, engineers, business modelers, and other personnel will form and shape into logical design components.

3.3. Global Airline Services — An Illustrative Example

Let us consider our hypothetical business organization, **Global Airline Services Inc**. This business organization has been in operation for the last 15 years with headquarters based in Fairfax, Virginia, USA, providing airline transportation services, both passenger and freight, to cities in the USA and abroad, as depicted in the high-level corporate view of Figure 1.

Global Services is characterized by an employee workforce of 6,750 people distributed globally, a main processing facility in Fairfax, and providing reservation services to domestic and international travel agencies. Competition for passenger and freight transportation services however has been fierce and two years ago the Global Services' Chief Executive Officer (CEO) and her top executive officers put together a plan for modernization of current business operations which was then

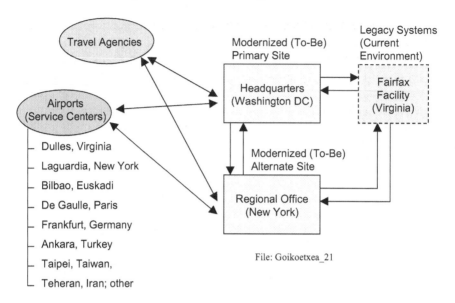

Figure 1. Global Airlines Services, a High-Level Corporate View

submitted to its own Board of Directors for consideration. The modernization plan included a detailed business plan for the next 5 and 10 year business periods, a set of business and engineering requirements, a proposed high-level enterprise architecture, a marketing plan, and a cost estimate.

Subsequently, the Board of Directors, approved the modernization plan, secured loans in the international banking community, and set up two bodies of corporate officers, business, engineering, and operations personnel, and community leaders to direct, approve incremental funding, and guide the modernization effort. One body is made up of business and community leaders, called the Enterprise Business Organization (EBO) responsible for business vision and strategy, setting up business process principles, assumptions, and constraints consistent with the approved business plan. The second body is made up of both engineering and business personnel and called the Information Technology Organization (ITO) which is responsible for setting up system requirements, coming up with the business systems that will house the applications that will implement the business processes, setting up the various engineering design teams and review boards, insuring that the to-be enterprise architecture adheres to current technology standards and best business practices, and scheduling the fielding of system functionality into 3 major "releases".

A high-level view of the proposed enterprise architecture is shown on Figure 2. It features web-based access by travel agents to a variety of enterprise services including airline seats, origin points, destination points, transfer of reservations to other airlines, travel packages, account application forms, earned miles programs, insurance forms, other via menus in a portal system.

Forms would be installed in web server farms while applications (software responsible for implementing more significant functionality) would be hosted on the Web application servers. These applications would send messages to the Enterprise Data System with specific instructions to post data to or read data from (i.e., queries) the enterprise database. Data on current individual and corporate accounts in the current system (i.e., legacy systems) will have to be migrated to the modernized system in Washington D.C. over a period of 18 months; in the meantime, new individual and corporate account applications will be processed immediately and stored in the modernized system.

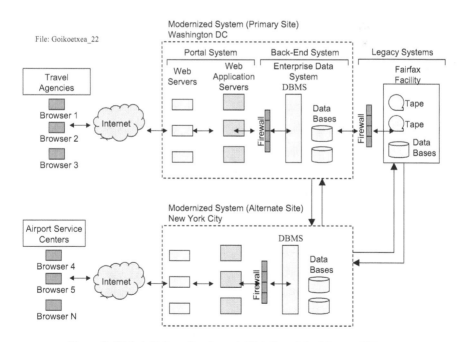

Figure 2. Global Airlines Services. A High-Level Architectural View

An alternate site will be built and located in the City of New York featuring all of the functional capability featured by the Washington D.C. site, the primary site. Additionally, a fail over-and-recovery capability will be designed to enable transfer of all functionality from the primary site to the alternate site and back to the primary site within a prescribed amount of time, per system requirements. The failover back and forth is needed to provide for scheduled maintenance, as well as to provide for unscheduled, disaster-and-recovery needs, e.g., floods, fire, power loss, other.

3.4. Vision and Strategy

The importance of the Vision and Strategy statement in forging the new, "to-be" enterprise architecture cannot 'be overestimated. Global executives sought the opinion and aspirations of the stockholders and members of the Board of Directors to arrive at the following statement:

> *Vision and Strategy: In order to meet the business, financial, and engineering challenges of the next 25 years Global Airlines Services is committed to the following: to double the passenger volume within 10 years and triple passenger volume by the 25-th year, increase freight volume by a factor of 10, improve passenger and operations security to the highest national standards each year, and expand airport operations to 10 new, major cities in Taiwan, China, Teheran, Ankara, Sidney, Mexico City, Buenos Aires, Kyoto, and Harare. To that end, the new, modernized architecture will expand web-based technology from its current level of 35% to 85% in all domestic and international operations, convert all its current stand-alone data stores and data management systems (DBMS) into a single, highly distributed, efficient, and high-performance relational enterprise data management system, provide for a primary site in Washington, D.C., to serve as headquarters for all business and engineering operations, and provide for an alternate site in New York City to enable disaster/maintenance failover and recovery operations. Additionally, Global Airline Services is committed to carry out Organizational Change (OC) within all its domestic and international operations in order to prepare for and align business and financial personnel and organizations with the market and engineering challenges listed above through new roles and responsibilities, training, revised financial and auditing services, and progressive corporate policies that reflect sound business practices in the service of our stockholders and the public at large.*

Accordingly, this enthusiastic yet realistic business content of the Vision and Strategy, its well-articulated marketing goals, and reference to specific technological innovations constitute the guiding light and force behind the enterprise architectural effort in this example.

3.5. Business Processes

The to-be business processes of Global Airlines are depicted on Figure 3 and organized into the following categories:

- Airline Ticket Sales
- Travel Services
- Database Services
- Accounting
- Financial
- Payroll
- Security
- Human Resources, and
- Infrastructure

Figure 3. Business Processes To-Be in Airline Example

Beyond a high-level description of these business processes in the enterprise modernization proposal, it is the responsibility of the Business Modeling Team to come up with detailed descriptions of each business process.

The Airline Ticket Sales business process, for example, has been designed to feature three grouping of business activities: Ticket Sales Information, Ticket Reservation, and Payment Processing, as shown on Figure 4. In turn, Ticket Sales Information is decomposed into Phone Call Queries, E-Mail Queries, Web-Site Queries, and Paper Queries, and so forth.

The Enterprise Database business process is responsible for storing, processing, and managing all data stores, as shown on Figure 5, and decomposed into two main categories of business activities: Initialize Database, and Data Administration

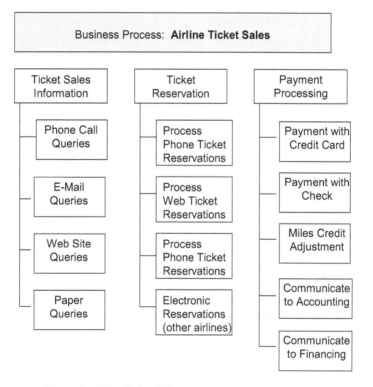

Figure 4. Airline Ticket Sales Business Process To-Be

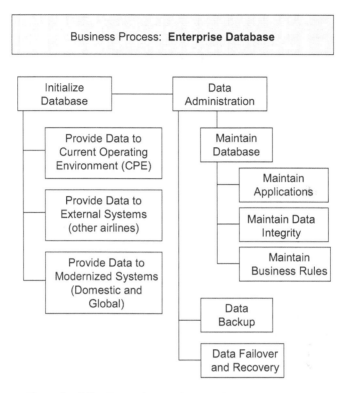

Figure 5. Airline Enterprise Database Business Process To-Be

Within Data Administration, for example, more specific business activities are:

- Maintain Database
    Maintain Applications
    Maintain Data Integrity
    Maintain Business Rules
- Data Backup, and
- Data Failover and Recovery.

The Financial business process understandably features its own set of business activities, as depicted on Figure 6, with two main categories of business activities:

- Account Information
    - Create New Individual Account
    - Create New Corporate Account
    - Validate Identification ID
    - Store Data
- Financial Account Activity
    - Validate Account Activity
    - Payment
    - Earned Credit Adjustment
    - Compute Tax
    - Account Balance and Controls, and
    - Store Data

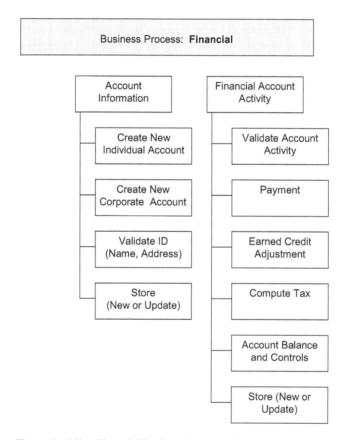

Figure 6. Airline Financial Business Process with Business Activities

3.6. System Requirements

An Enterprise Architecture modernization effort is no different from any other business, or engineering enterprise in that it must begin with a set of system requirements. The system requirements are the critical vehicle for the capturing, writing, and communication of the desired functionality. Everything begins with a set of requirements that will have to be *validated* by the owners of the modernization effort (stakeholders of Global Airlines) and placed under configuration management (CM).

Functional Requirements:

- SYS-1: GLOBAL shall migrate accounts that exhibit a balance of zero dollars or credit (overpaid balance) to the modernized system (primary site).
- SYS-2: GLOBAL shall identify and store the reason for account balance that has a value other than zero dollars.
- SYS-3: GLOBAL shall provide event-logging software for balance and controls of accounts.
- SYS-4: GLOBAL shall provide event-logging software for audit trail purposes.
- SYS-5: GLOBAL shall quote Federal and State taxes for each seat reservation request.
- SYS-6: GLOBAL shall incorporate Portal technology in the modernized EA design
- SYS-7: GLOBAL shall feature relational database technology in the modernized EA design.
- SYS-8: GLOBAL shall create a date stamp identifying executed transactions on a daily basis.
- SYS-9: GLOBAL shall incorporate business-rules technology to support applications.
- SYS-10: GLOBAL shall back up all its data by close of business (COB) daily.
- SYS-11: GLOBAL shall incorporate system failover-and-recovery between Headquarters (primary site in Washington D.C.) and New York City (alternate site).

Non-Functional (i.e., Performance) Requirements:

- SYS-11: GLOBAL shall be able to process up to 2.5 million queries to its database daily.
- SYS-11: GLOBAL shall be able to respond to each query within 8 seconds 98% of the time.
- SYS-11: GLOBAL shall be able to respond to paper requests for account application within 24 hours.
- SYS-11: GLOBAL shall provide be able to issue electronic seat tickets within 5 seconds 75% of the time and within 60 seconds 98% of the time.
- SYS-11: GLOBAL shall be able to implement a 48-hour recovery capability from alternate site back to primary site for scheduled maintenance purposes.

3.7. Business Process Principles

Several methodologies in the market today propose the issuance of a set of principles, assumptions, and constraints to guide the planning and design process. Global Airlines also subscribes to this approach and accordingly has mandated in its modernization program that changes be made in its organization structure, business processes, and technology infrastructure:

- Prompt response to request for services from travel agencies.
- Prompt response to request for services from airport service centers.
- Create a Web-based infrastructure nationally and globally.
- Create a modernized, integrated database system.
- Provide for intra site and inter site system failover and recovery
- Adopt up-to-date business practices.
- Adopt up-to-date independent accounting and auditing practices.
- Minimize the impact on the current system during modernization program.

3.8. Business Process Assumptions

The contractor, Integrated Technologies and Research Inc. (iTR), and Global Airlines have entered a contractual agreement that guides the modernization effort:

- Modernized databases and applications will be housed at both the primary site (Washington D.C.) and the alternate site (New York City).
- Seat reservation systems by travel agencies will not change.
- The modernization effort will incrementally migrate account files in the legacy systems to the primary site.
- Individual and corporate account information will reside in the modernized systems or the legacy systems but not in both systems.
- Up-to-date business accounting practices will apply to the modernized systems.
- Up-to-date business auditing practices will apply to the modernized systems; these practices and processes will be independent of those for accounting.
- Full security certification is the goal for the modernized systems.
- A coordinated and integrated release of architectural functional will be developed and managed.
- A software and test plan will be developed, applied, and managed.
- A development environment (DE) will be created, applied, and managed.
- A transition plan (i.e., move architectural components in the DE to an operational environment) will be created, applied, and managed.
- 3.9. Business Process Constraints

Global Airlines management has determined a set of constraints on business process development, strict adherence to Federal Aviation Administration (FAA) regulations, observance of local workforce union policies, and cooperation with transportation policies set forth by the European Community (EC):

- Business practices shall adhere to FAA policies and regulations.
- Business practices in Europe shall adhere to European Union (EU) policies and regulations.
- Changes to technology and operating procedures shall be negotiated with local workforce unions.
- Content of architecture releases shall reflect funding available.
- Organizational Change (OC) shall require adequate lead time to insure proper training, development of revised/new responsibilities, and staff adjustments.

3.9. Business Modeling Toolsets in the Market

Business modeling tools are essential to successful EA work today. Four EA tools in the market today are as follows:

- Toolset: FirstSTEP Designer: to model, simulate, and analyze business processes, from Interfacing Technologies Corporation, www.interfacing.com
- Toolset: System Architect, 2002, Telelogic Inc. www.telelogic.com
- Enterprise Architect, Unified Modeling Language (UML) tool, by Sparxsystems, www.sparxsystems.com
- Toolset: Rational Rose, 2002, www.rationalrose.com
- Rational Rose® software is a model-driven development tool that can be used to model business processes.

There is a substantial body of literature on methodologies for the modeling of business processes and some of these methodologies, including the Unified Modeling Language (UML), have been implemented into software tools that can then be applied to the design and implementation of business processes into software applications, i.e., coded programs. See Chapter 7 for an overview and illustrative application of UML with the Enterprise Architect (EA) tool

3.10. Selection of an EA Toolset

Criteria for EA tool evaluation and selection should be tailored to reflect intended use of the architecture, scope, levels of integration desired, number and content of work products, and other factors. Table 1 lists a set of multiple criteria for the selection and evaluation of EA tools available in the market today.

Table 1. EA Tool Evaluation and Selection Criteria (*Source*: Federal Enterprise Architecture: A Practical Guide, 2001)

Functional Area	Multiple Criteria
Development of EA Work Products	• Available platforms • Support for chosen framework • Support for modeling methods and techniques — e.g., object-oriented analysis and desing, IDEF, activity models, class models, information models • Import/export capability • Cost (initial and maintenance) and licensing • Vendor support (time, cost)
Maintenance of EA Work Products	• Interoperability with other enterprise engineering products and development tool and repositories (as in System Architect (SA), by Telelogic Inc.) • Traceability of requirements and other enterprise engineering artifacts • Configuration management (CM) support • Quality Assurance (QA) support
EA Design Support	• Business process modeling • Code design representation (e.g., UML representation with Enterprise Architect tool)
Distribution of EA Work Products	• Accessibility (e.g., software needed, access requirements) • Report generation (reports and presentations) • Media supported (e.g., Rational Rose, HTML, CD-ROM, XML, other) • Levels of access control (e.g., Read-only, Read-Write) • Use of hypertext links

3.11. Conclusions

In this chapter we set out to introduce the definition of a business process and its utilization in EA planning and design. Several observations are made:

(a) The EA community today is in agreement on the importance of defining and modeling the business processes in an organization early in the planning stages. In the case of EA work in the Federal sector, for example, the General Accounting Office (GAO), has repeatedly reported on and recommended the identification, definition, and modeling of business processes at the outset of EA planning
(http://www.gao.gov/sp/html/strobj426.html)

(b) A set of principles, assumptions, and constraints on the identification, definitions, and allocation of business processes and activities to components of the enterprise architecture has become an integral EA planning activity. When this set is stated early in the planning stages EA owners, decision makers, and contractor personnel are effectively able to agree on the relative importance of business processes and their subsequent implementation by business systems.

(c) The example of the Global Airlines Services was introduced to illustrate the development of the Business Process Architectural View in this chapter and the other four architectural views in subsequent chapters.

(d) The Vision-and-Strategy statement serves to guide EA planning right from the start. This importance of this statement is paramount as it articulates the desires and aspirations of the owners of the new or to-be-modernized EA. It sets the tone for those aspirations, identifies key technologies to be introduced, sets up a time frame (e.g., 5, 10 years, other), projects a set of goals to be achieved, and expresses financial commitment towards the attainment of those goals.

(e) System requirements, both functional and non-functional, are the basis for business processes in the enterprise while deriving direction and impetus from the Vision-and-Strategy Statement. Everything begins with, revolves around, and culminates with validation of system requirements through testing of EA components. Examples of functional and non-functional requirements were provided. The functionality content of business processes and activities must be captured in the language of the system requirements. In an iterative fashion business process modeling facilitates requirements definition and, vice versa, requirements definition encourages business process modeling.

(f) This section of Business Processes Architectural View now serves as a "building block" for subsequent chapters that present and inter-relate the other EA four architectural views.

3.12. Exercises

E3.1 Select a leading Airline Company and gather the following architectural descriptions:

(a) Organizational Chart (CEO, names of company executives, titles and placement in the organizational tree).
(b) A high-level view of its Enterprise Architecture (diagram).
(c) A list of main business processes.
(d) A statement of EA Vision and Strategy (look for it in the company's Annual Report).
(e) Size of workforce, annual sales, annual profit/loss (Annual Report).

E3.2 Conduct a search of the Web/Internet and describe four leading Enterprise Architecture (EA) toolsets and list the following:

(a)   Name of EA tool; name of vendor; URL.
(b)   Client tools (MS Visaul Interdev, SP3, other).
(c)   Middleware tools (MS Visual Basic, SP3, Windows COM+, other).
(d)   Database (SQL Server, other).
(e)   Web tools (MS Internet Information Server 5 running on Windows, other).
(f)   Operating system (Windows, NT, other).
(g)   Software (Sun Java, Netscape Navigator, Explorer, other).
(h)   Processor (mhz, MIPS, also manufacturer's name).
(i)   Memory.
(j)   H/D space.
(k)   Display (e.g., 17"@ 800x600, color settings).

(l) Database Server (e.g.,Windows, SQL Server).
(m) Web Server (e.g., Windows Server, COM+, other).
(n) Number of users.

E3.3 Apply EA tool selection criteria on Table 1 to the Global Airlines example presented in this chapter to rank the four EA tools identified in Exercise E3.2.

E3.4 Interfacing Technologies Corporation, a leading vendor in business modeling methodologies based in Montreal, Canada, has developed FirstSTEP, a toolset for business process modeling and management, as shown on Figure E3.3.

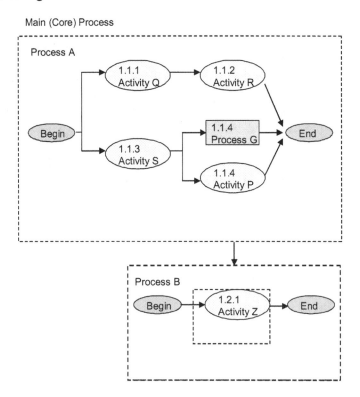

Figure   E3.3.   Process   and   Activity   Map   in   FirstSTEP   Methodology (*Source*: Levi and Klapsis, Interfacing Technologies, 2002)

(a) List and briefly define the basic steps in the FirstSTEP methodology (suggestion: contact Interfacing Technologies at www.interfacing.com)

(b) Discuss general applicability of the FirstSTEP methodology to capturing the vision-and-strategy activity in building an enterprise architecture

(c) Apply the FirstSTEP methodology to map the business processes and activities shown earlier in Figures 3-6 for the Global Airlines Services example.

E3.5 As the business modeler for your organization, Enterprise Business Modeling Inc., your task is to prepare briefing on institutional drivers of business process in the EA community.

(a) Search the published literature in the Federal sector (e.g., General Accounting Office (GAO)) for three organizations that promote the use of business process modeling in EA planning and design. List 1-2 relevant publications with one descriptive paragraph for each organization.

(b) Search the published literature in the Private sector (e.g., banks, airlines, manufacturing, other) for three organizations that promote the use of business process modeling in EA planning and design. List 1-2 relevant publications with one descriptive paragraph for each organization.

Chapter 4

The Business Systems Architectural View

Vision and Strategy
Business Processes Architectural View
System Requirements Development
Business Systems Architectural View
Data Architectural View
Applications Architectural View
Technology Architectural View

4.1. What is a Business System?

A *business system* is a logical representation of functionality to be executed by the enterprise in the course of carrying out a business activity or business process. A business process is made up of several business activities, and several business systems may be needed to carry out a single business activity, i.e., a business system houses services needed to carry out one or more business activities. In Chapter 3, we recall, we presented the Business Process Architectural View, a grouping of business activities identified and defined across major business areas in the organization such as financial, accounting, payroll, human resources, security, database services, infrastructure services, and others. In this chapter we look into the composition of the Business Systems

Architectural View, the identification and definition of business systems in this view, their organization and relationship to each other within a hierarchical business systems tree, their interfaces, and the eventual assignment of business systems to projects.

> *A business system is a logical representation of a portion of the functionality executed by the enterprise in the course of carrying out a business activity or business process. Typically, a business process is made of multiple business activities and a single business activity will require services from multiple business systems. In this manner, an enterprise architecture may consist of 200-300 business systems that provide a variety of services across major functional areas in the enterprise, e.g., Human Resources, Finances, Purchasing, other.*

The identification, definition, and interfacing of business systems often is a most challenging endeavor that calls for a team of individuals with very specific business and engineering skills, i.e., the *Business Systems Design Team*. This team is responsible for translating the Vision and Strategy document (i.e., work product), the set of business processes that describe the day-to-day business of the enterprise, and the set of system requirements into a complete and detailed set of logical entities that are called business systems. Initially, this team may have a short list of 5-10 business systems that are then presented to the rest of the engineering organization and the customer for validation. Over a period of weeks this short list typically can grow to have 200-300 business systems organized into a business hierarchical tree. How this hierarchical tree becomes a reality depends heavily on art and science, the experience of members of the Business Systems Design Team with other related enterprise architecture (EA) projects, the perseverance of a few highly dedicated business executives and chief architects, and the talents and hard work of the many individuals throughout the engineering organization. The following pages illustrate this most challenging process.

So far we have presented elements of the Vision and Strategy, System Requirements Development, and the Business Processes Architectural View (Chapter 3). Next, in this chapter, we proceed to discuss the challenges associated with the task of constructing the Business Systems Architectural View.

4.2. Why Business Systems?

Experience in the last 5-10 years with Enterprise Architecture (EA) planning in the government sector has shown that well-intended engineering efforts were doomed from the start because these failed to consider adequately the identification and representation of the business of the enterprise and, instead, these efforts jumped too quickly into a "technical solution" (GAO report GAO-02-234R). By now we have learned that it is of paramount importance in EA work to describe and document legacy business systems, proceed with the design of new (i.e., modernized) business systems, and then move on to the design of other EA components (Lucas and Mohr, 2002).

4.3. How this Chapter is Organized

This chapter builds on the business processes foundation developed earlier in Chapter 4 and proceeds to present a methodology for the identification and definition of business systems needed to support those business processes.

The Global Airline Services is developed further, this time to show a list of business systems at levels 1 through 4 in a business systems hierarchy. Even for a modestly complex enterprise the number of business systems needed to provide enterprise services can quickly grow to hundreds of business systems. Therefore, the need to identify business systems so that each one can provide services that are useful to multiple business processes. This section includes definitions for the terms interface, system input, and system output, as well as names for 15 interfaces allocated among business systems at Level 1.

A second section introduces the reader to the basic elements and philosophy of the Technical Reference Model (TRM). The TRM concept emerged within the government sector and over the past 10-15 years it has evolved in shape and content to guide the adoption of a set standards on software usability, hardware interoperability, and industry engineering practices in EA planning. Elements of the DoD and US Customs TRMs are discussed.

A third section discusses the challenges associated with the task of allocating business systems in the business systems hierarchy to projects. Business systems allocated to Project A, will be developed by engineering personnel in that project only. Business systems allocated to Project B, will be developed by engineering personnel in that project only. Should there be 3 projects, 5 projects, 20 projects or more? Should business systems be decomposed down to level 3 only or all the way to level 6 or higher, and what are the implications of this decomposition to the engineering organization and the customer in terms of business, engineering, and cost efficiency?

In the Exercises Section a set of exercises are presented to both students and instructor to consider additional design questions, options, and tradeoffs involved.

Finally, a References Section presents a list of related reference articles, books, and web sites.

4.5. Business Systems Hierarchical Tree – Example Continued

Based on a thorough understanding of the four artifacts listed above, the BSD team recommends that at the top of the business systems hierarchy of Global Airline Services three systems be recognized, let us say:

- Travel Services System (TSS).
- Corporate Management System (CMS), and
- Enterprise Infrastructure System (EIS).

Travel Services System (TSS) will be composed of business sub-systems that provide services for individual travel services, corporate travel services, domestic ticket sales, and international ticket sales, as shown on Figures 1 and 2. Corporate Management System (CMS) will be composed of business sub-systems that provide services for the internal management of the organization, namely the financial system, budget preparation, human resources, corporate asset management (e.g., airport facilities, equipment, parts, and real estate), procurement management, and business performance monitoring. The Enterprise Infrastructure System (RIS) is to be composed of business sub-systems that provide services for the portal, the database(s) and database management system (DBMS), the enterprise knowledge base, decision support systems, communication services (e.g., messaging middleware, protocol software, telephones, radio, etc.), platform services, security, directory services, weather forecasting services, and legacy transition systems.

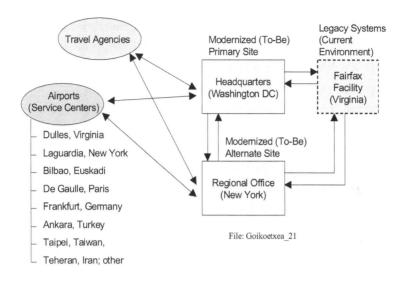

Figure 1. Global Airlines Services, a High-Level Corporate View

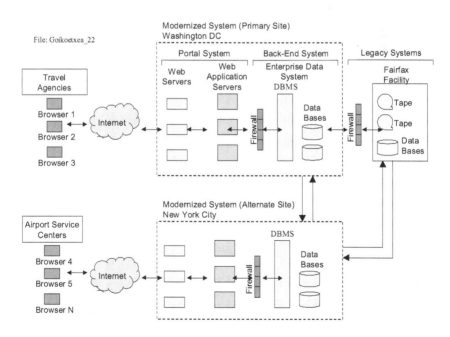

Figure 2. Global Airlines Services. A High-Level Architectural View

After several iterations over a period of 4-6 weeks the business systems hierarchical tree takes shape and form, as shown on Table 1.

> *A Business Hierarchical Tree is intended to be a listing of all business systems in the enterprise, distributed over 3-6 levels, with each business system defined in terms of business services (e.g., create new corporate account), with interfaces identified by type (e.g., FAX, e-mail, MQSeries message) and content (e.g., seat reservation request) so that it completely reflects and provides for the business functionality and performance stated in both the business processes and the system requirements.*

Several observations about the business tree on Table 1. There are three main, top business systems which are Travel Services System (TSS), Corporate Management System (CMS), and Enterprise Infrastructure System (EIS) which reside at Level 1 in the hierarchy. TSS itself is decomposed into four sub-systems: Individual Travel Services, Corporate Travel Services, Domestic Ticket Sales, and International Ticket Sales which reside at Level 2. In turn, International Ticket Sales is decomposed into three business sub-systems: Economy Ticket Sales, Business Ticket Sales, and Corporate Ticket Sales which reside at Level 3, and so forth.

From that textual hierarchical representation, the presentation of the business systems can then evolve to a graphical hierarchical representation, as shown on Figure 3.

4.6. Interfaces

Business systems need to talk to each other through data interchange across a physical media, i.e., pipeline, channel, a network. In this sense the *output* of business system A can serve as the *input* to business system B. Each interface must have a owner, be it a project or an organization on the customer side or an external system. Also, the design of an interface ought to have a release year in its time horizon:

> *Interface: Data interchange across a physical media, i.e., pipeline, channel, connector; both business and technical data*
> *can be interchanged; and types of interface media include phone line, FAX, message middleware, other.*
> *Output: Data and information flowing out of a business system that is needed to interact with a receiving business system.*

Table 1. Business Systems Hierarchical Tree for Global Airlines Services

Global Airlines Business Systems								Architecture Releases			
								EA	EA	EA	Project
ID	L1	L2	L3	L4	L5	L6	L7 Hierarchical Levels	1.0	2.0	3.0	
1	Travel Services Business System										
1.1		Individual Travel Services						X			CORE
1.1.1			Airline-Hotels Promotion Services								
1.1.2			Car Rental Promotion Services								
1.1.3			Airline-Amtrak Promotion Services								
1.2		Corporate Travel Services						X			CORE
1.2.1			Airline-Hotels Promotion Services								
1.2.2			Airline-Land Development Promotion Services								
1.2.3			Community and Local Government Promotion Services								
1.3		Domestic Ticket Sales						X			CORE
1.3.1			Economy Ticket Sales								
1.3.2			Business Ticket Sales								
1.3.3			Corporate Ticket Sales								
1.4		International Ticket Sales						X			CORE
1.4.1			Economy Ticket Sales								
1.4.2			Business Ticket Sales								
1.4.3			Corporate Ticket Sales								
2	Corporate Management System										
2.1		Global Financial System						X			CORE
2.1.1			Loans Management System								
2.1.2			Costs Management System								
2.1.3			Receipt Management System								
2.1.4			Payment Management System								
2.1.5			General Ledger Management System								
2.1.6			Corporate Financial Management System								IAA
2.1.6.1				Indpendent Accounting and Reporting System					X		IAA
2.1.6.2				Independent Auditing and Reporting System					X		IAA
2.1.6.3				Balance and Controls Services				X			IAA
2.2		Budget Preparation System									
2.2.1			Mechanical Facilities Maintenance Projected Costs				X				
2.2.2			Domestic Sales Promotion Costs								
2.2.3			International Sales Promotion Costs								
2.2.4			Proposed Budgets by Department								
2.3		Corporate Business Performance System							X		
2.3.1			Enterprise Executive Information Administration and Reporting System							
2.3.2			Internal Mgt Strategic Planning System								
2.3.3			Enterprise Strategic Planning System								
2.3.4			Internal Mgt Operations Planning and Reporting System							
2.3.5			Internal Mgt Knowledge Production System								
2.3.6			Internal Mgt Business Process Mgt System								
2.4		Human Resources Management System						X			
			Payroll Services System								
			Recruitment and Promotion Services System							
			Pension Plan Services System								
			Training Services System								
2.5		Corporate Asset Management System						X			
			Airport Mechanical Systems								
			Airport Information Systems								
			Travel Traning Centers Systems								
2.6		Procurement Management System						X			
			Contract Formation Systems								
			Contract Management Systems								
			Labor Union Relations and Contract Management Systems							
			Purchasing Systems								

Table 1. (*Continued*)

#	Name				Code
3	Enterprise Infrastructure Services				
3.1	**Global Portal System**	X			INFRACS
3.1.1	**Employee Portal Infrastructure System**	X			INFRACS
3.1.2	**User Account Services System**	X			INFRACS
3.1.2.1	User Authentication System	X			INFRACS
3.1.2.2	User Authorization System	X			INFRACS
3.1.2.3	User Preference Management System	X			INFRACS
	User Account Management System				INFRACS
3.1.2.4.1	New Account Registration System	X			INFRACS
3.1.2.4.2	User Account Update System	X			INFRACS
3.2	**Enterprise Data Warehouse**		X		
3.2.1	Enterprise Data Warehouse and Management System				
3.2.2	Legacy Extract, Transform and Load System				
3.2.4	Enterprise Data Warehouse Reporting System				
3.3	**Enterprise Knowledgebase**			X	
3.3.1	Enterprise Corporate Knowledgebase System				
3.3.2	Enterprise Knowledgebase Data Management System				
3.4	**Enterprise Infrastructure Planning and Management System**	X			GOPE
3.4.1	Domestic Enterprise Infrastructure Strategic Planning System				GOPE
3.4.2	International Enterprise Infrastructure Strategic Planning System				GOPE
3.4.3	Global Enterprise Knowledge Production System				GOPE
3.4.4	Global Enterprise Operations Planning and Reporting System				GOPE
3.5	**Global Data Analysis & Decision Support System**			X	GOPE
3.5.1	Global Data Mart Production and Mangement			X	GOPE
3.5.2	Global DSS Services and Reporting System			X	GOPE
3.6	**Communication Services**				
3.6.1	External Internet Gateway Network	X			
3.6.2	Registered User Intranet Network	X			
3.6.3	Internal Intranet Network	X			
3.6.4	Local Host-to-Host Networks				
3.6.4.1	Web Portal Local Host-to-Host Networks	X			
3.6.4.2	Corporate Data Center Local Host-to-Host Networks	X			
3.6.5	Storage Management Network	X			
3.6.6	Systems Management Network	X			
3.6.7	Development and Test Network	X			
3.6.8	Voice Network	X			
3.6.9	Video Network				
3.6.11	**Computer Telephony Services**				
3.6.11.1	Telephone Call Routing System	X			
3.6.11.2	Computer Telephony Integration Services	X			
3.6.12	**Communications Performance Measurement System**	X			
3.6.12.1	Network Performance Data Management System	X			
3.6.12.2	Network Performance Data Analysis and Reporting System	X			
3.7	**Storage Management Services**	X			
3.7.1	Online Storage Management System	X			
3.7.2	Near-line Storage Management System	X			
3.7.3	Archival Storage Management System	X			
	Airport Facility Services				

Input: Data and information received by a business system that is needed to interact with a sending business system.

Owner: Entity that funds the design of the interface and will be responsible for its maintenance throughout the life cycle of the interface.

Release Year: The year in which the interface will first be fielded and become operational.

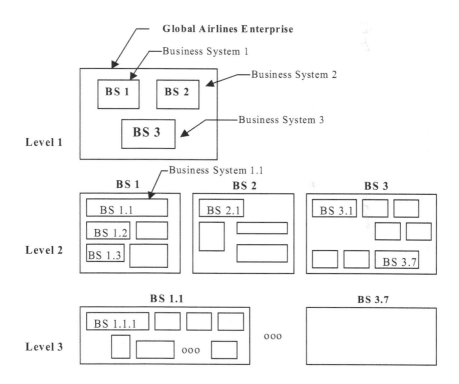

Figure 3. Business System Hierarchical Tree, Graphical Representation

Shown on Figure 4 are the Level 1 interfaces for our enterprise, Global Airline Services. We note, for example, that there are five interfaces between the Travel Services System (BS1.0) and the Corporate Management System (BS2.0):

IF1: Global Employee Profile Data
IF2: Requests and Actual Hires
IF3: Travel Discount Policy
IF4: Payments Received
IF5: Financial Accounting Records

Similarly, there are four interfaces between the Travel Services System (BS1.0) and the Enterprise Infrastructure System (BS3.0); two interfaces between the Corporate Management System (BS2.0) and the Enterprise Infrastructure System (BS3.0); two interfaces between the modernized Global Airline Services and Third-Party Travel Agencies; and two interfaces between Global Airline Services and Third-Party Airport Maintenance Facilities.

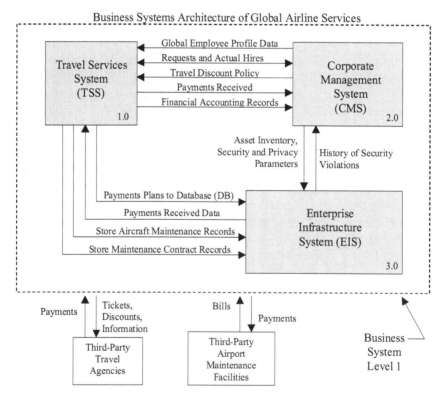

Figure 4. Interfaces at Level 1 of the Global Airline Business Systems Hierarchy

4.7. Technical Reference Model (TRM)

Within the government sector in the USA the Clinger-Cohen Act of 1996 (Public Law 104-106, OMB M-97-16) assigns responsibility to the Chief Information Officer (CIO) of each federal government department to develop, maintain and facilitate the implementation of an information technology architecture (ITA). One instrument of that policy is the Technical Reference Model (TRM) which attempts to provide a conceptual framework and context within which the designer can find a common technical vocabulary and recommendations for interface definition and location within a hierarchy of business systems. The general intent here is to provide technical support to Agencies, Centers, Institutes and Offices in the Department of Defense (DoD) to help coordinate design, development, and acquisition of information systems, i.e., to bring engineering, business, and economic efficiency to the acquisition process.

In general, the TRM provides a taxonomy for identifying a discrete set of conceptual layers, entities, interfaces and diagrams that provides for the specification of standards. The TRM is rooted in the concept of an open systems environment and through its application it supports portable, scalable, and interoperable applications through standard services, interfaces, data formats, and protocols. Specifically, the technical reference model establishes a framework for the identification of information services and standards:

> *The Technical Reference Model (TRM) identifies and describes the information services used throughout a government agency or organization by specifying set of standards on software and hardware behavior, called the Standards Profile; it guides the grouping and use of services as to produce and promote interoperability and economic efficiency throughout the enterprise.*

The basic concepts can be captured in the form of a generic TRM model, as shown on Figure 5. This generic TRM is made up of three components: the Application Software Entity, the Application Platform Entity, and the External Environment, with interfaces providing connectivity among these three entities. Software modules make up the Application Software Entity; this ought to be the architectural entity that contains a box of "thin applications" as well as a second box of general-purpose applications; the thin applications implement functionality that is very specific to a particular project (e.g., determine speed of incoming aircraft), whereas the general-purpose applications implement functionality that are useful to all projects (e.g., data conversion from one format to another, messaging, data storage, etc.). Processing servers (i.e., platforms) and hardware components make up the Application Platform Entity. The External Environment is made up of software and platforms that belong to external systems and users (i.e., third-party agencies, user community, etc.). Application Programming Interfaces (APIs) are then called by the thin applications to request the use of general-purpose applications and infrastructure services.

Among the government agencies involved in the development and promotion of TRM models we can cite the Department of Defense (DOD), US Customs, the Internal Revenue Service, and the Department of Health and Human Services.

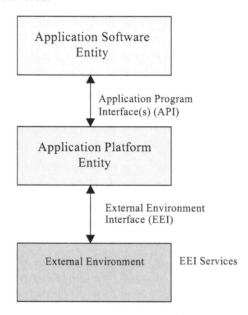

Figure 5. Generic Technical Reference Model (TRM)

4.8. DoD Technical Reference Model

Over the last 10-15 years, the Department of Defense (DoD) has produced a technical reference model that reflects several major architectural efforts, namely the Technical Architecture Framework For

Information Management (TAFIM, 1995). When blown up, this generic model of the DoD TRM takes the shape shown on Figure 6, which consists of four major sub-layers: The Mission Area Application, Support Applications, Application Platform, and the External Environment.

- **Application Software Entity:** There are two sub-layers at the top of the TRM. The Mission Area Applications sub-layer that contains all the mission-specific applications with code that immediately addresses mission requirements and provides the functionality needed to implement those requirements. The intent here is to allow software developers (i.e., contractors) to concentrate on building "thin applications" (i.e., software, code) that provides the specific functionality needed (e.g., target classification, vehicle speed determination, time required to re-configure aircraft, etc.) without having to address code for image re-formatting and presentation, data unit conversion, communication channel support, other. In this manner, applications can later call Application Programming Interfaces (APIs) to reach for varieties of infrastructure services, including common services. Engineering, mission, and operational efficiency is the desired outcome here.

- **Support Applications Entity:** This sub-layer contains those building blocks that support the mission applications, including multi-media, format conversion, communications, database management systems utilities, business processes, and other support applications.

- **Application Programming Interface (API):** Once the mission area applications are built and housed in the Mission Area Applications sub-layer these applications simply make use of APIs to access the support services. With this approach the software builder can immediately dig into the task of building code to implement mission functionality thus reducing development costs. Multiple software developers over the life cycle of the system can build mission applications that will "plug in" and perform well. The price to pay for this operational convenience is of course that of building the Support Applications sub-layer.

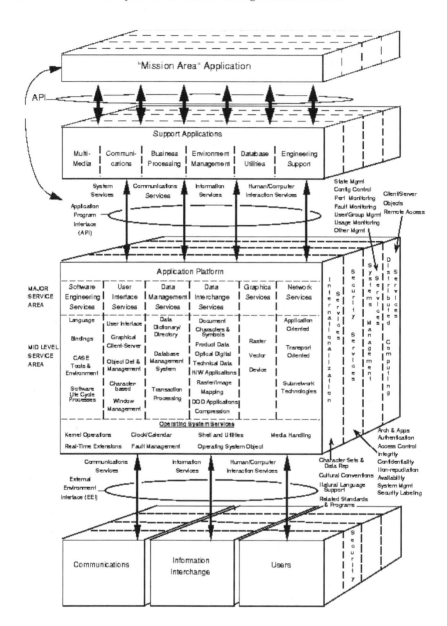

Figure 6. DoD's Technical Reference Model (TRM)

- **Applications Platform Entity:** This sub-layer houses the hardware and software resources that support the services on which the mission area applications will run. Services available through this sub-layer include:

  Data Management Services
  Data Interchange Services
  Software Engineering Services
  User Interface Services Graphics Services
  Network Services
  Operating System Services
  Internationalization Services
  Security Services
  System Management Services, and
  Distributed Computing Services

- **The External Environment Entity (EEI):** This sub-layer is the interface itself between the application platform and the external environment, across which information is exchanged with third-parties. It is often defined primarily in support of system and application software interoperability. The EEI specifies a complete interface between the application platform and the underlying external environment, and may be divided into the following groups:

  - **Human/Computer Interaction Services EEI:** This EEI is the boundary across which physical interaction between the user and the application platform takes place. Examples of this type of interface include cathode ray tube (CRT) displays, keyboard, mice, and audio input/output devices. Standardization at this interface can allow users to access the services of compliant systems without costly re-training, for example.
  - **Information Services EEI:** This EEI defines a boundary across which external, persistent storage service is provided, where only the format and syntax is required to be specified for data portability and interoperability.
  - **Communication Services EEI:** This EEI provides access to services for interaction between internal application software entities and application platform external entities,

such as application software entities on other application platforms, external data transport facilities, and devices. The services provided are those where protocol state, syntax, and format must be standardized for application interoperability.

4.9. U.S. Customs Service Technical Reference Model

Both the IRS and the U.S. Customs operate under institutional and architectural guidance of the U.S. Treasury. The Treasury Enterprise Architecture Framework (TEAF, July 2000) has its own TRM, as shown on Figure 7. It is relatively easy then to map services in the Customs TRM to services and entities in the DoD TRM. Do the TRMs presented above address all challenges of definition of business systems and optimal distribution of interfaces across the enterprise? Probably not. Is the general philosophy of engineering, business, and economic efficiency in EA planning captured in a TRM representation as promoted by Federal agencies and DoD organizations? Probably yes.

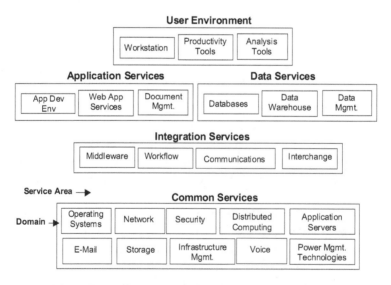

Figure 7. U.S. Customs Technical Reference Model (TRM)

4.10. Assignment of Business Systems to Projects

Now that the Business Systems Design BSD team finally has a set of business systems that are represented hierarchically, so that each business systems and interface is defined in terms of intended functionality (i.e., services to be provided) and validated by the Global customer, one may ask what is next. Who in the engineering organization will inherit these business systems and use them to proceed with the planning and design of the Enterprise Architecture (EA)? A next step is in fact that of breaking up the business hierarchy into groups of business systems that have an *business affinity* for each other and that can be organized and funded into projects of their own, as depicted on Figure 8. Several observations about the hierarchical tree:

- Each "parent" business system in the top level, Level 1, has been decomposed into several sub-systems or "child" business systems that reside in Level 2.
- Each "parent" business system in the top level, Level 2, has been decomposed into several sub-systems or "child" business systems that reside in Level 3, and so on, until a total of 200-300 child business systems are to be found in Level 4, the lowest level for our Global Airlines example.
- The BSD team, in coordination with other business and engineering groups within the PRIME organization, has grouped business systems that share in an affinity for a particular major function (i.e., database management, customer relations, corporate e-services, etc.) into sets of projects. Accordingly, business systems in Sets 2 make up Project A; business systems in Set 1 and Set 3 make up Project C, and so on.
- At the lowest level in the hierarchy (Level 4 in this example) each business system will be assigned to one project only, i.e., a business system cannot be owned by two or more projects.
- However, at the next higher level (Level 3 in this example) each "parent" business system can have a child business system that belongs to one project and another child business system that may be owned by another project, i.e., we see a "parent" system in Level 3 that is owned in part by Project A and in part by Project C.
- Next, interfaces among projects need to be identified, defined, and documented in work products.

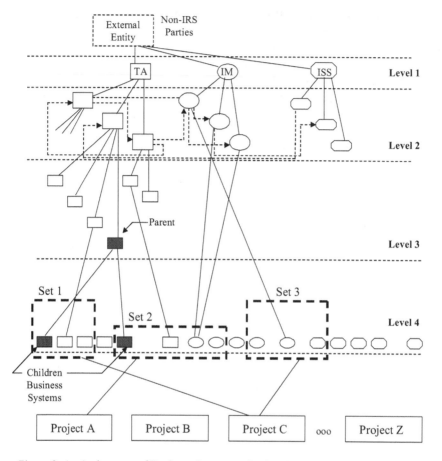

Figure 8. An Assignment of Business Systems to Project (*Source*: A. Goikoetxea, 2004)

- Multiple Projects in our Global Airlines Services example include:

   Global Account Transaction Engine (GATE) Project: Design, development, and fielding of a master relational database with individual and corporate accounts;
   Travel Reservations and Customer Account Management (TRAVEL) Project: Design, development, and fielding of a

seat reservation system with customer account management (CAM) capability;

Infrastructure and Common Services (INFRACS) Project: Design, development, and fielding of infrastructure services (e.g., local area network, data storage, data warehouse, etc.) and common services (e.g., security services, software release management, e-mail, etc.);

Weather Surveillance and Information Distribution (WEATHER): Design, development, and fielding of weather information fusion systems; and

Radar Data Processing (RDP) Project: The design, development, and deployment of a system that feature fast automatic track initiations, very accurate system tracks, avoidance of false/multiple track generation, fast maneuver detection, and uninterrupted and continuous aircraft tracking.

4.11. Conclusions

In this chapter the reader was introduced to a methodology for the definition and organization of business systems in a hierarchical tree.

(1) We learned that a business system is a logical representation of enterprise services, that each business system can house multiple enterprise services, and that one process will normally require services housed in multiple business systems (one-to-many relationship).

(2) There is no single, fail-safe, efficient approach to the identification, definition, and organization of the business systems hierarchy. Initially it is often a slow, painstaking, and frustrating experience, particularly if a large number of executives, decision makers, and engineers attempt to come up with a list with which everyone can agree. My experience has shown that a small group of 3-5 individuals can be most effective in generating an initial set of 25-35 business systems that can later be shared and validated with other decision makers and engineers.

(3) Is the Technical Reference Model (TRM) needed in EA planning? Yes. Not only it can guide the process of defining interfaces among the business systems and the optimal allocation

of these interfaces across the entire enterprise, but it is mandated by Federal regulations in the course of building EAs for government agencies. Can the TRM provide a simple, step-by-step approach to interface definition and allocation. No, it cannot, as it is intended as a guiding framework only.

(4) What is the relationship among business processes and business systems? Business systems exist to provide services needed in the execution of business processes and activities only. Business processes are a basis and driving force behind EA planning.

4.12. Exercises

E4.1 Consider the business systems hierarchy presented on Table 1 for the Global Airline Services enterprise. Add a total of 8 new business sub-systems at level 4 to business systems 1.1.2, 1.3.2, and 1.4.3

E4.2 You are a Chief Architect in the Global Airline Services organization. Since award of an EA modernization contract one year ago to Gasteiz International Inc., a multi-national information systems consulting organization, you have been working with the Business Systems Design team and the hierarchy of business systems has been designed and approved as listed on Table 1 with the condition that these business systems must be allocated to exactly three projects. Proceed to identify and define three projects of your choice and show your own allocation of business systems to these three projects (a) at Level 3 only, and (b) at Level 4 only.

E4.3 Discuss similarities and differences between the DOD Technical Reference Model (TRM) and the US Customs TRM.

(a) Briefly comment on the intended purpose(s) of the DOD TRM, followed by your critique on how well/poorly those purposes are accomplished.
(b) Does one TRM represent advantages over the other? Discuss.
(c) As a systems engineer in the Business Systems Design team of the EA modernization contract for Global Airline Services (a) identify three business processes in Corporate Management Systems and (b) map those business processes to business systems at Level 2 in Enterprise Infrastructure Services (EIS).

Chapter 5

The Data Architectural View

Vision and Strategy
Business Processes Architectural View
System Requirements Development
Business Systems Architectural View
Data Architectural View
Applications Architectural View
Technology Architectural View

5.1. Introduction

Data to an enterprise architecture is like blood to the human body: it is everywhere, it feeds all body parts, it requires storage, maintenance facilities, and it makes use of a network of production centers, pipelines, and processing centers. Additionally, data must be organized into various data types, stored in *database tables*, and these tables need to have *relationships* with each other so that specific *data elements* can be retrieved in fast and economic ways. As we are about to see in this chapter, the Data Architectural View is a key component in the development of the enterprise information architecture (EA) for a business organization in the private sector or a command and control system in the government sector. The Global Account and Travel

Services Engine (GATE) project, we recall from Chapter 4, is the project responsible for building the Architectural Data View and its physical implementation, i.e., the GATE database.

5.2. What is the Data Architectural View?

Data flows from one business system to another business system, and some of the data are stored in the form of data elements in database tables, as depicted in Figure 1.

Examples of data elements in the Data Architectural View, are:

Entity (Table): Individual Account
> d_1: Name (a "data element", also known as a "field" or "attribute")
>
> d_2: Address
>
> d_3: Telephone Number
>
> d_4: Balance (dollars)

Entity (Table): Airline Ticket Form
> d_4: Form_ID
>
> d_5: Account_ID

Entity (Table): Payment Received
> d_6: Amount (dollars)
>
> d_7: Account_ID
>
> d_8: Date of Receipt

Data elements, also called *fields* or *attributes*, make up tables (also known as *entities*), these tables are connected via foreign keys in ways specified during the logical data design effort, and the size in bytes of each data element is determined during the physical data design effort. Data flows represented in the Business Systems Architectural View should map to these data elements for purposes of posting data (as in transaction processing and posting of data to the database) or reading data (as in executing queries to the database). This View also contains tables that store information other than data element content such as *stored procedures* for query execution and the *data definition language (DDL)* that contains the code used to build the physical database itself. Typically 500-750 data elements may end up organized into 35-50 tables to constitute the Data Architectural View.

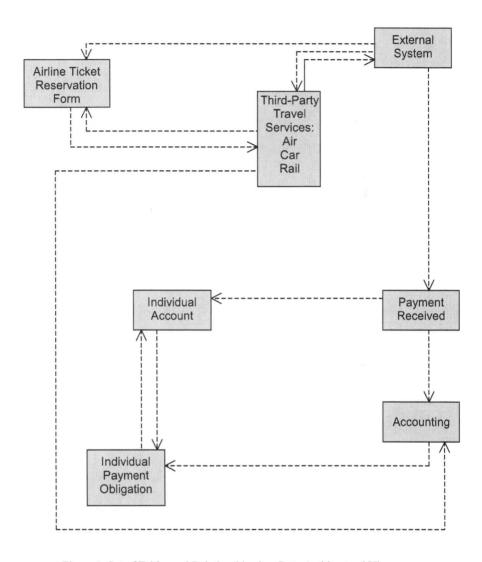

Figure 1. Set of Tables and Relationships in a Data Architectural View

DATA ARCHITECTURAL VIEW: A framework for the identification, definition, representation, organization, and management of data in the Enterprise Architecture (EA). Data are represented through the use of entities, attributes, and relationships.

ENTITY: Any person, organization, sub-system, or event that produces, gathers, uses, or distributes data in the enterprise or the external systems with which it communicates. Entities identified early in the design of the data architectural view generally end up as tables later on during the logical design phase. Examples of entities are Reservation Form, Payment, Payment Plan, Passenger, Cargo, Aircraft, Individual Account, and Accounting.

ATTRIBUTES: Characteristics or dimensions of an entity. An entity will usually have 5-10 attributes, depending on the detail and complexity to be captured during the modeling effort. Attributes are also known as data elements and fields. Examples of attributes in the Aircraft entity are Type (Boeing 747, Douglas D-123, Lockheed 711, Airbus 200, other), Seat Capacity (50, 75, 225, other), Owner (Global Airlines Services, United Airlines, Euskadi Airlines, other), Crew (4, 6, 8, or more).

RELATIONSHIP: A condition that is established by design between two or more entities. The relationship between the Payment entity and the IndividualPaymentObligation entity may be called "Is Applied to" to imply the flow of payment data from the Payment entity to the IndividualPaymentObligation entity.

5.3. How this Chapter is Organized

This chapter presents and illustrates a methodology for the planning and development of the Data Architectural View. Each step of this methodology is described and illustrated with the application of data concepts and definitions to the Global Airlines Services example that we are using throughout the book. Section 5.4 presents a 7-step development approach to building the Data Architectural View, and each step is illustrated with portions of the Data Architectural View for the Global Airline Services example.

Section 5.5 discusses the relationship of the Data Architectural View to the Business Process Architectural View, the Business Systems Architectural View, and the Applications Architectural View.

A Conclusions section reviews the lessons learned in the process of putting together the Data Architectural View. At the end of this chapter Section 5.8 on Exercises is presented to pose questions and to gain further insight.

5.4. A Methodological Approach to the Data Architectural View

Development of the Data Architectural View requires seven steps in the design effort, as depicted in Figure 2. As the design advances from one step to the next, data access standards are gathered and applied, the various legacy (i.e., the "old" sub-systems) and modern data stores are listed, data is organized by major data subject areas, relationships among these data subject areas are established, business data rules are created through interaction with the customer and the functional requirements, attributes are created and given specific characteristics, and each iteration of the Data Architectural View is communicated to the customer, business and engineering teams. Again, communication among the EA teams is essential.

In terms of time resource allocation to the planning phase of the EA, my engineering experience says to go with the following percentage estimates:

Vision and Strategy	10%
Business Process Architectural Vie	15%
System Requirements Development	10%
Business Systems Architectural View	10%
Data Architectural View	20%
Applications Architectural View	15%
Technology Architectural View	20%
	Total = 100%

So that for an EA planning effort of say 18 months, a total of (18 months)(0.20) = 3.6 months or 14 weeks, approximately, ought to be allocated to the planning portion alone of the Data Architectural View. In turn, those 14 weeks need to be allocated to the various steps and models where I would recommend the following guidelines:

Step 1: Data Organization Model	10%
Step 2: Data Diagnostic Model	5%
Step 3: Subject Area Data Model	10%
Step 4: Conceptual Data Model	10%
Step 5: Logical Data Model	15%
Step 6: Physical Data Model	25%
Step 7: Communicate Data Architectural View	25%
	Total = 100%

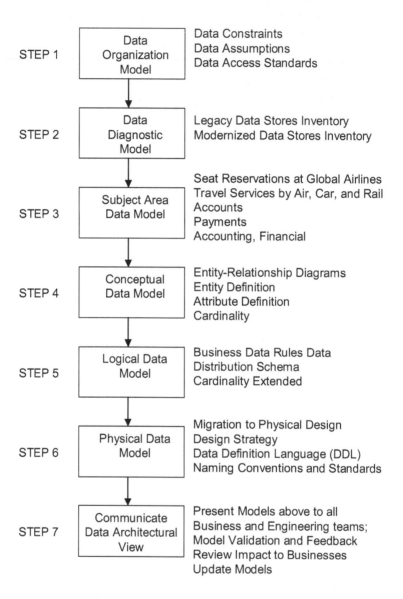

Figure 2. Methodology for the Construction of the Data Architectural View

As such, the amount of time to be allocated to Step 4, Conceptual Data Model, is (18 months)(0.20)(0.10) = 0.36 months or one-and-a-half weeks, approximately. Now, time allocation by itself, alone, is not very meaningful, and allocation of people resources across the various development teams needs to be considered as well. Depending on the number of people assigned to the Step4 the number of weeks needed to do the job will vary. See Chapter 19, EA Implementation Strategy, for a comprehensive discussion and a set of guidelines for resource allocation to EA planning, design, development, testing, pilot, and, release management.

Step 1: Create the Data Organizational Model
This most important step sets up the "working environment and mood" of the data model design effort by placing on the design board desired data principles, data constraints, data assumptions, and data access standards.

Data Principles
These data principles address customer data needs and requirements in areas of data consolidation and integration, naming conventions, minimal disruption of on-going legacy business processes, data privacy and security:

- The GATE database will conform to all Global Airline Services data privacy and security policies and regulations.
- GATE will house and manage all authoritative data on Global domestic (USA) and international data stores.
- GATE will employ relational database design principles, technology, and management practices to replace all legacy data stores and systems, both file and relational systems.
- GATE will conform to and support best financial accounting practices.
- GATE will conform to and support best financial auditing practices, and these will be performed independently of financial accounting practices.
- GATE shall adhere to naming conventions in the US Department of Defense (DoD) Database and Data Element Catalog.
- An integral component of the GATE design will be those to enable data back up, intra-site data failover and recovery, as well as inter-site data failover and recovery.

Data Constraints

Data constraints represent limitations and practices for designers to observe in the course of designing the GATE database and associated sub-systems:

- The GATE database and management system shall be able to communicate with legacy systems, and this capability shall be transparent to all domestic and international Global users.
- GATE must utilize legacy data formatting when posting data to or reading data from the legacy systems.
- GATE shall accept requests for data (i.e., queries) only from affiliated external systems.

Data Access Standards

Ways and means of accessing the GATE database are not arbitrary and instead need to be specified:

- GATE shall adhere strictly rules and guidance provided by the Global Data Access Standards notebook.
- All data requests from Global travel service centers must be authenticated and authorized.
- Third-party travel services centers cannot access the GATE database directly; instead, they submit requests for data and services through the Global Portal.
- All data access to GATE must use message middleware (e.g., IBM MQSeries, Tuxedo, other) and direct on-line access by any other means will be denied.

Data Assumptions

WHERE, geographically, within the enterprise will data be stored? And HOW data will be stored? Often these are considerations that must be addressed early in the design:

- The GATE database and data will be owned and maintained by Global Airline Services and housed in the Washington DC headquarters facility, the primary site, and the New York facility, the alternate site.
- The legacy data stores and data will be owned and maintained by Global Airline Services and housed in its current location, the Fairfax City facility.

- GATE will initially house new individual and corporate accounts only; eventually, however, all legacy accounts will be migrated to the GATE database and database management systems.

Step 2: Create the Data Diagnostic Model

This step identifies all the data assets, both legacy and planned, that are relevant to the GATE development effort, as depicted on Table 1. The intent here is to identify the list of all legacy data resources available, including tables and data elements in those tables, and then to make decisions on number of new geographical sites and distribution of planned, modernized data stores.

The task of figuring out which legacy databases can be "re-cycled" and used in the design of new modernized databases is not a trivial endeavor, but it is not an insurmountable task either. As many as 50%-75% of the legacy data elements will often be required to design, operate, and maintain the new modernized databases and as such the identification of these data elements and the data associated with them is a vital task. As the database designer sets to identify existing multiple databases that may contain the tables and data elements of interest to him/her several situations are possible, as depicted on Table 2. In the simplest case, Case 1, all desired data elements or objects (i.e., data elements, tables, stored procedures, other) reside in one data source so the design strategy is to utilize that single data source and no decision opportunity exists. In Case 2 all desired objects reside in multiple copies of the same data source. In Case 3 desired objects reside across multiple, distinct data sources, with no sharing of data objects across data sources. Finally, in Case 4 desired objects reside across multiple, distinct data sources, but some data objects are shared across data sources available. See Goicoechea (2001, 2000) and Chapter 9, Principles of Distributed Database Design, for an analytical perspective on the treatment of Case 4.

Step 3: Create the Subject Area Data Model

This step identifies for the first time the main subject areas in the data model design effort. This high-level view of subject areas allows data model designers to begin to "carve out" the design space into a finite number of boxes that are going to serve a place-holders for data attributes. In the case of our Global Airlines Services example the model is depicted in Figure 3 and the subject areas are as follows:

Table 1. Legacy and Modernized Data Assets

Data Asset	Location	Technology	Size	Description
I. Legacy Data Stores (Current State)				
Global Account Database (GAD)	Fairfax City, Virginia	Flat File on Tape	3.2 Million accounts using 45 GB	Both Individual and Corporate accounts
Global Human Resources Database (HRDB)	New York City, New York	Flat File on Tape	1,350 Employee files using 1.3 GB	Global Airline Services Employee files
Spare Parts and Maintenance Database (SPM)	Manassas, Virginia	Flat File on Tape	26.5 Million Parts using 14 GB	Manufacturer, parts, and maintenance records
		Total =	60.3 GB	
II. Modernized Stores within the GATE Datebase (Future State)				
Individual Travel Services Account Database (ITSA)	Washington, DC	Sybase Relational Database	2.6 Million accounts 27.5 GB	Individual accounts
Manufacturer and Spare Parts Database (MASP)	Washington, DC	ORACLE Relational Database	450 Vendors, 35 Million Parts using 10 GB	Manufacturer, parts records
Maintenance Database (MADA)	Washington, DC	ORACLE Relational Database	1.1 Maintenance Plans using 5.5 GB	Airline Unit and maintenance records
		Total =	43 GB	

Case No.	Distribution of Available Data Elements	Architectural Strategy	Optimization Criteria
1	All desired data elements/objects reside in one data source	Select single data Source	None. No decision opportunity exists
2	Desired data objects reside in one data source with exact replications in multiple sites	Select single data source	Select site that offers lowest system development cost. Other criteria: - performance
3	Desired data objects reside across multiple, distinct data sources; no sharing of data objects across data sources		Select entire set of data sources. No decision opportunity exists.
4	Desired data objects reside across multiple, distinct data sources; there is sharing of data objects across data sources		Select subset of data sources using optimization criterion: - Performance - Cost - Other

Table 2. Distribution Patterns of Data Elements Across Multiple Data Sources

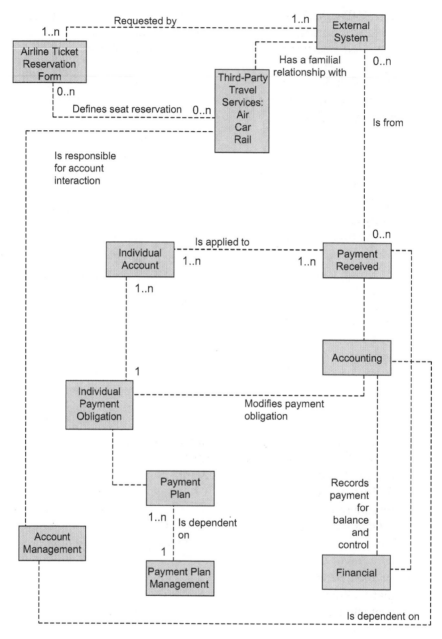

Figure 3. Subject Area Data Model, Global Airlines Services Example

- **Third-Party Travel Services**: Non-Global travel agents can request information on seat availability and other services (e.g., flight connection with other, airlines discount packages, car rental services, rail transfer, other) and electronic airline ticket reservation forms from Global Airline Services.

- **Airline Ticket Reservation Form:** This is an electronic ticket reservation form that can be requested by travel agents using computer consoles and HTML formatting from web servers owned by Global Airlines Services.

- **External System:** An external system can be any business or government entity that has a relationship with Global. A business entity can be a bank, a corporation, or a hotel. A government entity can be a local, state, or federal agency.

- **Individual Account**: It is the account assigned to an individual that is doing business with Global (e.g., purchasing an airline ticket, establishing a business travel account with a payment plan, etc.).

- **Account Management**: This entity manages the individual accounts; data attributes that characterize this entity are date when account was created, account ID, balance, and account authorizing Global individual ID.

- **Payment Received**: It is the dollar amount paid by an external system on behalf of an individual who has an account with Global.

- **Individual Payment Obligation:** This is the actual dollar amount owed by an individual after travel incentives (e.g., 10,000-Mile Club, travel referral compensation, voluntary seat release for over booking, etc) are applied to that individual's dollar balance.

- **Payment Plan**: An individual (or corporation) can request and subscribe to a payment plan with Global; this is the equivalent of Global granting credit privileges to that individual (or corporation).

- **Payment Plan Management**: This entity manages the payment plans associated with individual accounts; data attributes that characterize this entity are date when plan began, interest rates, number of months of plan, account ID, and authorizing Global individual ID.

- **Accounting:** This entity stores information needed to conduct the accounting function of Global, including payment (credit), date of payment, individual that sends payment, amount of travel service (debit), date of expenditure for travel service, and account ID.
- **Financial:** This entity stores information needed to conduct the financial function of Global, including account ID, request for payment received from Third-Party travel services, total credits earned across Global on a daily basis, and total debits received by Global on a daily basis across all accounts.

Step 4: Create the Conceptual Data Model

During this step in the creation of the Architectural Data View, the analysis continues to look at the overall data requirements of the proposed information system.

We are still looking at a high-level view of the entities but already we want to begin the task of identifying the attributes that characterize each entity and represent business relationships among these entities. Sure, later on as data modeling continues there will be changes to make to the conceptual model to reflect better, incremental understanding of the business requirements.

> *Conceptual Data Model (Schema): A detailed specification of the data entities, a list of attributes that characterize each entity, and a complete set of entity relationships that are technology independent. At this point it is recommended to have this conceptual model, also called schema, in graphical format, and entity-to-function mappings, as well as storing these specifications as metadata in a data dictionary or metadata repository.*

A typical set of entities and their attributes in the Global Purchasing Department of the same example, are shown on Figure 4 and Table 3, respectively. The entity SUPPLIER, for example, has four attributes: Supplier_Identifier, Supplier_Name, Supplier_Zipcode, and Supplier_Type; no need at this point in the design to define the attributes themselves in detail, beyond the purpose intended by the attribute name itself. The relationship "Sends" between the entity SUPPLIER and the entity SHIPMENT has cardinality "Mandatory One" to mean that there must be one supplier, otherwise the shipment cannot take place since the supplier will be sending the shipment, "Optional Many" indicating that there can be 0, 1, 2, 3, ...many shipments.

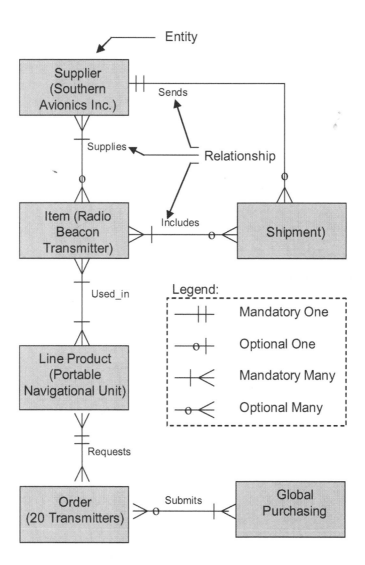

Figure 4. Entity-Relationship Diagram (ERD) for the Global Purchasing Department

Table 3. Data Attributes for Conceptual Data Model

	Attribute Name (i.e., data element name)
SUPPLIER	Supplier_ID Supplier Name Supplier_Zipcode Supplier Type
ITEM	Ball_Bearing_ID Ball_Bearing_Price Fastener Identifier Fasterner_Price
LINE PRODUCT	Product_Line_Name Product_Line_Sales_Goal Product_Line_Promotional_Status Product_Line_Partnership_Name
GLOBAL PURCHASER	Global_Purchaser_ID Global_Purchaser_Division_Name Global_Purchaser_Division_Country Global_Purchaser_Division_Airline_Code
ORDER	Order number Global_Purchaser_Identifier Order_Placement_Date Order_Shipment_Date
SHIPMENT	Shipment Identifier Shipment_Bill_of_Laden_Document_Identifier Shipment Content Order_Shipment_Date

Entity-to-Function diagrams (EFD) as the one shown on Figure 5 are also valuable representations of the Create (C), Read (R), Update (U), and Delete (D) data interactions between the business functions of the enterprise and the entities themselves (i.e., CRUD). We note that the entities in the Global Purchasing Department are already represented in this EFD and that, for example, the Airline Order Placement business function is recognized to have all four data interactions, i.e., CRUD. Similarly, in an actual data modeling effort the EFD would be extended to encompass all business functions (derived from the business processes of Chapter 3) and all entities in the conceptual data model.

Business Functions:	Individual Account	Corporate Account	Travel Services Center	Flight Reservation Order/Form	Flight Itinerary	Payment Received	Invoice Received	Ground Support Equiment	Supplier	Shipment	Line Product	Global Purchasing	Order	Spare Parts	Car Rental partnership
Market Research		CR	CR U		CR U				CR		CR UD	CR			CR UD
Business Planning		CR U			CR U						CR U		CR U		CR
Sales Training	CR U	CR	CR UD			CR	CR		CR U	CR U	CR U	CR U			
Travel Package Development															
Vacation Travel Incentives															
Car Rental Partnership Planning															
Rail Partnership Planning															
Airline Order Placement									CR UD			CU D	CR UD		
Airline Order Fulfillment									CR UD	CR U	CR UD	CR UD			
Spare Parts Order Placement									CR UD				CR UD		
Spare Parts Order Fulfillment										CR UD	CR UD				
Maintenance Planning															
Airport Asset Management															
Production Operations															
Security Asset Order Placement															
Security Asset Order Fulfillment															
Accounting															
Balance and Controls															
Financial Reporting															
Human Resources/Hiring															
Loan Management															
LEGEND: C = Create, R = Read, U = Update, D = Delete															

Figure 5. An Entity-to-Function diagram, Global Airline Example

Step 5: Create the Logical Data Model

Step 5 extends the modeling effort represented in the Logical Data Model to accomplish two very specific activities: (1) convert the information content of entity and attributes into a standard notation called *relations*, and (2) transform these relations into basic elements following a well established process called *normalization*. The result will be a complete set of specifications for organizing data into data elements, grouping these data elements into relations (i.e., tables), and then we provide the means for these relations to communicate with each other through the use of *relational keys*.

From Table 2 we can proceed to write down the schema for the entities in the Global Purchasing Department as shown on Figure 6. The order of the attributes within an entity is not important.

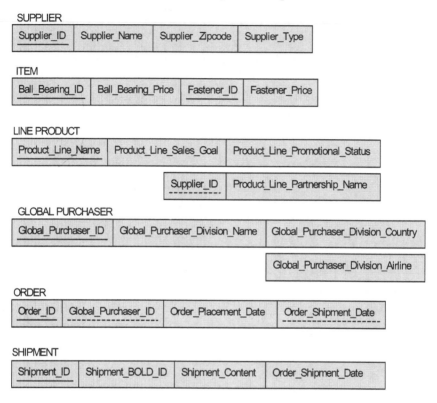

Figure 6. Schema for Six Relations in Global Purchasing Department, Global Airlines Services

Next, as we proceed to store instances of attribute values within a particular entity we end up with a relation which is a two-dimensional table of data, i.e., the table columns are attributes and the table rows are data records.

Codd's Basic Normal Forms

- Three main motivational forces behind the analytical and technological database management breakthroughs in the last 30 years are: (a) the desire to organize and store data efficiently (i.e., both cost and storage efficiency), (b) the desire to retrieve data in a fast manner, and (c) the desire to exercise control of changes to data over time (i.e., changes to one portion of the database are propagated appropriately to other portions of the database). The relational data model first introduced by E.F. Codd in 1970 contributed greatly to and paved the way for those breakthroughs (Codd 1990, 1970), in particular his concepts and process on *data normalization*. Data normalization is basically a formal process for determining which attributes should be grouped together in a relation in order to accomplish those three measures of efficiency.

Step 6: Create the Physical Data Model
This most vital step guides the designer in the conversion of the Logical Data Model into a full Physical Data Model by defining and quantifying fields that populate the various tables in the database (e.g., FirstName: CHARACTER (8)), identifying the primary and foreign keys, by agreeing on naming conventions for tables and fields, and by deciding on the database environment itself (i.e., Sybase, Oracle, DB2, etc.). Also, database performance optimization considerations may require "de-normalization" of some tables that were placed in Normal Form earlier during the logical design, depending on the structuring of queries that may read some data elements more often than other data elements; those data elements that are queried more often than others can be grouped into a few tables so as to improve query response times (i.e., shorter query response times are desirable). Accordingly, the following activities are carried out during design of the Physical Data Model:

- Name and define fields already identified in the Logical Data Model.
- Quantify fields by storage format also called *data type*. The selection of data type is guided by the desire to minimize storage space needed and to improve data integrity.
- Select *indexes* for efficient storage, connecting, and retrieval of records.
- Analyze historical data and new system functionality (i.e., new business processes built into the modernized enterprise architecture) to arrive at estimates of transaction volumes (create, update, and delete) and query volumes (reads of data elements

only); prepare estimates of the frequency of use of data elements by queries to the database; this knowledge of volumes and frequencies will assist the database designer in determining which data elements will be affected by CRUD activity (C = Create, R = Read, U = Update, and D = Delete) and group data elements accordingly; data elements with high use frequency will get grouped within the same table or set of few tables to minimize number of "joins" and search time as queries are executed.

- Identification and description of technologies (i.e., SQL-based relational databases, C++ based object-oriented databases) and database management systems that are best suitable for the enterprise (i.e., Oracle, Sybase, DB2, other).

Field Data Types

Each database management system (DBMS) may support slightly different data types. Access, for example, supports nine data types as shown on Table 4.

Table 4. Access Data Types (Source: Viescas 1997)

Data Type	Usage	Size
Text	Alphanumeric data	Up to 255 bytes
Number	Numeric data	1,2,4, or 8 bytes
Date/Time	Dates and times	8 bytes
Currency	Monetary data, stored with four decimal places of precision	8 bytes
AutoNumber	Unique value generated by Access for each new record	4 bytes
Yes/No	Boolean (true/false) data	1 bit
OLE Object	Pictures, graphs, or other OLE objects from Windows-based applications	Up to 1 gigabyte (GB)
Memo	Alphanumeric data – sentences and paragraphs	Up to 64,000 bytes
Hyperlink	A link address to a document or file in the WWW internet.	Up to 2048 characters

Oracle supports nine data types as shown on Table 5.

Table 5. Oracle Data Types

CHAR	Alphanumeric	Up to 255
DATE	Valid calendar dates.	From January 1, 4712 B.C. to December 31, 4712 A.D.
NUMBER	Signed number, plus decimal point and sign.	Up to 40 digits.
DECIMAL	Same as NUMBER	
FLOAT	Same as NUMBER	
INTEGER	Same as NUMBER	
LONG	Alphanumeric	Up to 2 gigabytes in length.
LONG RAW	Binary data, otherwise same as LONG	
MLSLABLE	Representation of a secure operating system	4 bytes
SMALLINT	Same as NUMBER	
VARCHAR2	Alphanumeric	Up to 200 bytes
VARCHAR	Same as VARCHAR2	

Next, entity graphical representation need to include information on attribute type and length, as shown on Figure 7.

Step 7: Communicate the Data Architectural View to Teams and Projects

The development of the Data Architectural View is a highly iterative process, one that ought to involve presentations to and discussions with all the engineering teams to insure the data across the enterprise are accurately, completely, and efficiently represented in the Logical Data Model and Physical Data Model, as presented above.

In this step the Data Architectural View is documented and communicated to other engineering teams and projects through reports, presentations, solicited written comments, and invitations to engineering and customer (EA owner) personnel to attend working sessions of the GATE project and the Enterprise Data Model team. A typical outline of a presentation for presentation of the Data Architecture View is shown on Table 6.

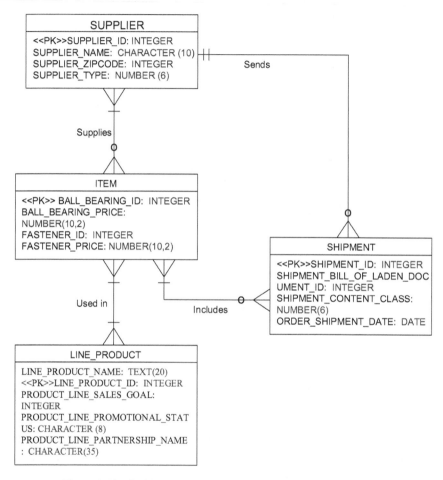

Figure 7. Physical Data Model of the Global Purchasing Department

Table 6. Outline of the Data Architecture View Presentation

- Enterprise Architecture (EA) Planning Phases
- Project Releases and Data Dependencies
- Status of Data Architectural View (e.g., Conceptual, Logical, and Physical Design)
- Impacts, Change Requests (CRs)
- List of Tables and Attributes in the EA
- Mapping of Requirements to Attributes
- Mapping of Legacy Attributes to Modernized EA Attributes
- Database Configuration Items (Cis)
- Database CI Test Planning
- Feedback from EA Development Team
- Feedback from EA Business Systems Team
- Feedback from Release Management
- Feedback from Modernization Projects.
  - CARGO Project
  - FLIGHTS Project
  - GATES Project
  - SEATS Project
  - SDC project
- Questions and Answers

While audience participation should be encouraged, audience composition should be managed to reflect personnel involved in the various steps of the data model methodology (the seven steps presented earlier). During the creation of the Data Organization Model (Step1), for example, it would be productive to invite engineering personnel from the Requirements Management Team and the Business Process Development Team, given that data principles and data constraints would be of general interest to that particular audience. Similarly, during the creation of the Subject Area Data Model (Step 3) it would be productive to invite engineering personnel from the Business Development Team who can then contribute their own insight on mapping of business systems and functions to proposed subject areas. And so on, as depicted on Figure 8.

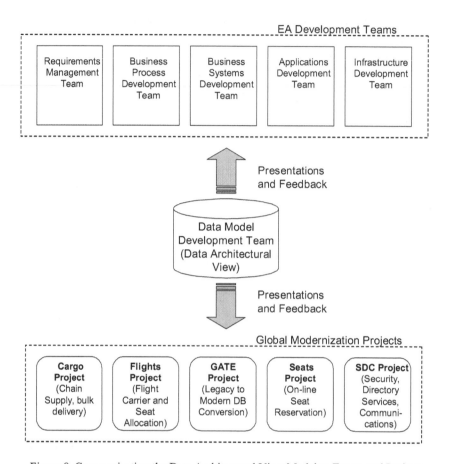

Figure 8. Communicating the Data Architectural View Model to Teams and Projects

Also, and most important, these presentations by the Data Model Development team should present an opportunity for planners, engineers, and subject matter experts (SMEs) from the various teams and from the customer side to come together, meet each other, and voice their needs, concerns, and expectations. In Chapter 4, Business Systems Architectural View, the reader may recall that business systems are allocated to projects, and that as a result these projects receive incremental funding to implement those business systems. It then becomes important to coordinate with project personnel to insure that business implementation in those projects is aligned with concepts, principles, and direction of the Data Architectural View. Content of data inputs, data outputs, and data flows on and across all projects must be coordinated through the Data Architectural View to insure adherence to data naming standards and traceability of requirements to agreed-upon subject areas and data element names.

5.5. Data Ownership and Stewardship

Increasingly today, the importance of data ownership and stewardship is being recognized in the EA community. This importance and awareness is being backed by workshop and conference activities that highlight the issues and call for corporate resources to define objectives and fund specific courses of action. It is recommended that a Data Ownership and Stewardship Group be created early in the EA planning phase and that such a group be encouraged to create a set of objectives, rules of operation, and clear lines of responsibility in coordination with the Enterprise Systems Engineering Board (ESEB; see Chapter 19, EA Implementation Strategy).

5.6. Relationship of the Data Architectural View to the other Architectural Views

In principle, all the EA development teams should talk with each other in an efficient manner during the planning and design stages. In reality this communication is not very effective for several reasons. For one the variables of design of the Data Model Team, these being the data elements, are not exactly at the top of the list of priorities of the other teams, and vice versa. This is so because the variables of design for design team A are different from the design variables for design team B, and only a few design variables are common among the design teams, i.e., the design variables for the Business Systems Development Team (e.g., number and type of interfaces, number of hierarchical levels, portal business system, etc.) are different from the design variables for the Data Model Team (e.g., number of fields, type of field, number of tables, etc.). As a result, the development teams do meet and give presentations to each other on the engineering activities being carried out within their respective teams, but what one team does and says is not easily related to the engineering activities being carried out by the other teams. End result: countless meetings and potentially countless bills to the customer.

Yes, "the East and West eventually meet", as we say, but at the cost of great many resources of money and time. Those of us who have labored in these design teams have witnessed the frustration and have felt helpless at times. At the University of Mondragon, Euskadi, we have put together a small research team at the Institute for Enterprise Architectures and Digital Administration (IEA) to look into ways to address this challenge. At the IEA we believe that part of the answer is to be found in the development of a mathematical foundation or framework for the engineering side of EA design. See Chapter 20, A Mathematical Foundation of Enterprise Architecture Design.

5.7. Conclusion

In this chapter we presented basic concepts, definitions, and design activities in the construction of the Data Architectural View of an enterprise information architecture. Several observations are made:

(1) We introduced the basic concepts of data element (i.e., attribute, field, or column), relational entity, key, and relationship towards the means to store, retrieve, and manage large amounts of data in a relational database environment.

(2) A 7-Step methodology was presented to guide engineering activity towards construction of the Data Architectural View. The engineering approach to dealing with the complexity of the data model is incremental in nature: do the Data Organization Model first to identify data constraints and data standards; next, do the Data Diagnostic Model to identify the inventory of legacy systems and data stores; next, do the Subject Area Data Model to determine the first cut at the entity names for the logical data model; and so forth. In the execution of each step engineers and planners in the various development teams work with each other in order to create and organize data elements that will support the functionality of business processes (i.e., Business Processes View) and business systems (i.e., Business Systems View).

(3) The importance and criticality of building a Conceptual Data Model first, followed by building a Logical Data Model, and eventually building a Physical Data Model was underscored. We want the Conceptual Data Model to feature all the entities in the enterprise so that the EA owners can look at this model and validate it through changes as needed before progressing to the next step. Next, are all entities finally built into the data model and are these entities normalized? If yes, proceed to building the Physical Data Model where substantial engineering resources will be committed to tailor data types, select and build indexes for efficient data storage and retrieval and optimal system performance.

(4) Communication among the various planning and design teams is key to the success of the EA effort. A sample agenda was created to highlight the paramount importance of this activity.

5.8. Exercises

E5.1 Consider the E-R diagram for the Purchasing Department of the Global Airlines Services Corporation, Figure 4.

(a) Develop a Logical Data Model (e.g., similar to Figure 1)
(b) Show the functional dependencies
(c) Develop a set of INF, 2NF, and 3NF relations.

E5.2 Table E1 contains data on suppliers and parts for the Global Airlines Services Corporation.

(a) Convert this relation to one named GLOBAL_SUPPLIER in its first normal form, 1NF. Illustrate the relation with the data shown on Table E1.
(b) List any functional dependencies in GLOBAL_SUPPLIER, as well as candidate key(s).
(c) For the relation GLOBAL _SUPPLIER identify an insert anomaly and a delete anomaly.
(d) Derive a 2NF relation(s) from GLOBAL_SUPPLIER.

Table E1: Sample Data for Suppliers and Aircraft Parts

Supplier Name	Address	Part_No.	Description	Unit Cost
Delta Avionics	Los Angeles	34112	Optical Cable	$275.00
Pacific Infrared	Bilbao			$260.00
Technologies				
Delta Avionics	Los Angeles	80001	VHF	$2,500.00
Flight Chips	Paris		Transceiver	$2,450.00
Cable Unlimited	Teheran			$2,109.00

E5.3 Euskadi Global Enterprises (EGE), a subsidiary of Global Airlines Services, has a number of employees, i.e., table EMPLOYEE. The attributes of the EMPLOYEE include employee ID, name, social security, number of years employed by EGE, and address. The company has several projects (see Chapter 5 for a description of these projects) funded by Global Airline Services: GATE (database modeling), Global Account Transaction Engine (GATE) Project, Travel Reservations and Customer Account Management (TRAVEL) Project, Infrastructure and Common Services (INFRACS) Project, Weather Surveillance and Information Distribution (WEATHER), and Radar Data Processing (RDP) Project. Attributes of these projects include ProjectName, StartDate, BillingRate, and SkillName. An employee can be assigned to 0, 1, or multiple projects. Every two weeks EGE mails a check to each employee who has worked on a particular project during that two-week period based on number of hours and billing rate for an employee.

(a) Draw an E-R diagram with relevant entities.
(b) Draw a class diagram that shows relevant classes, attributes, and relationships.

Chapter 6

The Applications Architectural View

Vision and Strategy
Business Processes Architectural View
System Requirements Development
Business Systems Architectural View
Data Architectural View
Applications Architectural View
Technology Architectural View

6.1. What is a Software Application?

In earlier chapters, we recall, we identified and discussed the makings and workings of the systems requirements, business processes, business systems, and data modeling in an enterprise information architecture (EA). In this chapter we address and discuss the software applications that make up the Applications Architectural View (AAV). Basically, the software applications are the physical means by which the functionality called for in the system requirements and business processes gets implemented (i.e., coded). It is this collection of software applications that are called upon to provide the enterprise services featured within the various business systems. Another way of saying this is: the software applications are housed within the business systems so that when these software applications are activated they provide the services associated with each of the business systems in the enterprise.

> *Software Application:* A software program or collection of software programs that can be activated to produce services needed by the business systems in the enterprise. A software program that automates the execution of a business function.

> *Applications Architectural View:* The set of software applications that are needed to provide the totality of computer-based services in an enterprise architecture, including definition of each application, rules for the design of the applications, an ordering of these applications according to the business systems that they will be supporting, and a plan for the distribution of these applications across physical components of the enterprise architecture. In this manner, an enterprise architecture may consist of 300-400 applications distributed across those physical components.

The identification, definition, language implementation, run-time automation, and distribution of the applications is also a major challenge for the designer of an enterprise architecture. This major task becomes the responsibility of the *Applications Development Team*. Initially this team will have a copy of the Vision and Strategy document with its high-level view of the functionality of the new or modernized enterprise architecture as envisioned by decision makers and architects on the customer side. Over the following weeks and months, this team will also have purview to early design of the business processes, business systems, the enterprise data model, and the technology architecture as these artifacts are developed by their respective design and development teams. Incrementally and progressively the Applications Development Team will arrive at a "general approach" that addresses number and types of applications, selection of computer languages to use to implement and code the applications, application design rules, and a plan for the distribution and allocation of the applications to the various physical components (i.e., hardware platforms) in the technology architecture.

> *Design and development of the Applications Architectural View ought to be independent of computer languages and choices to be made for physical components of the enterprise architecture, for the most part. This is not say that this design and development effort takes place in a*

vacuum and, instead, it is cognizant of the evolution of computer languages, the preference by manufacturers of computer technology for one computer language over another, even the financial status and prospects for corporate stability in the market of one manufacturer over another.

Then, it is the challenge of engineers and computer personnel in the *Applications Development Team* to design and implement a set of applications in a manner that sees that system functionality is fully captured, that is cost efficient, cognizant of the emerging technologies in the market, and knowledgeable of emerging technologies, computer languages, and language development tools and environments.

6.2. How this Chapter is Organized

This chapter begins with a description of 7 steps involved in the construction of the Applications Architectural View (AAV) in Section 3. Section 4 calls for the construction of "traceability matrices" to insure that applications are mapped to artifacts in the other architectural views, e.g., mapping of applications to business systems in the Business Architectural View.

Section 5 presents a high-level view of software standards applicable to EA planning. Section 6 illustrates the construction of an applications architectural view for the Global Airlines Services example. A Conclusions section, Section 7, reviews the main design points made in this chapter. Finally, an Exercises section and a Bibliography section conclude this chapter.

6.3. A Methodology for Construction of the Applications Architectural View

Development of the Applications Architectural View requires seven steps in the design effort, as depicted in Figure 1. As the design advances from one step to the next, the system requirements baseline is reviewed, the business systems hierarchy is revisited, an applications development model is adopted to set guidelines for the distribution of applications across the client portals, Web servers, Web application servers, mainframe(s), and database management systems (DBMS). In the process of doing all this the Technology Development Team (or

Infrastructure Development Team) makes sure that each iteration of the Technology Architectural View is communicated to the customer, business and engineering teams, and project personnel.

Time resource allocation to the planning phase of the EA may look as follows:

Vision and Strategy	10%
Business Process Architectural View	15%
System Requirements Development	10%
Business Systems Architectural View	10%
Data Architectural View	20%
Applications Architectural View	**15%**
Technology Architectural View	20%
Total =	100%

Accordingly, for an EA planning effort of, say, 36 months, a total of (36 months)(0.15) = 5.4 months or 22 weeks, approximately, ought to be allocated to the planning portion alone of the Applications Architectural View.

Steps involved in the construction of the Applications Architectural View may vary from one organization to another, depending on resources available and constraints, but a sequence of steps similar to the seven steps shown on Figure 1 may apply.

Next, those 22 weeks need to be allocated to the various steps and models, and a recommended guideline may be as follows:

Step 1: Review of Business Systems	5%
Step 2: Gather Application Principles, Constraints	15%
Step 3: General Applications Model	20%
Step 4: Application Design Rules	10%
Step 5: Application Templates and Tools	15%
Step 6: Allocate Applications to Architecture	10%
Step 7: Communicate Technology Architectural View	25%
Total =	100%

As such, the amount of time to be allocated to Step 3, General Applications Model, is (36 months)(0.15)(0.20) = 1.08 months or four weeks, approximately. Now, time allocation by itself, alone, is not very meaningful and programmer allocation across the various development teams needs to be considered as well. Again, see Chapter 17, EA Implementation, for a comprehensive discussion and set of guidelines for

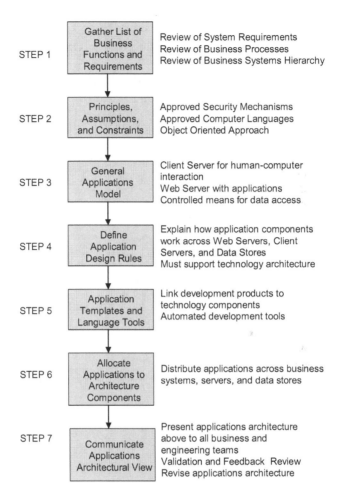

Figure 1. Steps in the Construction of the Applications Architectural View

resource allocation to EA planning, design, development, testing, pilot, and, release management. Next, we proceed to describe briefly each of the seven Steps.

Step 1: Gather List of Business Functions and Requirements

This step is undertaken by the Applications Development Team in order to become thoroughly knowledgeable of the set of system requirements, business processes, and the business systems as documented in their respective work products and already described in Chapters 4 and 5. From the beginning, application designers should be very familiar with all the requirements and business functions called by the proposed enterprise architecture. Later in the design effort, as subject matter experts (SMEs) join the applications design effort, application designers must become intimately cognizant of the functionality to be coded and implemented in the applications. In an Object-Oriented application design environment, for example, this intimate knowledge of business functions and business processes is needed in order to capture it fully in the following engineering activities:

- Definition of Elementary Business Processes (EBP)
- Definition of System Business Services (SBS)
- Creating EBP Scenarios and Storyboard
- Transitioning of the Application Design to Coding.

Step 2: Principles, Assumptions, and Constraints

This Step sets forth the application development philosophy for members of the Applications Development Team with regards to ways and means of getting applications talking to each other, gaining access to data, security concerns, and the optimal distribution of applications across platforms.

Application Principles

These are general guidelines for application design and development that reflect best-practices, the functionality called for in the system requirements, and the vision of the Applications Development (contractor) team:

- Modernized applications architecture is message-based and asynchronous (or synchronous connectivity among applications, as the system requirements may call for).
- Where possible and cost-effective commercially-off-the-shelf (COTS) code products shall be used by both legacy and modernized applications.
- Custom (i.e., non COTS) applications must conform to the set of applications templates approved by the Applications Development Team (see Step 5).

- Custom applications must use approved security mechanisms across interfaces.
- Only C++ and Java shall be used for modernized applications; this is only an example, the point being that application development teams across participating contractor groups (i.e., Prime and Contractor teams) must agree to use the same set of programming languages to attain desired levels of system interoperability, performance, and cost efficiency.
- GATES applications will eventually replace legacy applications.

Application Assumptions and Constraints

This set of application assumptions and constraints address key application-to-application communication paradigms that support the customer's concern for and philosophy on security and mechanisms for data access:

- Applications requirements for GATES will change during the development process due to new business paradigms that may be required to stay competitive in the airline industry (e.g., supply chain management, and changing/new Federal Aviation Administration (FAA) regulations)
- Business rules are to be used throughout the applications architecture; some of the business systems will be heavy users of business rules and may require the use of business rules engines to harvest and manage those rules throughout the enterprise; custom applications must compatible with business rules management systems (BRMS).
- Harvesting of business rules via interviews with subject-matter-experts (SMEs) and Global Airline Services executives will be challenging, may require time resources, and at times may slow down the applications design effort.
- Client platforms will require a common user interface (CUI) for all applications to be run/accessed on those platforms.
- In order to optimize application development and enterprise resource utilization (i.e., CPU, RAM, storage devices, other) the primary method of user interaction with the enterprise will be through thin, web-based presentation; these "thin clients" will call on application services rendered by applications housed in other platforms (e.g., Web Application Servers).

- A few "fat clients" will reside on servers that house applications and will make application services available to thin clients and other platforms via remote displays.
- The presentation layer will use a publish-and-subscribe paradigm.
- A Structured Query Language (SQL) layer of code will provide access to GATES and other data stores; custom and COTS applications will not be allowed to access data stores directly and, instead, they must communicate with the SQL data access layer via message queues and an asynchronous messaging protocol.

Step 3: General Applications Model

Economic efficiency, system performance, and resource management considerations require that applications be organized in some near-optimal fashion. In the last decade we have learned to group applications into "strata" according to affinity of services provided by the applications and support for each other, as Figure 2 depicts.

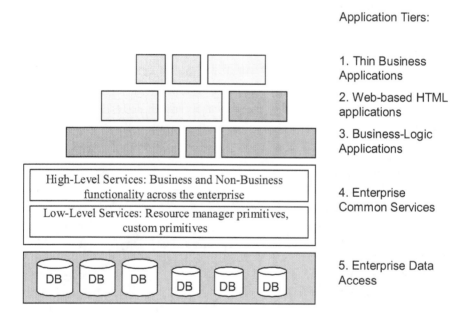

Figure 2. General Enterprise Applications Pyramid Architecture

In this applications pyramid model five strata or tiers are recognized. Within Tier 1 at the top of the pyramid reside very thin, mission-specific applications; these applications implement the functionality called for in the system requirements. Tier 2 houses Web-based HTML applications used mainly to support portals in client/server architectural frameworks. Business logic and business rules environments are more likely to be housed in Tier 3. The bulk of enterprise common services (i.e., infrastructure services such as data conversion, data access, queue messaging, data warehousing, decision support systems, other) are provided by applications in Tier 4, many of which will be COTS products). Finally, SQL-based and C++ applications in Tier 4 provide access to and manage the data stores in the enterprise.

A more detailed view of the same applications model is shown on Figure 3. At the front end of this applications model one finds the Client with its human-computer interface (i.e., browser, local file directory, and function menus); such thin client can be Web-based and will usually reside in a desktop or laptop platform. A Web server or farm of servers will store light HTML applications and will manage its interactions with the client. In terms of connectivity, messaging middleware can be used between applications and the platforms that host these applications; the queue messaging can be asynchronous between platforms to accommodate different operating systems (OS) or specific needs in business logic, e.g., message A cannot be retrieved from queue 1 by an application until events B and C have been triggered by other applications.

Mission-oriented applications can reside in a Web Applications Server, along with software agents that support the HTML and messaging applications. Common/infrastructure services are provided by fat applications that reside in the Enterprise Common Process Server; as mentioned earlier these services include data conversion, data access, queue messaging, data warehousing, security, and decision support systems. Access to data stores can be accomplished in several controlled ways. One data access mechanism is through the use of Application Programming Interfaces (APIs) that free the designer of the mission-specific applications from the burden of interfacing directly with other pieces of code, either modernized or legacy code; instead, the designer calls a particular API that accesses services in the Enterprise Common Process Server or the database management system (DBMS).

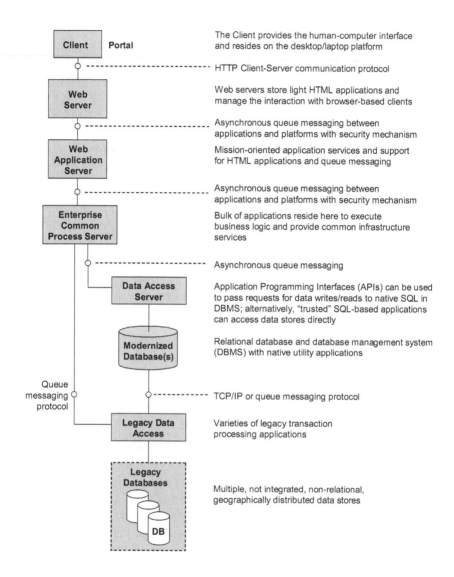

Figure 3. Web-Based General Applications Model

All enterprise architectures must deal with earlier legacy systems at one point or another in the enterprise modernization process; this is often a most challenging endeavor due to a number of reasons, including poor or missing documentation of legacy systems, stove-pipe systems and applications, procedure and labor intensive communication protocols, and a layer of convoluted organizational bureaucracy. Still, the modernized systems must communicate with the legacy system during the design and operational phases in the life cycle of the enterprise architecture via a variety of communication protocols (e.g., TCP/IP) and temporary "transition bridge" applications that eventually will have to be thrown away in part or fully.

Step 4: Define Application Design Rules

There are two main categories of design rules that the application designer needs to be aware of: (1) inter-application design rules, and (2) and intra-application design rules. Inter-application design rules address varieties of languages and communication frameworks among architectural components (i.e., use of Web-based interfaces between applications residing in platform A and platform B). Intra-application design rules deal with the specifics of a particular language development environment (e.g., software engineering standards, use of object-oriented constructs in C++).

> *Applications are designed and exist for the whole purpose of creating and/or supporting the services that are to be provided by the business systems identified earlier in the Business Systems Architectural View of Chapter 4 and nothing else. Accordingly, applications in the Applications Architectural View are designed to populate the various logical business systems and to make happen the variety of business system services that will be needed throughout the enterprise as advertised in the Business Systems Hierarchy.*

Inter-Application Design Rules

Inter-application design rules address varieties of languages and communication frameworks among architectural components (i.e., use of Web-based interfaces between applications residing in platform A and platform B).

- Client
  - "Thin" clients are preferred, with a minimum of application content to invoke computer-human interfaces (i.e., browsers), security services, and system administration services; "fat" clients to be the exception to this rule as these require duplication of applications across platforms.
  - for A few "fat clients" will reside on servers that house applications and will make application services available to thin clients and other platforms via remote displays.
- Web Server
  - HTML pages and other Web services are delivered using HTTP
  - Only approved APIs shall be called by Web services.
- Web Application Server
  - These applications will be used to support Web services including menu displays, receipt of user requests, format conversion, and forward requests for data.
  - House agents for approved messaging middleware and security services only.
  - Re-use of common application services (e.g., API frameworks, business logic components, business rules engines, and queue messaging) across as many business systems as possible.
- Enterprise Common Process Server
  - Common infrastructure services to be developed and controlled by each application, i.e., request for data from
  - data stores, request for directory services, posting of data to data stores, reformatting of data (e.g., from a DB2 relational format to a flat-file legacy data format).
  - The inventory of common infrastructure services is to be used by all applications as needed; the intent here is to attain economic efficiency by reducing duplication of common applications across platforms.
- Data Access Server
  - Access to data stores will be controlled separately by applications housed in the other servers, i.e., by mission-specific applications, security, and directory services.
  - All application development teams (i.e., all contractor teams) must use data access services residing in this server

category, including API calls; only "trusted" parties (e.g., corporate offices of Global Airline Services) can send in workloads of transactions for batch processing and posting to the GATES database.

Intra-Application Design Rules

Intra-application design rules deal with the specifics of a particular language development environment (e.g., use of object-oriented constructs in C++: Activity, Use Case, Sequence, Elementary Business Processes (EBP), Business System Service (SBS), Class Diagrams, etc.). In the early 1980's and 1990's the object-oriented community witnessed the appearance of a large number of design languages which carried a number of common features while each featured some unique design representations features as well.

Step 5: Applications Templates and Language Tools

This Step discusses the use of application templates and lists existing language development tools. Shown on Table 1, for example, is a list of prominent languages available today for applications development, along with a list of criteria for language selection and use. It is a function of the Enterprise Systems Engineering Board (ESEB) to propose and control the use of languages in the enterprise. This is to say that every development team must coordinate and comply with ESEB language use policy.

In terms of development tools, Table 2 lists a set of most prominent tools across languages, processes, and platforms. Again, it is a function of the Enterprise Systems Engineering Board (ESEB) to propose and control the use of language development tools in the enterprise and to see that every development coordinates and complies with ESEB language development policy.

Step 6: Allocate Applications to Business Systems

How does the designer (i.e., programmer, systems designer, manager, etc.) go about distributing applications across the hierarchy of business systems? This activity is also part engineering and part art. Generally, he/she goes about this task by applying experience and general guidelines that may be available within the EA organization. In this Step I like to propose what I call the *Five Competing Principles of Application Distribution in the Enterprise*:

Table 1. Criteria for Selection of Application Language(s)

Selection Criteria	Application Languages							
	Weight	C	C++	JAVA	Visual Basic	Cobol	HTML	XML
1. Ease of Code Generation	4		+					
2. Ease of Code Maintainability	3		+					
3. Follows Industry Standards	5	`	++					
4. Easy to Use Toolset	3		++					
5. Required Skills Available in the market	3		+					
6. Interoperability with existing legacy languages	2		0					
7. Interoperability with languages in modernized architecture components	5		++					
8. Likely to stay in market for next 5-10 years	5		++					
9. Robustness during run time	5		++					
10. Productivity	5		++					
11. Performance	5		++					
12. Cost of toolset	3		+					

Legend:
Weights: 1 – 5 Ratio Scale (Note: weights are subjective, vary from one decision maker to another.
Attribute Values: 0 = Not Applicable, + = Desirable, ++ Highly Desirable.

Table 2. Language Development Tools

Process	Languages	Development Tools	Intended Platform
1. Web Thin Client	JAVA Script, HTML	Internet Explorer 5.0 Netscape 4.7	NT Workstation Intel-Compatible
2. Web Fat Client	Visual Basic, C++	MS Visual Studio 6	NT Workstation Intel-Compatible
3. Applications Web Server	ISAPI, CGI, C++	Sun Visual Workshop 2.1 Netscape Enterprise Server 3.6	SUN E10000
	ASP, ISAPI, CGI, C++	MS Visual Studio 6 MS Internet Information Server 4	NT Server Intel-Compatible
4. Server Process	COBOL, C++	IBM VisualAge 2000	PCM Mainframe
	C++	Netscape Application Server 2.1 Netscape Enterprise Server 3.6 SUN Visual Workshop 2.1	SUN E10000
5. Batch	C++	SUN Visual Workshop 2.1	SUN E10000
	COBOL, C++	IBM VisualAge 2000	PCM Mainframe

- <u>Economic Efficiency Principle</u>: Applications shall be designed, implemented, and distributed across architectural components (i.e., processing servers, data management servers, routers, etc.) so as to maximize the ratio of number of business services to number of applications in the enterprise. We want to provide all the business services with a minimum number of applications possible.

- <u>System Performance Principle</u>: Applications shall be designed, implemented, and distributed across architectural components (i.e., processing servers, data management servers, routers, etc.) so as to minimize aggregate query response time subject to a specified system throughput requirement (i.e., volume of transactions processed per operation cycle, say a 24-hour operations cycle, other cycle duration).
- <u>System Resource Management Principle</u>: Applications shall be designed, implemented, and distributed across architectural components (i.e., processing servers, data management servers, routers, etc.) so as to minimize the ratio of resources used (e.g., CPU utilization, data storage in GB/TB, and random access memory (RAM)) to number of applications.
- <u>System Security Tolerance Principle</u>: Applications shall be designed, implemented, and distributed across architectural components (i.e., processing servers, data management servers, routers, etc.) so that security-related functions are provided resulting in a number of security violations that is bounded (say 1 security violation per 1 million accounts per month) with an associated degradation/cost in query response time of less than 10% (e.g., secured query responses are 10% slower than unsecured query responses).
- <u>System Robustness Principle</u>: Applications shall be designed, implemented, and distributed across architectural components (i.e., processing servers, data management servers, routers, etc.) so as to maximize business system availability in the face of scheduled maintenance (e.g., bring down a server for relocation or CPU upgrading), unscheduled maintenance (e.g., water flooding of a facility for a few days, A/C motor burns and fire fighting personnel must intervene and evacuate facility for a few hours), and disaster events (e.g., fire event destroys physical plant) triggering system failover to an alternate site.

These are competing principles in the sense that each principle can be fully realized only at the expense of one or more of the other principles. As such, these principles are intended only as general guidelines for the design, use, duplication, and allocation of applications across the enterprise architecture. The General Applications Model of Step 3 can guide the application allocation so that a satisfactory level of attainment of these five principles can be attained, i.e., each principle can be attained up to an individual level, and together these satisfactory levels produce a satisfactory allocation of application components across the enterprise architecture.

Step 7: Communicate Applications Architectural View

Again, the development of the Applications Architectural View is a crucial design step and decisions reached in it should be communicated to and shared with other team and project personnel.

In this step the Applications Architectural View is documented and communicated to other engineering teams and projects through reports, presentations, solicited written comments, and invitations to engineering and customer personnel to attend working sessions of the Applications Development team. A typical outline of a presentation for presentation of the Applications Architecture View is shown on Table 4.

Table 4. Outline of the Applications Architecture View Presentation

- Enterprise Architecture (EA) Planning Phases
- Project Releases and Data Dependencies
- Status of Applications Architectural View (e.g., Principles, General Applications Model, Design Rules, etc.)
- Impacts, Change Requests (CRs)
- List of Applications
- Mapping of Requirements and Business Functions to Applications
- Application Configuration Items (Cis)
- Applications CI Test Planning
- Feedback from EA Development Team
- Feedback from EA Business Systems Team
- Feedback from Release Management
- Feedback from Modernization Projects.
- CARGO Project
- FLIGHTS Project
- GATES Project
- SEATS Project
- SDC project
- Questions and Answers

Audience composition should be managed to reflect the seven steps in the construction of the Applications Architectural View in Figure 1. Personnel from the Requirements Management Team and the Business Process Development Team, for example, should be invited to attend and participate in this presentation to assure traceability of functionality to be built into the applications back to functionality called for in the system requirements and spelled out in greater detail in the business systems descriptions.

Alignment of applications development in the various projects with the Applications Architectural View is crucial. Actual application development in the CARGO, FLIGHTS, SEATS, GATES, and SDC projects must conform to and comply with the design rules identified earlier in Step 4, including use of approved computer languages and method of access of data in data stores (i.e., APIs, direct access, secured access, etc.). And so on, as depicted on Figure 5.

6.4. Alignment of Applications Architectural View

As the Applications Architectural View evolves, it is important to insure that its evolution does not happen in a vacuum and, instead, that it reflects content in the other five architectural views, as depicted on Figure 5. Applications exist, after all, only to implement the functionality called by the business processes in the Business Processes Architectural View. In turn, each business process is mapped to a business system in the Business Architectural View. One way of realizing this alignment is through the coordination of the effort in the Applications Architectural View with team and project personnel as called for in Step 7 above.

6.5. Software Engineering Standards

In Step 4 we addressed application design rules and we recognized the role of software engineering standards in the design process. See Moore (1998) for a detailed history of software standards development and a complete listing of standards and societies.

> *A standard can be : (1) an object or measure of comparison that defines or represents the magnitude of a unit; (2) a characterization that establishes allowable tolerances or constraints for categories of items; and (3) a degree or level or required excellence of attainment [SESC93].*

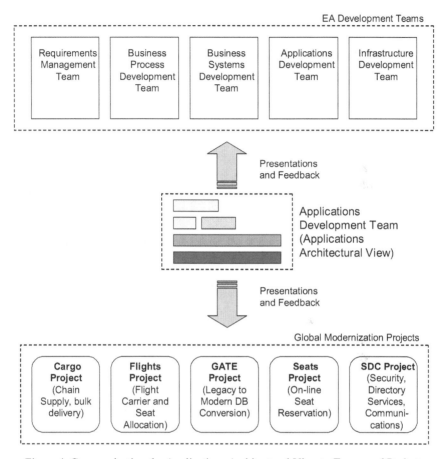

Figure 4. Communicating the Applications Architectural View to Teams and Projects

As Moore (1998) and Cargill (1997) point out, most software engineering standards have evolved following the principles of consensus development and voluntary adoption:

- Software engineering standards have been written by individuals or groups of individuals (i.e., committees)
- These standards have been exposed to discussion, feedback, change, and eventual adoption

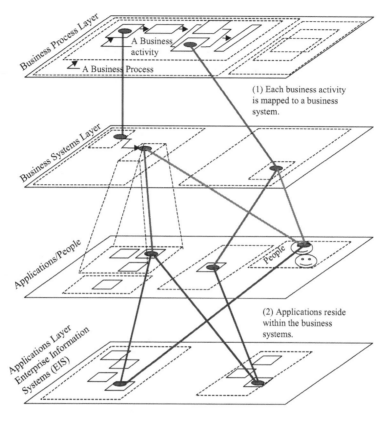

Figure 5. Alignment of Applications Architectural View with Other Architectural Views

- These standards are the product of consensus reached within committees in engineering professional organizations, academic community, and segments of industry.

Of all the software engineering standards, ISO/IEC 12207 is very prominent in the context of enterprise architecture planning as it addresses software analysis, design, coding, testing, integration and acceptance activities, as shown on Figure 6.

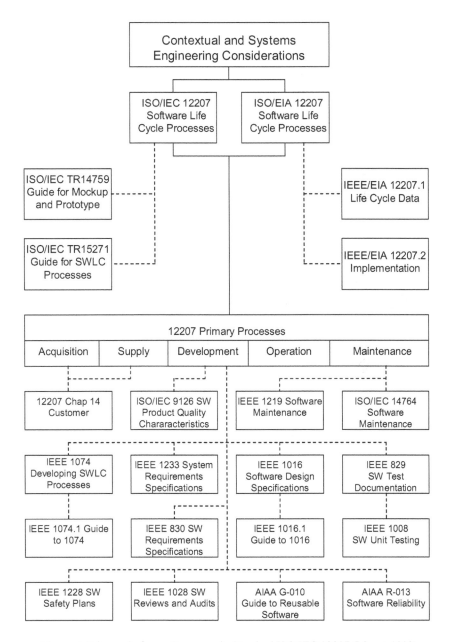

Figure 6. Primary Software Processes in Standard ISO/IEC 12207 (Moore 1998)

6.6. Representation of Software Design

This chapter on the Applications Architectural View would be incomplete without reference to methods and tools for software design representation, storage, and maintenance of the software design itself, i.e., the code design that implements the business services in a programming language. Of the various methods of representation, the Unified Modeling Language (UML) is probably the one most utilized in doing EA work today. See Chapter 7, The Unified Modeling Language (UML) in Software Design for an introduction to this universal method of representation, and a list of UML tools in the market today.

6.7. Conclusion

In this chapter we aimed to acquaint the reader with basic elements in the construction of the Applications Architectural View. Specifically, we learned that:

(1) An Applications Architectural View is a set of software applications that are needed to provide the totality of computer-based services in an enterprise architecture, including definition of each application, rules for the design of the applications, an ordering of these applications into categories according to the types of business systems that they will be supporting, and a plan (i.e., set of principles) for the distribution of these applications across physical components of the enterprise architecture. In this manner, an enterprise architecture may be consist of 300-400 applications distributed across those physical components.

(2) The design and development of the Applications Architectural View ought to be independent of computer languages and choices to be made for physical components of the enterprise architecture. This is not say that this design and development effort takes place in a vacuum and, instead, it is cognizant of the evolution of computer languages, the preference by manufacturers of computer technology for one computer language over another, even the financial and prospects for corporate stability in the market of one manufacturer over another.

(3) Every enterprise planning effort must be guided by a set of design principles, assumptions on how the business processes

will evolve subject to regulations (e.g., FAA in the case of our Global Airlines Services example), and constraints on funding resources. The earlier these guidelines are communicated across development teams and project personnel the greater the potential for cost efficiency and project success.

(4) A General Applications Model is a must-do in today's enterprise planning and development. If the enterprise is to be Web-based then it sets forth a sequence of processes that need to be observed, i.e., Client, Web Server, Web Applications Server, and so on, all the way to processes for access and retrieval of data from the data stores. This model insures that all development teams across the various projects "play by the same music sheets and rules".

(5) Legacy systems are a reality to be dealt with, not to be avoided, in applications development in most enterprise planning efforts. Options for posting and retrieval of data from legacy data stores must be considered, temporary "transition bridge" applications may be needed, and funding resources must be allocated accordingly.

(6) Alignment of the Applications Architectural View with the other five views must happen on a periodic basis to secure feedback and consensus from development personnel. This consensus must work both ways. The EA Applications Architectural View needs to be receptive to ideas and "waiver requests" from development teams to accommodate temporary or permanent deviation from design rules, languages, or data access mechanisms. Similarly, development teams must observe and comply with the general applications model and recommendations made by the EA Applications Architectural Team.

6.8. Exercises

E6.1 The role of an information system professional varies depending on whether such professional works in a Centralized Applications Development organization as in Figure E6.1 (a) or a Decentralized Applications Development Organization as in Figure E6.1 (b). In your opinion, discuss the pros and cons of both organizations with regards to:

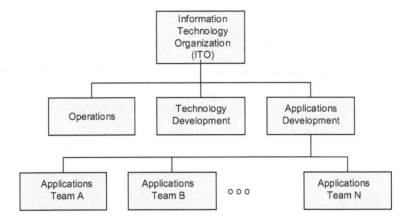

Figure E6.1(a) Organizational Chart for Centralized Applications Development

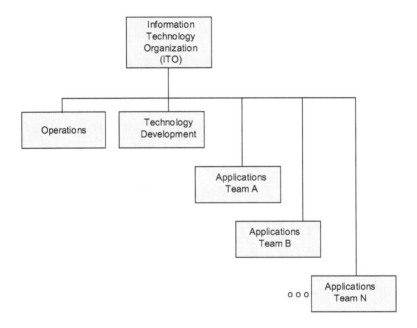

Figure E6.1(b) Organizational Chart for Decentralized Applications Development

(a) business process development
(b) Infrastructure development
(c) Enterprise Architecture planning
(d) Information processing and decision making
(e) Cost of applications
(f) Staffing needs in applications development teams.

E6.2 The exchange, processing, and harmonization (i.e., re-formatting of data) of aeronautical data, both before and during flight, is a prerequisite for secure and efficient air traffic management. Towards this end, Eurocontrol has proposed the Aeronautical Information Conceptual Model (AICM) shown on Figure E6.2. From a business point of view 80-90 per cent of the applications software must be COTS (code off the shelf) and the software must be usable in large-scale replicated environments or in single-location installation. Technologically the application must run on a variety of operating systems – different servers, working positions and browsers – with the possibility for an optimized two-tier or three-tier architecture." (Rudolph 2001).

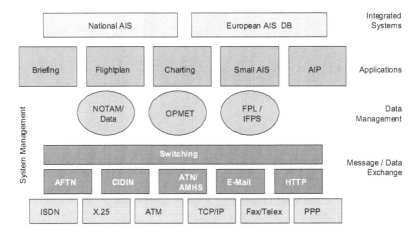

Figure E6.2 Applications Architecture of European Aeronautical Information Conceptual Model (AICM). Source: Air traffic Technology 2001

Legend:
AIS   European Aeronautical Information Services
NASR   National Airspace Resource System
AIP   Aeronautical Information Publication

As a member of the Center for Advanced Aviation Systems (CAAS) in your organization you have been given the task of researching this proposed architecture and briefing management on salient features, including:

(1) Definition of data harmonization and standardization in the context of commercial aviation;
(2) Definition of basic functions of meteorology, flight planning, briefing, charting, and static data;
(3) Description of ISDN, X.25, ATM, TCP/IP, and PPP protocols, and
(4) Describe main features of document DO-200A/ED-76, Standards for Processing Aeronautical Data by EUROCAE.

E6.3 Search the Internet for the technology "Business Rules":

(1) Prepare a ½ page description of this technology, including purpose and areas of application
(2) Discuss potential impacts to the Applications Architectural View.

Chapter 7

The Unified Modeling Language (UML) in Software Design

Illustrative example contributed by
students at University of
Mondragon, Euskadi:
  Aritz Oruesagasti
  Ania García de Salazar
  Juan López de Armentia
  Javier Sáez de Arregui
  Gorka Erlaiz
  Julen Capelastegui

7.1. Introduction

The design of the software applications in the Software Applications Architectural View of an Enterprise Architecture (EA) is made possible in great part thanks to the use of structuring and representation techniques, of which the Unified Modelling Language (UML) is a main leader today. As we are about to learn, UML is the result of countless hours of combined effort contributed by many individuals and organizations in the software community in the USA and many other countries in the last 8-10 years.

It is in the interest of EA owners and planners to become acquainted with the basics of UML: concepts, definitions, and diagrams in order to be able to better understand the analysis and design activities associated with the Software Applications Architectural View of an EA, as progress achieved in these activities is communicated by the contractor to EA owners and planners during regularly scheduled presentations and in formal published documents.

7.2. How this Chapter is Organized

This chapter presents an introduction to the Universal Modeling Language (UML) via concepts, diagrams, and an illustrative example. The Unified Process in the software life cycle is also presented in Section 7.5 and its importance in the analysis, design, and implementation of software is underscored. Section 7.6 takes the reader through a tour of the basics of use case diagrams, activity diagrams, and sequence diagrams, each time discussing the elements of each diagram, its use in software analysis and design, and providing guidance for its construction. An illustrative example contributed by students at the University of Mondragon is featured in Section 7.7 with detailed diagrams in an effort to share the insight gained in the analysis and design processes. A large list of UML tools in the market today is listed in Section 7.9, and finally a set of exercises is included in Section 7.10

7.3. Origins of and Ungoing efforts in UML

Software development is an intensive activity that requires planning, conceptual design, implementation, testing, and deployment in hardware (i.e., PCs, computers, and other support platforms). Over the last 10-15 years many people in the international software community have developed and applied diagrams and graphical representations of many types in an effort to guide and communicate the design effort among individuals in a design team and among design teams working in large projects. It was in the early 1990s that leading individuals and organizations began to meet with the idea to explore ways and means to gather the most promising graphs, diagrams, and procedures in a methodology that eventually would be called the Unified Modeling Language (UML), as illustrated in Figure 1.

Many peoples have contributed over the years to the creation of the UML methodology for the graphical representation of software design, of which Booch, Jacobson, and Rumbaugh (1999) have possibly contributed the most. Today UML is considered a key methodology for the graphical representation of software design, and this methodology has been implemented in many software support tools as shown in the following sections. The Object Management Group (OMG) oversees and guides the development of UML standards and practices.

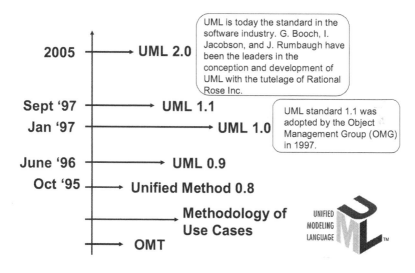

Figure 1. Origins of the Unified Modeling Language (UML)

7.4. Basics of the Unified Modeling Language (UML)

Many are the opportunities and challenges of UML representation in EA work today. The analysis and design of software systems continue to be complex and expensive due to challenges in the graphical representation of the design itself and the communication needs among the multiple design teams that collaborate in the planning, design, and assessment of enterprise architectures. Some of the facts:

- **What is UML?**
    - A standard notation universally accepted.
    - A collection of diagrams necessary for the description (i.e., representation) of the software design, including structural complexity and system behaviour.
    - A generic modeling language.
- **What is not UML?**
    - A programming language.

- – A business process modeling tool.
- – A replacement for design patterns and experience in solid, robust software design and implementation.

- **Theoretical advatages?**
  - – UML is a standard means of communication among multi-disciplinary design teams, including software, test, organizational change (OC), and infrastructure design teams.
  - – UML is supported by a growing variety of tools
  - – UML is an open standard, extensible, non-proprietary.
  - – It is applicable to a large variety of business domains, and compatible with many structural methods, and
  - – UML contributes greatly to knowledge representation and organization in EA work, e.g., economic efficiency in software design.
- **Posibles Disadvantages/Costs?**
  - – UML requires an initial corporate investment in money and time, e.g., license purchase, training courses, tools, etc., and this cost can be significant.
  - – For UML to become effective within an organization it requires upper management recognition and support, including commitment in the form of UML training and an administrator of UML-based tools.

7.5. The Software Life Cycle

An investment of high returns for the enterprise architecture EA planner is the time spent in getting acquainted with the basics of the software life cycle and its representation in the UML format, and how this UML format fits in the software design process called the Unified Process (UP), as illustrated in Figure 2.

Phases in the UP are Concept, Elaboration, Construction, and Transition. During the Concept phase system requirements for the enterprise architecture are analyzed and organized into groups so as to begin to ascertain the functionality to be designed and built into the architecture. This activity gains intensity during the Elaboration phase with the use of a variety of UML diagrams. Once, and only after the Elaboration phase is completed, the coding takes place during the

Construction phase, that is, the actual construction of the software code in one or several programming languages.

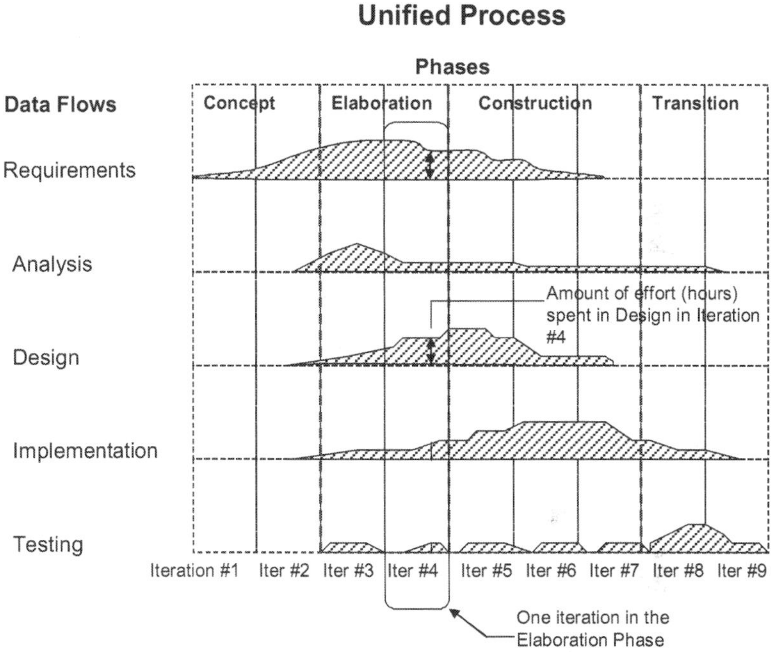

Unified Process

Figure 2. The Unified Process (UP) in Software Design

Finally, it is during the Transition phase that the code is housed in hardware components and these are deployed to parts and sites of the enterprise architecture, including different geographical locations.

During each phase five data flows occur: Requirements, Analysis, Design, Implementation, and Testing. System requirements must be "baselined" and available to the software design team during. These requirements are analyzed for individual functional ("what things to do") and non-functional ("when things must be done", with time requirements for system performance) content. In the process, use case diagrams, class diagrams, sequence diagrams and other UML diagrams are utilized in order to represent the design accurately and as completely as possible so that the various design teams and the owners of the enterprise architecture can follow and understand how the software design is evolving week after week and month after month. Months later and only after all the design teams and the EA owners agree that the software design is complete (i.e., both logical design and physical design have been completed, approved by the EA owners, and baselined), Implementation begins with the actual coding by skilful programmers assisted with programming tools and environments (e.g., Java, Borland C++ environments, .Net, other). Testing is often a most critical and decisive activity that must be carefully planned (a Test Plan must be carefully crafted months earlier) and executed (again, test scripts and test cases must be meticulously crafted and approved weeks and months earlier).

How is progress in the design of the software assessed? Software assessment is monitored in the form of *software design iterations* and their documentation releases. As Figure 2 points out, within each phase the progress made to date is documented in a collection of reports that constitute an *iteration activity*. During an iteration activity several documents may be prepared that contain text and graphics (e.g., UML) on the state of the design effort across all data flows. Generally 2-3 iterations may take place within each Phase, as illustrated in Figure 3.

> *Iterative Process: The UP is said to be an iterative process because with each iteration all the work flows are revised and updated. (Up and down flow in Figure 2).*

> *Incremental Process: The UP is said to be an incremental process because with each iteration new detail is created and new information is gathered, as the process moves forward in time (Left to right flow in Figure 2).*

Strategy of Functionality Releases

Functionality release is the term used to mean the fielding of portions of the new or modified architecture for operational use, after successful testing, after training of personnel, with all associated work products delivered to the EA owners on schedule. EA planners and contractor teams must carefully select dates to deliver "chunks" of the EA in a highly coordinated and orchestrated manner. Often an EA Delivery Strategy team is in place and charged with this responsibility, and 1-2 iterations of the work products may be required to insure that the functionality delivered with a release has been verified (i.e., a sub-set of the requirements have been verified through successful testing), technical and organizational change (OC) teams have been on-site to prepare to accept and integrate the new hardware and software into the operational system, and the community of stakeholders has been duly involved in the release activities from the very beginning.

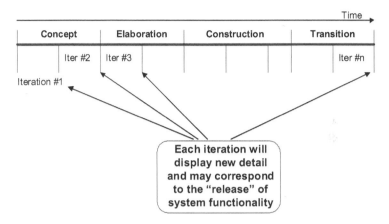

Figure 3. Work iterations support documentation and system releases

7.6. Basics of UML

A main strong point of UML is its rich variety of diagrams that are used to represent the evolving software design. These diagrams are intended to support analysis and design activities that take place during all the phases of the software life cycle. Next, we proceed to present highlights of each several of these diagrams.

Use Case Diagram

Two main purposes of an Use Case diagram are: (1) to present a high-level view of the system and its surroundings, and (2) to identify groupings of requirements called *Use Cases*. Not just any grouping, but grouping of requirements that have an "affinity" for each other. Shown on Figure 4 is a use case diagram intended to represent main activities in an automated teller machine (ATM) (i.e., the system), and its interaction with a Bank Clerk and a Credit Department (i.e., the environment).

The 2 human-like icons, a Bank Clerk and a Credit Department, are called *actors*. These actors represent things outside the system. The Bank Clerk can assist in the processing of activities in the system. The Credit Department can intervene in the activities of the system to approve or

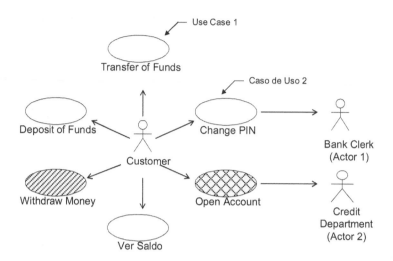

Figure 4. Use Case Diagram in an Automated Teller Machine (ATM) (*Source*: Boggs & Boggs 2002)

deny credit. Actors can be people or other systems. In this sense, the system is said to interact with people and/or other systems in its surroundings. How does the designer go about creating the various use cases? What are these use cases? As suggested earlier, as the system requirements are gathered these are organized into groupings that have an affinity for each other, that is, they contain functionalities that are related to each other (e.g., activities that support the transferring of funds from one account to another). Then each grouping is called a use case for that grouping of functionality. How many use cases to have in a design? The answer to this question varies with the number of requirements, and, to some extent, with the moneys and time available in a contract to design a system. For relatively small systems 5-10 use cases may be adequate, whereas for larger systems each subsystem may require those many use cases.

Activity Diagram

For each use case, an activity diagram is recommended. For the use case Open Account in Figure 4, for example, the activity diagram in Figure 5 has been constructed to show all the activities from the time a customer applies for an account in a bank to the time a bank clerk approves the issuing of credit and proceeds to open an account with its own account number, terms and conditions of the credit. These activities are sequential in the sense that one activity follows another until all the activities are completed, and these are organized into swim lanes: Service Representative, Credit Department Manager, and Customer.

One essential concept in analysis and design is that of *a scenario*. A scenario is a set of conditions that exist in a system and that can determine a particular sequence of activities. Shown on Figure 5 are two scenarios: credit is approved (scenario 1), and credit is denied (scenario 2), for example.

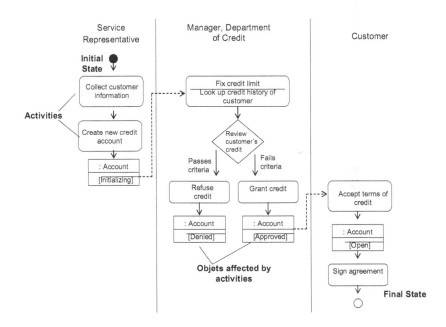

Figure 5. Sequence Diagram for Use Case "Open Account" in ATM example (*Source*: Boggs & Boggs 2002)

Sequence Diagram

A third type of diagram in UML is a sequence diagram, as shown on Figure 6. Typically, each use case is "expanded" with one activity diagram and one sequence diagram. Once an activity diagram has been completed, the next step is to construct a sequence diagram to capture much of the detail already contained in that activity diagram and to add detail on *messages* from one object to another. Also, this type of diagram places emphasis on both the sequencing of messages and the time interval between these messages. How is a sequence diagram constructed, what are the elements of construction in a sequence diagram? Basically, a sequence diagram features actors, objects, and messages, and these require the designer to advance his understanding of the structuring of the system being designed and to propose software objects that will carry out those activities, issue messages to other objects, and receive messages from other objects.

Examples of objects are Read Card, ATM Screen, Xabier´s Account, and Dispenser of Euros/Dollars.

An actor called Xabier initiates a sequence by placing his card within the system. An object called Read Card reads the account number, sends a message (message 2) to ATM Screen to open request opening a screen for the customer to view, and another message to Xabier´s Account with the account number information to be compared against other account numbers in database. I Xabier´s account number is already in the database then ATM Screen sends a message to the actor Xabier requesting a personal identification number (PIN), and so on.

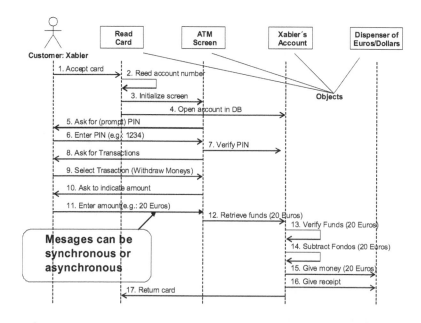

Figure 6. Sequence Diagram for use case "Withdraw Money" in ATM example

UML representation can allow for synchronous and asynchronous messages. Messages are synchronous if an object sends a message to two or more objects at the same time. Messages are asynchronous if an object sends a message to one object and them some time later it sends other messages to other objects (e.g., as in asynchronous databases). Messages are depicted horizontally and moving "downward" to account for the time dimension. In this manner, message 5 is shown to occur after message 4; message 6 occurs some time after message 5, and so forth. In the design of real time systems, for example, a time scale in fractions of a second would be shown running vertically on the left side of the sequence diagram to show the time in milliseconds from the time one message is completed to the time a new message is initiated.

Collaboration Diagram

Still another UML diagram is a Collaboration Diagram. This diagram is derived directly from a sequence diagram to show the same information content but this time it is represented differently, as shown on Figure 7 for the use case Withdraw Money.

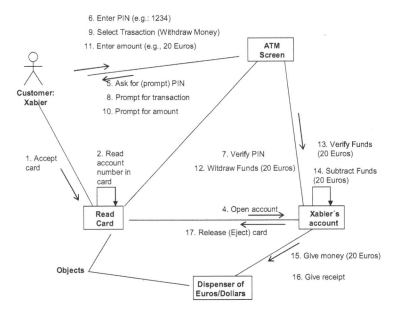

Figure 7. Collaboration Diagram for use case "Withdraw Money" in ATM example (*Source*: Boggs & Boggs 2002)

This type of diagram is often preferred by performance engineers given, rather than sequence diagrams, given that it shows more clearly those objects that have the largest number of messages coming in and going out, which is an indication of the demand for processing resources (i.e., CPU time, internal memory, and Input/Output resources) of those objects.

Types of UML Diagrams and their Use

UML tools are a must-have in the enterprise architecture (EA) industry today. Fortunately for EA owners, planners, and designer, the EA vendor community has responded well to needs in the modernization of EAs in industry and government and as a result there is rich content and variety in these tools. Most UML tools feature a large number of diagrams, from use case diagrams to fielding diagrams, as noted in Figure 8.

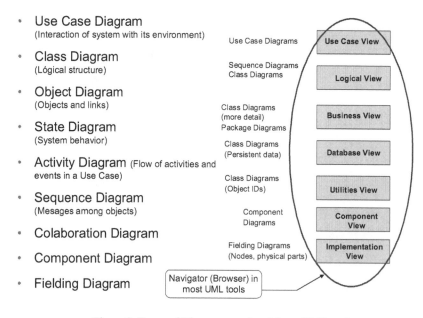

Figure 8. Types of Diagrams produced in an UML tool

A Management Section in the Enterprise Architect tool (EA, by Sparx Systems, Inc.), for example, allows the user 3 options to initiate a design session as shown on Figure 9:

- Open a Model File (an existing file)
- Create a New Model, or
- Connect to Server Repository

A Recent Models window displays the list of most recently used files. On the left of the interface, a list of icons is featured for each one of the UML diagrams (shown on Figure 9 are the icons needed to build a Use Case Diagram).

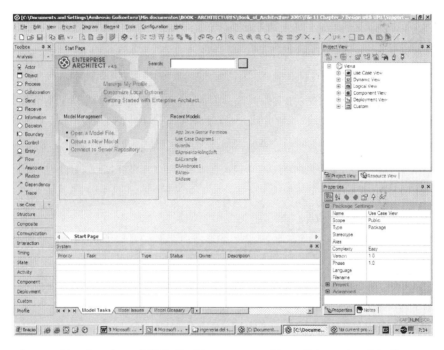

Figure 9. User Interface of UML Tool Enterprise Architect (EA) version 4.5, (Courtesy of Sparx Systems Inc.)

On the right hand side of the interface, directories for the various Views of UML diagrams are available:

- Use Case view
  - o Business Process model
  - o Use Case Model
- Dynamic View
  - o Interactions (Sequence Diagrams)
  - o State Case Model

- Logical View
  - Data Model
  - Logical Model
- Component View
  - Component Model
- Deployment View
  - Deployment Model
- Custom View
  - Formal Requirements
  - Non-Functional Requirements
  - Performance
  - User Interface

Tutorial sections are also a must-have fearure in modern design representation tools. EA features the following tutorials under Getting Started in the home page, as noted on Figure 10:

- Set Up the EA
- The UML Language
- Using Enterprise Architect (EA)
- Modelling UML
- Model Management
- Project Management with EA
- Forward and Reverse Engineer Code
- Modelling Database
- Generating Documents
- Automated Interfaces
- Glossary of Terms

7.7. An Illustrative Example on the Use of UML

Consider now an illustrative example on the use of UML in the design of a relatively simple application by the name of Building Access Control (BAC) System. The contractor, Mondragon Works, Inc (the contractor) has won the bidding and has been awarded a contract to design, implement, and deliver this system. This example has been contributed by our students at the University of Mondragon, Department of Computer Sciences, Euskadi (Basque Country), who developed it as a project in a course titled Software Design with UML Representation.

Statement of need (37 system requirements, only a narrative statement of these follows):

R1: The customer, Euskadi Enterprises, Inc. (the client), requires a system to control and manage the opening and closing of doors in a building where basic research is being carried out. This control and management is to be exercised via a computer program and hardware devises (i.e., the system).

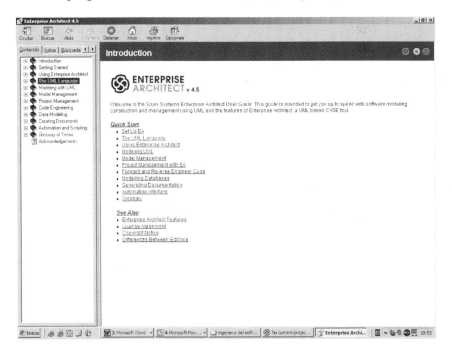

Figure 10. User Interface of UML Tool Enterprise Architect (EA) version 4.5, (Courtesy of Sparx Systems Inc.)

R2: An authorized person would use a card on a reading device to attempt to open a door and gain entrance to a research facility.

R3: When a person wants to enter a room or facility, he/she uses the card by running it through a control device by the door. Next, the system reads the data in the card, compares these data against data in a database, and if this database shows that such person has permission to enter the facility the door will open up, otherwise the door will remain closed.

R4: A computer (software) application will be created to manage facility entrance permits via a database. A database administrator will have the authority to add and delete data to the data base such as name of a person and rooms that he/she can enter. Figure 1 shows a "sketch" of the proposed system as prepared by the contractor design team and presented to its client to begin the concept phase.

R5: The programming language is to be in JAVA (determined by the client, to maintain compatibility with other systems in the client's domain), with JDBC (JAVA DataBase Connectivity) to access the database. Also, within the list of system requirements provided by the client it is stated that the contractor will use Enterprise Architect (EA, by Sparx Systems Inc.), a UML tool for software design and its representation.

After a preliminary analysis of the requirements, the contractor design team recommends to the client the high-level design shown on Figure 11. The software sub-system is envisioned as consisting of several software

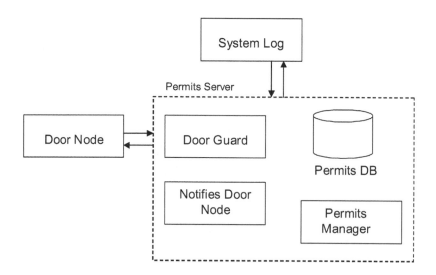

Figure 11. Initial Concept for Building Control System (BCS)

modules. A Door Node module will be installed by a door (one Door Node for each door in the building) to read a card. Information in the door card will be compared against data in a Door Guard that resides on a Permits Server (located in the same building or a different bulding); if the card´s owner has permission to enter that room, the door will open, otherwise it will remain closed. Permits are stored in a database, the Permits DB, the Permits Manager adds and deletes permits from the database (DB).

Once changes to the DB have been made the Notifies Door Node module communicates these changes to the Door Guard. All Door Node events are logged in the System Log for security control and management.

Door Guard:
Attends to multiple persons attempting to enter a room or facility
- Up to 100 simultaneous door accesses (enter a room).
- After each attempt to access, the person is notified whether he/she can enter (the door opens) or not (the door remains closed).

Maintains updated data:
- The Door Guard has its own memory to store permits and other data transferred from the Permits DB
- This information is updated as soon as the data in the Permits DB is updated by the DB administrator.

Responds to needs of the Permits Manager
- Responds to requests by the Permits Manager to change or update data (add/delete/modify names and permits)
- Data in memory (cache) by the Door Node remains blocked while such data is being updated.

Permits Manager:
- Notifies the Door Guard and the Door Node of changes to the DB
- Provides a window so that the DB administrator can create, remove, update, or delete (CRUD) names and permits statuses (approved, not approved) from cache memory.

Permits BD:
- Resides in the server, under Linux with MySQL
- Table Persons (ID, First Name, Last Name, Password, Administrator)
- Table Permits (ID, Door)
- Table Rooms (Door, Building)

System Log BD:

- Stores information on events related to requests to enter rooms (Detail: allowed, not allowed)
- Table Log (ID, Date, Hour, Room, Detail1)

Software System Design with Enterprise Architect (EA)

Following approval by the client of the high-level design shown on Figure 11, the design teams proceeds to advance the design. The following UML diagrams were constructed to conduct the software design.

The Mondragon Works design team examined the 37 system requirements and organized these into 4 groups so that requirements in each group had "affinity" (i.e., related) for each other. Next each group was represented as a Case Study using the Enterprise Architect UML tools, as shown on Figure 12. Diagrams constructed with Enterprise Architect can later be easily exported for use in other tools and documents. One such exported diagram is the use case diagram presented on Figure 13.

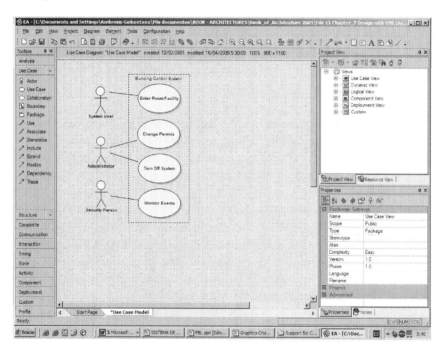

Figure 12. Software Design Representation with UML Tool Enterprise Architect (Courtesy of Sparx Systems Inc.)

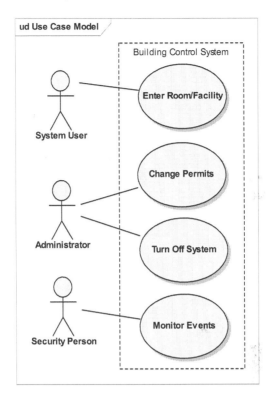

Figure 13. Use Case Diagram with 3 Actors and 4 Use Cases, Illustrative Example (Courtesy of Sparx Systems Inc.)

Enter Room/Facility Use Case: This use case represents functionality involved with the entering and closing of a door to gain access to a room or facility. This use case makes use of another use case called Valid Login, and this condition is generally shown with another "bubble" named Valid Login with an arrow pointing to the Enter Room/facility bubble and the text <includes> next to the arrow.

Change Permits Use Case: This use case represents functionality involved with the issuing and denial of permits to enter a room or facility.

Turn Off System Use Case: This use case represents all functionality involved with turning on and off the software system.

Monitor Events Use Case: This use case represents all functionality involved with the monitoring of room entry and exit events, so that statistics on room entry, exits, and possible violation attempts can be studied.

System User (Actor 1): The System User is the person that uses his/her card to enter a room or facility.

Administrator (Actor 2): The person responsible for administering room entry permits in the database.

Security Person (Actor 3): The person that monitors room entry and exits and looks for illegal entry events.

Sequence Diagrams

The Mondragon Works design team decided that 5 classes ought to be represented in the sequence diagram for the use case Valid Login: InterfaceLogin, DBConnect, DBPermits, Begin, and Persons, as shown on Figure 14. Eventually, later on during the design phase, each class will be given attributes (local and global variables) and methods (functions that carry out specific tasks such as computation, comparison of things, sending and returning lists of things among the classes). The InterfaceLogin class passes ID and password information to the DBConnect class, for example.

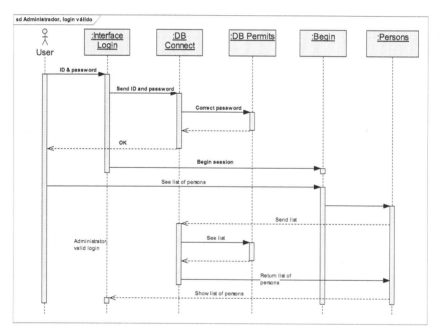

Figure 14. Sequence Diagram, Use Case: Valid Login (Courtesy of Sparx Systems Inc.)

Represented in Figure 14 is the functionality requested in requirement R1 for a system administrator. The administrator starts up the system application and a screen appears requesting user ID and password (this screen is generated by the software class :Interfaced Login); system compares this information against data already stored in a database and if both the user ID and password are correct then the login is valid and the administrator can proceed to conduct administrative tasks (e.g., add, delete persons form list of users allowed to use the facilities, request IDs for new persons, etc.). A person may present valid user ID and password but this person may have permission to carry out certain operations only, so that if the person is an administrator then the system will recognize this condition (class :DB Permits carries out this functionality) and allows him/her to carry out administrative tasks only, whereas if the person is a user then he/she can request other information (e.g., schedule of hours of operation of lab facilities).

Deployment Diagram
Eventually the design is nearly completed and a next step is that of deciding where and how the various software pieces will be distributed and housed within the hardware pieces of the system. For our illustrative example the Mondragon Works design team decided that the software classes cited in the earlier diagrams ought to be allocated to nodes in the system as depicted in Figure 15.

Accordingly, the class :Guard is housed within hardware located adjacent to a door (each doors has its own hardware and a replica of :Guard). The :Guard Chief, :Permits, :Permits Manager, and :Permits DB classes are housed within a server named PermitServer located in a central office. The class Notifier is housed in a second server named ChangesNotifier, and finally the class :EventManager is housed within a server named EventManager. The servers themselves can be housed in a single room or in different rooms and different buildings depending on other design, performance, architectural, and contractual considerations.

7.8. Conclusions

Following our presentation of salient features of UML, several points may be appropriate to make:

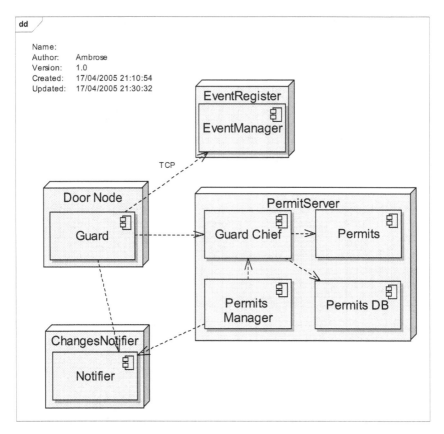

Figure 15. Deployment Diagram with nodes that host software for illustrative example (Courtesy of Sparx Systems Inc.)

- We set out to present an introduction of UML concepts, diagrams, and guidance to constructing these diagrams. Hopefully this introduction will encourage the reader to delve deeper into UML as a design representation methodology and tool.
- The art, science, and technology of software design continue to evolve. UML today does not specify exactly which set of diagrams to use, and instead it is up to individuals in a design team to decide which types of diagrams to use (e.g., use case diagrams, sequence, state, activity, other) and how many. Experience is key to the determination of a final mix of diagrams that will guide the design effort.

- Chief architects in an organization need to be able to relate to software design engineers. Design engineers and EA owners need to communicate with each other. Design engineers propose design features and it is up to EA owners to approve or reject those proposed design features. UML is then the common means of communication among design engineers and EA owners.
- Now-days a UML tool is a must-have item in the design of a new enterprise architecture or the modernization of an existing one. Most EA owners request an EA tool along with another 10-15 tools to automate some design processes and to gain economic efficiency in the software process and in the construction of the EA itself. In fact, EA owners specify the use of the UML tool and other tools (e.g., tool for system requirement management) in the EA contract itself.

7.9. Exercises

E7.1 Consider the use case diagram for a catalog sales system shown on Figure E7.1:

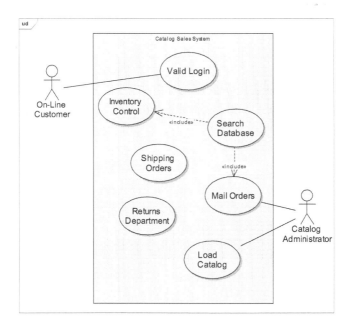

Figure E7.1. Use Case Diagram for the Catalog Sales System.

(a) Propose an activity diagram for the use case Mail Orders
(b) Propose a sequence diagram for the use case Mail Orders.

E7.2 A new building in Brussels is to house members of the European Parliament, and this building is to have two elevators:

(c) Construct a use case diagram
(d) Propose a set of rules (i.e., an algorithm) for use by the elevator scheduler to determine which of the two elevators to send out to pick up a person(s) waiting on a floor; use the information on Table E7.2 to guide this process and illustrate your proposed set of rules.

Table E7.2. People waiting for elevator

Event	Time (Hours)	Number or Persons waiting to be picked up	Floor of Origin	Destina-tion Floor
1	10:15	1	3	5
2	10:20	2	0	3
3	10:21	2	4	0
4	10:25	3	0	2
5	10:27	1	2	5
6	10:28	2	0	3
7	10:35	2	5	0
8	10:36	2	0	3
9	10:38	1	2	5
10	10:45	2	5	0

(e) For each person, per designed set of rules, determine:
  • Time of arrival to desired floor
  • Waiting time on each floor
  • Traveling time
  • Number of floors travelled by each elevator in the time period 10:15 – 10:45

Initial Conditions:
- At time 10:15 the two elevators are empty and waiting at the Lobby (Plant)
- Total of 5 floors and lobby floor
- Time to open/close the elevator doors is 5 seconds
- Time of travel of one elevator to another floor is 30 seconds.

E7.3 Consider the state diagram for an elevator shown on Figure E7.3:

(f) Draw an arrow from one state to another, as appropriate, to indicate a valid transition from one state to another (e.g., from Elevator Idle to Elevator Moving)
(g) Open up your Enterprise Architect UML tool and build this state diagram.

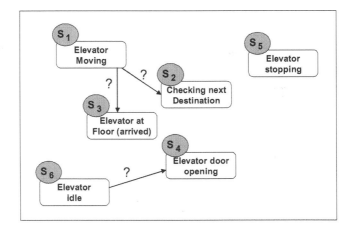

Figure E7.3. Number of possible states in an elevator system.

Chapter 8

The Technology Architectural View

Vision and Strategy
Business Processes Architectural View
System Requirements Development
Business Systems Architectural View
Data Architectural View
Applications Architectural View
Technology Architectural View

8.1. What is a Technology?

This chapter discusses the concept of a "technology" and how groupings of technologies are used to constitute the Technology Architectural View in an Enterprise Architecture (EA). Towards that end, a main objective of this chapter is to present a methodology for building the Technology Architectural View via a step-by-step approach where each step is decomposed into a number of tasks carried out by personnel in a technology team, often called the *Infrastructure Development Team.*

A technology is a collection of methods and physical means that make use of physical laws to achieve a product that is deemed valuable by a human being (i.e., a carpenter, shoe maker, a farmer, engineer, computer scientist, a musician, other). In that sense, a shovel represents a "technology" as it enables a farmer to dig into the soil and plant a seed; once the metal plate and the wooden stick are put together (i.e., method of assembly), the farmer is able to point downward to strike the ground, make a whole, and plant the seed (i.e., agricultural method). Later on, as he buys a tractor to open the soil and plant larger amounts of seed over a larger area of land he moves to a "higher technology", i.e., tractor technology. Similarly, *middleware software* (e.g., IBM's MQSeries software) is a technology that enables platform-to-platform communication. A database management system (DBMS) makes use of multiple information technologies such as software technology and data storage technology in order to store and retrieve data. A Global Airlines Services portal makes use of HTML technology and local area network (LAN) technology in order to retrieve information on flight schedules for a particular day and time window. And so forth. The terms "technology" and "vendor product" are used synonymously throughout this chapter.

> *A technology:* *A collection of methods and physical means that make use of physical laws to realize a product or service that is deemed valuable by a human being (i.e., a carpenter, shoe maker, a farmer, engineer, computer scientist, an accountant, a musician, etc.). Examples of technologies are data storage devices, local area networks, cable TV, and messaging middleware.*

8.2. What is a Technology Architectural View?

This chapter addresses the use of information technologies in order to implement the various architectural views discussed in earlier chapters for purposes of carrying out a collection of business processes. That is, in this chapter we set out to identify a variety of information technologies that can be arranged in some near-optimal fashion – that we are going to call the Technology Architectural View – for purposes of implementing the Business Process Architectural View, the Business Systems Architectural View, the Data Architectural View, and the Applications Architectural View.

> *Technology Architectural View:* *A set of information technologies (i.e., physical means) that are grouped in a manner prescribed by a set of principles (e.g., methods) in order to implement a set of business systems (Business Systems Architectural View), a data model (Data Architectural View), and a set of applications (Applications*

Architectural View) that will make possible the execution of a set of business processes (Business Process Architectural View). Typically, an enterprise architecture may consist of hundreds and even thousands of technologies.

The identification, definition, and assessment of these technologies in development and prototyping environments, and allocation to the business systems is a major challenge for the designers of an enterprise architecture. This major task becomes the responsibility of the *Technologies Assessment/Development Team.*

8.3. How this Chapter is Organized

Sections 1 and 2 guide the reader through a definition of a technology and a few examples of technologies. Section 3 presents a methodology for building the Technology Architectural View, the main topic of this chapter. A total of 12 Steps are proposed in this methodology, ranging from Step 1, Review of Business Systems Hierarchy, to Step 12, Communicate Technology Architectural View to Teams and Project Personnel. Next, each step is decomposed into several tasks which are described in detail with more illustrative examples. Concepts and objectives of this chapter are summarized in a Conclusions section. At the end of this chapter an Exercises section is presented.

8.4. A Methodology for Building the Technology Architectural View

Development of the Technology Architectural View requires a number of engineering steps to carry out and, as a recommendation, a sequence of twelve steps in the design effort, is depicted in Figure 1. As the design advances from one step to the next, the Business Systems baseline is reviewed, the business applications architecture is revisited, applications are mapped to business systems, a set of technology principles, assumptions, and constraints is adopted, and a list of candidate technologies and platforms is put together.

Time resource allocation to the planning phases of the EA may look as follows:

Vision and Strategy	10%
Business Process Architectural View	15%
System Requirements Development	10%
Business Systems Architectural View	10%
Data Architectural View	20%
Applications Architectural View	15%
Technology Architectural View	**20%**
Total =	100%

Accordingly, for an EA planning effort of say 36 months, a total of (36 months)(0.20) = 7.2 months or 29 weeks, approximately, ought to be allocated to the planning portion alone of the Technology Architectural View.

Steps involved in the construction of the Technology Architectural View may vary from one organization to another, depending on resources available and constraints, but a sequence of steps similar to the 12 steps shown on Figure 1 apply.

Next, those 29 weeks need to be allocated to the various steps and models, and a recommended guideline is as follows:

Step 1:	Review of Business Systems	5%
Step 2:	Review of Applications Architecture	5%
Step 3:	COTS Strategy	10%
Step 4:	Map Applications to Business Systems	10%
Step 5:	Technology Principles, Constraints, and Assumptions	5%
Step 6:	Identify Candidate Technologies and Platforms	10%
Step 7:	Map Technologies to Business Systems	10%
Step 8:	Principles of Technology Segmentation	5%
Step 9:	Technology Segmentation and Distribution Model	10%
Step 10:	Logical Technology Design	10%
Step 11:	Physical Technology Design	5%
Step 12:	Communicate Technology Architectural View to Teams	5%
	Total =	100%

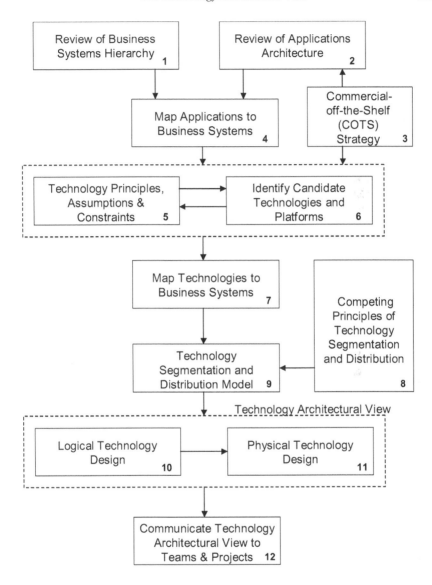

Figure 1. Steps for Building the Technology Architectural View (*Source*: Goikoetxea 2003)

As such, the amount of time to be allocated to Step 9, Technology Segmentation and Distribution Model, is (36 months)(0.20)(0.10) = 0.72

months or 3 weeks, approximately. Now, time allocation by itself, alone, is not very meaningful and people resource allocation across the various development teams needs to be considered as well. See Chapter 19, EA Implementation Strategies, for a comprehensive discussion and set of guidelines for resource allocation to EA planning, design, development, testing, pilot, and, release management.

Step 1: Review of Business Systems Hierarchy

In Chapter 4, we may recall, a hierarchy of business systems was gathered in order to identify categories of service providers (i.e., the business systems) and the services themselves. The business systems then are the logical representations of those categories of business and the services would be made available via applications. The applications implement the functionality called by the system requirements, the applications render services, the business processes make use of these services, and the applications live inside the business systems. Typically, a business process is made of multiple business activities and a single business activity will require services from multiple business systems. In this manner, an enterprise architecture may consist of 200-300 business systems that provide a variety of services across major functional areas in the enterprise. See the the business systems hierarchy identified earlier in Chapter 4 for the Global Services Airline Example. Three tasks are envisioned in carrying out this Step:

> **Task 1**: *Business Systems development team and Infrastructure Development team meat to review the Business Systems Hierarchy.* Personnel from the Infrastructure Development Team are to meat with personnel from the Business Systems Development Team for purposes of reviewing the contents of the business systems hierarchy identified months earlier. The implication here being that much of the business systems hierarchy has been defined prior to the work to be performed by the Infrastructure Development Team: that of identifying and evaluating candidate technologies and platforms. Incomplete definitions of business systems already identified in the hierarchy must be completed by personnel in the Business Systems Development Team; these complete definitions include textual descriptions of the services that will be provided by the business systems. This information and understanding is vital to

members of the Infrastructure Development team as they meet with vendors to learn about the specific functionality of their respective products.

Task 2: *Review recent developments and trends in vendor technologies.* Vendor technology may also have an impact on the current business system hierarchy. The business system hierarchy may be 4-6 months old by the time the Infrastructure Development Team comes into play in the EA planning and design phases, and it is quite possible for modified or new technologies to emerge in that time and to offer the potential to streamline the business systems hierarchy, i.e., reduce the number of business systems. This task makes sure, therefore, that the business systems hierarchy is up to date, is mature and robust in the face of proven technology, flexible and able to incorporate changes in one area (e.g., customer account management) with none or only minor changes required in other areas (e.g., directory services).

Task 3: *Adjust interfaces among those business systems that may be impacted by technology improvements or new technologies.* Changes in interface type (i.e., FAX, messaging middleware, phone, etc.), data volume, and frequency of data inputs need to be incorporated in the review of the business systems hierarchy.

Step 2: Review of Applications Architecture

By now the applications architecture already exists, as discussed in Chapter 6, and it is time to update that architecture to reflect direction and insight gained in the process of building and putting together the Technology Architectural View. Vendor presentations of candidate platforms and software products are very likely to bring improved or new perspectives and trends on business paradigms and COTS technology that personnel from the Infrastructure Development Team may want to use to modify the existing EA applications architecture, shown earlier in Chapter 6.

Task 1: *Verify that all applications proposed earlier in the applications architecture have been defined fully in terms of purpose, inputs, and outputs.* Also, each application should be traced back to one or more system requirements.

Task 2: *Balance of custom-made and COTS software products.* How many of the applications ought to be custom-built by contractor programmers, and how many of the applications ought to be purchased as commercial-off-the-shelf (COTS) products? The answer is not immediately available and it varies from one enterprise organization to another due to technical, administrative, financial, and/or strategic reasons, as we address in greater detail next in Step 3. However, it is important to realize that in the initial development of the applications architecture the emphasis ought to be in the definition of the applications that will provide the various business services required in the enterprise regardless of how the applications themselves will eventually be built, i.e., via actual coding by contractor personnel or via COTS acquisition and integration. The activities associated with the construction of the Technology Architectural View are in fact the ones that drive the determination of that balance of custom-made and COTS software products in the applications architecture.

> *Balance of mix of custom-made and COTS software products: The first draft of the applications architecture ought to concentrate on the definition, inputs, and outputs of each application, and the functionality it implements. This effort is independent of the means to build and acquire the applications, i.e., via custom-made or COTS software. The time to make this determination must wait until the Technology Architectural View work begins, as vendor presentations and vendor products are evaluated within an enterprise planning framework that includes an enterprise-wide COTS acquisition strategy.*

Task 3: *Adaptability of application architecture to proposed changes and tools for change management.* Changes to the applications architecture will come from several places, including changes in the requirements and insight gained into vendor software products and new commercial business practices. This is reality. This task, however, addresses the need for tools that store and manage information on the applications architecture so that those changes to the applications architecture are easily implemented and managed. See Appendix A for a description of commercial tools that can support the development and management of the applications architecture (e.g., System Architect tool)

Step 3: Commercially-off-the-Shelf (COTS) Software Strategy

Many are the factors to consider in the decision to purchase or not purchase COTS products, and the trend is for enterprise organizations to develop and apply their own home-grown COTS acquisition strategies. Some of the activities involved in acquiring and applying a COTS acquisition strategy are as follows.

Task 1: *Conduct a Gap Analysis.* What are the differences between enterprise user procedures and COTS product capabilities? Owners of business systems across the enterprise will often propose a preference for a particular COTS product and the need exists to gather a list of such products into a matrix of product capability against user requirements (King 2001; Taub 2001). Interviews with business owners can often help in determining degree of willingness to consider a product, trade willingness to integrate "black-box" complexity in the applications architecture against a full set of ready-to-go functional capabilities, an assessment of understanding of risks involved, timeframe to field products, etc. This matrix (gap analysis matrix) provides decision makers with an enterprise-wide view of the demand for COTS products, their potential application to functionality required across multiple business systems, and product capabilities.

Task 2: *Talk to current users of COTS products.* Once interest for a particular COTS product shows up in the matrix in Task 1 the next logical step is to identify current users of that product to ascertain product performance and user satisfaction. Phone calls, interviews, e-mail, and paper surveys can be alternative instruments to gather this type of information and store it in the same gap analysis matrix.

Task 3: *Put together a list of multiple criteria for COTS evaluation and selection.* What are the criteria (i.e., factors) to consider and apply to evaluate COTS products, the weights for relative importance of the criteria, and how is the information to be collected to be synthesized to arrive at a recommended product? There is a well-established body of methods for decision making in the published literature that can be readily applied to conduct this task (Goicoechea 2001, 1990, 1982). A preliminary step to using these methods is that of preparing a table such as that on Table 1 that displays the multiple criteria (left-hand column) and the amount of customization required by the COTS vendor.

Table 1. COTS Product Evaluation and Selection Criteria

#	Evaluation Criteria	Weight of Criterion (an example, only)	Minimal Customization	Customization with Plug-in Support	Extensive Customization	Not Supported	Comment/ Explanation
A	**Functional Requirements**						
1	Supports harvesting of business rules	6	☐	☐	☐	☐	
2	Ability to generate forms A through Z in format XX	8	☐	☐	☐	☐	
3	Ability to translate transaction content from format A1 to A2	6	☐	☐	☐	☐	
4	Ability to support manual and automatic routing of transactions to multiple field points	5	☐	☐	☐	☐	
B	**Performance Requirements**						
5	Able to process 5.5 million transactions per day	10	☐	☐	☐	☐	

Table 1. (*Continued*)

#	Evaluation Criteria	Weight of Criterion (an example, only)	Minimal Customization	Customization with Plug-in Support	Extensive Customization	Not Supported	Comment/ Explanation
6	Query response times of 2 seconds or less 95% of the time	10	☐	☐	☐	☐	
C	**Security**						
7	Ability to support X.500 directory services	8	☐	☐	☐	☐	
8	Ability to assign data access privileges to partners	5	☐	☐	☐	☐	
D	**Licenses and Costs**						
9	Willingness to negotiate pricing for multiple licenses across the enterprise?	10	☐	☐	☐	☐	
10	Cost per CPU	8					
Weight ratio scale 1-10 points, with 10 = most valuable, 1 = least valuable							

Task 4: *Identify Sources of Risk. Risks are inherent in the adoption of COTS products in the enterprise architecture including:*

- Operational requirements: Risks associated with using a COTS product to meet functional and non-functional (i.e., performance) system requirements (Clapp, 2001).
- Technical approach: Potential adverse impact of a COTS product on system integration, application development, applications testing, and lifecycle maintenance. COTS plug-in functionality is not a reality today and vendors and enterprise architects/programmers must work together in order to effectively integrate a COTS product into the enterprise architecture.

- Business strategy: Will a vendor continue to provide support for a particular COTS product as the market shifts from one business practice to another? What happens if the vendor goes out of business sometime after the COTS product is adopted and integrated in the enterprise architecture?

Task 5: *Develop techniques and measures for controlling COTS risk.* Risk mitigation measures include market research, early and frequent user involvement, early and frequent integration, and planning for replacement and obsolescence (Clapp, 2001). An integral component of the enterprise architecture planning function is to see that a body of COTS risks and mitigation measures has been developed, agreed upon and applied across business units in the enterprise.

Task 6: *Participation in Government-Industry collaborative initiatives.* Department of Defense (DoD) organizations and federally funded research and development centers (FFRDC) such as MITRE Corp. are continuously learning new ways to participate in or launch collaborative efforts with industry in order to influence COTS design in areas of mutual interest. "The government strategy, in general, has been to share the cost of the modifications with the vendors, to provide expertise when needed, and to give the COTS developer the data rights (i.e., ownership) to the extensions and hence the future profits" (Clapp 2001).

Task 7: *Participation in Standards organizations.* The International Standards Organization (ISO), the Institute of Electrical and Electronics Engineers (IEEE), and the International Council for Systems Engineering (INCOSE) review, refine, and propose standards that can have an impact on the design of COTS products in industry. It can be a lengthy process requiring months and years of collaborative effort among interested parties in industry, academia, Federal agencies and Department of Defense (DoD) but eventually standards are published and often adopted by COTS vendors. These standards can affect design and development of many architectural components, including interfaces, operating systems, and communications protocols.

Task 8: *Know how to negotiate COTS licensing terms and costs.* "Computer systems must be more flexible, scalable, and configurable to satisfy the changing needs of the military, and software must be upgraded and replaced more frequently than ever imagined…thus the importance and complexity of negotiating adaptable, cost-effective licensing agreements cannot be underestimated", (Taub 2001). Have all license terms and conditions been considered? Will the software products listed under license A run on platforms listed under license B? How will updates and maintenance impact cost? Etc. Acquisition personnel can help answer these and related questions and issues once the vendor interviews and presentations demonstrate a match between system requirements and vendor product capabilities.

Task 9: COTS Selection Schedule. A recommended sequence of activities leading to COTS product evaluation and selection is as follows:

- Vendors receive requirements package, i.e., request for proposal (RFP)
- Vendors provide client reference contacts
- Enterprise contractor conducts reference checks
- Vendors return a written response to the requirements package
- Enterprise owner and contractor review business process with vendors
- Demonstration of vendor prototypes
- Vendor's technical and business proposals are due to the enterprise contractor
- COTS product evaluation, selection, and recommendation to enterprise owners.

These activities can take place over a 4-6 week timeframe, approximately.

Step 4: Mapping of Applications to Business Systems

We recall that the business systems hierarchy and the applications were determined in Chapter 5 and Chapter 6, respectively. In this step we proceed to "populate" a business system with a set of applications that will provide the business services for that particular business system. Repeat this activity until all business systems have been populated with appropriate applications. Here it is recommended to prepare and document a mapping of applications to the business systems.

> **Task 1:** *Members of the Applications Development Team and the Business Systems Development team meet for purposes of determining the allocation of applications in the Applications Architectural View to business systems in the Business Systems Architectural View*, as depicted in Figure 2. Not one but several meetings and iterations will be required by these two teams in order to achieve this mapping activity. Business system 1.1, for example, has been populated with applications 15, 24, 2, 13, and 1.

> **Task 2:** *Next, insight gained in Step 3 into the functionality provided by COTS technologies is applied to the iterative process of mapping the applications to the business systems.* We recognize, then, the fact that COTS technologies will invariably impact this mapping.

> **Task 3:** *Applicability of the various COTS technologies across the enterprise itself also ought to play a role in the ultimate mapping of applications to the business systems.* This Step calls for coordination of effort with the Enterprise Systems Engineering Board (ESEB) which is knowledgeable of all COTS needs across all projects in the enterprise. COTS products that offer the potential for use across multiple projects will be favored over those COTS products that have applicability in only one project, for example.

Step 5: Technology Principles, Assumptions, and Constraints

Functional efficiency, performance, cost, and maintenance considerations drive the search for a set of principles, assumptions, and constraints that offer the potential for guiding the planning and design of the Technology architectural View:

- Evaluate operating systems and platforms together as a complimentary set.
- Organize and allocate categories of labor and processing to special-purpose platforms:

  - High Volume on-line transaction processing (OLTP), batch processing, and storage of large amounts of primary data to be housed on tier-1 platforms (e.g., IBM Z900 mainframes, DEC 8400 mainframes, etc.).
  - Storage and retrieval of supporting data, medium and high volume application services, and medium to heave web services to be housed in tier-2 platforms (e.g., SUN E15000 platforms).
  - Fat client services, thin client services, and remote displays to be housed on tier-3 platforms (e.g., Windows 2000/NT).

- Gather and/or adopt a set of standards that reflects preferences for choices among competing products in areas of messaging middleware, communication protocols, application programming interfaces, and computer languages. Apply these standards consistently across projects in the enterprise architecture.
- Ideally, a variety of platforms, vendors, operating systems, and communication protocols can be implemented throughout the enterprise architecture towards achieving architectural robustness, i.e., failure of one particular product does not require massive replacement of that product in architectural sub-systems.
- In reality, a small number of vendor products may end up in the architecture, the reasons being:

  - Only a small number of vendors may have enduring market strength and presence.
  - Economies of scale in transaction processing, database management, and operations support may be found in a few set of vendors only.
  - Funding limitations often favor the selection of a small number of interoperable vendor products as opposed to a large number of products.

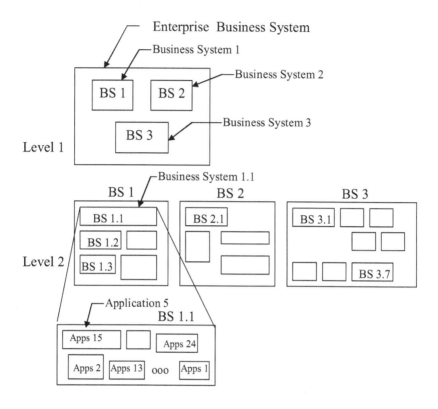

Figure 2. Mapping of Applications to Business Systems (*Source*: A. Goicoechea, 6/8/2002)

Step 6: Identify Candidate Technologies and Platforms

This step calls for the identification of candidate technology products. A set of well defined system requirements ought to be communicated to vendors as these are invited to meet with the Technology Assessment/Development Team in order to present business capabilities, limitations, and cost associated with a particular product (e.g., TCP/IP communications protocols, JavaScript, message middleware, IBM OS/390 mainframes, DB2 database management systems, etc.).

Step 7: Mapping of Technologies to Business Systems

This step calls for the mapping of candidate technologies to the existing hierarchy of business systems in the form of a "traceability matrix". At this point there ought to be multiple candidate technologies mapped to each business systems. Subsequent steps will determine, however, which candidate technologies are more preferable than other candidate technologies with regards to the evaluation criteria on Table 1, Step 3.

Step 8: Competing Principles of the Technology Architectural View

How does the designer (i.e., programmer, systems designer, manager, etc.) go about distributing technologies across the hierarchy of business systems and applications architecture? Should technologies be selected and distributed across an architecture of physical technologies, or should it be the other way around? In reality, the distribution happens both ways: The technologies are selected to reflect attributes and functionality of an application architecture, while an on-going effort in the Applications Development Team selects software modules and capabilities that are often linked by vendors to specific hardware platforms. It is, then, an iterative effort among the architects in the *Infrastructure Development Team* and the architects in the *Applications Development Team*. One may want to consider that a technology usually represents a grouping of several applications, and in this sense the principles proposed for the distribution of applications across business systems (Chapter 6) are also recommended here for the distribution of technologies across business systems with minor text modification, as depicted in Figure 3 and defined next:

- Cost Efficiency Principle: Technologies shall be identified, evaluated, and distributed across the applications architecture so as to maximize the ratio of number of applications to the number of technologies in the enterprise, i.e., Select the smallest set of technologies that would be needed to implement all the applications.
- System Performance Principle: Technologies shall be identified, evaluated, and distributed across the applications architecture so as to minimize aggregate query response time subject to a specified system throughput requirement (i.e., volume of transactions processed per operation cycle, say a 24-hour operations cycle, other cycle duration).

- <u>System Resource Management Principle</u>: Technologies shall be identified, evaluated, and distributed across the applications architecture so as to minimize the ratio of resources used (e.g., CPU utilization, data storage in GB/TB, and random access memory (RAM)) to number of applications.
- <u>System Security Tolerance Principle:</u> Technologies shall be identified, evaluated, and distributed across the applications architecture so that security-related functions are provided resulting in a number of security violations that is bounded (say 1 security violation per 1 million accounts per month) with an associated degradation/cost in query response time of less than 10% (e.g., secured query responses are 10% slower than unsecured query responses).
- <u>Architectural Robustness Principle</u>: Technologies shall be identified, evaluated, and distributed across the applications architecture so as to maximize business system availability in the face of scheduled maintenance (e.g., bring down a server for relocation or CPU upgrading), unscheduled maintenance (e.g., water flooding of a facility for a few days, A/C motor burns and fire fighting personnel must intervene and evacuate facility for a few hours), and disaster events (e.g., fire event destroys physical plant) triggering system failover to an alternate site.
- <u>Variety-of-Technologies Principle</u>: Technologies shall be identified, evaluated, and distributed across the applications architecture as to maximize the ratio of number of different vendors and technologies to the number of applications. If one technology fails or one vendor is not available to provide service (i.e., the vendor fails commercially and it goes out of business), its adverse impact on other technologies in the architecture is contained. Variety of technologies contributes to architectural robustness.
- <u>Division-of-Labor Principle:</u> Technologies shall be identified, evaluated, and distributed across the applications architecture so as to require technical support from a finite, well delineated, and manageable set of skills (e.g., data storage, communications, security, message middleware, etc.).

These are competing principles in the sense that each principle can be fully realized only at the expense of one or more of the other principles (once the Technology Architectural View has reached its Pareto Frontier, as is discussed in Chapter 20). As such, these principles are intended only as general guidelines for the design, use, duplication, and allocation of technologies across the enterprise architecture.

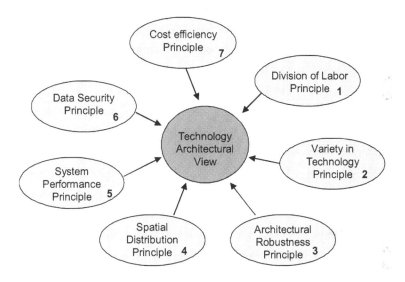

Figure 3. Competing Principles in the Technology Architectural View

Step 9: Technology Segmentation and Distribution Model

This step is responsible for segmenting the totality of technologies proposed into a finite set of groupings, for example:

- Communications Segment
- Platform Segment
- Storage Segment
- Data Backup and Restore Segment
- Disaster Recovery Segment
- other

Note that technologies within each segment have a functional affinity for each other (e.g., the Storage Segment is made up of data tapes, databases, database management systems, and data replication servers). Also, this step benefits from the application of the Division-of-Labor principle cited earlier.

Step 10: Logical Technology Architecture Design

Vendor independent technologies can be represented in logical diagrams, as shown in Figure 4.

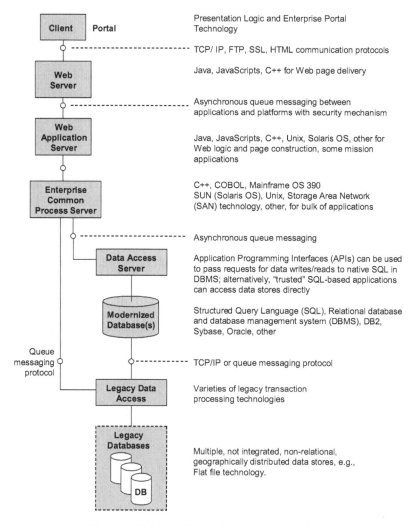

Figure 4. Web-based Logical Technology Model

This logical diagram, for example, shows a portal-based architecture with generic categories of technologies as transactions originate at the portal, move on to a Web server, a Web application server, data access box, and finally data is posted either to a modernized database or a legacy data store. For our Global Airlines example the logical technology architecture is shown on Figure 5

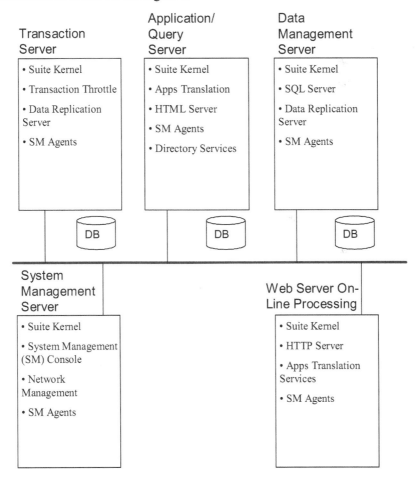

Figure 5. Logical Architectural Model, Global Airlines Services

Step 11: Physical Technology Architecture Design

Vendor dependent technologies are now represented via physical diagrams as shown on Figure 6 for the Global Services Airline example.

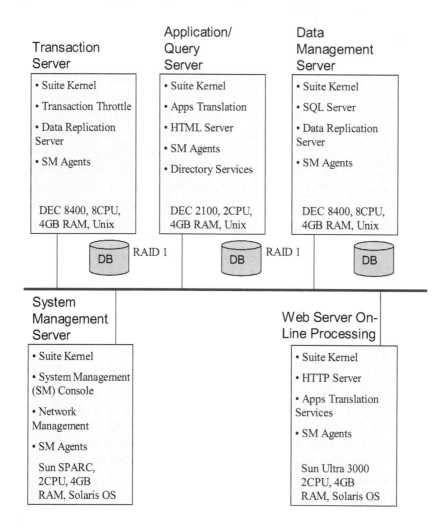

Figure 6. Physical Architectural Model, Global Airlines Services

This time the physical diagram for this portal-based architecture shows actual vendor products, so that the transaction server box is known to be a DEC 8400 computer system (from Digital Equipment Corporation Inc.) with 8 CPU, 4GB of random access memory (RAM), and a UNIX operating system.

Step 12: Communicate the Technology Architectural View

Development of the Technology Architectural View is a crucial design step and decisions reached in it should be communicated to and shared with other team and project personnel.

In this step the Technology Architectural View is documented and communicated to other engineering teams and projects through reports, presentations, solicited written comments, and invitations to engineering and customer personnel to attend working sessions of the Technology Integration team. A typical outline of a presentation for presentation of the Applications Architecture View is shown on Table 2.

Table 2. Outline of the Technology Architectural View Presentation

• Enterprise Architecture (EA) Planning Phases
• Project Releases and Data Dependencies
• Status of Technology Architectural View (e.g., Principles, General Applications Model, Design Rules, etc.)
• Impacts, Change Requests (CRs)
• List of candidate technologies
• Mapping of Requirements and Business Functions to Applications
• Application Configuration Items (Cis)
• Applications CI Test Planning
• Feedback from EA Development Team
• Feedback from EA Business Systems Team
• Feedback from Release Management
• Feedback from Modernization Projects.
• CARGO Project
• FLIGHTS Project
• GATES Project
• SEATS Project
• SDC project
• Questions and Answers

Audience composition should be managed to reflect the seven steps in the construction of the Technology Architectural View in Figure 1. Personnel from the Requirements Management Team and the Business Process Development Team, for example, should be invited to attend and participate in this presentation to assure traceability of functionality to be built into the applications back to functionality called for in the system requirements and spelled out in greater detail in the business systems descriptions.

8.5. Conclusions

In this chapter we aimed to acquaint the ourselves (e.g., the planner, the architect, the owner of the EA, others) with basic elements in the construction of the technology Architectural View. Specifically, we learned that:

(a) A technology is a collection of methods and physical means that make use of physical laws to realize a product or service that is deemed valuable by a human being. Examples of technologies are data storage devices, local area networks, cable TV, and messaging middleware.

(b) Technologies can then be grouped to form a Technology Architectural View of the enterprise architecture. These technologies are the physical means and procedures needed to implement a set of business systems (Business Systems Architectural View), a data model (Data Architectural View), and a set of applications (Applications Architectural View) that will make possible the execution of a set of business processes (Business Process Architectural View). Typically, an enterprise architecture may consist of hundreds and even thousands of technologies.

(c) Software, whether in-house built or commercially procured (e.g., COTS products), must run in physical environments made up of technologies and methods. A 12-step methodology was presented where each step is decomposed into several specific tasks that personnel in an infrastructure development team will then carry out to identify and evaluate alternative technologies, interview vendors, recommend selection of some technologies, and finally show how these technologies will work together in order to meet both functional and non-functional system requirements. Logical and physical diagrams are means of representation of the interactions among individual technologies.

(d) Allocation of technologies across the enterprise architecture is a most challenging activity for personnel in the Infrastructure Development Team. There are available, however, a number of principles that can be applied in order to build a number of desirable attributes into the EA such as robustness, ease of maintenance, security, and system performance.

Chapter 9

Distributed Database Design with Multiple Criteria

9.1. Introduction

Increasingly today, many information systems in Enterprise Architectures (both commercial and military) are being designed to access multiple bodies of data available not in a single data source (i.e., a database) but in multiple data sources distributed over several/many programs and systems within the Department of Defense (DoD) community. This chapter addresses the following questions:

- What are the options available to the database designer as he/she considers **multiple data sources** potentially available? Should a "preferred" set of data sources be identified, and how can this be done in some optimal fashion?
- If database segments are to be designed by contractors and submitted to DISA's DII COE program, what ought to be the guidelines and criteria to follow during the database design process and "segmentation process"?
- How are segments to be integrated to create a system? Should the segmentation process "encourage" the production of several/many small segments or just a few large segments to be subsequently integrated to create a system?

The motivation for these questions stems from text content in DISA's Defense Information Infrastructure (DII) Common Operating Environment, Integration and Runtime Specification (I&RTS) (Version

4.0, October 1999). We review portions of that text, pose two specific problems, and we proceed to obtain solutions to these two problems.

9.2. Database Segment Development

The DII COE document does contain general guidelines that database segment developers can use to meet data requirements:

- Use existing data stores at runtime (this requires acquisition of access rights). Data stores can be used as-is or changes can be negotiated with the data store owner.
- Review the database segments on the COE Data Emporium for potential reuse. For example, if the Emporium contains a database segment that contains the common representation for Organizations, then that segment should be used.
- Attempt to have existing segments updated to satisfy the new requirements. Use similar enterprise segments (preferred) or Community of Interest segments if available.
- Create new segments to extend the existing segment(s) as necessary to meet the requirements.
- Create a new data segment by reusing as much existing schema as possible and augmenting it to meet the requirements.

Other factors are recommended as well towards determining the structural contents of a database:

- Which tables can be conveniently managed as a unit.
- Which tables are defined to support a functional area.
- What are the sources of data, and
- What are the database object dependencies.

"An advantage of multiple shared database segments is that the segments are more granular, therefore allowing a shared data server to be configured to support mission applications without having to carry superfluous data and can be handled as separate configuration items. A disadvantage of multiple shared database segments is the management of database object dependencies that can be created by such things as *foreign key constraints*. These inter-segment dependencies complicate the management of segment installation and, moreover, the removal of segments." These guidelines, however, do not offer specific ways or mechanisms that a designer can follow to select a preferred subset of data sets or to partition a database into segments while minimizing the number of foreign-key dependencies.

9.3. How this Chapter is Organized

At the outset, this chapter identified two specific problems in distributed database design. In Problem 1 the need exists to partition a very large database (say 25 tables of more and a total of 100 fields or more) into several smaller databases. In Problem 2 the desired fields are available in several databases that are geographically distributed, so that there are many subsets of these databases that would collectively contain a list of needed fields. Section 9.5 presents a methodological approach that is new in the use of non-linear mathematical programming to obtain a best solution to Problem 1. Section 9.7 shows how to use mathematical representation and multiple criteria to obtain a solution to Problem 2 and in the process determine the Pareto or Efficient "curve".

9.4. Statement of the Problem

This paper addresses two specific distributed-database design problems:

Problem 1: Given a determination to partition a database into database segments (i.e., subsets of tables), what are the design options available to the developer, and what are the trade-offs involved in terms of development costs, data sharing, system interoperability, system performance, other criteria? The designer begins with one large database and proceeds to partition it into several smaller databases or segments, i.e., a "one-to-many" database segmentation problem.

Problem 2: Given multiple, alternative data sources, how does the database designer select a best subset of data sources? Part of the system design may be the formation of an "integrated, virtual database" or a system interface that enables queries of the various data sources. If query performance (i.e., non-functional requirement) is important then the design solution may identify a particular set of data sources. If keeping system development costs down is a primary concern then the design solution may identify a different set of data sources and this design will not necessarily yield high query performance. The designer begins with a large collection of databases and proceeds to select portions of each database to form a single, composite database, i.e., a "many-to-one" database segmentation problem.

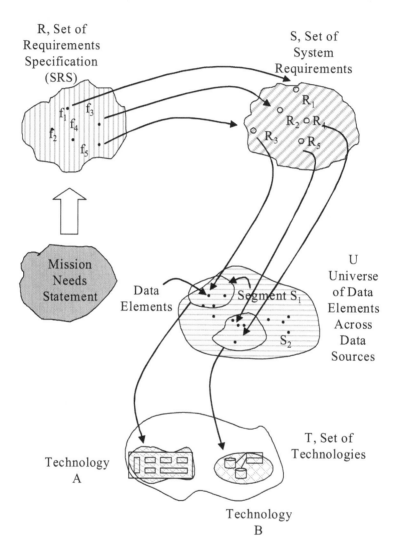

Figure 1. Mapping of System Requirements to Data Elements in a Distributed Database Environment

9.5. Methodological Approach

Mission requirements drive the selection of data sources, database design options reflect alternative solutions in a "solutions-space" (i.e., one single, large database system; several small databases; single site; multiple site, distributed database environment; etc.), while development costs and non-functional requirements (i.e., system performance, security, reliability, etc.) contribute to identifying "a preferred system", as depicted in Figure 1 and Figure 2. See Ozsu and Valdiriez (1991) and Simon (1995) for a presentation of design issues and a preview of emerging technologies for distributed database design. Also, see Goikoetxea (2001) for greater detail on the methodological approach and solution.

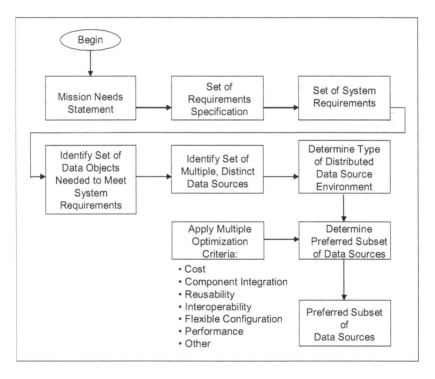

Figure 2. General Framework for Database Design in a Distributed Database Environment

Multiple criteria such as cost, component integration, reusability, interoperability, and performance must be considered in the final determination of the preferred subset of data sources, as will be illustrated next.

9.6. Problem 1: One-to-Many Database Segmentation

"A disadvantage of multiple shared database segments is the management of database object dependencies that can be created by such things as foreign key constraints. These inter-segment dependencies complicate the management of segment installation and, moreover, the removal of segments" [DII COE].

An approach suggested here is to decompose the database (i.e., a set **S** of tables) into multiple segments (i.e., a database segment S_i is made up of a subset of the tables in **S**, so that $S_i \in S$) so that a table appears in one and only one segment and the union of all segments is the set **S,** as depicted on Figure 3.

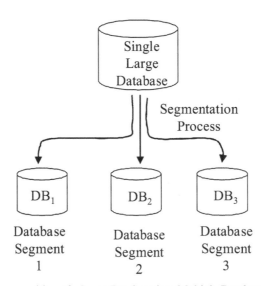

Figure 3. Decomposition of a Large Database into Multiple Database Segments

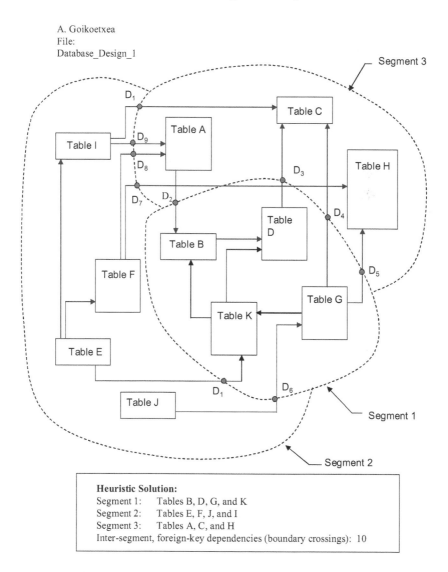

A. Goikoetxea
File:
Database_Design_1

Figure 4. Three Segments with a Total of 10 Boundary Crossings

The following observations are made:

(a) Consider the database to be segmented shown on Figure 4. A 4-table segment candidate in Figure 4 has 6 foreign-key dependencies, i.e., 6 segment boundary "crossings"; an arrow points to the child-end of a relationship between two tables; the other 4-table segment also has 6 dependencies, and the 3-table segment has 8 dependencies; counting the total number of crossings yields a total of 10 foreign-key dependencies.

(b) Formulation of the "segmentation design problem" shows that the number of possible pairwise dependencies (i.e., at least one foreign key is involved between two tables) is the number of combinations given by the binomial coefficient. For the example database in Figure 4 this possible maximum number is 55, that is:

$$\binom{11}{2} = \frac{11!}{9!\,2!} = \frac{(11)(10)}{2} = 55$$

However, the actual number N_1 of table pairs with dependencies (boundary crossings) is only 15:

A-B	D-K
A-I	E-F
A-F	E-I
B-K	F-H
B-D	H-G
C-I	I-C
C-D	I-E
C-G	

(c) The number of "segment dependencies" N_2 is 10 which is smaller than the number of "table dependencies", i.e., $N_2 < N_1$.

(d) Number of segments possible, 3 or 4 tables each:

$$\binom{10}{4} = \frac{10!}{6!\,4!} = \frac{(10)(9)(8)(7)}{(4)(3)(2)} = 210$$

$$\binom{6}{3} = \frac{6!}{3!\,3!} = \frac{(6)(5)(4)}{(3)(2)} = 20$$

Out of the set of 10 tables, for example, 210 segments could be constructed with 4 tables each; of the remaining 6 tables 2 segments could be constructed with 3 tables each; the total number of possible designs (i.e., one design consisting of one 4-table segment and two 3-table segments) would be $(210)(20) = 4,200$, a very large number of segment designs indeed.

Mathematical Formulation:

One way of obtaining a best, optimal set of segments is to apply mathematical optimization. Let $X_{ji} = 1$ if table i belongs to segment j, 0 if table i does not belong to segment j, and such that i = A, B, ...K, L, and j = 1, 2, and 3 as depicted in Figure 3.

Then, the optimization problem can be stated as follows:
Minimize:

$$\sum_{i,j,k,l} X_{ij} X_{kl} \cdot \delta_{jk}$$

where $\delta_{jk} = 1$ if dependency exists between tables j and k; $\delta_{jk} = 0$ if dependency does not exist between tables j and k; k, j = A,B,C, ...L, the names of tables, but k $\neq$ j; also i,l = 1, 2, and 3, the names of the segments, but i $\neq$ l, subject to constraints:

$X_{1A} + X_{1B} + X_{1C} + ... + X_{1k} = 4$
to require only four tables in segment 1;
$X_{2A} + X_{2B} + X_{2C} + ... + X_{2k} = 4$
to require only four tables in segment 2;
$X_{3A} + X_{3B} + X_{3C} + ... + X_{3k} = 3$
to require only 3 tables in segment 3;
$X_{1A} + X_{2A} + X_{3A} = 1$
to require that table A belong to one segment only (either segment 1, 2, or 3);
$X_{1B} + X_{2B} + X_{3B} = 1$
to require that table B belong to one segment only;
$X_{1C} + X_{2C} + X_{3C} = 1$
to require that table C belong to one segment only; and so forth for all other remaining tables; also,
$X_{ij} = 1$ or 0 for all i and j.

Solution:

The optimal solution to this non-linear, binary problem was obtained using the mathematical programming capability in Solver, in Microsoft Excel:

$$X_{1C} = 1 \qquad X_{1G} = 1 \qquad X_{1I} = 1$$
$$X_{1J} = 1 \qquad X_{2B} = 1 \qquad X_{2K} = 1$$
$$X_{2D} = 1 \qquad X_{2E} = 1 \qquad X_{1K} = 1$$
$$X_{3A} = 1 \qquad X_{3F} = 1 \qquad X_{3H} = 1$$

and all other variables are zero, i.e., do not select. This mathematical representation can also accommodate other constraints such as week entities, business rules, and groups of tables that the user wishes to be contained within the same segment. This time the number of crossings has been reduced from 10 to 7, which is in fact the optimal solution for this design problem. A graphical representation of this solution is shown in Figure 5.

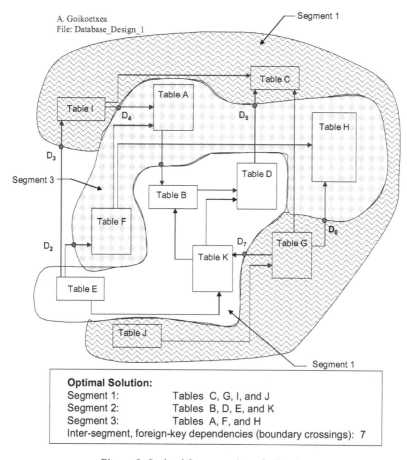

Figure 5. Optimal Segmentation of a Database

9.7. Problem 2: Many-to-One Database Segmentation

As the database designer sets to identify existing multiple databases that may contain the tables and data elements of interest to him/her several situations are possible, as depicted on Table 1. In the simplest case, Case 1, all desired data elements or objects (i.e., data elements, tables, stored procedures, other) reside in one data source so the design strategy is to utilize that single data source and no decision opportunity exists. In Case 2 all desired objects reside in multiple copies of the same data source. In Case 3 desired objects reside across multiple, distinct data

	Table 1. Distribution Pattern of Data Elements Across Multiple Data Sources		
Case No.	**Distribution of Available Data Elements**	**Architectural Strategy**	**Optimization Criteria**
1	All desired data elements/objects reside in one data source	Select single data Source	None. No decision opportunity exists
2	Desired data objects reside in one data source with exact replications in multiple sites	Select single data source	Select site that offers lowest system development cost. Other criteria: - performance
3	Desired data objects reside across multiple, distinct data sources; no sharing of data objects across data sources		Select entire set of data sources. No decision opportunity exists.

	Table 1. (*Continued*)		
Case No.	Distribution of Available Data Elements	Architectural Strategy	Optimization Criteria
4	Desired data objects reside across multiple, distinct data sources; there is sharing of data objects across data sources	Select subset of data sources	Select subset of data sources using optimization criterion: - Performance - Cost - Other

sources, with no sharing of data objects across data sources. Finally, in Case 4 desired objects reside across multiple, distinct data sources, but some data objects are shared across data sources available.

We proceed to consider a decision problem in Case 4.

Selection of Preferred Subset of Data Sources

Next, we consider an illustrative example of Case 4 where there are a total of 7 desired data elements, {1,2,4,5,7,9,10}, distributed over 5 data sources as shown on Figure 6. A decision point occurs given the opportunity to select a "preferred subset" of n data sources (i.e., databases) that meets the following criteria:

(1) all the desired data elements are represented in this preferred subset,

(2) it contains the smallest number of data sources needed to provide all the data elements in the "design subset of data elements" in Figure 2,

(3) it results from optimization of a criterion (e.g., minimize design cost, minimize aggregate query response, other), and

(4) it is a Pareto solution (i.e., a non-dominated solution in n-dimensional Pareto space; see Goicoechea et al., 1992, 1982).

From this illustrative problem we can see that three possible solutions exist:

Solution 1:	Choose sets: A + B + C
Solution 2:	Choose sets: A + D
Solution 3:	Choose set: E

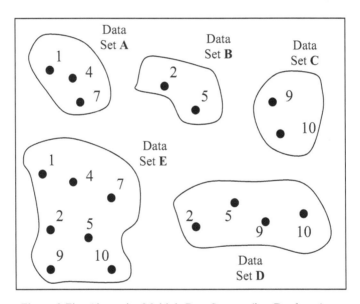

Figure 6. Five Alternative Multiple Data Sources (i.e., Databases)

That is, solution 1 yields a choice subset consisting of data sources A, B, and C; solution 2 yields a choice subset consisting of data sources A and D; and solution 3 yields a choice subset consisting of data sources E only. We note that each of these three solutions contain the entire design set of data elements, {1,2,4,5,7,9,10}.

9.8. Multiple Criteria

In a real-world situation, the number or alternative data sources may be large and simple enumeration of the possible solutions may not be practical. Mathematical programming (MP) is one approach to solving this design problem, as shown next.

Multiple criteria in distributed database design can include:

- Cost
- Performance (query response time, other)
- Reuse/sharing of data sources
- Flexibility of configuration

See Goicoechea et al. (1992, 1982) for a description of multiple criteria in engineering design and business decision problems.

Design variables: Let

X_{ij}	= data element j in data source i,
X_{A1}	= data element 1 in data source A
X_{A4}	= data element 4 in data source A
X_{A7}	= data element 7 in data source A
X_{B2}	= data element 2 in data source B
X_{B5}	= data element 5 in data source B
X_{C9}	= data element 9 in data source C
X_{C10}	= data element 10 in data source C
X_{D2}	= data element 2 in data source D
X_{D5}	= data element 5 in data source D
X_{D9}	= data element 9 in data source D
X_{D10}	= data element 10 in data source D
X_{E1}	= data element 1 in data source E
X_{E2}	= data element 2 in data source E
X_{E4}	= data element 4 in data source E
X_{E5}	= data element 5 in data source E
X_{E7}	= data element 7 in data source E
X_{E9}	= data element 9 in data source E
X_{E10}	= data element 10 in data source E

Decision problem

A decision problem is formulated next via mathematical programming (MP). A decision variable is assigned to each data element in the "choice sub-set of data elements" with a range of possible values of 1 (i.e., select this data element and its data source) and 0 (i.e., do not select this data element and its data source). The MP technique proceeds to find a combination of data elements and data sources that minimizes cost, i.e., an *optimal solution*. Cost and query response time parameters are as shown on Table 2 for this illustrative example.

Table 2. Cost and Query Response Times

Design Variable	Coefficient C_I	
	Cost ($,Dollars)	Query Response Time (Seconds)
X_{A1}	2	4
X_{A4}	2	4
X_{A7}	3	3
X_{B2}	10	3
X_{B5}	12	3
X_{C9}	1	2
X_{C10}	1	2
X_{D2}	3	3
X_{D5}	3	3
X_{D9}	3	3
X_{D10}	3	3
X_{E1}	2	15
X_{E2}	2	20
X_{E4}	1	15
X_{E5}	2	20
X_{E7}	2	20
X_{E9}	2	15
X_{E10}	1	15

Minimize overall system cost function:

$$F_{cost} = C_1 X_{A1} + C_2 X_{A4} + C_3 X_{A7} + C_4 X_{B2} + \ldots + C_{19} X_{E10}$$

Subject to the following constraints:

$X_{A1} + X_{A4} + X_{A7} + X_{B2} + ... + X_{E10}$ $= 7$,
total number of desired data elements is 7;
$(X_{A1} + X_{A4} + X_{A7})/3$ $= 0,1$
binary constraint, i.e., select all or none of the data elements in data
source A;
$(X_{B2} + X_{B5})/2$ $= 0,1$
binary constraint, i.e., select all or none of the data elements in data
source B;
$(X_{C9} + X_{C10})/2$ $= 0,1$
binary constraint, i.e., select all or none of the data elements in data
source C;
$X_{A1}, X_{A4}, X_{A7}, ...X_{E10}$ $= 0,1$
all decision variables are binary;

The solution to this illustrative problem was obtained via mathematical
programming (MP) in Excel's Solver:

X_{A1}	$= 1$		X_{D2}	$= 1$
X_{A4}	$= 1$		X_{D5}	$= 1$
X_{A7}	$= 1$		X_{D9}	$= 1$
			X_{D10}	$= 1$

and all other variables are set to zero, thus identifying data sources A and
D as the choice subset, which corresponds to Solution 2 shown earlier.
However, if the design criterion is to minimize aggregate query response
time across all data sources to be selected (i.e., maximize performance)
then the solution is given by data sources A +B +C, which can be
verified by inspection of Table 2 and which corresponds to Solution 1
identified earlier.

Next, we proceed to apply both cost and performance criteria:

Minimize: $\mathbf{F} = w_1\mathbf{F}_{cost} + w_2\mathbf{F}_{performance}$
$= w_1[C_1X_{A1} + C_2X_{A4} + ... + C_{18}X_{E10}]$
$+ w_2[R_1X_{A1} + R_2X_{A4} + ... + R_{18}X_{E10}]$

subject to the same constraints since the "design space" remains the
same. The solution to this multi-criteria design problem with *criterion
weights* $w_1 = 0.6$ and $w_2 = 0.4$ yields:

X_{A1}	$= 1$	X_{D2}	$= 1$	X_{D10}	$= 1$
X_{A4}	$= 1$	X_{D5}	$= 1$		
X_{A7}	$= 1$	X_{D9}	$= 1$		

which corresponds to Design 2. Other sets of weights can be tried such that $w_1+w_2 = 1.0$ until all non-inferior solutions in the Pareto frontier have been identified. In our example there are only three possible designs, and these are now presented on Table 3 and Figure 7.

Table 3. Multiple Design Criteria and Database Designs

Criteria	Design 1	Design 2	Design 3
1. Cost ($)	31	19	12
2. Performance (Total Query Time, Sec.)	21	23	120

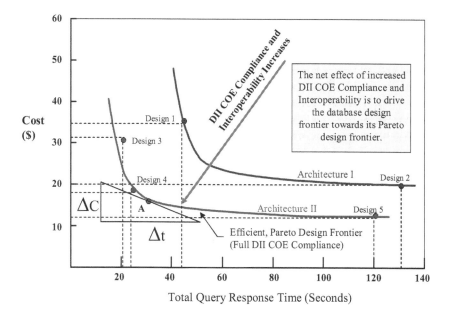

Figure 7. Pareto Frontier in Database Design

Several observations can be made now. First, the optimization procedure above generated the three possible solutions/designs in this illustrative example, and these solutions make up the *Pareto design frontier*. The DB designer aims at obtaining designs that are *Pareto-optimal*, that is, designs that are part of the Pareto design frontier. Solutions over this frontier are such that as one moves from Design 1 to Design 2, the cost decreases from \$31 to \$19 at the expense of query performance (i.e., total query time increases from 21 sec. to 23 sec.). A tangent to the design frontier at point A is $\Delta C/\Delta t$, which is the *criteria tradeoff* at that point; at point A, for example, an improvement in query performance in the order of 20 seconds costs \$10, approximately.

It would not be immediately apparent to the DB designer working with say hundreds of data sources, whether he/she is obtaining DB designs that are "above", "below", or "on top" of the Pareto frontier, and it then becomes necessary to obtain and compare several solutions. Solution B, for example, is "inferior" to Solution C because whereas both offer the same performance, solution C has a lower cost. Solution D has still a lower cost but is not technologically possible. As the designer maintains performance at a fixed level and continues to make design changes each lowering the total, eventually he will not be able to make further designs changes that translate into a lower cost. It is at that point that he has reached the Pareto design frontier. Each technology (e.g., flat file database design and operation, Oracle DBMS, Sybase DBMS, etc.) has its own Pareto design frontier.

9.9. Conclusions

- Database segmentation presents many challenges to the database engineer in his/her efforts to satisfy system requirements while applying multiple design criteria. Minimizing server administrative overhead, cost, number of table joins needed to execute a query, and physical distance to data source, for example, is desirable. On the other hand, maximizing data source availability, database performance (through record indexing at the data source, efficient schema design, efficient reference data set design, containment of database fragmentation, other) is desirable. Identification of these often conflicting criteria, relationships among them, and providing the means to measure criteria values of alternative designs early in the database design phase should yield a positive payoff later during database development and eventual field deployment and operation.
- Systems engineering can provide a framework for effective analysis of requirements, selective utilization of optimization

techniques, and multiple criteria tradeoff analysis of alternative database designs.

- It is possible to consider the general design problem of partitioning a large database into a desired number or database segments in such a way that the number of foreign-key dependencies is the smallest number possible. This smallest number of foreign-key dependencies can have a beneficial impact on overall system performance, including a decrease in database server administrative overhead. This approach can now be applied to large databases containing hundreds of tables.

- It is relatively straight forward to apply multiple-criteria decision making (MCDM) techniques to virtual database design. Hundreds and possibly thousands of data sources may be initially available to the database designer as he/she searches for the best selection of a relatively small number of data sets. This approach can guide the database designer in the search of Pareto database designs (best selection of data sources) that feature desired, multiple criteria levels and tradeoffs.

- Topics for future research applying the problem representation and solution techniques demonstrated above can include data sharing and system inter-operability in a multiple-project, multiple-client distributed database environment.

Chapter 10

Performance and Capacity-Based Architecture Planning: Concepts, Principles, and Measurement Tools

10.1. Introduction

Enterprise Architectures (EA) are functionally complex, their construction takes place over long time frames (often several years), are difficult to measure and assess due to changing requirements or new ones over various architecture releases, can involve large number of business processes and activities distributed over multiple systems, and rely on new component technologies from a fast-paced vendor community. On top, the need to measure, assess, and monitor progress during the EA lifecycle ought to be crucial and of the highest interest to all parties involved, e.g., EA owners, contractor teams, and overseeing organizations.

This chapter presents and discusses an enterprise-wide performance and capacity engineering model (EPCEM). Generally, construction of an EA requires construction, monitoring, and performance assessment of several projects. As such, program-level (i.e., EA level) EPCEM needs to provide for integration of all project-level EPCEM activities, as we shall see in this chapter. Definitions of tasks, roles of people participating in EPCEM, and information that must be collected and delivered to overseeing organizations (e.g., OMB E300 exhibits, as stated in the Performance Reference Model (PRM)) will be listed. Additionally, the EA work products identified in earlier chapters need to demonstrate and adequately document EPCEM activities and models as to be able to present a coherent, integrated, and complete view of the Enterprise.

The purpose of the EPCEM is to provide information to the application designers, infrastructure designers, Modernization and IT management team at each design decision point as to the viability of proposed application designs, expected performance levels for specified levels of resources, and/or the level of resources required to provide specified levels of performance when processing projected workloads. The models are also intended to provide the basic information required to support application performance improvement and performance tuning efforts. They will be validated against performance test and benchmark and other performance data collected during the various systems tests.

10.2. Objectives of this Chapter

The objectives of this chapter are to assist the EA performance and capacity engineer to set up an EPCEM in the EA organization capable of supporting the various analysis, design, implementation, testing, and fielding activities. Specific objectives are:

- To project impacts of workload scenarios and new/modified requirements on architecture sub-systems and components.
- To evaluate how the architecture supports functional and non-functional requirements.
- To identify alternative architectural options in areas of distributed database environments, processing power and utilization (CPUs, RAM, I/O), disk storage, data backup, and inter-site failover and recovery, other).
- To identify flaws in architecture design, ability of architecture to meet requirements, implementation issues, and actively communicate this information to various EA teams.
- To communicate to EA owners the importance of EPCEM activities and resources EARLY in the EA effort. A mistake commonly made by EA owners is to wait for design and coding to be well underway and then try to bring EPCEM into the effort.
- To recommend to EA owners to establish and secure working arrangements with other organizations (e.g., government agencies, vendor community) that have testing facilities for purposes of sharing and using those facilities to test proposed COTS products and EA sub-systems.

10.3. How this Chapter is Organized

This chapter presents and discusses key activities in the enterprise-wide performance and capacity engineering model (EPCEM). Section 10.4 shows the 7 EA lifecycle phases during which a total of 15 capacity and performance activities will take place, both at the project level and the enterprise level. Section 10.5 presents an EA system performance evaluation approach that takes the reader trough a series of performance modeling activities and actual testing activities; modeling results are compared with actual test results and modeling parameters are then adjusted accordingly. A list of business modeling and system performance tools in the market today are presented in Section 10.6. Also, a list of roles and responsibilities in the EPCEM model are given in Section 10.12.

10.4. EPCEM Approach to Life Cycle EA Planning

Crucial to successful life cycle EA planning is the implementation of an enterprise-wide performance and capacity engineering model (EPCEM) early in the life cycle, as illustrated in Figure 1.

The cycle phases in EA planning are:

- *Phase 1: Vision and Strategy*: During this phase individual inputs from EA owners and executives are gathered regarding strategic goals of the new EA (i.e., the "To-Be", future, modernized EA), new business processes and activities, marketing, expanded facilities, and new business partners. Also, a set of system requirements begins to emerge in this phase. An EPCEM should be drafted by PRIME contractor and presented to the EA owners and executives for consideration and eventual acceptance with changes as needed; characterization of a preliminary workload (i.e., volume of transactions, queries to databases, other inputs to be processed). *Milestone 1* is reached when all activities in Phase 1 are completed.
- *Phase 2: Conceptual Design*: Once a set of strategic goals is known, this phase prepares a high-level view of an architecture and system capable of meeting the new system requirements. New vendor technologies and business paradigms are considered for possible integration in a new architectural design. EPCEM

activities should include a rough-order-of-magnitude (ROM) of processing resources (e.g., CPU, internal memory, and input/output (I/O) rates) and disk data storage capacity. Milestone 2 is reached when all activities in Phase 2 are completed.

- *Phase 3: Logical Design*: This phase is about the dentification, definition of initial relationships among database tables/entities, fields within each table, and the initial baselining of system requirements into a Systems Requirements Report (SRR). Business processes are fully defined so that the design is able to proceed to the creation of a hierarchy of business systems that will house those business processes. Software/code classes are already defined. Portal and web server technologies and products are proposed by engineering teams as components to the EA; subsequently vendors submit bids through a product acquisition office; best technologies and products are recommended to EA owners. First draft of the EPCEM should contain high-level capacity and performance models that show how the non-functional (i.e., performance and capacity) system requirements will be met; a high-level disaster recovery (DR) design is completed; draft of the EPCEM is delivered to EA owners for review, eventual acceptance and approval. Milestone 3 is reached when all activities in Phase 3 are completed.

- *Phase 4: Physical Design*: Database fields are assigned data types and character number lengths are determined, table/entitie relationships are characterized fully, main keys are identified, multiple alternative designs are prepared and evaluated (e.g., 3-5 alternative plans, ideally). Begin to provide OMB with E300 reports. Software/code classes are fully defined in terms of behavior, internal and external functions, input and output parameters. EPCEM activities should include end-to-end modeling of business processes and activities, fully developed performance and capacity models; Disaster recovery system design is fully validated by EA business owners. Milestone4A is reached when all activities in Phase 4 are completed.

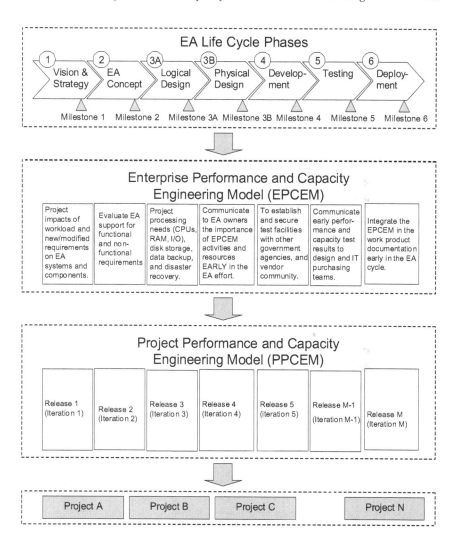

Figure 1. Elements in an Enterprise Performance and Capacity Engineering Model (EPCEM)

- *Phase 5: Development:* Coding of classes is completed and integrated with vendor technology and components ((i.e., commercial off the shelf or COTS) products, code is delivered to test teams to prepare for quality testing. EPCEM should include refined performance and capacity models with projections on processing resources for future EA releases. Software/code classes are already defined. Provide OMB with E300 reports. Milestone4B is reached when all activities in Phase 5 are completed.

- *Phase 6:* Integration Testing and Deployment: Test cases and scripts are written and applied to verify system requirements during Acceptance Quality Testing (AQT), end-to-end System Integration Testing (SIT) by PRIME contractor, and System Acceptance Testing (SAT) by EA owners. Test results are entered into the EPCEM and compared against earlier performance and capacity projections, model parameters are adjusted accordingly; document performance and capacity baseline at the EA and project levels; end-to-end pilot operations, security plan is signed by EA owners; disaster recovery design has been tested in the pilot. Provide OMB with E300 reports. Milestone5 is reached when all activities in Phase 6 are completed.

- *Phase 7:* Operations and Maintenance: Conduct and complete facility readiness reviews, project sub-system readiness review, deploy and run new system. EPCEM activities should contain full performance and capacity models, projected vs. actual system throughput. Monitor operation and maintenance of new system, build database to store operations, scheduled and un-scheduled maintenance data (e.g., component down time, repair time, etc.)

Central to the concept and philosophy of the EPCEM is that it must be instituted early in the life cycle of the EA. Why so, and what often happens in the practice? Ideally, as stated earlier, an EPCEM model and process should be designed, funded, and built into the EA life cycle to insure that both functional and non-functional requirements are considered in all major decisions regarding analysis, design, and evaluation of COTS products (software) and hardware platforms being considered for purchasing and eventual integration into the EA system. In practice this does not always happen for a number of reasons:

- The need to show EA progress early in the game. Some EA owners are of the belief that once funding for the EA begins it is important to show results to the EA stockholders as soon as possible (understandably so), and that functional requirements ought to be the main consideration during the analysis and design phases. "Let us do the functional requirements first and later we will take care of the non-functional requirements, for sure", one can often hear.

- EA owners (i.e., the client) work on the EA for 1-2 years and then they move on. A reality of EA building is complex and it responds to some very real and dynamic scenarios. During the analysis, design, and coding phases some EA owners and managers often feel that in order to show progress in the EA effort during their tenure it is best to concentrate on the implementation of the functional requirements, and that planning for and implementation of the non-functional requirements may hinder their best efforts. "Build the most functionality during those 1-2 years, get promoted, and then move on to higher and greener pastures in the EA organization,...let the next guy worry about system performance and capacity issues", can be a prevalent feeling.

- Testing begins and the brutal reality emerges. Often, as new EA owners and project managers begin their tenure and the EA effort enters the testing phase, the awakening can be brutal as test results begin to reveal that processing and time response capabilities of the system being built fall short of meeting performance requirements. By then some major decisions have been made and implemented on coding, the purchasing of platforms, and their integration into the EA system. "Fine tuning of the system" may not work this late in the game. Replacement of some low-yielding components or sub-systems begins to be considered, painfully. Scheduled EA releases are delayed. Performance engineers are then sought frantically. Precious time may have been lost.

- Engineers eventually get the job done, despite short falls on the part of management. Engineers on both sides of the picture do come together and save the day. One of the most redeeming and satisfying experiences about being part of an EA building effort is seeing performance engineers on the EA owners side, and performance engineers and software developers on the contractor side come together and work intensely over a period of several months until the needed design changes are made and the system finally delivers the goods. The EA and its system do meet all functional and performance requirements and the system is ready for release and deployment, finally.

The OMB reference models do provide guidance on solid planning, though. Preparation of the OMB E300 exhibits now include a requirement that alternative designs must be analyzed for comparison with the proposed design. OMB E300 exhibit requirements, however, ought to be extended to include capacity and performance test results of critical system components against workload requirements during the design, implementation, and testing phases.

10.5. General EA System Performance Evaluation Approach

So what are some of the specific performance and capacity activities that are carried out during the EPCEM? Shown in Figure 2 are main performance and capacity activities that ought to be planned for by EA owners and carried out by EA designers:

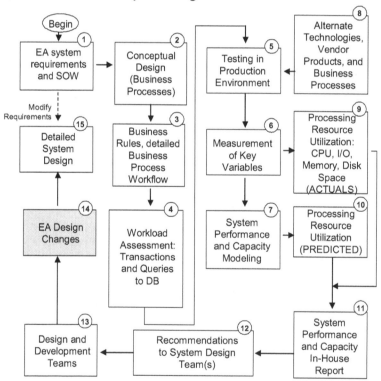

Figure 2. Activities in the Enterprise Performance and Capacity Engineering Model (EPCEM)

Step 1: To begin with, a set of EA system requirements must be well under way, already baselined or nearing this event; also, the Statement of Work by EA owners has gathered considerable detail to support definition of functional and non-functional requirements.

Step 2: The Business Processes Team has documented the business processes in the EA to lend support to a conceptual design of the EA system. As noted earlier in Chapters 3 and 4, the business processes are now represented by their various business activities and these activities have been distributed among the logical business systems. Additionally, the applications that carry out the business activities have been allocated to hardware platforms in the conceptual EA system.

Step 3: The Performance and Capacity Team works with the Business Processes Team to insure that business rules are already identified and part of the several/many process workflows in the conceptual EA system. One by one, each of the process workflows must be documented and process dependencies (e.g., DB access, memory utilization, I/O resource utilization, etc.) are well known. Typically, members of the two teams meat over several weeks to go over diagrams (Powerpoint, Visio, UML, other) to make sure that the various workflows needed to carry out the business activities are well understood, that the various sub-systems and components come into play as required, and that processing resources will be in place and on demand.

Step 4: Workload assessment. This is a most critical step in the EPCEM program, because information on number of transactions and queries to the database(s) to be processed per hour must be computed. How this workload varies from hour to hour over a 24-hour period must be characterized, and possible peaks in these numbers must be identified. By now the EA organization has allocated funding for a Performance and Capacity Report or Section that documents the workloads that the EA system will have to process over that 24-hour period, as well as variations in peak loading over the 12 months of the year.

Step 5: Testing in a Production Environment. An EA sub-system has been assembled in the production environment (i.e., a lab facility that replicates part or all the to-be EA system), predetermined workloads are processed, workflows are established, and test results are collected, analyzed, and documented. Workflows that could not be carried out during this exercise are identified and a trouble report is prepared with detail on what went wrong (e.g., the DB was not loaded correctly with data at the outset of the exercise).

Step 6: Measurement of Key Variables. Percentage of CPU utilization, internal memory usage, disk space used, and I/O utilization over the time required to run a test are measured, analyzed, and reported in the Performance and Capacity Section of the EA System document, a main EA work product. Of particular interest to EA owners and planners ought to be the CPU utilization charts for peak loads over a 24 hour time period: when the peak load appears the CPU utilization percentage ought not to exceed 80%-85% as to allow another 15%-20% CPU capacity for unscheduled loading that can come from external systems due to a variety of reasons (e.g., an external system experienced a backlog of transaction processing due to some component failure of its own and when that component "came up" the external system released its large load of transactions to the EA system over a short time period of, say one hour.)

Step 7: System Performance and Capacity (P&C) Modeling. Essential to the EPCEM program is a set of P&C tools and modeling capabilities. P&C testing and modeling go together. One cannot do without the other. Accordingly, EA owners and planners ought to invest in P&C tools with which to model the workloads and workflows of the to-be EA system early in the EA program. Understandably, this is an essential and crucial investment in people, money, and time as EA sub-systems are modeled piece-by-piece, workloads are scheduled, and model parameters (i.e., variables such as CPU utilization, MIPS available, I/O rates, MIPS required per transaction, many other) are estimated based on earlier testing and loaded into the P&C

model. Finally, the models in the P&C tools are run and results are analyzed to yield a picture of the performance of the evolving EA system, i.e., the PREDICTED behavior of the EA system.

Step 8: Alternate Technologies, Vendor Products, and Business Processes. Critical to the design and implementation phases is the ability to try proposed vendor products (i.e., COTS products) in a testing and production environment (Step 5) in order to verify vendor claims and to learn how to integrate the vendor products in the evolving system. Also, new business paradigms (e.g., Customer Relationship Management (CRM) technologies and products) appear in the market and it is in the interest of EA owners and planners to be able to test these new business paradigms in realistic production settings.

Step 9: Processing Resource Utilization: CPU, I/O, Memory, Disk Space (ACTUALS). Among the key variables measured in Step 6 are CPU percentage utilization, input/output rates, internal memory usage, and disk space. Values measured for these variables in the production environment then provide a picture of the true, current performance capability of the system, i.e., the set of ACTUALS. In turn, these variable values are used as inputs to the performance and capacity tools for the next round of modelling and testing. With each new round of modelling and testing, larger transaction loads and additional sub-systems are integrated and tried in the production environment.

Step 10: Processing Resource Utilization (PREDICTED). Once the performance and capacity modelling tools are loaded with realistic parameter values (the set of ACTUAL values in earlier production runs), the tools are run, this time with larger transaction loads and additional sub-systems or components. Again, the tools provide reports on CPU percentage utilization, input/output rates, internal memory usage, and disk space utilization which constitute the current set of PREDICTED values. Next, when the same transaction load and additional sub-system configuration will be tested in the production environment to obtain a set of ACTUALS which will then be compared against the set of PREDICTED values. If the difference between PREDICTED and ACTUALS is small, then small changes in model parameters (i.e., arrival rate of transactions, time actually required to process transaction type A, transaction type B, other) are made. If the difference is large, then the modelling done needs to be examined carefully, model parameters are adjusted accordingly, and the tools are run again until the difference between PREDICTED and ACTUALS is shown to be small. At this time, the models in the tools are said to be calibrated and ready for the new system configuration and round of testing.

Step 11: System Performance and Capacity In-House Report. This activity gathers the analyses conducted on the comparison of PREDICTED with ACTUAL system performance and capacity values in order to comment on current ystem configuration, explain system shortcomings, and recommend changes on sub-system configuration or relative value of proposed vendor products (i.e., COTS). Also, and often most significant, software deficiencies are identified and reported to the software design and development teams for proper correction.

Step 12: Recommendations to System Design Team(s). Findings in the system performance and capacity in-house report (Step 11) are communicated to the software design and development teams for correction. Detailed test case results must be documented with identification number, time of testing, system configuration, name of tester (person), and comments by tester.

Step 13: Design and Development Teams. By this time in the implementation and testing phases, the design and development teams are playing a most crucial role: working closely with the testing team(s) to make necessary adjustments in the software so that the system configured in the production environment can meet the non-functional requirements (i.e., performance and capacity requirements).

Step 14: EA Design Changes. If the software design is sound to begin with, then the software changes will be minor. If the software design is flawed to begin with, then minor software changes "will not do", production testing will have to be stopped, and production and delivery schedules will have to be modified to allow time for the software design and hardware changes to take place, which can be a worst scenario greatly costly to and feared by EA owners, EA planners, and the contractor teams. In this worst scenario everyone involved loses: delivery schedules cannot be met and "fielding of new functionality" needs to be delayed by months (e.g., 3 months, 6 months, and even a year or more), EA owners will require additional funding, and EA contractor teams eventually may lose their contracts.

Step 15: Detailed System Design. The reporting of actual test results and recommendations made in the in-house performance and capacity report may call for major system design changes, as indicated in Step 14. Occasionally the EA owners may be able to relax some of the performance and capacity requirements but this opportunity seldom materializes given that the baselined requirements initially did undergo several iterations and the content of each requirement was closely considered and determined. Rarely do difficult non-functional requirements get relaxed, "they just get moved to the next Release", the saying goes in the EA industry. A lot of words said above in order to get to the punch line: EA owners would be wise to incorporate an EPCEM program early in the EA work so that later on they do not have to experience the pain and frustration of seeing critical performance and capacity requirements endlessly move from one EA release to the next EA release at great cost to their professional reputations and to the taxpayer.

10.6. Use of Business Modeling and Performance Simulation Tools

As indicated above in Step 7, business modeling and system performance simulation are essential activities in capacity and performance EA planning and design. A more detailed view of this step is given in Figure 3. How does the EPCEM team go about selecting a good set of modeling and simulation tools? There are a number of factors to consider. First of all, the number and types of non-functional requirements (i.e., capacity and performance) should give a clear indication of the relative importance in these in system planning and design. If transaction processing is a main functionality, then capacity and performance are most likely to be key factors and an appropriate set of modeling and simulation tools ought to be procured.

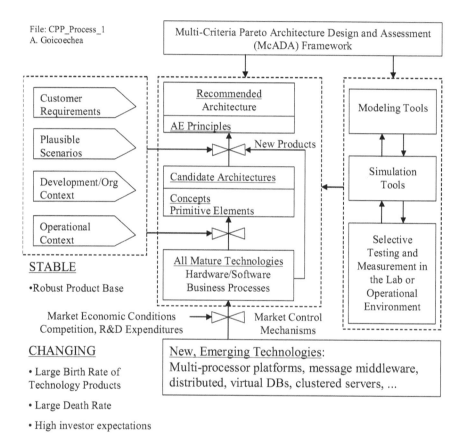

Figure 3. Factors to consider in the selection of business modeling and system performance simulation tools

New business paradigms may be contemplated in the new enterprise architecture. When this is the case, this is another indication that modeling and simulation tools will be needed throughout the EA lifecycle. Customer Relationship Management (CRM), for example, is a business paradigm that most likely comes in the form of a COTS product (i.e., a component in software design terminology) and will require business modeling in order to assess its interplay with other COTS or sub-systems in the EA.

New and emerging technologies may be contemplated in the new infrastructure architectural view, e.g., a newer and faster processor. Again, when this is the case the impact of these new technology products on the rest of the architecture needs to be assessed via modeling, simulation, and actual, selective testing in a development facility.

How much business modeling and system performance simulation ought to be conducted? System performance sensitivity to technology type (i.e., structural complexity of proposed COTS product), product cost, and interoperability requirements ought to be obtained. Therefore, technology type, product cost, and interoperability can be multiple criteria to consider in the selection and exercise of modeling and simulation tools in an EA project and program. Also, as illustrated on Figure 4, other criteria are as follows:

Workload characterization:
- Transaction baseline load (to determine)
- Mail volume
- Queries baseline load

Processing resource utilization
- CPU utilization (and number of CPUs)
- Database page number and management
- Network bandwidth
- Disk space usage
- Web server capacity and load balancing

System performance throughput
- Transactions volume processing
- Transactions processing times (individual)
- Query volume
- Network traffic rates
- Web server traffic rates

Other
- Security guard server capacity
- Data replication traffic rates, and
- System failover recovery times achieved.

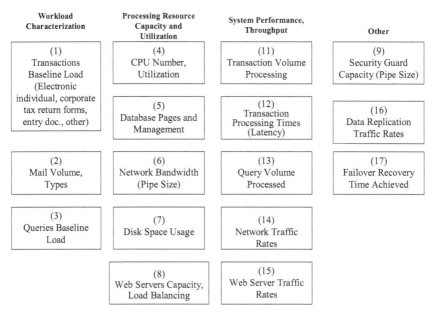

Workload Characterization	Processing Resource Capacity and Utilization	System Performance, Throughput	Other
(1) Transactions Baseline Load (Electronic individual, corporate tax return forms, entry doc., other)	(4) CPU Number, Utilization	(11) Transaction Volume Processing	(9) Security Guard Capacity (Pipe Size)
	(5) Database Pages and Management	(12) Transaction Processing Times (Latency)	(16) Data Replication Traffic Rates
(2) Mail Volume, Types	(6) Network Bandwidth (Pipe Size)	(13) Query Volume Processed	(17) Failover Recovery Time Achieved
(3) Queries Baseline Load	(7) Disk Space Usage	(14) Network Traffic Rates	
	(8) Web Servers Capacity, Load Balancing	(15) Web Server Traffic Rates	

Figure 4. Multiple criteria and categories of modeling and simulation activities in an EPCEM program

10.7. Measurements and Analysis

Carry out measurements and analysis of each main activity in an EPCEM project and program. You´ve got to measure things. Modeling and simulation alone, by themselves, are of limited value and consequence. Testing and measurement alone, by themselves, are of limited value. However, put these two sets of activities together and you have a very powerful EPCEM program working towards the success of an EA program. Figure 5 provides an example of the graphical representation of measurements that ought to be carried out in an EA program in order to provide near-real-time feedback to engineers and architects working in the various EA teams. These measurements, then, can provide critical information on system capacity and performance, which in turn can be used to recommend changes to software design and the adoption (or rejection) of COTS products being proposed and tested.

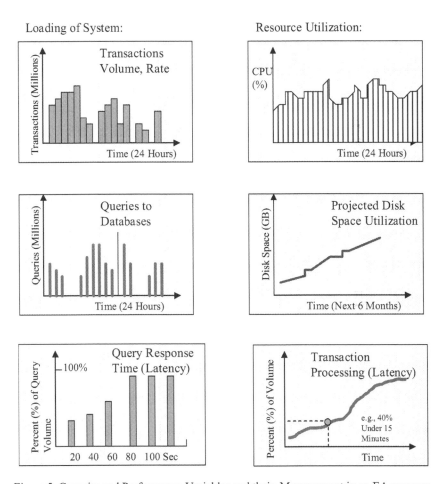

Figure 5. Capacity and Performance Variables and their Measurement in an EA program

10.8. Illustrative Example — What Needs to be Modeled

In the Global Airline example, we recall, the GATE project is responsible for the planning, design, implementation, testing, and fielding of the main database and associated subsystems. As such, the

GATE applications structure and flow, the GATE database design, sales account processing loads, and all proposed new structural changes need to be modeled. This is to help ensure that the final design will meet end-state peak performance requirements within acceptable computing resource utilization constraints, and to help estimate the target maximum computing resource requirements for GATE production.

Additionally, each GATE release needs to be modeled to ensure ongoing Capacity Planning is adequate, to establish release-specific target computing resource utilization budgets, and to ensure each GATE release design can perform within release-specific computing resource utilization budgets.

The outcome of this modeling and simulation effort should generate:

- Evidence that the GATE Design will likely scale to end state loads
- Computing resource utilization budgets for each major GATE component (e.g. TP, Filter, COMM2C, etc.) for each release
- Capacity Planning guidance for each GATE Release.

A Capacity Planning and Performance baseline needs to be articulated in adequate detail in terms of specific things measured (e.g., CPU, memory, I/O, disk utilization) AND attribute trade-off charts and analysis. It is not enough for the a PRIME contractor to produce an occasional performance "point", but instead a family of points must be produced to generate multiple design curves (e.g., query response time as a function of volume of queries processed over a 24-hour time period and DB design cost, as illustrated in Figure 5) for use in scalability analysis, inter-project design, and acquisition strategy analysis. At a minimum, the following information ought to be baselined several months (ideally monitored throughout the entire Release and certainly documented 2-3 months before release target date) before each GATE release target date:

(1) Measure, report, and document:
- Transaction workloads: Volumes, frequency (how many times in a day and time windows), units (i.e., no. of files, no. of transactions of various types), peak loading, and bytes volume.
- Transaction processing times.
- Target processing windows at the production environment.

- Timeline distribution across all software configuration items (CIs), i.e., budgeting processing time across all configuration items (CIs) in the applications architectural view.
- MIPS/CPU usage.
- I/O rates.
- DB statistics.
- Internal memory usage.
- Disk space requirements, including rate of increase over time within each Release.

(2) Measure, report, and document all parameters in (1) for each of the following EA sub-systems:
- DB initialization.
- Router/Filter.
- Transaction Processing.
- Business Rules (BR) environment.
- Sales Event and transaction, and
- MQSeries messaging middleware.

(3) System performance and storage capacity projections for subsequent releases.
- How will the GATE sub-system scale up to performance and capacity requirements for subsequent releases?
- Processing resources at the Current Processing Environment (CPE), namely the Fairfax-CPE, the primary (Washington DC) site, and the alternate site (New York) resources that will be available on a timely basis to provide adequately for capacity and performance (C&P) needs in future releases.
- A list of C&P mitigation measures proposed and the risks involved.
- Projections of disk space for each table in the GATE DB2 database for each release, and
- Projections of queue depth for each queue in the MQSeries messaging middleware sub-system for each release.

Simulation models are often developed in stages, becoming more refined as the design is driven to a more detailed level and portions of the system are coded. The estimates at each stage become more reliable than the prior versions. Once portions of the system are constructed, the models can be further refined using data from actual testing. These refined models can be used to get more accurate projections of the initial deployment, and to help assess the impact of future changes to system requirements or workload volumes.

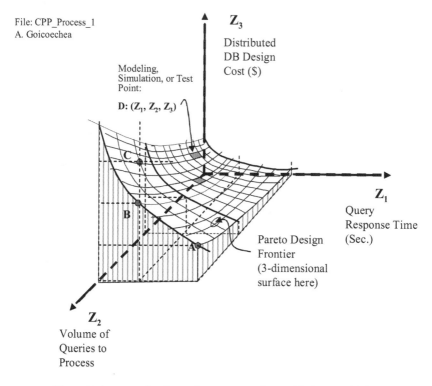

Figure 6. An example of a performance envelope with three variables

Ultimately, a key contribution of an EPCEM program ought to be a series of measurements and recommendations on sub-system and architectural changes that make possible the achievement of Pareto designs and variable tradeoffs, e.g., rate of queries returned and costs.

Messaging middleware (e.g., IBM's MQSeries) has a strong presence in enterprise architectures, both legacy and new, given its ability to connect platforms of different operating systems and its asynchronous operation. A significant benefit we get from messaging middleware is the ability to interconnect tens and possible hundreds of legacy platforms that may have different operating systems due to earlier technical, contractual, and procurement decisions. Another major benefit is that many of these platforms can now work asynchronously (one platform processes a transaction and sends it to a "transaction queue" where it waits along with other transactions until a second platform "gets it" for additional processing, and so on the next platform).

The price to pay for these benefits is in the form of an added software layer (the software middleware itself) and additional CPU resources. A task of the EPCEM team is, therefore, figure how to include messaging middleware detail in the business modeling and system performance simulation activities. Figure 7, presents detail on the messaging middleware used in the Global Airline Services (GAS) example that we have been discussing throughout this book. Depth of the queues (i.e., number of transactions that accumulate in a messaging middleware queue) must be simulated in response to transaction volumes anticipated, as well as time to "put" transactions in the queues, time to "get" transactions from the queues, the balancing of queue depths, and associated processing resources used up (CPU, memory, and I/O rates).

10.9. Testing and Simulation in a Virtual Lab Environment

Test facilities do not have to be located in one single facility, and instead there may by multiple test facilities geographically distributed and available to the EPCEM team. Some subsystems are being developed in facility A run and operated by contractor A, some subsystems may be scheduled for development and testing in facility B being run by contractor B, and so forth. On top, all those subsystems can be run and executed from facility C. When this is the case, a virtual lab environment is said to exist. Activities to conduct in a virtual lab environment can include business process modeling, Web load modeling, transaction processing analysis, sub-system availability and reliability, and benchmark testing, as shown on Figure 8.

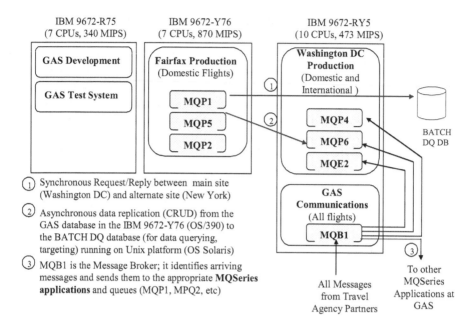

① Synchronous Request/Reply between main site (Washington DC) and alternate site (New York)

② Asynchronous data replication (CRUD) from the GAS database in the IBM 9672-Y76 (OS/390) to the BATCH DQ database (for data querying, targeting) running on Unix platform (OS Solaris)

③ MQB1 is the Message Broker; it identifies arriving messages and sends them to the appropriate **MQSeries applications** and queues (MQP1, MPQ2, etc)

Figure 7. Modeling and simulation of Messaging Middleware in an Enterprise Architecture

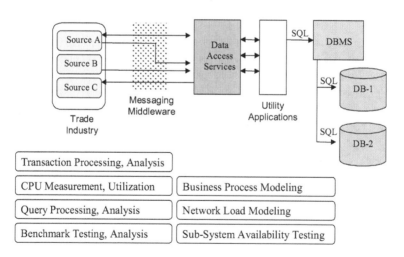

Figure 8. Testing and Simulation Activities in a Development Lab

10.10. Web Load Generation for Simulation and Performance Analysis

Of particular usefulness in EA planning and desing is Web load modeling and testing, as illustrated in Figure 9. Web servers, query servers, and transaction servers can be exercised through the creation and launching of synthetic loads with tools such as WebLoad Tool (by RADVIEW Software). A few specific types of queries can be generated in a Web load tool. Next the EPCEM engineer can ask the tool to generate thousands of copies of those few types of queries and to have these "launched" from the tool at specific times over a 24-hour period to simulate a realistic scenario. Through the LAN these transactions are directed to a variety of servers for processing.

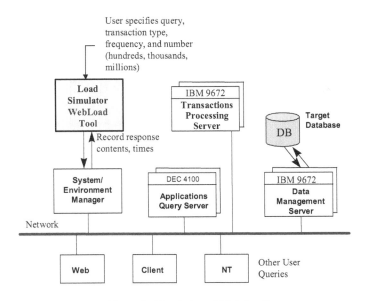

Figure 9. Simulation of Web loading

10.11. P&C Measurement Tools

There are a number of performance simulation tools in the market that allow for flexibility in the scope and depth to be designed into a modeling-and-performance-simulation task. This flexibility can be achieved in:

- Level of detail modeling desired, e.g., modeling needed to support business rules development; CI-interaction (interface data exchange); CICS modeling, etc.
- Load scenario generation to reflect how tax processing third parties step in over time to make use of modernization projects
- Distribution of load over system components and over time windows, etc.

Most tools available today can be used to do performance simulation and, if desired, business process modeling. A partial list of such tools includes:

- ARIS Tool, www.ids-scheer.com
- HyPerformix Workbench and Strategizer (formerly called SES/workbench) http://www.hyperformix.com/products/workbench.htm
- Savvion Process Modeler, http://www.savvion.com/products/
- Proforma, http://www.proformacorp.com/provision/intro.asp

A tool such as **SES/Strategizer** can be used to perform a variety of client/server modeling tasks, modeling of entire enterprise with software and hardware components, user load behavior, LAN topology and performance, and Web Server modeling, as illustrated in Figure 10.

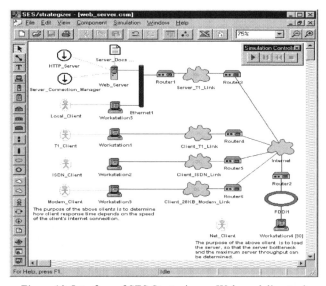

Figure 10. Interface of SES Strategizer, a Web modeling tool

10.12. P&C Roles and Responsibilities

All the capacity and system performance activities described above require a variety of skills and personnel. Table 1 presents a list of roles often found in EPCEM teams.

Table 1. A list of roles in EA capacity and performance planning
(Source: R. Will, 2004)

Role	Definition
Performance Requirements Specialist	Knowledgeable of the kinds of capacity and performance requirements on IRS systems. Such knowledge helps facilitate a discussion with the business owners of the project toward selecting performance requirements that are meaningful, testable, unambiguous, and complete
Project Capacity Modeling Specialist	Defines resource consumption relationships for project workload analysis.
Enterprise Capacity Modeling Specialist	Defines resource consumption relationships for enterprise workload analysis.
Project Architecture Specialist	Understands the technical architecture of the project in terms of its software-based processes and how they will be mapped to the hardware and middleware as well as the data flow within and among these processes.
Project Performance Modeling Specialist	Experienced in performance modeling and will acquire in-depth knowledge of the design features and performance requirements of the application being developed.
Enterprise Performance Modeling Specialist	Experienced in performance modeling. This specialist will need to be able to integrate the models of the subsystems from the projects into a higher-level enterprise model, retaining the basic features of the subsystem models without including excessive detail .
Infrastructure Hardware and Middleware Specialist	Has knowledge, skills, and experience in the hardware and middleware components that are utilized in the EA systems.
Performance Testing Specialist	Provides assistance to the developers in instrumenting the application for performance data collection and assistance to the testers in measuring performance in order to verify that performance requirements are being met.

Table 1. (*Continued*)

Role	Definition
Infrastructure Modeling Specialist	Defines resource consumption relationships in terms of functional workload for the infrastructure.
PEMV Specialist	Responsible for generating the Performance Engineering Model View report.

10.13. Conclusions and Recommendations

The importance of EA system performance and capacity planning cannot be overemphasized. Several points were made:

- Crucial to successful life cycle EA planning is the implementation of an enterprise-wide performance and capacity engineering model (EPCEM) early in the life cycle.
- Some EA owners and managers often feel that in order to show progress in the EA effort during their tenure it is best to concentrate on the implementation of the functional requirements, and that planning for and implementation of the non-functional requirements may hinder their best efforts. "Build the most functionality during those 1-2 years, get promoted, and then move on to higher and greener pastures in the EA organization,…let the next guy worry about system performance and capacity issues", can be a prevalent feeling.
- Testing begins and the brutal reality emerges. Often, as new EA owners and project managers begin their tenure and the EA effort enters the testing phase, the awakening can be brutal as test results begin to reveal that processing and time response capabilities of the system being built fall short of meeting performance requirements. By then some major decisions have been made and implemented on coding, the purchasing of platforms, and their integration into the EA system. "Fine tuning of the system" may not work this late in the game. Replacement of some low-yielding components or sub-systems begins to be considered, painfully. Scheduled EA releases are delayed. Performance engineers are then sought frantically. Precious time may have been lost.

- Engineers eventually get the job done, despite short falls on the part of management. Engineers on both sides of the picture do come together and save the day. One of the most redeeming and satisfying experiences about being part of an EA building effort is seeing performance engineers on the EA owners side, and performance engineers and software developers on the contractor side come together and work intensely over a period of several months until the needed design changes are made and the system finally delivers the goods.
- EA owners would be wise to incorporate an EPCEM program early in the EA work so that later on they do not have to experience the pain and frustration of seeing critical performance and capacity requirements endlessly move from one EA release to the next EA release at great cost to their professional reputations, to the taxpayer (in the case of EA work in the Federal Agencies and the armed services), and the stockholder (in the case of EA work in the Private Sector).

Chapter 11

Disaster Recovery Planning

11.1. Introduction

The "unbelievable" happened on August 2003 when the lights went out across much of the Northwest of the USA, Toronto and other major cities in Canada to become the largest blackout in the history of these two countries. Canadian Geographic (2003, www.canadiangeographic.ca) went on to report that "as the energy system in Ontario and several states slowly powers up, authorities are struggling to answer how such a massive blackout, the largest in North American history, could have occurred.... Research by the North American Electric Reliability Council, a non-profit, energy watch-dog for Canada and the United States, showed that it began with the failure of three transmission lines in Northern Ohio. The resulting deficit in energy would normally have been supplemented by energy imports from the surrounding bi-national grid. However, the line failure triggered a chain reaction that shut down everything from the bright lights of Broadway in New York to streetcars in Toronto".

Earlier, the "unthinkable" happened on September 11, 2001 when the two World Trade Center towers in New York's business and financial center were targets of terrorist attacks and destroyed completely, with thousands of lives lost thus sending shock waves throughout DoD and entire global business communities. As a result, thousands of organizations today are earnestly engaged in the assessment of vulnerabilities and risks to their information infrastructures, the preparation of disaster recovery plans, and the allocation of resources to implement those plans.

What is a disaster event, how can it be characterized, and most important what can be done to recover from these disaster events? The types of disasters that can cripple and/or stop completely operations of large infrastructures can include flooding, fires, hacker attacks on servers, terrorist attacks, and power failures, as noted on Table 1. Disasters are unpredictable in terms of when, where, how they will occur, the number and sequence of architectural components to be affected. Disasters inevitably result in loss of business continuity, loss of revenues, and decreased quality service. Now, whereas the planner cannot predict when, where, and how the disaster can occur he/she can prepare for it in a variety of ways as we shall see in this chapter.

Table 1. Ten Worst U.S. Information Technology Disasters
Source: 3 through 11 are from *Information Week*, January 10, 1994

Rank	Description	Date	Data Centers Hit
#1	Electric Grid Black Out in the North East	August 15, 2003	2000+
#2	Terrorist attack on N.Y. World Trade Towers	Sept 11, 2001	500+
#3	Nationwide Internet Virus	May 1988	320
#4	Chicago Flood	April 1992	175
#5	New York Power Outage	August 1990	150
#6	Chicago/Hinsdale Fire	May 1988	90+
#7	Hurricane Andrew	Sept 1992	90
#8	Nationwide Pakistani Virus	May 1988	75
#9	San Francisco Earthquake	Oct 1989	64
#10	Seattle Power Outage	August 1988	
#11	Chicago Flood	August 1987	

In the case of enterprise architectures within the government Agencies and Department of Defense (DoD) the Office of Management and Budget (OMB) Circular A-130 provides guidelines for the storage, access, and management of data: "Agencies will ensure the ability to access records regardless of the form or medium, …reduce risk by avoiding or isolating custom designed components (COTS), using components that can be fully tested or prototyped prior to production, and insuring involvement and support of users..." (OMB Circular A-130).

11.2. How this Chapter is Organized

A list of most recent disasters that impact the EA community and a definition of Disaster Recovery (DR) kick off this chapter. Next, Sections 11.3 and 11.4 presents a business case on the need to have a set of DR requirements and a DR contingency plan validated and approved by EA owners; a total of 8 basic steps are outlined and recommended as the core of such a contingency plan, ranging from the assignment of low, medium, and high priorities to business activities in the EA, to regularly scheduled DR readiness auditing. The basics of intra-site recovery planning and inter-site recovery planning are presented in Sections 11.7 and 11.8, respectively; here, we examine the basic concept of having a primary site and a secondary site in the operation of an EA, how most of the day-to-day business activities are carried out in the primary site with hourly data replications to the secondary site. Highlights of a survey of companies in the Private Sector are reported in Section 11.10 and, last, an IT audit checklist is provided in Section 11.11 that can be used as a "primer" for the development of a full-scale IT audit plan for a corporation in the Private Sector or a government agency in the Public Sector.

11.3. What is Disaster Recovery Planning?

What can be done to prepare for a disaster in an IT center? What are the activities that a large (or small) enterprise architecture (EA) with critical information technology (IT) infrastructure assets can do to prepare for the eventuality of a disaster? Can the EA survive a disaster, recover, and get back to the business of the day? These are some of the questions that individuals working in disaster recovery planning groups and organizations must address.

> *Disaster Recovery Planning is the engineering and business function that addresses the types of potential catastrophic and unscheduled events that can result in the loss of business continuity in one or multiple parts of an enterprise architecture and that, accordingly,*

proceeds to identify and describe points of risk and vulnerability, a set of disaster recovery requirements, a disaster recovery contingency plan, and a disaster recovery plan.

EA executives, owners, and managers cannot predict the type of disaster to occur, the gravity of impacts to the ability of the system to continue delivering business services day in and day following such a catastrophic event, of course not. However, they can certainly come up with a list of types of plausible disasters, a list of scenarios within which those disasters might unfold, a list of critical and non-critical business functions, and the sequence of subsequent engineering activities that can lead to eventual recovery of part or all of the enterprise architecture.

11.4. Developing a Disaster Recovery Plan

Development of a Disaster Recovery Plan (DRP) calls for gaining an understanding of the day-to-day business activities that an enterprise needs to conduct (see Chapter 3, Business Processes Architectural View), the identification of those parts of the architecture that are vulnerable to threats, and a determination of the level of disaster recovery capability desired. Accordingly, the following steps are suggested in the development of a DRP:

(1) Gather and set of disaster recovery (DR) requirements and validate these through interaction with and participation of the owners of the business processes in the EA;
(2) Identify risks and vulnerabilities to software and hardware systems of the enterprise architecture;
(3) Identify risks and vulnerabilities to business systems, services, and continuity in the enterprise architecture;
(4) Develop a list of high-priority, medium-priority, and low-priority for business services, software, and hardware systems;
(5) Talk to the owners of the business systems and services to ascertain time allowable to recover these; some organizations like to specify *a recovery time objective (RTO)*, the time following the incidence of a disaster or major disruption within which applications and data that support those business systems and services must be restored (e.g., 48 hours). Also, *a recovery point objective (RPO)* is often specified and measured from a

point in time prior to the time the disaster occurs, i.e., "the age of backup tape data shall not exceed 36 hours".

(6) Learn about the technologies available for disaster recovery, including options for intra-site data recovery, inter-site data recovery, and data backup; next, conduct trade-off analyses involving costs, RTO, and technology risks; next, communicate findings in trade-off analysis to business owners in the EA organization;

(7) Conduct "DR Readiness" auditing periodically; a DR readiness checklist can be an effective way of identifying vulnerable points in the architecture and identifying disaster preventive/corrective measures;

(8) Prepare a DR Contingency Plan that identifies roles and responsibilities among personnel involved in DR work, plausible disaster scenarios, sequence of events to follow, DR reporting and documentation needs.

11.5. DR Requirements

A set of disaster recovery (DR) requirements essentially specifies how much business functionality must be recovered and the time frame of recovery (e.g., hours, days, weeks, other). Also, although these requirements need not say how the functionality is to be recovered they may go as far as saying that one or more alternate sites are needed. A short list of DR requirements may read as follows:

DRr1: *There shall be a primary processing site and an alternate processing site.*

DRr2: *Replication of master files from computer center A to alternate center B shall occur on a daily basis.*

DRr3: *The system shall maintain a list of high-priority, medium-priority, and lower-priority business applications.*

DRr4: *All high-priority business applications and their services shall be recovered fully within 36 hours.*

DRr5: *All medium-priority business applications and their services shall be recovered fully within 48 hours.*

DRr6: *All low-priority business applications and their services shall be recovered fully within 72 hours.*

11.6. Basic Elements of a Contingency Plan

A contingency plan for disaster recovery must contain the following elements:

- *Data Back up:* Procedures to establish, maintain, and monitor a software and hardware environment for data back up –data storage and retrieval on an agreed upon frequency, e.g., daily, weekly, other. Often organizations will require the use of flexible and scalable storage area networks (SAN) technology to store data; similarly, network attached storage (NAS) can provide high-performance storage appliances that provide shared data to client servers over a network.

- *Uninterruptible Power Source (UPS):* Procedures for the installation, operation, and maintenance of UPS at both the primary and the alternate sites. Large computer infrastructures require uninterrupted and controlled power sources so that if the power is lost momentarily (i.e., hours or days), the data and programs stored in semi-conductor primary storage is safe and operational. Often these UPS consist of batteries and diesel power generators.

- *Connectivity to external trading partners:* Procedures for the operation of communication links to External Trading Partner's production sites. Redundant paths may be required to insure network availability during the transmitting and receiving of data in a disaster event.

- *Security:* How is the privacy and integrity of data to be secured during disaster recovery proceedings? Both data and procedures for disaster recovery may be considered to be "of a sensitive nature" and, accordingly, only selected personnel may have access to those data and procedures. Often these security procedures for the handling of sensitive data and procedures are spelled out within the Technical Contingency Planning Document (TCPD).

- *Organizational Change:* Identification of key personnel and their participation in a disaster event and subsequent recovery proceedings. The preparation of procedures that must be carried out by key personnel becomes then a most significant component of a contingency plan for disaster recovery.

11.7. Basics of Intra-Site Data Failover

Most basic to the concept of disaster recovery planning is having a *primary processing platform* that is responsible for all or most of the processing of transactions and *an alternate or backup processing platform* that takes over processing operations in case of failure or sidelining of the primary processing platform, as shown on Figure 1.

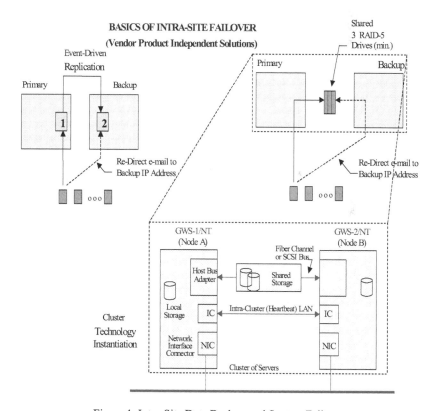

Figure 1. Intra-Site Data Backup and System Failover

Both the primary and the backup platforms reside within the same site, in this case. Also, hardware for the storage of data can reside on one or the other platform, on both platforms, or can be shared by both platforms. In the case of e-mail, for example, each time it arrives to the primary platform for processing it is immediately replicated to storage in the backup platform, this way when the primary fails the e-mail and associated software is immediately available in the backup platform.

Now whereas the primary platform is always running and processing transactions, the backup platform may be running only a few basic functions to be responsive to questions and commands from enterprise management systems (ESM) to ascertain its availability (i.e., a "hot" backup), or it can be totally inactive but remaining in place in the local area network (i.e., a "cold" backup). Obviously, a cold backup platform may require less maintenance than a hot backup but it would also contribute to longer system recovery times. Integral to this data backup concept is continuous communication between the primary and backup platforms via a "heartbeat" over the local area network. This heartbeat consists of a signal that send to each of the two platforms every fraction of a second to verify that both systems are alive; when the primary fails to send back a heartbeat, due to any disaster or condition, ESM activates the backup processing platform thus maintaining business continuity in the enterprise. Processing is then said to fail from one platform to the other, i.e., system *failover* occurs.

11.8. Basics of Inter-site Failover

Next, we consider the case where the enterprise's ability to survive a disaster is augmented by the creation and existence of not one but two sites that are identical or nearly identical in functionality. Additionally, each of these two sites is able to process transactions, and these are stored in database partitions 1 and 2, as depicted in Figure 2.

This architecture would provide for significant gains in availability and reliability while achieving reduced recovery times. The price to pay is higher than that for a single site, understandably, as an additional site and data storage are required. Still, some enterprise architectures actually consider multiple sites, going from two sites to three sites, as depicted in Figure 3.

As the number of sites increases to 3 sites and beyond the costs of acquiring and maintaining the enterprise increase exponentially due to additional data storage, data replication software and hardware, enterprise management systems, and training.

BASICS OF INTER-SITE FAILOVER
(Vendor Product Independent Solutions)

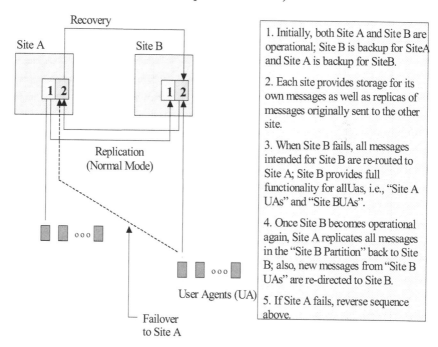

1. Initially, both Site A and Site B are operational; Site B is backup for SiteA and Site A is backup for SiteB.

2. Each site provides storage for its own messages as well as replicas of messages originally sent to the other site.

3. When Site B fails, all messages intended for Site B are re-routed to Site A; Site B provides full functionality for allUas, i.e., "Site A UAs" and "Site BUAs".

4. Once Site B becomes operational again, Site A replicates all messages in the "Site B Partition" back to Site B; also, new messages from "Site B UAs" are re-directed to Site B.

5. If Site A fails, reverse sequence above.

Figure 2. Inter-Site Data Backup and System Failover

11.9. RAID Technology for Data Backup

Data storage devices today are able to achieve very high reliability due to breakthroughs in redundant arrays of inexpensive disks (RAID) technology, as depicted in Figure 4 through Figure 7.

With RAID technology an array of four or more physical disk drives function as a single logical disk drive. Now, space in those multiple disk drives can be used to store data only or to store data and error correction code. *Error correction code* can be used to detect errors in data stored in the *stripes* and to reconstruct damaged portions of the data stripes. The RAID-0 configuration, for example, uses four input/output (I/O) streams, one for each physical disk, with no data redundancy and no error correction code, thus enabling fast storage and retrieval of data. In

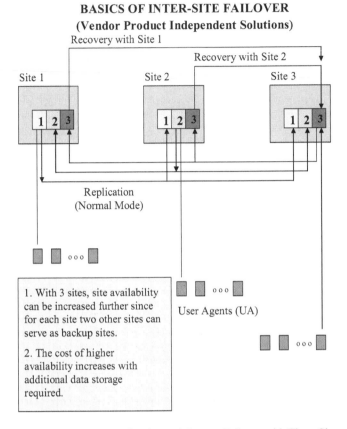

Figure 3. Inter-Site Data Replication and System Failover with Three Sites

RAID-1 all data stored in one disk drive is mirrored (i.e., duplicated) in another drive, thus offering data redundancy capability but consequently educing storage capability by half. RAID-2 uses disk space to store data, data mirroring, and error correction code, thus providing further gains in data reliability at the expense of volume of data that can be stored in the disk drives. Still, when very long data records exist that require more than one stripe RAID-3 may be the preferable configuration for data storage; for the configuration in Figure 7, for example, data is stored in disks 1, 2, and 3, while error correction code is stored in disk 4; additionally, one output stream is only possible to read data from disks 1, 2, and 3.

RAID-0

- An array of four/more physical disk drives that function as a single logical disk drive.

- Segments of data called **stripes** cut across all of the disk drives; a stripe is the set of pages of data in a RAID design which are the same relative distance from the beginning of the disk drive.

- It uses all disks for data storage only.

- Fastest Parallel Write/Read access.

- No redundancy: if one disk drive fails data in that disk is lost.

- No error correction.

- Useful for for applications requiring extensive I/O activity.

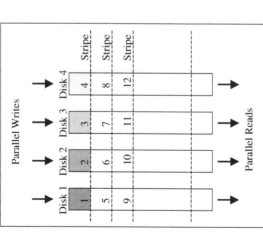

One Logical Disk Drive with Four Physical Disk Drives

Source: McFadden, Hoffer, and Prescott, Addison-Wesley Press 1999.

Figure 4. Basics of RAID-0 Technology

RAID-1

• An array of four/more physical disk drives that function as a single logical disk drive.

• Segments of data called **stripes** cut across all of the disk drives; a stripe is the set of pages of data in a RAID design which are the same relative distance from the beginning of the disk drive. Potentially many records in one stripe.

• It uses all disks for data storage only.

• **Disk data storage is cut in half** compared to RAID-0.

• **Fully redundant storage**: if one disk drive fails data in that disk is available in a second disk drive; data in disk 1 is **mirrored** in disk 2.

• No error correction.

• Useful for for applications requiring extensive I/O activity.

• **Multiple users** can read data simultaneously, i.e., in parallel.

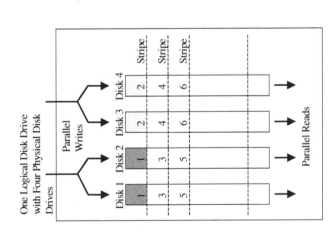

Figure 5. Basics of RAID-1 Technology

RAID-2

• An array of four/more physical disk drives that function as a single logical disk drive.

• Segments of data called **stripes** cut across all of the disk drives; a stripe is the set of pages of data in a RAID design which are the same relative distance from the beginning of the disk drive.

• Half of the disks used for data storage, the other half for error correction code (ECC). Data storage is half that of RAID-0

• Data redundancy is achieved through **error correction code** stored in some of the disk drives. Data is not mirrored.

• Each write (I operation) uses all drives in parallel and may require multiple stripes (for very large records).

• Each read (O operation) uses all drives in parallel, i.e., single user only.

• Useful for for applications requiring extensive I/O activity.

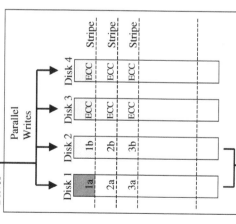

Figure 6. Basics of RAID-2 Technology

RAID-3

- Each record of data spans all data disks. RAID-3 is used when **very long records exist**, such that one record requires one or more stripes.

- Segments of data called **stripes** cut across all of the disk drives; a stripe is the set of pages of data in a RAID design which are the same relative distance from the beginning of the disk drive.

- One disk is used for error correction code (ECC) only; used to recover damaged data or drive in stripe.

- More **disk data storage** compared to RAID-2.

- Each write operation uses all drives (data and ECC) in parallel.

- Each read operation uses all data drives in in parallel.

- Only one program has access to disk array at a time.

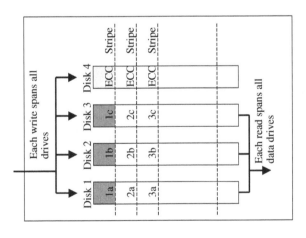

Figure 7. Basics of RAID-3 Technology

11.10. Disaster Readiness

Since the attacks on the World Trade Center of Sept. 11, 2002 half of all companies in the USA have significantly altered their way of thinking, their approaches, or policies related to business continuity. In a survey of over 1,500 business technology managers 53% reported that their business organizations are now adequately prepared and able to recover from a physical disaster, while 39% of the respondents felt they were not ready, with the remaining 8% responding with a "Don't know", as shown on Figure 8 (Information Week Research, 2002).

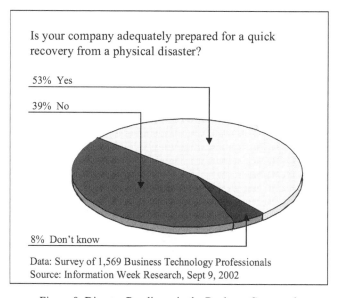

Is your company adequately prepared for a quick recovery from a physical disaster?

53% Yes

39% No

8% Don't know

Data: Survey of 1,569 Business Technology Professionals
Source: Information Week Research, Sept 9, 2002

Figure 8. Disaster Readiness in the Business Community

Similarly, the same survey reports that as many as 66% of business organizations today are prepared and able to deal with a security-related disaster, as depicted in Figure 9.

A portion of that same survey addressed turnaround times, as noted on Figure 10. Instantaneous failover to a hot backup or standby online system was reported by 8% of the respondents, restoration in a matter of a few hours was reported by 16%, within 24 hours by 32%, and restoration in a matter of days by 30%.

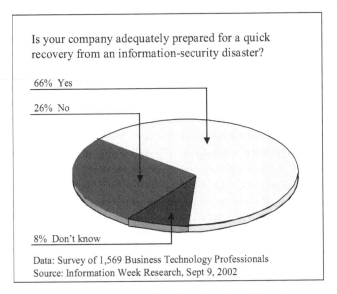

Is your company adequately prepared for a quick recovery from an information-security disaster?

66% Yes

26% No

8% Don't know

Data: Survey of 1,569 Business Technology Professionals
Source: Information Week Research, Sept 9, 2002

Figure 9. Data Recovery from Security-related Disasters

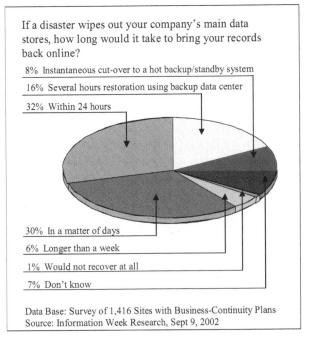

If a disaster wipes out your company's main data stores, how long would it take to bring your records back online?

8% Instantaneous cut-over to a hot backup/standby system

16% Several hours restoration using backup data center

32% Within 24 hours

30% In a matter of days

6% Longer than a week

1% Would not recover at all

7% Don't know

Data Base: Survey of 1,416 Sites with Business-Continuity Plans
Source: Information Week Research, Sept 9, 2002

Figure 10. Turnaround Time for Business Continuity

11.11. IT Audit Checklist

Each information technology organization within the enterprise also needs to have its own information technology (IT) checklist and audit in order to inquire and assess the status of readiness of system components in diverse areas such as access to computing facilities, access control to communications center, electric supply, business continuity planning, communications, personnel, and fire control. Table 2 provides one example of such a checklist.

Table 2. Information Technology (IT) Audit Checklist to support Disaster Recovery Planning
(*Source*: modified from Reynolds (1995))

Access Control to the Computer Center
1. Is the location readily identifiable as a computer center?
2. Is there a secure means to control access to the computer center?
3. Must visitors request an appointment in advance?
4. Is the movement of visitors restricted or controlled?
5. Do employees challenge unfamiliar visitors?

Access Control to the Communications Center
1. Are areas that provide electronic communication to the processing center adequately protected?
2. Are there locks on all phone company connection rooms?
3. Are there multiple routing paths for critical communication lines?

Access to Computing Resources
1. Are vital software and documentation kept in a safe and secure location in case a disaster (e.g., fire, earthquake, other)? destroys or disables the data center?

Fire Protection
1. Are there heat and/or smoke detection devices installed?
2. Are personnel trained in firefighting?
3. Does insurance cover losses due to fire, water, or smoke damage?
4. Are fire-resistant materials used for partitions, walls, doors, and furnishings?
5. Is smoking restricted?

Flooding or Water Damage
1. Is any part of the facility located in a flood zone?
2. Does overhead steam or water pipes exist?
3. Is there drainage under the floor of the computer room(s), on the floors above, or adjacent areas?
4. Does insurance cover flood and water damages?

Air Conditioning
1. Does the data center have its own dedicated A/C system?
2. Does the emergency power-off switch include A/C circuits?

Table 2. *(Continued)*	
2. Is access to essential software and documentation restricted to a need-to-know basis? 3. Are changes to software documented as to who made them and when for traceability purposes? 4. Are passwords required to identify terminal users? 5. Are users required to change their passwords frequently? 6. Does the operating system (OS) have built-in protection to prevent bypassing security software? **Personnel Considerations** 1. Is a background check performed on job applicants before hiring? 2. Is there a manager in charge of computer security with clear and well-defined responsibilities and procedures? 3. Are there policies and procedures that relate to computer security and data backup operations? 4. Is there a list of authorized vendor personnel services and phone numbers in a secured yet known place? 5. Are vendor personnel supervised while in the data center? 6. When an employee is terminated or re-assigned, are passwords, procedures, and locks changed to deny access to that employee thereafter? Create and manage a directory of employee, contractor, and supplier permits, passwords, system login events.	3. Are temperature and humidity in data center regulated and monitored? **Business Continuity Planning** 1. Has a formal disaster recovery plan written and approved? 2. Is there a manager and team in charge of business continuity planning with clear and well-defined responsibilities and procedures? 3. Have the various application systems been classified as to their relative priority in the event of limited processing (both computer and personnel) resources? 4. Is there a backup data center and/or alternate site(s) included in the disaster recovery plan? 5. Are extra copies made of critical files, data sets, and databases – both master files and transaction files? If so, are these extra files stored at a location other than the primary data center? 6. Are extra copies made of program source code, program load modules, and program documentation under configuration management (CM)? If so, are these stored at a location other than the primary data center?

Table 2. (*Continued*)	
Electric Power 1. Are there in place Uninterruptible Power Source (UPS), and if so are there procedures for their installation, operation, and maintenance? 2. In the event of a power outage, how long would it take to have power restored to your facility (e.g., no. of hours, days, longer)?	7. Is there at least an annual simulation and drill of a complete loss of the data center and a thorough testing of the entire disaster recovery plan?

11.12. Cost-Availability Trade-Offs

Ability of an enterprise architecture to achieve a recovery time objective (RTO) in a matter of hours rather than days will depend in great part in the data storage and replication technology utilized. An architecture that relies on data tapes to transport data from a primary site to an alternate site miles away, via truck, railroad or aircraft, will have to be satisfied with an RTO of 2-3 days at best, as depicted on Figure 11. On the other hand, an architecture that makes use of data replication technology (e.g., Symmetrix data replication platforms by EMC Corp.) can expect to achieve system recovery in only minutes or hours.

During the planning phase it is often useful to generate a graph similar to that in Figure 11 to identify the various data backup and replication technologies and associated costs. As such, a *course of action* # 1(COA-1) may call for data backup to be done with tapes every 24 hours for subsequent transport to an alternate site; should a disaster occur at the primary site, the data in the tapes in the alternate site can be recovered in say 5 days and business continuity is recovered 3 days later for an RTO of 8 days. For course of action # 3 (COA-3), on the other hand, data backup is accomplished with replication software and platforms that send a copy of each data posting in the primary site to a database in an alternate hot site. Thus, enterprise owners, executive decision makers, and managers can weigh the value of business requirements and RTOs against an array of technologies and associated

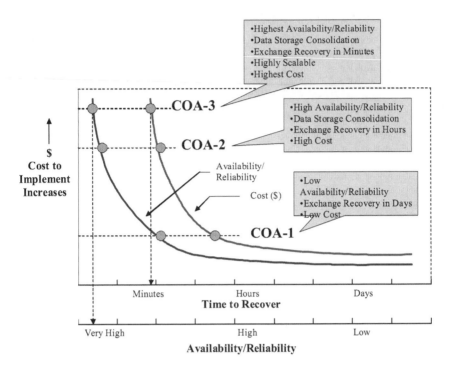

Figure 11. Cost-Recovery Time Trade-Offs for Alternative Courses of Action and Technologies

costs. Invariably, early in the planning phase, decision makers often want unrealistically low RTO times with relatively small capital outlays.

Once a disaster recovery analysis is conducted and information is presented in graphs such as the one presented in Figure 11, decision makers generally become more reasonable and settle for the disaster recovery plans and enabling technologies that are commensurate with available funding resources.

11.13. Global Services Airline, An Example

We use the example of Global Services Airline (GSA) that we have carried from one chapter to the next to illustrate the design of a disaster recovery plan for an enterprise architecture. The high-level view of the enterprise architecture for the Global Services Airline, you may recall, is as shown on Figure 12. Washington D.C. is the primary site that houses the portal and database management systems, with legacy systems located in Fairfax City, Virginia. A backup, hot site currently exists in New York City that is also able to duplicate all of the functionality in the primary site.

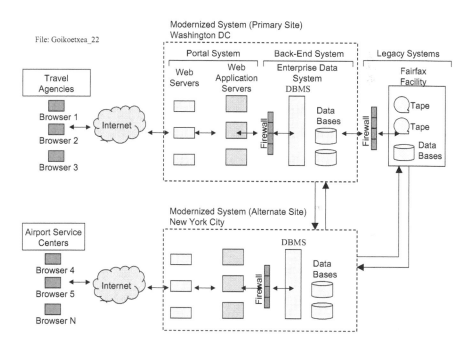

Figure 12. A High-Level View of the Global Services Airline Enterprise Architecture

The "AS-IS" enterprise architecture, shown on Figure 13, backs 5 gigabytes of data into 10 tapes every 24 hours (i.e., at the end of each business cycle) and has a contractor pick up the tapes and deliver these via GSA aircraft to the alternate site in New York. Should a disaster occur, the data tapes in the New York facility are loaded onto its own the database management system (DMBS) over the next 5 days. Data validation procedures take place over the next 3 days. Recovery objective time (ROT) is achieved in 8 days.

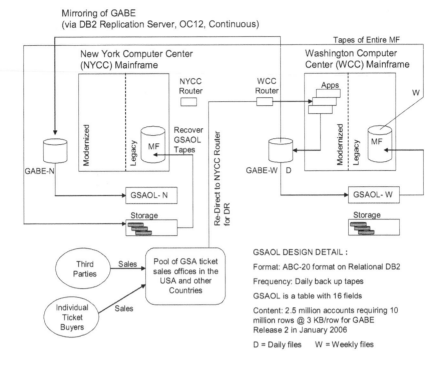

Figure 13. "As-Is" Disaster Recovery Architecture for the Global Services Airline Example

The "To-Be" enterprise architecture in the modernization program for the GSA, on the other hand, calls for the use Symmetrix technology (EMC Corporation, URL www.emc.com) as shown on Figure 14. As transactions are processed and data are posted to master files (MF) database at Site A, a mirror image of the database updates are sent to the alternate site immediately thereafter.

11.14. Conclusion

Disaster Recovery (DR) planning is a major IT, business, and organizational investment, precisely because it is indispensable in successful EA planning and operation. Too much is at stake in the running of EA centers in terms of data stored, IT infrastructure, and

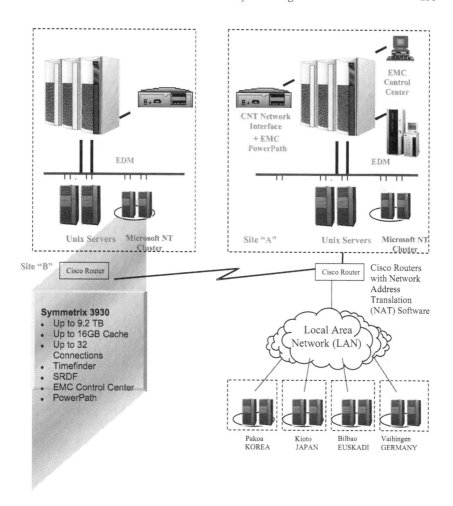

Figure 14. "To-Be" Disaster Recovery Architecture for the Global Services Airline Example

customer trust to be left without safeguards and system recovery capabilities. The cost to EA planners and the taxpayer of not having an operational DR capability in place is simply too high.

11.15. Exercises

E.11.1 Prepare a one-page summary of Circular 1-130 noting specific reference and direction in disaster recovery for (a) Federal Agencies, and (b) Department of Defense (DoD).

E.11.2 For a Federal, State, or local agency of your choice:

- Generate its organizational chart.
- Identify the business unit(s) responsible for disaster recovery (DR) planning in that organizational chart.
- Present salient components of its disaster recovery plan (DRP).
- Find out whether such DRP has been used in the past and what is a summary of the sequence of events leading to the disaster and steps taken that led to system recovery, if available.

E.11.3 Conduct a search on the Internet to gather a basic list of costs and capabilities of the Symmetix 3930 technology (suggestion: look into EMC corporation, www.emc.com).

Chapter 12

The Open Group's Architectural Framework (TOGAF)

12.1. Introduction

Earlier in Chapter 2, we may recall, the motivation and impetus for the Enterprise Architecture Frameworks (EAF) in the USA was already discussed and they were found to be in three most significant sectors: Federal Agency Sector, Department of Defense (DoD), and the Private Sector.

In this chapter we take a second look at that synergism among those three most significant sectors for purposes of learning about the genesis of The Open Group's Architectural Framework or TOGAF, its main characteristics, and how it is finding its way into applications in the Private sector

The Development of The Open Group's Architectural Framework (TOGAF) begins in 1994 "at the instigation of The Open Group's User Council" (Perks and Beveridge, 2003). Originally based on TAFIM already developed by DoD. Basically, Dod gave the Open Group "explicit permission and encouragement to create TOGAF by building on TAFIM"; since then, the Open Group's Architecture Forum has published several versions of TOGAF in the Open Group's public web site http://www.opengroup.org/public/arch/. In this chapter we set out to present and discuss the basic elements, characteristics, and steps in TOGAF, we proceed to relate some of these characteristics against those in the architectural components of other architectural frameworks (e.g., C4ISR), and finally present an example to illustrate its application.

12.2. Organization of this Chapter

This chapter presents basic principles and main development elements of the Open Group's Architectural Framework (TOGAF), including the Standards Information Base (SIB), Technical Reference Model (TRF), and the steps in the Architectural Development Method (ADM). An example of a manufacturer and distributor of confection goods is borrowed from Perks and Beveridge (2003) to illustrate some of the seven phases of ADM.

12.3. Technical Architecture Framework for Information Management (TAFIM)

By 1990 it had already become apparent to many armed services in the Department of Defense (DoD) that military systems and architectures were becoming increasingly complex and that the need existed to help guide the design, implementation, operation, management, and evolution of these systems. Accordingly, in circa 1991 DoD created the Technical Architecture Framework for Information Management (TAFIM) in order to provide guidance for the evolution of DoD technical that meet specific mission requirements while providing for multiple desired system characteristics such as interoperability, portability, and scalability. Accordingly, the TAFIM consisted of multiple bodies of information and guidance:

- A *Technical Reference Model (TRM)* to provide a conceptual model for information system services and their interfaces in the architecture. See Chapter 4 for a detailed description of the TRM.
- Architecture Concepts and Guidance Design with concepts and guidance for the design and integration of architectural components.
- A DoD Standards-Based Architecture Planning Guide for the translation of functional requirements into business services, standards, components, configuration of these components, their phasing, and the acquisition of products and services to implement them.

- A DoD Goal Security Architecture (DGSA) that addressed security requirements derived from mission statements and threat descriptions.
- An Adopted Information Technology Standards (AITS) intended to guide DoD acquisition and the migration of legacy systems while supporting multiple TAFIM objectives such as interoperability, reduced life-cycle costs, and security.
- A DoD Human Computer Interface (HCI) Style Guide which provided a common framework and set of concepts in HCI design and implementation.

12.4. Emergence of TOGAF

While TAFIM did serve well the armed services community over the years, there were already visible signs of challenges and difficulties, and on January 7, 2000 it was cancelled by the Architecture Coordinating Council (ACC) "in response to a shifting in the strategic direction of all architectural efforts in DoD", although no public reason has been communicated as of today (DoD, 2000). Parks and Beveridge (2003) and others, however, have conjectured and have offered some observations regarding possible potential difficulties with TAFIM:

- Time in years required to build a TAFIM architecture makes it obsolete from the very beginning.
- Considerable IT and business modeling expertise required, thus often times the final product was difficult for business oriented professionals to follow and understand; and

The TRM, however, was retained by DoD directive. As intended by its creators in the Open Group, TOGAF is both a framework and a methodology for architectural development while maintaining many of the desirable elements of TAFIM. This is to say TAFIM aims to focus on the production of a valid, reasoned, deployable, and maintainable architecture for an organization or enterprise. Main elements of TOGAF include:

- A technical reference model (TRM)
- Standards information base (SIB), and
- An architectural development method (ADM)

12.5. Technical Reference Model (TRM)

As already discussed in Chapter 4, the Technical Reference Model (TRM) is a taxónomy of logical services that need to be provided in order to support the business and IT infrastructure of the enterprise architecture. Categories of services include operating systems, messaging middleware (e.g., MQSeries, Tuxedo, other), database access services, database management systems, business applications, network services, file formatting, multimedia translation services, security, user interface, and communications services. Typically, these categories of services are identified for the intended/target architecture and depicted in a box-and-arrow diagram along with the types of interfaces needed across associated systems.

12.6. Standards Information Base (SIB)

Basic to all architectural frameworks is the creation, availability, and maintenance of a set of standards on services and technologies recommended for the construction of enterprise architectures. Such is the case with TOGAF's SIB, a database of facts and guidance about information systems standards originating from several sources, including formal standard bocies such as ISO and IEEE, authoritative standards makers such as the Internet Society, and from other consortia, like the World Wide Web Consortium and the Object Management Group OMG).

The Standards Information Base has three main uses (source: http://www.opengroup.org):

(1) Architecture development: For an organization that is creating an architecture for its information systems, the Standards Information Base provides a valuable source of information about standards that may be used to populate the architecture.

(2) Acquisition/Procurement: An organization that is planning a procurement (whether or not based on an architecture) will find that the Standards Information Base can help ensure that the procurement gives a clear statement of technical requirements, with an assurance of conformance; and

(3) General information: Finally, it can simply be a source of information about relevant IT standards, for use by anyone at any time.

12.7. Architectural Development Method (ADM)

TOGAF's Architectural Development Method organizes knowledge into seven phases, as depicted in Figure 1:

- Phase A: Initiation and Framework
- Phase B: Baseline Description
- Phase C: Target Architecture
- Phase D: Opportunities and Solutions
- Phase E: Migration Planning
- Phase F: Implementation
- Phase G: Architecture Maintenance

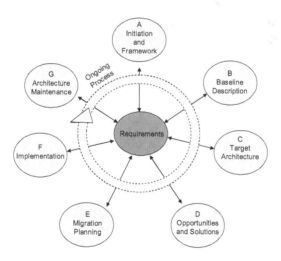

Figure 1. TOGAF'S Architectural Development Method (ADM) (Perks and Beveridge 2003, with kind permission of Springer Science and Business Media)

It may be worthwhile noting that the creators of ADM envisioned it to be cyclic in nature, so that completion of one phase proceeds to the beginning and completion on the next logical phase in an ongoing process of discovery, replenishment, and maintenance over time. Salient features of each phase are outlined on Table 1, while further detail and elaboration on the content of each of each phase are provided via the following illustrative example.

Requirements gathering is seen as central to the ADM method, with all activities in each phase feeding that information gathering activity. Over the next few pages we proceed to describe the essential activities in each phase of this ongoing process.

Table 1. Phases in the Architectural Development Method

Phase	Name of Phase	Description
A	Initiation and Framework	This most important initial phase sets the stage for the architectural analysis and design. The following elements are captured and defined: • Business goals and/or strategic drivers. • Architecture vision. • Architectural principles and constraints. • Set of system requirements (business, organizational, and technical). • Work product acceptance criteria. • Managerial approach. • Program plan and schedule. • Institutional buy-off and support. • Request for Proposal (RFP). • Terms of Reference (TOR). • Architectural Board for governance and control.
B	Baseline Description, i.e., "As-Is" Architecture	The objective of this phase is to build a high-level description of the main characteristics of the current environment, including business environment and the current processing environment (CPE). Specific documentation (output) includes: • IT operational documentation. • As-is business systems hierarchy and interfaces.

Table 1. (*Continued*)

Phase	Name of Phase	Description
		• Network system. • Security framework and control procedures. • High-level view of the TRM. • Interviews with business owners, development, and operations, and management personnel to identify current system issues, and • Interviews with key system users.
C	Target Architecture, i.e., "To-Be" Architecture	During this phase, the effort concentrates on realizing alignment of the system requirements, discovery, and analysis work with the architectural foundation, i.e., TOGAF. Steps in this phase include: • Brainstorm architectural principles and mechanisms. • Produce affinity groupings of functionality using TOGAF TRM. • Highlight inter-dependencies among groupings. • Conduct high-level gap analysis to ensure that all current systems are considered and modify existing business systems hierarchy accordingly. • Identify and refine definitions of interfaces. • Build a Standards Information Base (SIB) to describe the technologies and standards that support the TRM's services. • Key questions and traceability of requirements to all ATD phases • E-business strategy . • Selection criteria for service portfolio and choice technologies. • Logical and physical directory service. • Organizational Change (OC) requirements updated. • Technology Model View (Output).

Table 1. (*Continued*)

Phase	Name of Phase	Description
D	Opportunities and Solutions	This phase is responsible for uncovering the various techniques needed to transition from the current (As-Is) architecture to the target (To-Be) architecture. Phase steps are: • Impact analysis. • List of new e-commerce services, initiatives, and technologies in the market. • Identify changes to latest-cut at the target architecture, both logical and physical changes. • Organizational change (OC) management is instituted. • Project identification and classification, i.e., identify work units needed to support the transition to the target architecture (Output).
E	Migration Planning	The objective of this phase is "to sort the various implementation projects into priority order. Activities include assessing the dependencies, costs, and benefits of the various migration projects", as defined in TOGAF. Order and extent of execution of these activities involve decision making in project management. Activities include: • Cost-benefit-risk analysis. • Asset management decision-making to support project prioritization, including Multiple-Criteria Decision Making (MCDM). • Project release strategy, i.e., "project roadmap"
F	Implementation	The objective of this phase is "to formulate recommendations for each implementation project and construct an architecture contract to govern the system implementation and deployment", as defined in TOGAF. Categories of projects can be: • Policy development (e.g., security, tax processing, capital investment, other).

Table 1. (*Continued*)

Phase	Name of Phase	Description
		• Product customization. • Data storage, retrieval, and management. • Customer communications, relations management (CRM). • Organizational change (OC). • Performance benchmarking. • Other.
G	Architecture Maintenance	Business change inevitably happens over time. The objective of this phase is "to establish a maintenance process for the new baseline that is achieved at the completion of the implementation phase. This process will typically provide for the continual monitoring of such things as developments in technology and changes in the business environment, and for determining whether to formally initiate a new architecture evolution cycle", as defined in TOGAF. The target architecture becomes the current architecture and a new evolution cycle begins. Steps in this phase include: • Conduct architectural governance control to manage technology change and implementation, i.e., migration of new product versions. • Scheduled and un-scheduled product replacement, and • Monitor architectural compliance with SIB.

12.8. An Illustrative Example – A Manufacturing Environment

In order to describe the key concepts and developmental steps in TOGAF, we borrow an overview of an illustrative example (the Crunchy Frog LTD) by Perks and Beveridge (2003). For a detailed development of the TOGAF methodology refer to this excellent publication replete with historical background, lessons learned on TOGAF, and examples.

Crunchy Frog Ltd. (CFL) is an initially family-owned manufacturer of confections that began in the 1955 in the USA with headquarters in

New Orleans. Thirty distribution and selling centers in the USA, recently expanded to the United Kingdom and Germany. CFL's IT group reports to the Chief Information Officer (CIO) and she reports directly to the CFL Leadership Team and the Chief Executive Officer (CEO). Total of 10,000 employees in the USA and 50 employees in the international market, approximately, as depicted in Figure 2.

Why does CFL want an Enterprise Architecture (EA)? After all, CFL has been doing business comfortably well for the past few years and there are no major difficulties to be seen in the immediate horizon. Well, for one there have been a number of internal indicators that are of concern to the CFL Leadership Team and, accordingly, an external consultancy group was commissioned to conduct a study.

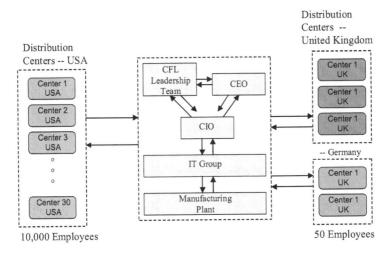

Figure 2. High-Level View of CFL, an Illustrative Example (Perks and Beveridge 2003, with kind permission of Springer Science and Business Media)

Main results of this study are as follows:

- <u>Non-alignment of IT to business</u>: Some key IT processes (initialization and procurement) were ad hoc and not aligned with either the business strategy or the IT strategy.
- <u>Lack of measurement ability:</u> IT could not measure its costs and benefits to business goals.
- <u>Legacy systems difficult to maintain</u>: Main platforms (e.g., IBM AS/400s) were becoming increasingly difficult to maintain and evolve.

- Costs higher than industry benchmarks: Eroded management efficiency, non-unified approach to application development, and labor intensive systems integration procedures resulted in higher costs across the CFL environment.
- Arbitrary allocation of logical business systems: No defined hierarchy of logical business systems, business processes, and the allocation of these to the various departments in the CFL organization. A result was duplication of the same information function across multiple departments, and
- Non-efficient technology distribution: Technology procurement was not coordinated across departments resulting in duplication and higher costs.

12.8.1. Phase A: Initiation and Framework

Next, a series of interviews with stakeholders, business, and IT personnel were conducted resulting in the creation of the following documents:

- Information Systems Strategic Plan (ISSP)
- Business Strategic Plan
- E-Business Strategic Plan
- Cursory Business Systems Architecture

Information Systems Strategic Plan (ISSP)
This plan, it was observed, did document the IT goals and made an effort to map these to the business objectives that had been listed in the Business Strategic Plan. Overall, the ISSP appeared to have been structured reasonably well with an appropriate planning horizon. IT objectives included:

- Manage the business globally
- Deliver outstanding customer services, goods, and support, and
- Continue to identify growth opportunities, both in the USA and in the international markets.

Business Strategic Plan
This plan also documented a set of high-level business plans for the domestic and international markets where CFL already had distribution centers. Some specificity would have been appropriate, however, particularly, in the articulation of percentage increases in productivity and sales volumes over the next, say, 5, 10, and 15 years.

e-Business Strategic Plan

This plan described a number of new e-business projects that would bring in new technology needed to support the organizations business strategic plan. However, neither the business nor the IT sides of CFL could describe accurately the readiness of the technical environments if these were to adequately support the proposed e-business projects. A reliable basis for conducting cost-benefit analysis did not exist. Nevertheless, the proposed e-programs are as follows:

- Bring in e-based supply-chain technology in order to electronically connect CFL with its major suppliers.
- Offer a catalog browsing service to CFL customers
- Offer electronic ordering to CFL customers.

Cursory Business Systems Architecture (BSA)

The hierarchy of business systems in place for CFL was not particularly well structured and defined. Mostly a series of "box-and-arrow" diagrams with incomplete definitions for the busines systems themselves, their associated business systems, and their interfaces, as shown on Figure 3. Also, the relevance of some existing business processes to emerging, highly competitive markets was questionable.

Information needs for the CFL were captured in Table 2 via interviews. It was noted, for example, that although there was an

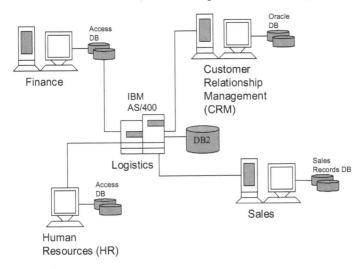

Figure 3. Legacy Business Systems Architecture for CFL (Courtesy: Perks and Beveridge, 2003, Springer Publishers)

Table 2. CFL Functionality Across Business Systems

Information Need:	Type: S = Strategic T = Tactical O = Operational
Finance Department	
Budget	T
Capital needs forecasting	S
Gross income	T
Cash flow actual	T
Cash flow projected	S
Debt servicing	T
Creditor, total current	T
Profit by customer	T
Profit by distribution center	O
Depreciation	T
Fixed assets	S
Sales Department	
Commission by sales person	T
Sales by center, salesperson	O
Lead time for delivery	O
Price structure	S,T,O
Marketing Department	
Competitor analysis	S
Gross profit	O
Sales forecast, volume	S
Revenue by center, salesperson	O
Product life, by unit ID	T
Logistics Department	
Transportation costs	O
Inventory volumes, by product type	O
Labor costs	O,T
Direct material costs	T
Manufacturing capacity	S,O
Down time	O

adequate balance of strategic, tactical, and operations needs across functions in the Financial Department these functions were often disjointed from the other organizational units, i.e., Human Resources (HR), Sales, and Customer Relationship Management (CRM).

CFL Team members conducted interviews with directors and managers to gather requirements in the categories noted on Table 3.

Table 3. Requirements Gathering
(Source: Perks and Beveridge 2003)

Key:	Provision Assessment:		
IS = ISSP Strategy BS = Business Strategy ES = e-Business Strategy ER = e-Business Requirement AP = Architectural Principles C = Constraint	1 = Not provided for in current processing environment (CPE) 3 = Some aspects exist in CPE 5 = Fully provided for in CPE		
Strategic Element	Provided Through	Current System Impacted	Provision Assessment
Support the development of high-value products for continued growth (BS)	Provide CFL with the capability to develop faster solutions for future business problems (ES) Provide a gateway into the internal buisness-to-business processes to high-value customers (ES) e-business initiatives are scheduled to be presented to the market in 6 months (C) Offer a catalog browsing service to customer (ER) Internet: establish an internet infrastructure to support e-business (ES)	Internet infrastructure, Logistics, Sales, Network	1 1 n/a 1 2
Be a best-cost producer (BS)	Reduce the cost of business transactions	Logistics, Internet	1

Table 3. (*Continued*)

Key: IS = ISSP Strategy BS = Business Strategy ES = e-Business Strategy ER = e-Business Requirement AP = Architectural Principles C = Constraint		Provision Assessment: 1 = Not provided for in current processing environment (CPE) 3 = Some aspects exist in CPE 5 = Fully provided for in CPE	
Strategic Element	Provided Through	Current System Impacted	Provision Assessment
	(ES)	infrastructure	
Manage the business globally	International coverage; extend the CFL IT environment to the international offices (IS) A UK support center is required (C)	Network, Systems Management	3 1
Deliver oustanding customer service	Improve response time to customer (ES) 24x7 manufacturing operation is a "must" (C)	Internet infrastructure, Logistics	2 5
Streamline internal business processes for best cost (BS)	Align technical architecture with CMA standards (AP) Control technology total cost of ownership and operation (IS) Insure quality of information and reliability across all interfaces (IS)	All IT systems	1 1 3

Architectural Principles

CFL's Chief Information Officer (CIO) contributed a list of architectural principles that she felt were most important in guiding the architectural effort:

- Adopt best-of-breed, proven technology
- Centralize processing and database(s) at headquarters (HQ) if possible and desirable
- Applications must work together, no stove-pipe software systems
- All computers must be integrated via a network system
- Computer platforms and services must be reliable, able to deliver accurate information in a timely and efficient manner
- Platforms, networks, and procedures needed to access data must be transparent to users.

12.8.2. Phase B: Baseline Description

This phase is intended to capture the current IT environment, including arrays of platforms, the data model, data warehouses if any, and the communications network i.e., the "As-Is" IT environment. Although TOGAF emphasizes here the IT environment, there is an opportunity in this phase, however, to continue understanding and documenting the current business systems hierarchy and its interfaces, a significantly challenging and time-consuming task in most EA efforts.

Cataloguing the Current Processing Environment (CPE)

Why document legacy systems? There are a number of very legitimate reasons for wanting to prepare new documentation on existing systems (i.e., legacy systems, often stove-piped with little or no integration infrastructure). Often a clear understanding of how the various components of an existing architecture relate to and communicate with one another is fragmented or missing, as can be the case with systems and databases distributed geographically and marketing environments that reflect different sales regulations (e.g., domestic vs. international markets). Also, and possibly more significant, a total view of the way the organization is able to conduct business today is needed in order to propose and implement new, cost-effective, and successful new business processes and technologies. In fact, not one but multiple views may be required to gain this understanding and make a "leap" into an improved or new way of doing business. Information on component functionality ought to come from various sources:

- Policy and procedures
- Business processes and activities
- Standards adopted for EA development and maintenance
- Types of interfaces among business systems, such as application progamming interfaces (APIs), Object-oriented methodology for software development, communication protocols, XML, HTML, and mixed media storage.

As described in other chapters, multiple views of the enterprise can be most effective in capturing, organizing, and relating categories of information:

- Newtork view
- Security environment view
- Data model view
- Business systems view, and
- Applications view (e.g., e-mail, services directory, file sharing, etc.)

The study did manage, however, to produce a high-level view of the interface topology of CFL, as depicted in Figure 4.

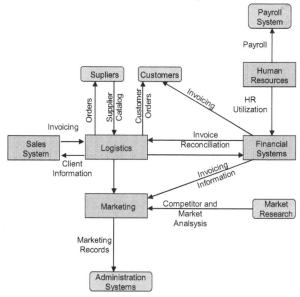

Figure 4. Interface Topology and Business Systems for CFL (*Source*: Perks and Beveridge 2003, Springer Publishers)

The Sales System and Logistics system interface, for example is lightly characterized by "Invoicing" and "Client Information" information flows. Granted, not much detail was found in the existing CFL documentation and this is a main point to make here: The task of documenting the existing IT environment can be frustrating and full of challenges and, yet, an honest effort must be made to gather and document all the information available by searching through existing fragmented documentation and interviews with operations personal.

Fortunately, documentation on the Sales System itself gathered during the study was more abundant, as shown on Figure 5. This system counts with Customer Relationship Management (CRM) software installed in several PCs and sales laptops. Sales information is then replicated and sent via match mode to an Oracle database using a corporate network (with TCP/IP protocol) and the Internet.

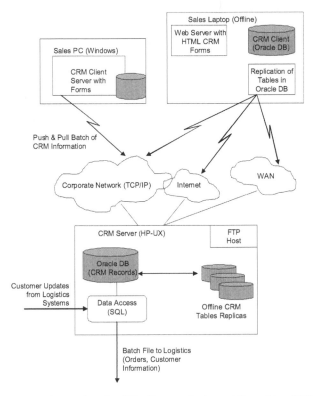

Figure 5. Sales Technology View for CFL (*Source*: Perks and Beveridge 2003, Springer Publishers)

12.8.3. Phase C: Target Architecture

This Phase C consists of a series of activities leading to the new, future, target architecture: the TOGAF architecture. In other words, we already know what the "shape" of the future architecture will be and there remains the task of modifying some old business processes, throwing out some old business processes that can not be adapted, creating some new business processes and arranging then all to fit into the TOGAF main components: the TOGAF TRM and the Standards Information Base (SIB).

Building the TOGAF TRM follows the steps stated earlier in Chapter 4, The Business Systems Architectural View. Building the Standards Information Base (SIB) consists of mapping and cataloguing the technologies that will provide the logical business services and, as such, it also contains technology selection criteria and procurement guidelines when working with vendors and providers of technologies. Once the SIB is created, a Gap Analysis can be conducted to identify overlaps and gaps in business services between "where we are today" and "where we want to be tomorrow" in the new TOGAF architecture. Speaking of technologies, EA work in countries in the European Union (EU) are still laboring to define their own EA frameworks but already there is a rich fabric of new, emerging technologies referred to as the new Technologies of Information and Communication (TICs). See Chapter 17, Digital Administration, for a description of these technologies.

A set of business goals must be gathered and documented. This activity ought to be the one presented earlier in Chapter 3, The Business Processes Architectural View, which describes the use of business systems hierarchy and architectural principles. In this sense, based on the knowledge gained through the study of that chapter, we already know how to construct a "TOGAF Business Strategy" for a particular organization. Table 4 presents a summary of detail collected for the Logistics Sub-system.

12.8.4 Phase D: Opportunities and Solutions

Just like phase C was about building the landscape of the target architecture with business processes and business systems that constitute the WHAT of the target architecture, this next phase is about HOW to get to the target architecture, i.e., the TOGAF architecture. Accordingly, this phase is about:

Table 4. SIB Analysis, CFL Information System Logistics
Application Type: Business Application
X = Business sub-category already exists in the current architecture

Service Category	Business Sub-Category	Current	Technologies Implemented
Operating system services	Kernel services		OS/400
Network services	Data communications		SNA, TCP/IP, X.25, frame relay
	e-mail		Proprietary custom application
	Distributed data	X	DB/2 replication
Software engineering services	Language support		COBOL
Security sevices	Identification and authentication	X	RACF
Transaction processing	Transaction management		OS/400 interactive
User interface	Character based		3270 green screen

- Identifying new services and new technologies.
- Designing an Organizational Change (OC) Management Plan.
- Identifying top-level projects that will enable the TOGAF teams to move from the current architecture to the target architecture.
- Designing an Implementation Plan that will guide the many engineering and OC activities towards accomplishing the requirements of the target architecture. In TOGAF terms, a high-level view of the process and activities involved is provided by the wiring diagram shown on Figure 6.

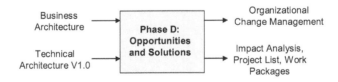

Figure 6. TOGAF's Opportunities and Solutions Wiring Diagram

Organizational Change (OC) Management

Changing and advancing the business services and technologies in the current architecture to evolve to the target architecture is a challenge of major proportions, but one that cannot occur successfully without another type of change: Organizational Change (OC). Over the last 8-10 years of EA work we have learned that this work moves forward best when it involves both technological change and organizational change simultaneously, in parallel.

> *Organizational change management is about anticipating resistance and anxiety among people within an organization that is experiencing technological change to meet new business objectives, and then conducting activities to explain change, propose new roles and responsibilities, and to gain consensus to move forward together as a team.*

Where is the resistance to technological change coming from? Several and many can be the reasons for resisting technological change, both real and perceived:

- Some people in the organization undergoing change fear they may lose their jobs after years of service.
- More technology may "get things done faster and possibly better", thus needing less people to get the same amount of work done, can be the thinking of some individuals.
- Often people fear the unknown.
- People may fear that upper management will use the technological change as an excuse "to get rid of older and marginal workers in the organization".
- "The organization is planning on reducing the cost of products and services in order to become more competitive and consequently some employees will be laid off", can also be recurring thought among anxious personnel at all levels in the organization.

This fear of change, whether real or imaginary, can then evidence itself in various forms of resistance to the architectural change:

- People may opt for leaving the organization to find employment elsewhere, thus contributing to the loss of valuable, experienced employees.
- The presentation of elements of the architectural views (e.g., vision and strategy, set of requirements of the new architecture, concept design, other reviews and documents) can be looked at with suspicion, thus not receiving all the enthusiasm and energy that employees would otherwise be able to give to the new plans for change.
- "The EA team is being unrealistic in their demands for change and think they know better than the rest of us", and "The EA team will get rid of my job, I can see it happening", can be the perception of some individuals and teams within the changing organization.
- Scheduling of new "pilot activities" fail due to varied reasons, including new equipment and programs not being available on time, training of personnel for new activities is lethargic, and requirements can not be successfully validated and are simply moved on to future releases.

What are specific activities and strategies within an Organizational Change (OC) Management Plan? While the literature on OC is ample and has been available for several decades now it has been only in the last 6-8 years that successful OC planning has happened:

- Set up an "OC Team" early in the EA planning with adequate resources of people, money, and time to get the OC job done well.
- Empower the OC team to prepare and deliver presentations to the various EA stakeholder and user groups on how the EA work will progress over time.
- Seek actively and involve the various EA stakeholder and user groups in the validation of some EA design elements (e.g., the EA transition strategy, new pilot operating procedures, co-signing of EA work products, other).
- Communicate to workers, supervisors, and directors detail on how and when new subsystems will be installed and provide for new training ahead of time throughout all EA phases and releases.

- Training by personnel in the OC team ought to include courses on new tools (e.g., UML training for software engineers, DB2 database operation for database engineers and data entry operators, other) and new business practices (e.g., Customer Relationship Management (CRM) technology) for marketing personnel.
- Identification, creation, definition, and support of new roles and positions such as database administrator (DB administrator), Office of the EA Architect, information security administrator, other.

EA Work Packages

A substantial number of Work Packages needs to be prepared, validated, and delivered to the EA client during this phase, as noted on Table 5, including the System Requirements (SYR) document, Use Cases Architecture document, Business Case (BC) document, Logical Business Systems Hierarchy, Physical Design, and the Capacity and Performance Plan.

Table 5. Work Products (i.e, Deliverable Documentation)

Work Package	Description	Service Supported
System Requirements (SYR) Document	Listing of all system functional and non-functional (i.e., performance) requirements.	All services
User Cases Architecture Document	Definition of terms and listing of all User Cases, including decomposition of these into activities, sequence diagrams, internal and external systems.	All services
Business Case (BC) Document	Cost-Benefit analysis, Net Present Value (NPV) analysis, and investment return projections for each	Economic, Policy, Governance

Table 5. (*Continued*)

Work Package	Description	Service Supported
	project identified in modernization effort.	
Business Processes Architecture		
Logical Business Systems Hierarchy		
Logical Design Document		Technical
Physical Design Document		Technical
Capacity and Performance Plan		Technical
Business Rules Catalog		
Software Development Plan		
Infrastructure Services Architecture		
Pilot Plan		
Organizational Change Management Plan		Change Management
Project Management Plan		Management
Release Management Plan		Management

12.8.5. Phase E: Project Initiation and Migration Planning

As its name implies, during this phase potential projects are identified, cost-benefit analysis is conducted on each potential project, potential projects are ordered in order of priority (i.e., priority setting), and an orchestrated effort is made to begin to form and document an implementation plan of these projects. In TOGAF terminology, these activities are depicted in Figure 7.

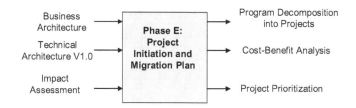

Figure 7. TOGAF's Project Initiation and Migration Wiring Diagram

Project Initiation

By now the TOGAF EA effort has already identified a hierarchy of business systems, as the wiring diagram of Figure 8 indicates. Next, this business hierarchy is examined to identify groups of business systems that have an affinity for each other. Thus, the analyst may find 15-18 business systems that involve database functions and as such this group may end up being promoted as "the database engine project". Another set of 25-30 business systems may involve communication protocols, local area network services, security services, firewall services, etc., and as such this second group of business systems may be recommended to constitute "the infrastructure project". This process of association is depicted in Figure 11.

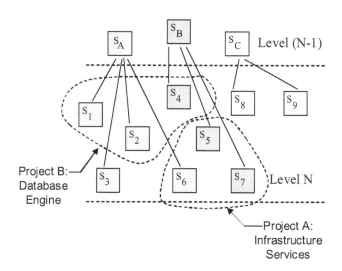

Figure 8. Decomposition of Business Hierarchy into Projects

We may note that this process of grouping business systems into projects is what we already presented in Chapter 4, The Business Systems Architectural View. Accordingly, we may want to take a second look at that chapter to help with our understanding of project initiation in TOGAF's Phase E.

Cost-Benefit Analysis

Once all the potential projects are identified and we are on our way to building the new, target architecture (i.e., the TOGAF architecture), do we find financing for all these projects and proceed to build them one at a time, or all at the same time? Well, as we already suspect, the owner of the architecture (i.e., administrators in a government agency or the board of directors of a corporation) has limited moneys at any fiscal year, enough to begin funding on 2-3 projects while the rest of , say, the other 4-6 projects may have to be scheduled for funding in later fiscal years. Also, even if there were enough moneys to finance all the proposed projects, the owner of the architecture would not want to do just that and, instead, would proceed with caution by implementing an "incremental approach" by building a few projects first, learning what works well, how mistakes can be avoided, and then building another batch of projects. This incremental approach is one that is most often applied in actual, real-world EA work and one that we recommend highly in this book.

How is the relative importance or priority of recommended projects determined? A number of factors or criteria must be considered as illustrated in Figure 9. At the outset, high-level requirements of the architecture as well as detailed requirements at the project level must be considered. If the target architecture is intended for a government agency then public services are a high priority (not all requirements are equally important), and digital services are likely to be deemed highly desirable; consequently that project that will provide for Web-based transaction processing and other digital services will likely end up receiving a high priority for its funding and construction. If the target architecture is intended for an airline corporation then that project that will provide for a modernized data base and auxiliary subsystems will likely end up receiving a high priority for its funding and construction, and so on.

Benefits and Costs for each project need to be identified and assessed applying well known benefit/cost (C/B) techniques, including Present

Value (PV) and Internal Rate of Return (IROR). If the ratio of benefits to costs over a time frame (5, 10, 15, or more years) is less than 1.0 the project is discarded, otherwise it is considered feasible. Accordingly, projects are ranked from higher B/C ratios (higher priorities) to lower B/C ratios. Project "dependencies" enter the analysis as well. If Project A (Project e-Services) is one that will provide digital services to customers but it requires to access data in the databases of Project B (Project GATES), then Project A is said to have a dependency on Project B. Accordingly, if Project A is given a high priority then Project B will likely be given a high priority as well.

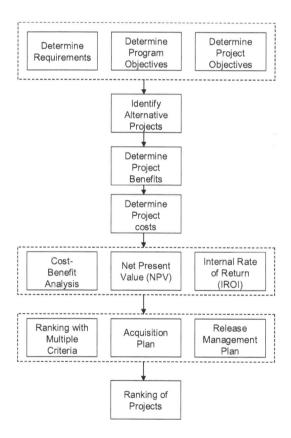

Figure 9. Ranking of Projects Using Multiple Criteria

Other criteria such as business commitments established with other business partners or government agencies, availability of funding, training of personnel, maturity of technology products proposed by vendors, and preferences of the stakeholders for one type of functionality (e.g., Web-based services) over another (e.g., a second manufacturing plant) need to be considered as well in the ranking of projects. By now there are a number of well established multiple-criteria decision-making (MCDM) methods that use these multiple criteria in the ranking of projects, including MATS (multi-attribute trade-off system), PROTRADE, ELECTRE, AHP, and Expert Choice (Goikoetxea et al., 2004, 1982; P. Vincke et al., 1992; Saaty, 1990).

12.9. Conclusions

In this chapter we set out to describe the basic elements of the TOGAF architectural framework, and we illustrated these elements with an example produced earlier by Perks and Beveridge (2003). Several observations may apply:

- The TOGAF architecture comes about after a long learning process during the early TAFIM days.
- It is fairly well streamlined, with a set of well defined steps, and associated with each of these steps there is a number of work products to complete and deliver to the owners of the architecture.
- It should be of interest and highly applicable in organizations in the Private Sector (e.g., banks, manufacturing enterprises, learning centers, other) that are not bond by government EA guidelines.
- This model ought to be adaptable to organizations with limited funding, so that a limited set of work products can be prepared and delivered.
- It is early yet, and few statistics are available on the costs and savings of implementing TOGAF versus any of the other EA frameworks we have studied in this book.
- The TOGAF methodology and practice, however, rests on a strong theoretical and practical foundation led by the OMG and its ample repertoire of standards and documentation of EA best practices.

Chapter 13

The Department of Defense Architecture Framework (DODAF)

Co-authored with Kathie Sowell

13.1. Introduction

The *Department of Defense Architecture Framework* (DODAF) is the guiding document that provides a common language for describing architectures across all segments of the United States Department of Defense (DoD). A common language, or technique, for describing architectures was deemed necessary in the DoD in order for architectures developed by different Services and Agencies to be understood by all involved parties, compared, and integrated as necessary.

This framework has had a long development history, starting out in 1996 as the C4ISR *(Command, Control, Communications, Computers, Intelligence, Surveillance, and Reconnaissance) Architecture Framework*, as illustrated in Figure 1. In 1997 a second version of the framework was developed and in 1998 it was made mandatory for all C4ISR architectures developed within DoD. In 2003 another version was produced, and in acknowledgment of its applicability beyond C4ISR, the title of the document was changed to the *Department of Defense Architecture Framework*

It is important to understand that, although the DODAF was originally developed for use by several military organizations, its constructs and techniques are more broadly applicable. As evidence of this broad applicability, many organizations outside of the DoD, and even outside of the United States, have adopted and adapted the essentials of the DODAF. In fact, the DODAF constructs can even be used in conjunction with other frameworks and methodologies such as the Zachman Framework, the Federal Enterprise Architecture Framework, Spewak's Enterprise Architecture Planning method, and The Open Group Architecture Framework.

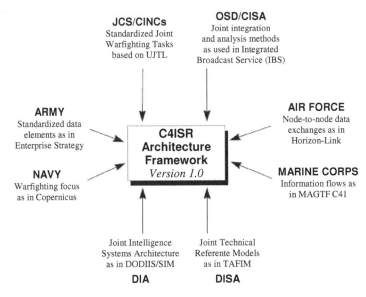

Figure 1. Multiple and combined origins of the C4ISR Architecture

Accordingly, the objective of this chapter is twofold: (1) to present a summary of the DODAF, and (2) to relate concepts and elements of this framework to concepts and elements presented in earlier chapters.

13.2. Organization of this Chapter

Section 13.3 describes the structure and major constructs of the DODAF. Section 13.4 lists the architectural principles that constitute the DODAF philosophy. Section 13.5 describes a recommended high-level process for using the DODAF to build an architecture description. Section 13.6 lists some of the automated tools used today in the development and documentation of the products, and describes the capabilities of each tool. Section 13.7 presents a table of all 26 of the DODAF products, along with a brief description of each. Section 13.8 provides details for a few of the DODAF products that are used most often in architectures. Section 13.9 offers a comparison of the DODAF with Zachman's schema, while Section 13.10 gives one possible mapping of the DODAF products onto Spewak's four-layer architecture planning methodology. Finally a set of conclusions and exercises closes this chapter.

13.3. Structure of the DODAF

The DODAF is based on the principle that any architecture can be described in terms of three *views*, as shown on Figure 2. A view is a perspective on the architecture, in which only certain aspects of the architecture are described. Each view consists of several *work products* A work product is a model that describes some defined portion of the architecture. A product has a specified graphical presentation format and contains specific information about the architecture. The three views of the DODAF are the Operational View, the Systems View, and the Technical Standards View.

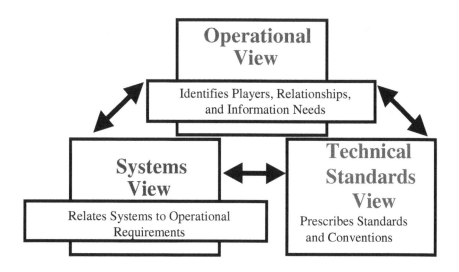

Figure 2. The Three DODAF Views and their Linkages

The Operational View describes the participants (players), the activities they perform, and the information they need to exchange. The Systems View describes the hardware and software that the participants use in order to accomplish their activities. The Technical Standards View lists the interface standards that the systems must satisfy, or other rules governing their implementation. In turn, each of these three main views is decomposed into relevant products. In addition to the view-specific products, there are also two products that relate to the architecture as a whole, not to any one view. These products are described individually in Section 13.7.

13.4. Guiding Principles of the DODAF Philosophy

The following principles provide insight into the philosophy of the DODAF:

- Architectures should be built with a purpose in mind.
- Architectures should facilitate, not impede, communication among people
- Architectures should be readable, comprehensible, comparable, and people ought to be able to integrate multiple architectures.
- Every architecture should comply with the Framework sufficiently to facilitate the first three principles above (see Chapter 17, EA Implementation, Compliance, and Governance).

13.5. The Six-Step Architecture Description Process

In accordance with the DODAF philosophy, architecture description is envisioned as a six-step process, as depicted in Figure 3.

Initially, the architect must have a clear purpose in mind, such as to propose funding for a new element in an existing architecture, to fully modernize an existing architecture, or to create and implement a new capability. Functional areas to be addressed, geographical bounds, and technologies to be considered are some dimensions of scope for the architecture. Linkages and detail needed across the three views spell out the content of the necessary products. During the product-building phase

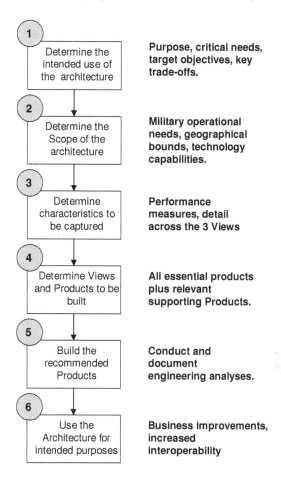

Figure 3. A Six-Step Process for Building an Architecture

and afterwards, conduct informal and formal analysis. Finally, draw conclusions and make recommendations that support the original purpose for building the architecture description.

13.6. A Set of Automated Tools

While the DODAF is intentionally tool-independent, there are some tools that can help with the development of the products better than other tools. A list of choice tools currently used in the DODAF community include:

System Architect (by Telelogic Inc., originally created by Popkin Inc., http://www.telelogic.com)
- Most widely used EA tool in the EA global community today.
- Fully integrated collection of models and documents across four key architecture domains: Business, Information, Systems, and Technology.
- Alignment of Business Processes and IT Systems to Business Objectives.
- Planning, Modeling, and Execution of Business Processes.
- Readily available, flexible software license terms.
- Rapid response to Business Change and Organizational Change (OC)
- Placed as a leader EA tool in Gartner´s Magic Quadrant for EA development.

netViz Tool
(http://www.netviz.com/solutions/regulatory_compliance.asp)
- Originated for communications network design/troubleshooting, can build other DODAF products as well.
- Graphics supported by a database, can be imported to other databases, e.g. Access database.
- Uses "data-driven graphics"
  - o Changes to data fields modify graphical appearance
  - o Useful for color-coding link types, activity types, etc.
  - o Drawings linked via drilldown capability
  - o Useful for drilling down from operational nodes to the systems at the nodes.
- Allows user to see multiple models at the same time.
- Exports to PowerPoint and Visio, imports from Visio.

Visio Tool (by Microsoft)
- Family of products.
- Customizable drawing capabilities.

- Oversize drawings via plotter.
- Database support.
- See also description of this and other EA tools in the IFEAD web site (http://www.enterprise-architecture.info/EA_Tools.htm)

Metis Tool (Computas North America, acquired by Troux Group, see article on www.forrester.com)
- EA Repository with directories for text and graphics content in various EA views.
- Support to EA and IT governance processes.
- Built on XML metamodel-driven, object-oriented technology (as opposed to other EA tools that use relational database technology).
- Web-enabled modeling solution (Version 3.0).

Proforma Tool (www.profromacorp.com)
- With modeling software ProVision to evaluate impact of technological change on business performance.
- Business process modeling capability.
- Support for EA requirements analysis.

13.7. Description of the Product Types (i.e., Work Products)

Next, we proceed to identify and briefly describe the complete set of products. For a detailed description the interested reader is encouraged to visit the website: http://www.defenselink.mil.nii.doc/DODAF

Table 1 lists and describes the products. The first column in the table identifies the view to which the product belongs; the second column contains an identifier for the product (e.g., AV-1" means "product number one that relates to all the views," "OV-1" means "product number one of the Operational View," etc.); the third column contains the product's formal name; and the fourth column contains a short description of the product. Essentially, these are the views implemented and available in System Architect, the EA tool by Telelogic Inc and available in CD format (Limited license) in the back end of this book.

Table 1. DODAF Work Products

Applicable View	Framework Product	Framework Product Name	General Description
All Views	AV-1	Overview and Summary Information	Scope, purpose, intended users, environment depicted, analytical findings
All Views	AV-2	Integrated Dictionary	Architecture data repository with definitions of all terms used in all products
Operational	OV-1	High-Level Operational Concept Graphic	High-level graphical/textual description of operational concept
Operational	OV-2	Operational Node Connectivity Description	Operational nodes, connectivity, and information exchange needlines between nodes
Operational	OV-3	Operational Information Exchange Matrix	Information exchanged between nodes and the relevant attributes of that exchange
Operational	OV-4	Organizational Relationships Chart	Organizational, role, or other relationships among organizations
Operational	OV-5	Operational Activity Model	Capabilities, operational activities, relationships among activities, inputs, and outputs; overlays can show cost, performing nodes, or other pertinent information
Operational	OV-6a	Operational Rules Model	One of three products used to describe operational activity—identifies business rules that constrain operation
Operational	OV-6b	Operational State Transition Description	One of three products used to describe operational activity—identifies business process responses to events
Operational	OV-6c	Operational Event-Trace Description	One of three products used to describe operational activity—traces actions in a scenario or sequence of events
Operational	OV-7	Logical Data Model	Documentation of the system data requirements and structural business process rules of the Operational View

Table 1. (*Continued*)

Applicable View	Framework Product	Framework Product Name	General Description
Systems	SV-1	Systems Interface Description	Identification of systems nodes, systems, and system items and their interconnections, within and between nodes
Systems	SV-2	Systems Communications Description	Systems nodes, systems, and system items, and their related communications lay-downs
Systems	SV-3	Systems-Systems Matrix	Relationships among systems in a given architecture; can be designed to show relationships of interest, e.g., system-type interfaces, planned vs. existing interfaces, etc.
Systems	SV-4	Systems Functionality Description	Functions performed by systems and the system data flows among system functions
Systems	SV-5	Operational Activity to Systems Function Traceability Matrix	Mapping of systems back to capabilities or of system functions back to operational activities
Systems	SV-6	Systems Data Exchange Matrix	Provides details of system data elements being exchanged between systems and the attributes of that exchange
Systems	SV-7	Systems Performance Parameters Matrix	Performance characteristics of Systems View elements for the appropriate time frame(s)
Systems	SV-8	Systems Evolution Description	Planned incremental steps toward migrating a suite of systems to a more efficient suite, or toward evolving a current system to a future implementation
Systems	SV-9	Systems Technology Forecast	Emerging technologies and software/hardware products that are expected to be available in a given set of time frames and that will affect future development of the architecture

Table 1. (*Continued*)

Applicable View	Framework Product	Framework Product Name	General Description
Systems	SV-10a	Systems Rules Model	One of three products used to describe system functionality—identifies constraints that are imposed on systems functionality due to some aspect of systems design or implementation
Systems	SV-10b	Systems State Transition Description	One of three products used to describe system functionality—identifies responses of a system to events
Systems	SV-10c	Systems Event-Trace Description	One of three products used to describe system functionality—identifies system-specific refinements of critical sequences of events described in the Operational View
Systems	SV-11	Physical Schema	Physical implementation of the Logical Data Model entities, e.g., message formats, file structures, physical schema
Technical	TV-1	Technical Standards Profile	Listing of standards that apply to Systems View elements in a given architecture
Technical	TV-2	Technical Standards Forecast	Description of emerging standards and potential impact on current Systems View elements, within a set of time frames

13.7.1. Overview and Summary Information (AV-1)

This product contains basic nomenclature for the identification of all architectural products, their contents, and findings:

- Identification of Architectural Product
    - Name
    - Architect
    - Organizations involved
    - When developed

- Purpose
    - Analysis needs
    - Decision support needs

- Scope
    - Views and products used
    - Time frames addressed

- Context
    - Mission
    - Geographical detail
    - Rules, criteria, and conventions followed

- Findings
    - Results
    - Recommendations

- Tools and file formats used

13.7.2. Integrated Dictionary (AV-2)

This product is a central source of all terms and metadata (data about data itself, i.e., the data that should be captured in each product) used in all the products of the architecture, i.e., a dictionary of terms and their relationships, as depicted in Figure 4. **The System Architect (SA) Tool** has a directory allocated to this product.

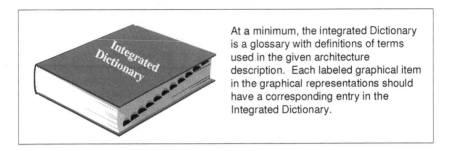

At a minimum, the integrated Dictionary is a glossary with definitions of terms used in the given architecture description. Each labeled graphical item in the graphical representations should have a corresponding entry in the Integrated Dictionary.

Figure 4. Integrated Dictionary (AV-2)

13.7.3. High-Level Operational Concept Description (OV-1)

This is a very visual, high-level product used to give a general description of the architecture in a flexible format. It is rich in graphics with some supplementary text. It is intended to introduce the concept of the architecture and to orient the audience to the architecture that will be described in more detail in other products. Figure 5 is an example of a High-Level Operational Concept Description taken from the DODAF. It illustrates a general concept for missile defense.

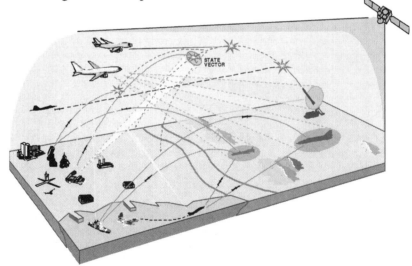

Figure 5. High-Level Operational Concept Graphic (OV-1), as shown in DODAF, v. 1

13.7.4. Operational Node Connectivity Description (OV-2)

This product depicts the operational nodes, that is the people, roles, or facilities that perform activities in the architecture. The operational nodes do not mention the hardware/software systems that are used at or by the operational nodes.

The operational nodes are graphically connected by arrows called "needlines." These needlines indicate which nodes provide information and which nodes need to receive that information. The needlines do not imply that the information is sent directly, in a point-to-point fashion, from one node to the next. A needline is a rollup that represents an aggregation of all the types of information that may be produced by one node and received by another.

Figure 6 illustrates a very simple example of an Operational Node Connectivity Description, for a sales enterprise.

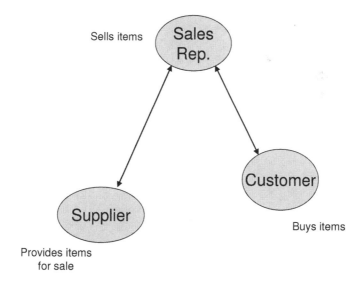

Figure 6. A Simple Operational Node Connectivity Description (OV-2)

As shown on Figure 6, the operational nodes or participants are the sales representative, the supplier, and the customer. The figure tells us that the supplier provides items for sale and produces information that the sales representative needs; the sales representative sells items and provides information that the customer needs, and also needs to receive information that the customer provides; and that the customer buys items and provides information that the sales representative needs.

13.7.5. Operational Information Exchange Matrix (OV-3)

The Operational Information Exchange Matrix details each needline from the Operational Node Connectivity Description. Each needline is decomposed, as necessary, into individual information exchanges and each of those information exchanges is further described in terms of several descriptors. No hardware or software is mentioned; only the information need itself is described. Table 2 presents an example template for the Operational Information Exchange Matrix.

13.7.6. Command Relationships Chart (OV-4)

This product documents information on the hierarchical relationships among organizations and their resources in an architecture, as depicted in Figure 7.

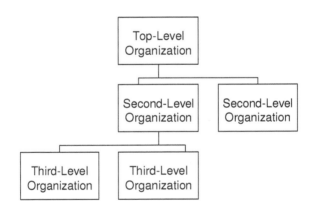

Figure 7. A Template for a Command Relationship Chart (OV-4)

Table 2. A Template for the Operational Information Exchange Matrix

Identifier/ Name of Operational Needline Supported (from OV-2) *	Identifier/ Name of Information Exchange *	Nature of Transaction								Purpose/ Triggering Event *	Information Source		Information Destination	
		Mission/ National Scenario *	Language (For Multi-National Operations)	Description (Content) *	Size	Units	Media *	Collaborative (Y/N)?	LISI Level Required		ID of Producing Node (facility or logical node) *	ID/name of Producing Activity *	ID of Receiving Node (facility or logical node) *	ID/name of Receiving Activity *
1	e.g., 1-a ··· 1-a													
2	e.g., 2-a ··· 2-a	···	···	···	···	···	···	···	···	···				
···	···	···	···	···	···	···	···	···	···	···				
n	···									···	···	···	···	···

CONTINUED

Identifier/ Name of Operational Needline Supported (from OV-2) *	Identifier/ Name of Information Exchange *	Performance Attributes			Information Assurance Attributes				Threats			Physical Environment			Remarks/ Other
		Frequency *	Timeliness *	Throughput	Security Classification (& Declassification/ Restrictions, if app.) *	Priority or Criticality *	Integrity Checks Required	Assured Authorization to Send/ Receive	Physical (includes weather, terrain)	Electronic (jamming, hackers, etc.)	Political/ Economic	Aerospace	Land	Sea	
1	e.g., 1-a ··· 1-a														
2	e.g., 2-a ··· 2-a	···	···	···	···	···	···	···	···	···	···	···	···	···	···
···	···	···	···	···	···	···	···	···	···	···	···	···	···	···	···
n	···														

*Indicates minimum recommended attributes

13.7.7. Activity Model (OV-5)

The Activity Model is most often hierarchical in nature and it describes the activities associated with the architecture. The model begins with single box that represents the overall activity and it proceeds successively to decompose the activity to the level required for the purpose of the architecture (level N) as in IDEF0 diagrams (cite IDEF0 reference here). Figure 8 depicts the use of the Activity Model to represent a generic customer service operation. (Sowell 2006).

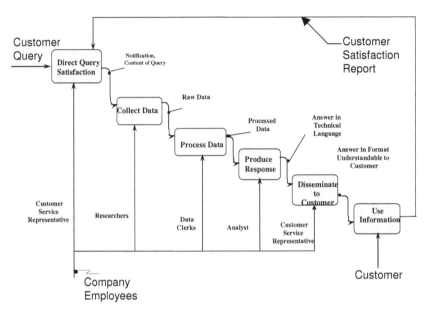

Figure 8. Example of an Activity Model (OV-5) for an Aspect of Customer Service

13.7.8. Systems Interface Description (SV-1)

The Systems Interface Description moves the architecture description from the Operational View to the Systems View. In this product, the hardware/software used at or by the operational nodes is overlayed onto the nodes to show what systems facilitate the activities.

Figure 9 illustrates a very simple System Interface Description, in which a sales representative and a supplier use telephone and fax to exchange information, and the sales representative and the customer use telephones. This example Systems Interface Description depicts the systems interfaces that connect systems across nodes. It is often necessary to delve deeper and to show the interfaces between systems within the individual nodes as well, and even the components that make up each system. The level of detail chosen for a given architecture depends upon the purpose for which the architecture was built.

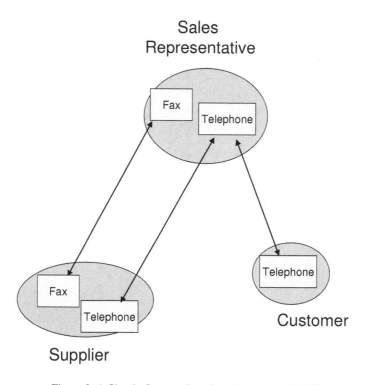

Figure 9. A Simple-Systems Interface Description (SV-1)

13.7.9. Systems Communications Description (SV-2)

This product adds detail to the Systems View by documenting specific communication systems and the connection paths among them. The following two figures, Figure 10 and Figure 11, illustrate the Systems Communications Description in the inter-nodal and intra-nodal perspective, respectively.

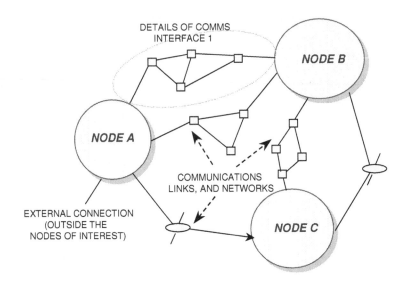

Figure 10. Systems Communication Description, Internodal Perspective

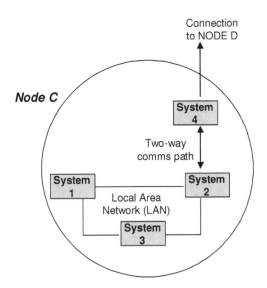

Figure 11. Systems Communications Description, Intranodal Perspective (SV-2)

13.7.10. Technical Standards Profile (TV-1)

This product documents the technical standards that apply to the architecture and how they need to be implemented in a time-phased manner. Table 3 illustrates a Technical Standards Profile.

Table 3. Technical Standards Profile (TV-1), an Example

Service Area	Service	Standard
Operating System	Kernel	FIPS Pub 151-1 (POSIX.1)
	Shell and Utilities	IEEE P1003.2
Software Engineering Services	Client Server Operations	FIPS Pub 119 (ADA)
	Object Definition and Management	DoD Human Computer Interface Style Guide
	Doalogue Support	Project Standard
	Window Management	FIPS Pub158 (X-Window System)
Data Management	Data Management	FIPS Pub 127-2 (SQL)
Data Interchange	Data Interchange	FIPS Pub 152 (SGML)
	Electronic Data Interchange	FIPS Pub 161 (EDI)
Graphics	Graphics	FIPS Pub 153 (PHIGS)

13.7.11. Standards Technology Forecast (TV-2)

Forecasting of availability of new and emerging technologies is equally important in the description of an architecture, as depicted on Table 4 for the data production portion of an architecture.

Table 4. Standards Technology Forecast, an Example (TV-2)

Service Areas	Service	Status	As of 12/05	Expected by 12/06	Expected by 12/08	Comment
Operating System	Kernel	Now	FIPS Pub 151-1		FIPS Pub 151-3	Very likely
	Shell & Utilities	Now				
	Near Real Time Extension	Future			FIPS Pub 151-3	Possibly, market direction not clear today.
Program-ming	5th Generation Programming Languages	Future		FIPS Pub 119 –Ada extended		
User Interface	Voice recognition	Future		New FIPS Pub		Very likely
Data Manage-ment	Data directory services	Future		FIPS Pub 127-1 with Links to examples		Very likely

13.8. Comparison of DODAF with Zachman's Framework

By now we have seen much detail on Zachman's architectural framework expanded in Chapters 1 through 10. We have also stated earlier that the DODAF Framework products can be used in conjuction with other Frameworks. In order for this to be true, the DODAF must be compatible with other Frameworks.

We are now ready to pose an important question: are the DODAF and the Zachman Framework compatible with each other? For convenient reference, the Zachman's Framework is shown again in Figure 12.

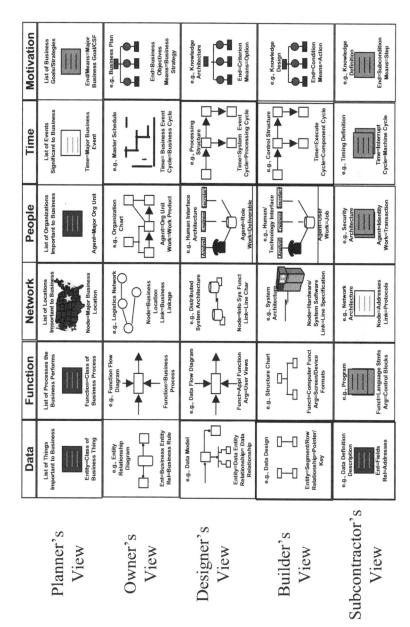

Figure 12. The Zachman EA Framework

In her study for the MITRE Corporation, Sowell (2004, 1999) reviewed Zachman's schema and arrived at the following conclusion: "The DODAF and the Zachman Framework are compatible, that is they each can describe the same facts about a given architecture." This compatibility can be understood in light of several critical facts:

- Each Zachman cell contains only one kind of data.

- Each DODAF product contains multiple kinds of data combined to describe a given aspect of the architecture.

- Each DODAF product has a specification that prescribes what kinds of data (facts) are to be captured in that product.

- Therefore, the DODAF products can be mapped to Zachman cells, but the mapping will not be one-to-one

Graphically, these findings are illustrated on Figure 13. This figure overlays a representative sampling of the DODAF products onto the Zachman cells that each product "satisfies." The DODAF products are shown as colored ovals: blue ovals for products of the Operational View, yellow ovals for products of the Systems View. This is a general mapping only for this reason: each Zachman cell contains only one kind of data, but each DODAF product contains several kinds of data, combined to describe a given aspect of the architecture. Therefore, a true one-to-one mapping between the Zachman Framework and the DODAF could only be accomplished at the DODAF product content specification level.

> The C4ISR Architecture Framework is a descriptive technique that can be used alone or in conjunction with other frameworks, methods, and languages. Some examples include: Zachman Framework, Federal Enterprise Architecture Framework, and Spewak's Enterprise Architecture Planning methodology.
>
> Kathie Sowell (1999)

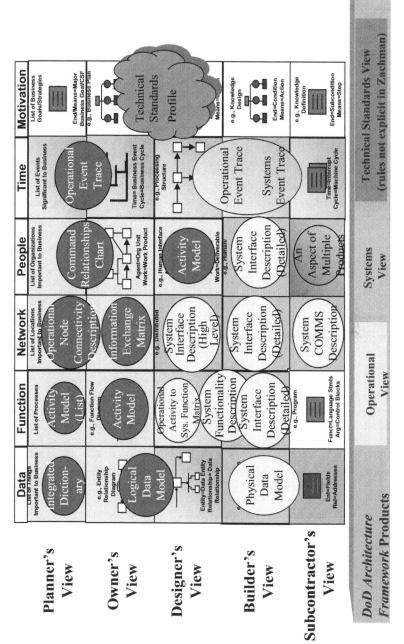

Figure 13. Mapping of DODAF Products to the Zachman Framework (Sowell, 2006)

Although this is a general mapping, and does not show all the DODAF products, some patterns can be seen from the overlay of DODAF products onto the Zachman Framework.   It can be seen tht the Operational View products (blue ovals) fall mostly in the top rows of Zachman, and the Systems View products fall mostly in the lower rows of Zachman. On the other hand, Sowell believes, the rules embedded in DODAF's Technical Standards View are not explicit in Zachman's schema, and this View can only be very generally mapped to Zachman's Motivation column.

13.9. Comparison of DODAF with the Federal Enterprise Architecture Framework

The Federal Enterprise Architecture Framework (FEAF) is an architecture framework built on a modified Zachman Framework schema.   It was developed in the US in 1999 under the auspices of the Federal CIO (Chief Information Officers/) Council, now known as the US CIO Council. The FEAF was originally intended to be mandatory for multi-agency Government architectures in the US.   It is no longer mandatory but is still widely used. Shown on Figure 14 is the Zachman-like structure of the FEAF today.

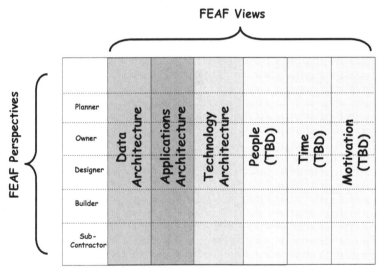

Figure 14. The FEAF's Zachman-Like Structure (Sowell, 2006)

EA planners may find useful still another view of the FEAF, as shown on Figure 15.

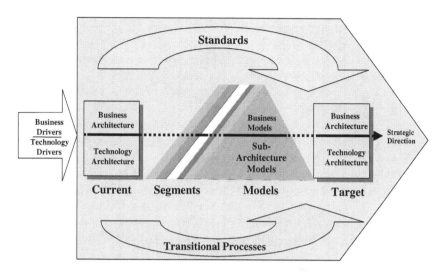

- Business Architecture corresponds to Operational view
- Technology Architecture corresponds to Systems view
- Description of Standards - corresponds to Technical Standards view

Figure 15. Another View of the FEAF Structure

Because the DODAF products can be mapped to the Zachman Framework, and the FEAF structure is based on the Zachman Framework, it follows that the DODAF products map similarly to the FEAF. Therefore, the DODAF is compatible with the FEAF as well as with the Zachman Framework

13.10. Comparison of DODAF with Spewak's Enterprise Architecture Planning

Another notable architectural publication is that by Spewak (1992). Spewak's perspective is that of a four-layer architecture planning methodology, as shown on Figure 16 affectionately known as Spewak's "architectural wedding cake" At the broadest and lowest level there is a

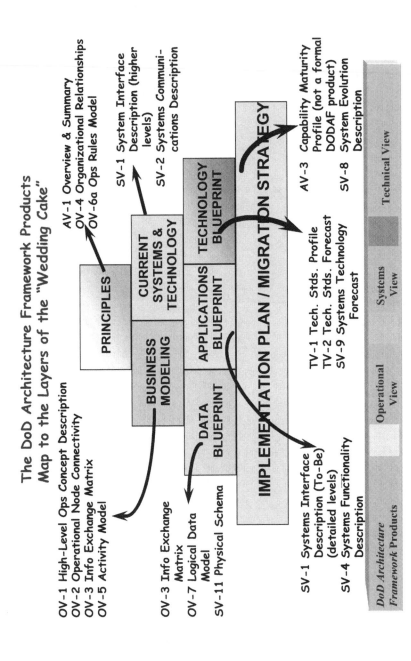

Figure 16. Mapping of DODAF Products to Spewak's "Wedding Cake" Architecture (Sowell 1999)

collection of products (work products) that make up the Implementation Plan and its Migration Strategy. Above this layer there is another layer made up of Data Blueprint, Applications Blueprint, and Technology Blueprint products. Next, riding this layer, there is a third layer made up of the Business Modeling and the Current Systems & Technology products. Finally, at the very top, the fourth layer is made up of a Principles product. Also shown on Figure 16 are Sowell's interpretation of how the various DODAF products map onto Spewak's Framework. For example, DODAF's OV-1, OV-2, OV-3, and OV-5 products map onto Spewak's Business Modeling in the third layer.

13.11. Conclusions

As indicated at the outset of this chapter, the DoD Architecture Framework is the framework used today throughout the numerous US Armed Services (e.g., Air Force, Navy, Army, etc.), and as such it is the largest development effort of its type ever in DoD's history. It involves all the Military Services, it employs thousands of people, and it is funded by the US Congress with millions of taxpayer's dollars year after year. In addition to its mandatory use by DoD, the DODAF is also used voluntarily by other Government Agencies in the US and other countries as well. In the process of reviewing the basic objectives, concepts, products, and implementation of the DODAF we reached several conclusions:

- The DODAF effort is indeed guided by a set of principles and a sequence of steps towards the development of 26 architecture products that populate and describe three architectural views: The Operational View, the Systems View, and the Technical View.

- There are several EA tools in the market today that can be advantageously used to help with the development and documentation of those 26 architecture products. In turn, these EA tools support a wide number of methodologies such as UML, IDEF0, and relational database schema.

- The DODAF is mappable to the Zachman Framework.

- The Federal Enterprise Architecture Framework utilized the DODAF's predecessor, the C4ISR Architecture Framework, as a referenced resource.

- The Federal Enterprise Architecture Framework uses the Zachman Framework as a foundation.

- The Federal Enterprise Architecture Framework divides an architecture into Business Architecture (corresponds to DODAF's Operational view) and Technology Architecture (corresponds to DODAF's Systems view).

- The Federal Enterprise Architecture Framework calls for the description of Standards which corresponds in a general way to DODAF's Technical Standards View.

- The DODAF products readily map into Spewak's four-layer architecture framework.

- The combined 26 DODAF products constitute a major engineering, management, funding, and "knowledge organization" achievement by any standard. Whether this effort can be streamlined, re-structured, and otherwise modified to achieve greater efficiencies (i.e., organizational and economic efficiencies) has not been explored in this chapter, although we like to think that this is a topic for future research.

13.12. Exercises

E13.1 Visit the *DoD Architecture Framework, Version 1.0 website: http://www.defenselink.mil.nii.doc/DODAF*

(a) Describe why it is important to articulate the purpose of your architecture before you begin to build the products.

(b) Give a summary of the Universal Joint Task List (UJTL), its purpose and main elements. (Description located in the DODAF Deskbook).

(c) Discuss why it is important that in a large organization such as the US Department of Defense all architects use the same Framework.

(d) Prepare a 1-2 page summary of Levels of Information Systems Interoperability (LISI) Reference Model (Description located in the DODAF Deskbook).

E13.2 If one considers the fact that the Federal Enterprise Architecture Framework (FEAF) was developed in the Federal Agency Sector and that DODAF was developed by DoD, please comment on the following:

(a) Did these two major architectural development efforts start out independently, when, and who were the main players (e.g., individuals, agencies, organizations, etc.) on each side?

(b) What are the main 2-3 similarities between these two architecture frameworks? Please explain.

(c) What are the main 2-3 differences between these two architecture frameworks? Please explain.

E13.3 Visit the Internet and comment on the role, if any, the General Accounting Office (GAO) played in the assessment (e.g., engineering practices, management practices, investment efficiency, etc) of:

(a) The planning and development of the FEAF-compliant architectures.

(b) The planning and development. of DODAF-compliant architectures.

E13.4 The DODAF's OV-5 Activity Model makes use of IDEF0 models:

(a) What individual or organization first created these diagrams and supporting methodology, when, and for what client? Suggestion: look up this topic in the Internet?

(b) What are the main concepts in the IDEF0 methodology?

(c) You are the new chief architect in Integrated Technologies and Research (iTR), draw the first three IDEF0 diagrams (levels A Minus Zero, A Zero, and the decomposition of each activity on the A Zero diagram) for the process "system requirements analysis". Provide your own definitions of inputs, outputs, and mechanisms.

E13.5 Download an evaluation copy of the **System Architect (SA)** software tool (by Telelogic Inc.) and comment on the following:

(a) Status of implementation of DODAF in this tool, e.g., which products are currently implemented and which ones are still under development (e.g., OV-1, OV-2, TV-2, etc.)

(b) Are other architecture frameworks implemented or being considered for implementation in SA besides DODAF and which are these other architecture frameworks?

(c) Does **SA** have a Unified Modelling Language (UML) modelling capability to support software design representation, and what level of detail is provided (e.g., use case diagrams, activity diagrams, sequence diagrams, etc.)?

Chapter 14

Colombia's SENA Enterprise Architecture:
A First EA Design and Roadmap

14.1. Introduction

In November 2004 our Institute for Enterprise Architectures (IEA) at the University of Mondragon received a request to study the current architecture at Colombia's *Servicio Nacional de Aprendizaje* (SENA), the largest vocational school system in this Latin American country with 124 vocational centers geographically distributed nationwide over its 27 Departments, and to present a first proposal for a modernized architecture. The invitation to IEA came from ALECOP Coop., a local corporation based in Mondragon-Arrasate, Euskadi that specializes in the design and sale of classroom teaching and vocational equipment, with a 10-year history of providing workshop teaching and lab equipment to SENA; ALECOP Coop. is an entity in the group of corporations known as Mondragon Cooperativa Corporacion (MCC), the largest cooperative organization in Euskadi today. A third participant in this proposal effort was TKNIKA, a research center of the Basque Government that lends technical and managerial support to vocational centers in Euskadi. The IEA accepted this opportunity to apply the body of knowledge and experience gained by the EA community over the last 5-8 years, and a first EA design was prepared by the IEA team over the next 6 months in the form of a proposal with recommendations that was presented to SENA in November 2005. The body of the proposal was equally contributed by IEA, ALECOP, and TKNIKA personnel. This chapter is a summary of the work proposed to the SENA to transform and modernize its current enterprise architecture.

14.2. How this Chapter is Organized

This chapter is intended to illustrate main features of an EA proposal to the SENA organization, namely an outline of main sections in the proposal, only. As such, Section 14.3 presents historical background on the creation and development of the SENA organization over the last 50 years in Colombia. A partial list of SENA high-level EA requirements is listed in Section 14.4, while an organizational diagram is presented in Section 14.5 to underscore the vital importance of identifying, recognizing, and involving the community of EA owners and EA users in all phases of an EA program. Finally, Section 14.6 takes the reader through a description of the main features in each one of the four architectural views detailed in this EA proposal to the SENA organization.

14.3. SENA Background

The SENA was created by Act (*Decreto*) 118 of 1957, to establish vocational centers that would produce skilled labor for its growing producing sectors, so that today, half a century later, it is the largest public vocational institution in Colombia with 124 Centers distributed over its 27 Departments, with 200,000 graduates in 2004. The student age range is 14-18 years. Its vocational program includes the following fields:

- Tele-Communications
- Agriculture
- Nursing
- Fishing Industries
- Industrial Technologies
- Hotel Services
- Other

A research and collaboration agreement was signed between SENA and Mondragon Cooperative Corporation (MCC) in 2004 to assist SENA with the modernization of its *Formación Professional* (FP) program (i.e., vocational program) in order to promote the development of curricula in several service areas, including:

- Educational development of new teachers.
- The use of the new technologies of information and communication (TICs) in the classroom and the SENA administration.
- Engineering design, development and application, and
- Business management of its 124 vocational centers.

A partial list of on-going SENA-MCC projects includes:

- *Tecnologia Basica Transversal (TBT) Project:* The application of the TICs to vocational courses across the areas listed above.
- *Diseño y Desarrollo Curricular con base en Competencias Laborale Project:* Design and development of trade capabilities (e.g., agricultural, fishing, and manufacturing skills), and
- *Long Distance Learning (LDL) Project* for SENA teachers.

14.4. Architecture Requirements

The national director of SENA and the Center directors provided a set of high-level architecture requirements to guide the planning of the new architecture:

- R1: The new enterprise architecture (EA) shall serve as a guiding framework, able to guide the creation, planning, and funding of multiple projects; all these projects, when completed, will constitute the new architecture.
- R2: The new EA will serve to promote a rich and diversified set of educational and research activities in engineering, telecommunications, organizational change, law, human resources, inland and coast-line fishing, finance management, agricultural development, and business management.
- R3: The new EA shall support SENA's strategic goal of excellence in vocational teaching and the development of programs that offer skills needed by local industries.
- R4: The new EA shall support the *Red de Centros Integrales de Formacion Professional (FP)* by participating in industry-based skills certification programs.

- R5: The new EA shall be flexible enough to adapt to mandates in local, regional, and national governments and how these mandates may change over time (i.e., funding of SENA's programs by government entities is currently irregular, subject to government appropriations which in turn are determined by government priorities).
- R6: The new EA shall be flexible enough to be able to respond to changes in demand for professionals and sets of skills in industry, agriculture, manufacturing, and fishing.
- R7: The new EA shall improve greatly the organization's ability to consider new technologies offered by the vendor community and make effective purchase decisions that benefit the entire EA and not just a few components (i.e., Centers).
- R8: The new EA shall support SENA's strategic goal of working closely with representatives from sindicatos (labor unions), individual corporations, and professional associations of corporations.

14.5. SENA's Organization and EA Stakeholders

It is recommended that all EA proposal efforts identify and recognize at the outset the EA owners and the EA stakeholders, as shown on Figure 1 for the SENA organization.

14.6. SENA's Proposed Target Architecture

In order to arrive at a design of SENA's target architecture, the Mondragón IEA team was of the opinion that several key elements had to be incorporated into the thinking and planning of the new EA, including:

- The organizational structure of SENA and its Directors – The *owners* of the architecture (Figure 1)
- The number and variety of SENA supporters, i.e., individuals and organizations in the Private Sector and Public Sector that look after the interests of SENA and otherwise benefit from the output of its vocational programs – The architecture *stakeholders* (Figure 1).

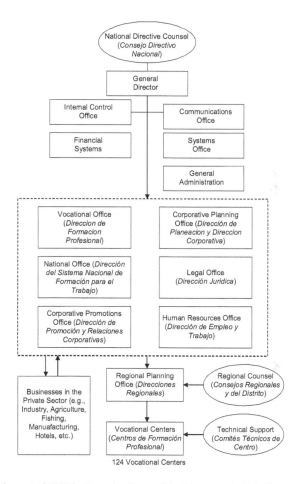

Figure 1. SENA's Organization and Architecture Stakeholders

- Dependency of SENA on regional and national public institutions for funding and general support.
- A migration plan (how to transition from the "old" architecture to the new, target architecture) that would be acceptable to the SENA stockholders.

Owners of the SENA Enterprise Architecture

Key processes involved in the make up and direction of SENA include:

- Regional and National Legislation on Education. SENA is a direct result of enacted legislation and it must respond to changes in the existing legislation.
- Internal politics of SENA. Given that the SENA organization currently has 124 vocational centers geographically distributed over all the 27 Departments in Colombia, a demand for teachers, lab equipment, and teaching supplies that increases each year, and a fixed amount of capital resources available, it is not surprising that SENA directors must work with and respond to many demands for EA services.
- Vision and Strategy of SENA directors. This is an on-going effort to look into future needs of SENA in response to future needs of its constituents over the next 5, 10, and 20 years.
- A model of sustainable growth.

Regional and National Legislation on Education

As noted earlier, since the creation of the the the SENA by the Act 118 of 1957, the SENA must reflect yearly legislative initiatives on education. In this sense the new SENA architecture must be flexible enough to respond to those new initiatives on education.

SENA's Vision and Strategic Plan

The SENA EA Owners are guided by the document *Vision del SENA al 2006*, dated 22 September 2002, where strategic directions are listed:

- Decentralization of some administrative functions, including student enrolment, Center resources management, and local employment of graduated students.
- Delegation of responsibility and authority currently concentrated in the Office of the Director of SENA (*Direccion General del SENA*) to Center Directors.
- Client-oriented educational services so that the skills needed by local industry, agriculture, manufacturing, and fishing are reflected in SENA's programs and curricula.
- Increase the importance and recognition given to Organizational Change (OC) and its management within SENA.
- Improve the organization's ability for self-governance.
- The promotion of strategic alliances with other vocational centers and universities nationwide, including research

cooperation with universities and research centers in other countries.

- Increase the use of the TICs and its efficiency in FP.
- Extend and improve the process of certification of skills *(certificación de competencias laborales)*.

Included in this Vision and Strategy is a concern for sustainable growth of SENA as an architecture, its programs, and output (skilled students that are employable in local industries):

- SENA's architecture and system ought to be grow steadily, evolve with time, and respond to organizational and technological change.
- With regards to digital services and the use of the TICs, these ought to be implemented across the SENA organization, including:
  o Administrative Services
  o Pedagogical Programs and Services
  o Interfaces among projects
  o Technological infrastructure
  o Software architecture, administrative and operational
- Extension programs (*Universidad extendida*) that promote interaction between SENA and corporations in the form of teaching and research agreements, exchange of personnel, visiting professors, and SENA's participation in the launching of new businesses.

Proposed SENA Enterprise Architecture

The IEA team working with SENA representatives over a period of 4-6 weeks felt that it was advantageous to present a first draft of the target EA with diagrams that had the same "look-and-feel" of diagrams shown in earlier chapters, diagrams with which SENA representatives were already familiar. Accordingly, the proposed framework featured four architectural views, as shown on Figure 2:

- A Functional Architectural View
- An Information Architectural View
- An Organization Architectural View, and
- A Technology Infrastructure Architectural View

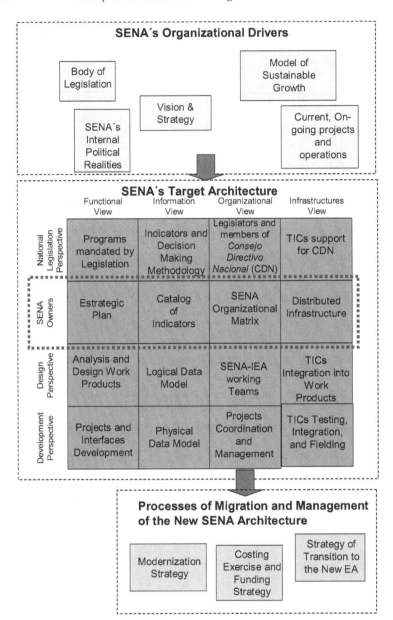

Figure 2. Architectural Views of the Proposed SENA Architecture

On the "Row" side of the EA representation, it was felt that the following perspectives were most relevant:

- National Legislative Perspective
- SENA's Owners' Perspective
- Design Perspective, and

Development Perspective Next, a list of 12 *work products* was proposed to populate the "Rows" and "Columns" of the proposed EA similar to the list of work products in Chapter 19, EA Implementation Strategies. We remind ourselves that what is "inside" each cell in the architecture matrix of Figure 2 is a collection of *work products,* i.e., documents that contain the engineering analyses, diagrams, graphics, procedures, mappings, etc. that would need to be conducted and carried out to produce the design of the target, new SENA architecture.

14.6.1. The Organizational Architectural View

This view gathers and documents information on people (WHO) and legislative framework (WHAT) that have managerial authority and responsibility for the running of SENA. The proposal represented detail at three levels of policy making: (1) at the national level, (2) at the regional (departmental level since Colombia is made up of *Departamentos*, i.e., regional States), and (3) at the vocational center level, as shown on Figure 3.

At the national level, a *Consejo Directivo Nacional* is integrated by educational and political appointees and guided by a National Administrative Policy as it makes decisions on SENA's issues and needs, i.e., registration policy, vocational programs to promote, how fast to grow as an educational and vocational institution, etc. At a regional level, Regional Councils adapt national policy to specific vocational needs, i.e., agriculture, fishing, mining, manufacturing, etc. Finally, the FP Centers implement national and regional policy through the development of curricula, teaching, and vocational how-to-do instruction to all students enrolled in the SENA system.

How are the Vocational Centers themselves to be structured? The IEA Team recommended to align lines of responsibility at the Centers as shown in the organizational matrix of Figure 4. That is, strategic business units such as *Formacion Professional Integral* (FPI), Continuing Education, Innovation, New Businesses Incubation, Employment and Job

Figure 3. SENA's Organizacional View

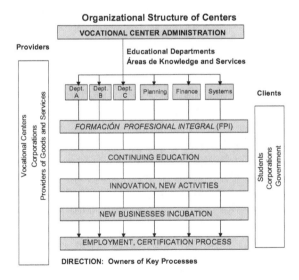

Figure 4. SENA's Organizacional View, Vocational Center Level, *Formación Profesional Integral* (FPI)

Certification Processes to appear horizontally, while the educational Departments (e.g., engineering, information, electrical, etc.), Planning, Finance, and Systems would appear "vertically". In this matrix, then, Departments would implement operational goals created by the strategic business units.

Business Providers are recognized in this organizacional view because they play an important role in the supply of workshop, lab, and educational modules and equipment to the strategic business units and the Departments. Similarly, *Clients* are the corporations that hire SENA students upon graduation and are recognized as essential third parties and players.

14.6.2. The Information Architectural View

Central to the Information View is a list of *indicators of performance* of major components of SENA;s architecture, as shown on Figure 5.

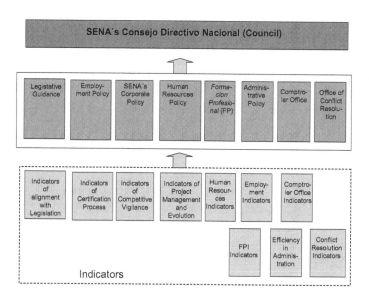

Figure 5. Categories of Indicators in SENA's Information View

As stated earlier, these indicators would be applied to all major SENA functions to measure performance, to monitor alignment with SENA's strategic goals, and to provide decision makers with up-to-date information on resources utilization and operational needs as a basis for effective decision making during construction of the new EA.

14.6.3. The Infrastructures Architectural View

Our IEA team recommended that this view be integrated by two layers of knowledge: (1) a software layer, and (2) a communications hardware layer, as shown on Figure 6 and Figure 7, respectively.

Software Infrastructure Layer

This infrastructure layer is populated by software applications that support all the operational, administrative, and strategic *business systems* (i.e., business activities and processes) within the SENA.

- *Vocational (Formación Profesional Integral, FPI) software Applications.* Within this Business System reside all the applications that support the *Formación Professional Integral* functionality, including curriculum planning, design, prototype testing, fielding and follow through, monitoring and evaluation of courses and programs.
- *Continuing Education Support Applications.* Applications integrated in this business system support all business activities and processes in Continuing Education (i.e., adult education), including course and program certification.
- *Innovation Support Applications.* Applications integrated in this business system support all business activities and processes in applied research and development (applied R&D).
- *New Business Support Applications.* Applications integrated in this business system support all new business activities and processes, including planning and creation of new Centers, student internship initiatives with local businesses and corporations.
- *Job Placement Support Applications.* Applications integrated in this business system support all business activities and processes associated with student job placement in local businesses and corporations.
- *SENA's Administrative Support Applications.* Applications integrated in this business system support all business activities and processes associated with human resources (employment,

employee evaluation, professional development, health, employment retirement benefits, etc.), student financial support, budget planning, and auditing.

- *SENA's Strategic Direccion Applications.* Applications integrated in this business system support all business activities and processes associated SENA's strategic planning function al all three levels: National, Regional, and Centers.
- *Infrastructure Application Systems.* Applications integrated in this business system provide software utility support (e.g., messaging middleware, formatting conversion, software maintenance support, other) for all infrastructure technologies, including local area networks (LAN), routers, servers, firewalls, and database systems.

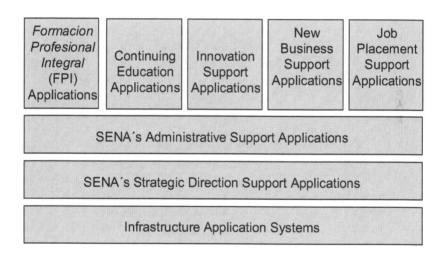

Figure 6. Proposed SENA's Software Infrastructure Layer

Communications Hardware Layer

This layer is integrated by all the hardware pieces that host the software applications, in the categories depicted in Figure 7:

- *Infrastructure Services.* Hardware systems that enable a wide variety of infrastructure services such as video conferencing, audio multi-media streaming, and unit security monitoring (e.g., intrusion detection).

- *LAN.* Local Area Network (LAN) services to provide communication among hardware and software systems within each Center, i.e., intra-center communication.
- *WAN.* Wide Area Network (WAN) services to provide communication among hardware and software systems among Centers, inter-center communication. Figure 8 depicts a generic collection of hardware units (e.g., personal computers, servers, printers, hand-held PC units, firewalls, etc) attached to the backbone of a WAN.
- *Servers.* Servers host the vast majority of software business applications, monitoring tools, and provide directory space for file access and retrieval.
- *Databases.* This layer is to be integrated by a database management system (DBMS) that hosts all databases in the SENA organization. Migration of data currently distributed in 20-30 databases across SENA Centers and headquarter facilities (in Bogotá city) to a single DBMS is a major project proposed by the IAE team.

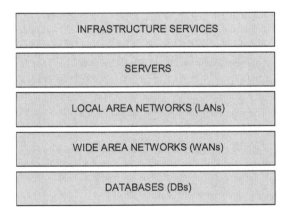

Figure 7. Proposed SENA's Hardware Layer, Infrastructures View

14.6.4. The Functional Architectural View (Business Processes and Systems)

Similar to what we describe on Chapter 3, The Business Process Architectural View, the IEA team met with SENA teachers, engineers, and directors to capture information of the existing business processes and, following the concepts presented in that earlier chapter, went on to propose a re-structuring of business process, as shown on Figure 8.

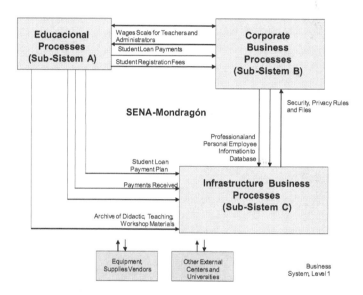

Figure 8. Proposed SENA Functional (Business Processes and Systems) View

We see that the three main categories (i.e., families) of business processes presented earlier in Chapter 3 are able to accommodate the business needs in the SENA organization:

- Educational Business Processes (EBP)
- Corporate Business Processes (CBP), and
- Infrastructure Business Support Processes (IBSP)

The category of Educational Business Processes (EBP) itself is integrated by all those business processes that support educational services in all three levels: National, Regional, and Operational Centers, such as:

- Creation and management of educational programs (e.g., agriculture, fishing, manufacturing, etc.).
- Pedagogical program development and certification processes.
- Management of performance and quality indicators, including their compilation and distribution to Directors at al three SENA levels.

The category of Corporate Business Processes (CBP) itself is integrated by all those business processes that provide and support corporative services, including:

- Human Resources (HR): Employment Benefits, Health, Retirement Benefits, etc.
- Organizational Change (OC)
- Corporate Finances, and
- Liaison with other Universities

Finally, the category of Infrastructure Business Support Processes (IBSP) is integrated by all those business processes that support the technology infrastructure, including:

- Storage and retrieval of data (e.g., student files, corporate files, supply inventory files, etc.).
- LAN and WAN service support.
- Format Conversion (textual and graphical), and

Next, each of the three categories of business processes is "exploded" into its own hierarchy of business processes, as shown on Table 1. Again, as we remember from Chapter 4, The Business Systems Architectural View, this is not an easy task, by any means, and accordingly the IEA team recommended interviews with numerous SENA Center directors, teachers, and administrative personnel in order to identify, first, the existing primary business processes and, second, to identify and propose a number of new business systems so that the new hierarchy of business processes and systems would enable the new SENA architecture to reach the goals and business targets set forth in the updated SENA Vision and Strategy document.

Accordingly, shown on Table 1 is Business System 1.1, Creation and Management of Course Curricula, which is scheduled to appear in the Release 1 (R1) of the SENA Enterprise Architecture (EA) as part of Project PITAGORAS.

Table 1. SENA's Hierarchy of Business Systems

Business Systems		Releases			Project
		R1	R2	R3	
1.	**Formacion Profesional Integral (FPI)**	X			
1.1	Creation and Management of Course Curricula	X			PITAGORAS
1.1.1	Courses, Center Level	X			PITAGORAS
1.1.2	Courses, Regional Level	X			PITAGORAS
1.1.3	Courses Development and Quality Control	X			PITAGORAS
1.2	Quality Control and Certification Systems		X		PITAGORAS
1.2.1	Vendor Supply Systems		X		PITAGORAS
1.2.2	Student Internship Programs		X		PITAGORAS
1.2.3	Community and Local Government Support		X		PITAGORAS
1.3	Indicators Business System		X		PITAGORAS
1.3.1	Vocational, Performance		X		PITAGORAS
1.3.2	Administrative, Regional		X		PITAGORAS
1.3.3	Administrative, Centers		X		PITAGORAS
1.3.4	Relationship with Participating Corporations		X		PITAGORAS
1.4	Professional Development, SENA Employees		X		PITAGORAS
1.4.1	Teachers, Development (training, new tools, etc.)		X		PITAGORAS
1.4.2	Administrators, Development (new training, tools)		X		PITAGORAS
1.4.3	Workers, Development (training, new equip.)		X		PITAGORAS

Similarly, Business System 1.4.1, Teacher Development, is scheduled for Release 2 of the SENA Enterprise Architecture as part of Project PITAGORAS. And so forth.

The proposal ends with a list of 4 projects to be completed during a 1-year Phase I of the proposed EA work intended to achieve specific goals:

- SENA EA Requirements (Work Product, iteration 1)
- SENA Organizational Change (OC) modules and workshops
- SENA Concept of Systems Operations (Work Product)
- SENA Center Management Tool Design (Work Product), and
- SENA Center Pilot Plan (Work Product).

Acknowledgements

The author wishes to thank Osane Lizarralde, Urtzi Markiegi, and Jose Maria Iriarte, University of Mondragon, Iñaki Pagonabarreaga, Angel

Txabarri, Nieves Alcain, and Jesus Rosel of ALECOP Coop., Jose Mari Elola, and Bittor Arias of TKNIKA for their participation and valuable contributions in the design of the proposed SENA architecture and the writing of the actual proposal to the SENA.

Chapter 15

Multiple Criteria for EA Framework Selection and/or Tailoring: Or What is the Best EA Framework for your Customer?

15.1. Introduction

A variety of Enterprise Architecture (EA) frameworks are emerging today in response to an array of needs in organizations in the Federal Agency, Department of Defense (DoD), and the Private Sector. These needs reflect a rich mosaic of institutional settings, congressional mandates, capital availability for public investment, timeframe, complexity of business processes involve, system processing and performance requirements, stakeholder's composition, and system release strategies, to mention a few. To a significant extent, the decision on which EA framework to select will impact the ability to plan for, design, and deliver a successful system to the customer on a timely and cost efficient manner.

The purpose of this chapter is to three-fold: (1) to introduce and briefly describe the variety of EA frameworks available today to the EA planner and designer, (2) to create and present a set of criteria for EA framework selection among a set of well defined frameworks (e.g., Federal Enterprise Architecture Framework (FEAF), The Open Group's Architectural Framework (TOGAF), DoD's Framework, etc.), and (3) to create and present a set of guidelines for tayloring a selected framework to meet specific or unique customer requirements (e.g., limited funding, an accelerated system release strategy, multi-agency institutional setting, other).

In this chapter we also develop a methodological approach to EA selection and/or tailoring that includes criteria identification, determination of relative importance of these criteria (i.e., customer preference elicitation and input from "lessons learned" already available, say, in documents or databases.

15.2. How this Chapter is Organized

As indicated at the Introduction, this chapter reviews and compares a list of most prominent EA frameworks available today to the EA planner. Each EA framework is briefly described in Section 15.3, including a diagram of structural elements, a list of "advantage attributes" and a list of "disadvantage attributes". A definition of a "best EA" is given in Section 15.4. Next, Section 15.5 presents a list of categories of EA knowledge that the EA planner needs to consider in selecting and tailoring a best EA. An EA selection methodology is described in terms of steps to follow to arrive to a best, tailored EA framework in Section 15.6. Finally, Sections 15.7 and 15.8 present a set of conclusions and exercises.

15.3. Alternate Architectural Frameworks

There is a number, granted not a very large number, of Enterprise Architecture (EA) frameworks available to the EA planner and designer. This list of architectural frameworks includes:

- The Zachman Framework
- IBM's Architectural Description Standard (ADS)
- Object Management Group (OMG) Model Driven Architecture (MDA)
- ISO 15704 and GERAM
- The Open Group Architectural Framework (TOGAF)
- Department of Defense C4ISR
- CAP Gemini's Integrated Architecture Framework (IAF), and
- Federal Enterprise Architectural Framework (FEAF)

Accordingly, over the next few pages, we are going to present salient features of each one of these architectural frameworks.

15.3.1. The Zachman EA Framework

As we already learned in Chapter 1, Introduction, Zachman (1987) is among the pioneers of EA work who has described an EA framework as a "simple, logical structure of descriptive representations for identifying models that are the basis for designing the enterprise and for building the enterprise's systems".

The seven columns in Zachman's matrix organize architecture information into the categories of Data, Function, Network, People, Time, and Motivation as shown on Figure 1. The five rows in this matrix organize architecture information into the categories of Planners's View, Owner's View, Designer's View, Builder's View, and Subcontractor's View. For more information visit Zachman's web page: www.zachmanframework.com

Advantage Attributes:

- Zachman's EA framework is relatively easy to understand and communicate.
- Five architectural views only, a relatively small number.
- It has been around for 20 years, more or less, and many planners have heard of it, may be familiar with its shape and form, and know that this framework inspired other EA frameworks.
- Low, reasonable knowledge organization requirements. For more information please see Zachman Institute for Framework Advancement, www.zifa.com

Disadvantage Attributes:

- It provides minor guidance on how artifacts in one view relate to artifacts in another view.
- It does not come with "a kit" that has a list of instructions on which analyses to conduct, no indication of level of detail to gather in each analysis, or set of tools to model business processes.
- There are no documented EA efforts in industry or government that have applied directly Zachman's framework.

15.3.2. Reference Model for Open Distributed Processing (RM-ODP)

The RM-ODP framework defines a framework for architecture specification of large distributed systems, basically, as is depicted in

	Data	Function	Network	People	Time	Motivation
Planner's View	List of Things Important to Business / Entity=Class of Business Thing	List of Processes the Business Performs / Function=Class of Business Process	List of Locations Important to Business / Node=Major Business Location	List of Organizations Important to Business / Agent=Major Org Unit	List of Events Significant to Business / Time=Major Business Event	List of Business Goals/Strategies / End/Means=Major Business Goal/CSF
Owner's View	e.g., Entity Relationship Diagram / Ent=Business Entity Rel=Business Rule	e.g., Function Flow Diagram / Function=Business Process	e.g., Logistics Network / Node=Business Location Link=Business Linkage	e.g., Organization Chart / Agent=Org Unit Work=Work Product	e.g., Master Schedule / Time=Business Event Cycle=Business Cycle	e.g., Business Plan / End=Business Objectives Means=Business Strategy
Designer's View	e.g., Data Model / Entity=Data Entity Relationship=Data Relationship	e.g., Data Flow Diagram / Funct=Appl Function Args=User Views	e.g., Distributed System Architecture / Node=Info Sys Funct Link=Line Char	e.g., Human Interface Architecture / Agent=Role Work=Deliverable	e.g., Processing Structure / Time=System Event Cycle=Processing Cycle	e.g., Knowledge Architecture / End=Criterion Means=Option
Builder's View	e.g., Data Design / Entity=Segment/Row Relationship=Data Pointer/Key	e.g., Structure Chart / Funct=Computer Funct Args=Screen/Device Formats	e.g., System Architecture / Node=Hardware/System Software Link=Line Specification	e.g., Human/Technology Interface / Agent=User Work=Job	e.g., Control Structure / Time=Execute Cycle=Component Cycle	e.g., Knowledge Design / End=Condition Means=Action
Subcontractor's View	e.g., Data Definition Description / Ent=Fields Rel=Addresses	e.g., Program / Funct=Language Stmts Args=Control Blocks	e.g., Network Architecture / Node=Addresses Link=Protocols	e.g., Security Architecture / Agent=Identity Work=Transaction	e.g., Timing Definition / Time=Interrupt Cycle=Machine Cycle	e.g., Knowledge Definition / End=Subcondition Means=Step

Figsure 1. Zachman's Matrix of Architectural Views (Zachman 1987)

Figure 2. It uses the term "viewpoint" instead of "vista" to represent a category of EA knowledge such as *enterprise knowledge, computational knowledge, engineering knowledge, information knowledge,* and *technology knowledge.* It recognizes the importance of modeling as a process in gathering those types of knowledge, the need for composition roles, and the relevance of standards and nomenclatures. The ISO (*International Standards Organization,* www.iso.ch/) and IUT-T (International Telecommunications Union, known as CCITT before, www.itu.int/) have worked together on standardization needs under the heading of ODP (Open Distributed Processing). It is this emphasis on standardization, the ODP believes, that helps create infrastructures within which support for distribution, interoperability, and portability can be integrated successfully (Vallecillo, 2005; Blanc et al., 1999). For more information visit Telematica Instituut, www.telin.nl

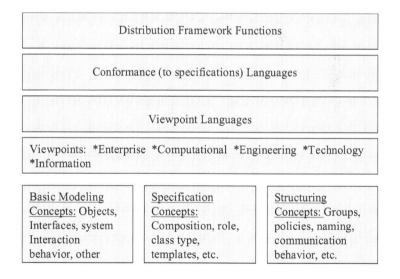

Figure 2. Building Blocks in the RM-ODP Architectural Framework

We want to add that in order to specify the services that ODP objects offer, the standard ISO/IEC 14750(ITU-T X.920) defines a textual language to describe object interfaces, known as the ODP Interface Definition Language (ODP-IDL).

Advantage Attributes:

- The RM-ODP architectural framework is relatively easy to understand and communicate.
- It promotes basic modeling of processes, specification concepts, and naming conventions in the organization of EA knowledge.
- It provides basic instructions on how to model distributed systems in an EA environment or program.
- It provides significant detail for building inter-operability, portability, and distribution capabilities into open, integrated, flexible, secure, and transparent systems.
- Standards-based
- Rich in analytical framework and concepts
- Only five viewpoints to organize EA knowledge
- It lends to treatment by several formal specification techniques, e.g., LOTOS, Estelle, SDL, Z, other.

Disadvantage Attributes:

- The emphasis is on software architecture development, and not so much on enterprise architecture development as a whole. That is to say, software architecture development takes place in one of the 5-8 views of EA planning and design.
- It provides little guidance on how artifacts in one view relate to artifacts in another view.
- Viewpoints limited to IT needs, little guidance for organizational change (OC) issues.
- Business process modeling not a main objective.
- Its structural complexity and high level of abstraction may discourage some people from its effective use in building open distributed systems.

15.3.3. IBM's Architectural Description Standard (ADS)

The International Business Machine (IBM) organization opted for a model that placed an emphasis in functional and operational concerns in its Architectural Description Standards (ADS) as it focuses on business solutions, as illustrated on Figure 3.

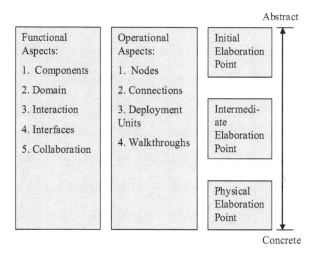

Figure 3. IBM's Architectural Description Standard

This ADS is intended to define a formal metamodel for architecture description based on IBM's best practices and experience in the field that could be understood by a broad range of IT architects (Mc David 1999; Youngs et al., 1999). The business dimension, then, comes out loud and clear in this approach. Several are the themes that have contributed to the technical strategy in this model:

An Architecture Development Language (ADL). A formal language able to describe and relate the various architecture components and concepts, including connections and protocols.

Integration of application development with infrastructure design. A lesson learned in earlier IBM work was that success of major development projects depended critically on the integration of application and infrastructure.

Exploitation of IBM's existing best practices, including:

- WSDDM-OT (Worldside solution design and delivery method-object technology)
- WSDDM-ISD (infrastructure desing), which incorporates the early End Infrastructure Design Method, and
- ESS, a major asset base of IBM reference architecture concepts and methods.

Use of Industry Standards. Since the 1990's the Object Management Group (OMG) was most influential in producing the Unified Modeling Language (UML), and IBM decided to adopt UML (v1.1) as the basis for ADS concepts, terms, and notation. ADS is rich in components and relationship diagrams, where a *component* is defined as a modular unit of software functionality, accessed through object interfaces, and its representation is preferably done via UML notation, concepts, and artifacts.

Advantage Attributes:

- It is based on IBM's rich and successful history of software development methods, lessons learned, and best practices.
- It provides a formal language through the definition of terms, its relationships, and guidance in their application to software engineering needs.
- It makes use of a rich mosaic of industry standards that *architecture work products* must adhere to.
- UML concept-rich environment.
- Software development is prominent.
- It also relies on the creation and application of patterns (or templates) that occur across components and that can be used over and over in many systems to improve efficiency in software development.

Disadvantage Attributes:

- Functional and Operational aspects address IT needs mostly; organizational change and corporate culture needs in an EA are not addressed.
- Representation of business processes is not a very prominent activity in the framework.
- The emphasis is on software architecture development, and not so much on enterprise architecture development as a whole; it does not address the other architectural layers, e.g., databases, business processes, and infrastructure.

15.3.4. The Spewak EA Framework

Enterprise Architecture Planning (EAP), it can be said, is different from the traditional method of systems planning used over the history of business computing, in the sense that the traditional planning approach is "technology driven" whereas EAP is "business driven" (Spewak 1992). Some of us who are familiar with Spewak's book like to think of it as a set of experience-based practical steps to EA planning, with useful checklists, tables to use to gather a list of existing hardware equipment, software applications, and suggested agenda content to carry out meetings among participating engineering and business teams. These are indeed very practical activities that EA owners and planners can follow during the early planning stages. As Figure 4 illustrates, the Spewak framework places at the "top" of its pyramid a set of planning activities and guidelines (Level 1), followed by planning activities that emphasize business modeling and the identification of current systems technology that my be selected to implement the business processes themselves (Level 2). Next is a layer that is responsible for planning activities that support data modeling, applications modeling, and technology studies intended for the To-be enterprise architecture (Level 3). Finally, a set of EA planning activities address EA migration needs and risk mitigation planning (Level 4).

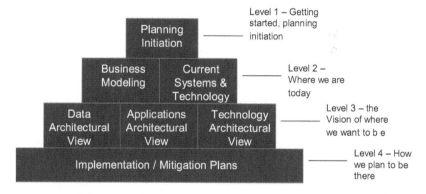

Figure 4. Elements in Spewak's Architectural Framework

Advantage Attributes:

- Practical, down-to-earth approach to EA planning.
- Emphasis is on planning, resource allocation, consensus building, and intended for EA owners mostly who need to come up quickly on the EA learning curve.
- Process-rich approach.

- Ample use of checklists across all 4 levels.
- Many examples of tasks throughout framework to illustrate planning process.

Disadvantage Attributes:

- Minor guidance on how to do EA design.
- Little guidance on how to conduct performance and capacity planning.
- Intended to be of help to EA owners and planners, mostly, with relatively little detail on design, software engineering, and system performance planning.

15.3.5. Generalized Enterprise-Reference Architecture and Methodology (GERAM)

On the European side, there is the Generalized Enterprise Reference Architecture and Methodology (GERAM) model, that opts for an assembly of EA methods and tools, as shown on Figure 5.

The origins of the GERAM framework are to be found in the work of the International Federation of Automatic Control (IFAC) and the International Federation for Information Processing (IFIP) of circa 1990. This joint task force was formed by a group of manufacturing engineers, computer scientists, and information technology managers "to study, compare, and evaluate the different available architectures for enterprise integration which were available in the published, open literature" (Williams, 2005). Among the studied architecture frameworks were:

- CIMOSA: As developed by the AMICE consortium under the ESPRIT Program of the European Community.
- PERA: The Purdue Enterprise Reference Architecture as its associated Purdue methodology, and
- GRAI-GIM: Work and methodology of the GRAI Laboratory of the University of Bordeaux, Bourdeaux, France, under contract work to develop production management systems

Advantage Attributes:

- EA European connection: Adheres to International Standard ISO 15704; makes use of concepts and constructs created earlier in work done on CIMOSA, PERA, and GRAI-GIM programs.

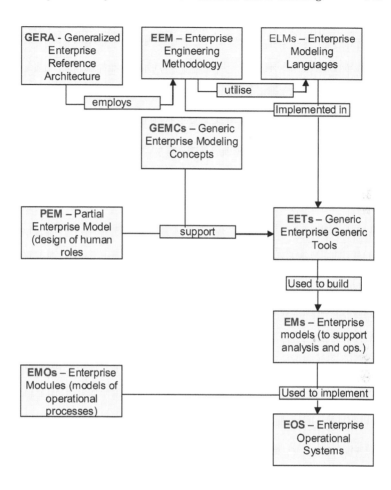

Figure 5. Elements in the GERAM Architectural Framework (Source: GERAM v1.6.3)

- Strong base of concepts and definitions.
- Guidelines for EAs to be considered complete and compliant
- Process-rich approach
- Ample use of checklists across all 4 levels.
- Many examples of tasks throughout framework to illustrate planning process.

Disadvantage Attributes:

- Not well known in the USA.
- Not very well known in the European Union (EU).
- Lessons learned with this EA framework not documented.
- Little guidance on how to conduct performance and capacity planning.
- Does not capture the concept of *multiple views* of an enterprise architecture.

15.3.6. The Open Group Architecture Framework (TOGAF)

We are already familiar with the TOGAF architecture framework presented earlier in Chapter 12 and depicted again in Figure 6.

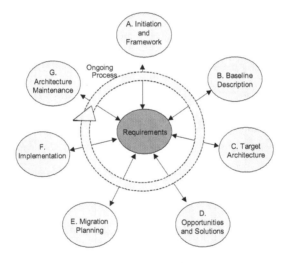

Figure 6. Basic Steps in The Open Architecture Framework (TOGAF)

The Development of The Open Group's Architectural Framework (TOGAF) begins in 1994 "at the instigation of The Open Group's User Council" (Perks and Beveridge, 2003). Originally based on TAFIM already developed by DoD. Basically, Dod gave the Open Group "explicit permission and encouragement to create TOGAF by building on TAFIM"; since then, the Open Group's Architecture Forum has published several versions of TOGAF in the Open Group's public web site http://www.opengroup.org/public/arch/. TOGAF's Architectural Development Method (ADM) organizes knowledge into seven phases: Initiation and Framework (Phase A), Baseline Description (Phase B), Target Architecture (Phase C), etc., as depicted in Figure 6. It is worthwhile noting that the creators of ADM envisioned it to be cyclic in nature, so that completion of one phase proceeds to the beginning and completion on the next logical phase in an ongoing process of discovery, replenishment, and maintenance over time. The scope of TOGAF v8.1 Enterprise Edition features all aspects of EA planning and development.

Advantage Attributes:

- TOGAF evolved from DoD's Technical Architecture Framework for Information Management (TAFIM, circa 1990) and its database of EA lessons learned.
- TOGAF is both a framework and a methodology for architectural development while maintaining many of the desirable elements of TAFIM.
- It has finding application in the Private Sector, even though it got started in the Government Sector.
- Each of the seven phases in the ADM is well delineated in the framework.
- Proponents claim that TOGAF takes less time and $ resources to implement than other EA frameworks.
- It is an industry standard architecture framework that be freely used by any developing enterprise architecture project in the Private Sector.

Disadvantage Attributes:

- Lessons learned with this EA framework are still being documented.
- Costs and benefits of doing TOGAF EA work, and how these compare against those costs and benefits of other EA frameworks are still being documented.

15.3.7. DoD's C4ISR Architectural Framework (DODAF)

Certainly the longest standing architectural framework is the Department of Defense (DoD) model: Command, Control, Communications,

Computers, Intelligence, Surveillance and Reconnaissance (C4ISR) architectural framework, as presented earlier in Chapter 13, An Overview of the C4ISR Framework, and depicted briefly again on Figure 7.

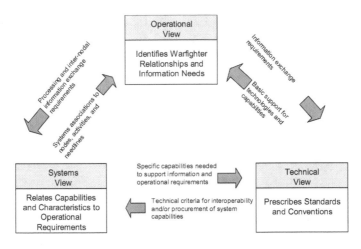

Figure 7. Elements in the C4ISR Architecture Framework

In October 1995 the Deputy Secretary of Defense directed that a DoD-wide effort be conducted "to define and develop better means and processes for ensuring that C4I capabilities meet the needs of warfighters", such as military aircraft, ships, and tank units. Towards that end, an integration task force (ITF) was formed under the direction of the Assistant Secretary of Defense for C4ISR consisting of representatives from the Joint Chiefs of Staff, the military Services, and DoD agencies. In 1998, the DoD mandated the "C4ISR Architecture Framework" for all ongoing and future contracted architectures. This Framework serves as a set of rules and requirements for ensuring that architecture descriptions developed by the Commands, Services, and Agencies are interoperable and can be integrated across Joint and combined organizational boundaries. Organizations wishing to integrate their technology into DoD systems must comply with the requirements of this Framework. They must also understand how to integrate legacy and future C4ISR systems into new C4ISR architectures to meet the DoD's new interoperability mandate.

Advantage Attributes:

- A strong base of EA concepts, definitions, standards, and procedures.
- Certainly the most technically complex EA framework, replete with architectural views, linking to multiple command levels, interfaces to countless military services, and having a most extensive documentation body.
- Guidelines for EAs to be considered complete and compliant
- Process and schematic-rich approach.
- Ample use of checklists across all 3 top views.

Disadvantage Attributes:

- Lessons learned with this EA framework not yet documented
- More guidance is needed on how to conduct "tailoring" to a set of customer needs in the Armed Services.

15.3.8. The Cap Gemini Integrated Architecture Framework (IAF)

The Integrated Architecture Framework (IAF) is also one that comes to us via what I like to call the "European Connection", from Cap Gemini organization in the Netherlands. Its first version appeared in 1996 as it was influenced by the Zachman Framework and Spewak's ideas (Schekkerman 2004). A representation of its structural elements is shown on Figure 8.

IAF	Business	Information	Information-Systems	Technology Infrastructure
Contextual	*What is the context? Description of the Environment*			
Conceptual	*What is required? Description of the challenge*			
Logical	*How can it be realized? A stable design of the system*			
Physical	*With What can it be realized? The possible realization at this moment*			

Figure 8. Elements in Cap Gemini's Integrated Architecture Framework (*Source*: Jaap Schekkerman, 2004)

There are four main areas in the IAF framework:

- Business or Organization: Starting point and expressing of business elements in an enterprise organization; this belief in the critical importance of the business dimension is deep rooted in the framework.
- Information: This elements addresses information needs and flows across functions and units of the enterprise.
- Information-Systems: This element represents equipment, methods, and people teams responsible for the automated support of business processes and functions.
- Technology-Infrastructure: Physical things such as local area networks, servers, databases, etc., are represented by this element.

Also shown on the left-hand column of Figure 8 are the five levels of "concern" addressed in IAF:

- The Contextual level, which describes the context of the organization in terms organization changes to make, where it fits within a larger organization, the scope and depth of the EA program to be undertaken.
- The Conceptual Level, which addresses the Requirements to be met and satisfied by the new/modified architecture.
- The Logical Level, which addresses logical solutions being proposed.
- The Physical Level, addressing instantiations of a best logical solution in the form of products, procedures, and people teams.
- The Transformation Level, describing the impact of changes in the organization on the proposed solutions.

There are some experiences with the use of the IAF, such as the C3I architecture study done for the Royal Netherlands Army (PHIDEF 1997)

Advantage Attributes:

- In the IAF places major emphasis is on business processes and services as these are represented in the modeling of the enterprise architecture, i.e., a SERVICE-BASED architecture.
- It focuses on the interdependency between business and information technology (IT)

- Services classification: IS-Business services, IS-Infrastructure services, and IS-Technical
- A **Private Sector** EA effort, proposed by CAP Gemini Consulting of the Netherlands, Europe.

Disadvantage Attributes:

- Only a few applications of IAF so far.
- Little documentation of lessons learned in IAF projects.

15.3.9. Federal Enterprise Architecture Framework (FEAF)

We are already quite familiar with this very prominent EA framework since we discussed it in detail in Chapters 1 and 2. The FEAF has its origins in the Cohen Act of 1996, the Office of Management and Budget (OMB) Circular A-130, and the Federal Enterprise Architecture Framework (FEAF) of 1999, as illustrated in Figure 9. "Work Products" are identified and described as the bodies of knowledge that make up the enterprise architecture frameworks (EAF), truly substantive, even monumental at times, volumes of text and graphics that document how an EA is supposed to be put together, how parts relate to each other across various architectural views, and how projects and subsystems will be fielded and deployed according to a multi-year schedule.

It is through the FEAF mandate that the USA Federal Government:

- Promotes information sharing across Federal Agencies (e.g., Internal Revenue Service, U.S. Customs, etc.) and associated organizations.
- Encourages the development of enterprise architecture frameworks within the individual Federal Agencies that follow FEAF guidelines (i.e., EA compliance)
- Promotes efficiency in public administrations and improvements in services to citizens (e.g., faster response time to request for service, web-based access to public information, etc.)

In order to assist Federal Agencies in the planning, design, construction, and assessment of their own enterprise architectures, the Office of Management and Budget has designed a set of "reference models" that address needs in several key categories:

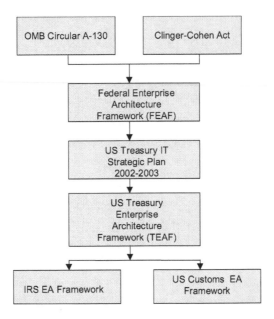

Figure 9. Enterprise Architecture Framework Development in the Federal Sector

- Performance Reference Model (PRM)
- Business Reference Model (BRM)
- Service Reference Model (SRM)
- Data and Information Reference Model (DRM)
- Technical Reference Model (TRM)

Advantage Attributes:

- Achievement of economies of scale by providing services that can be shared across multiple agencies (e.g., IRS, old US Customs)
- Improvement of consistency, accuracy, and timeliness of information technology (IT)-managed resources
- Capture and dissemination of elements in the vision and mission of the organization for effective investment planning and decision making Use of the EA by business planners and owners for purposes of strategic planning, coordination of operations across multiple agencies

Disadvantage Attributes:

- It requires substantial governance oversight.
- It is not clear yet where the economies-of-scale are paying off
- Lessons learned so far point to challenges in EA documentation (sheer volume, other), EA release strategies, false starts, interfacing of multiple EA projects within same EA, other.
- Substantial financing over multi-year EA programs is needed, available to Federal Agencies only.
- Too complex, expensive, and likely unnecessary structure for non-federal, non-government organizations and corporations that, instead, may find more appropriate frameworks in TOGAF, IAF, other.

15.4. A Definition of a Best Enterprise Architecture

Now that we have identified and briefly described the set of most prominent enterprise architecture frameworks available today, how does the EA planner know how to proceed and select the framework that fits best his/her EA needs. Also, even after the planner has identified a "best" framework it may need some adjustments, i.e., some tailoring. In order to do this, we are going to need to define some terms, create a list of criteria, and then use these criteria as we proceed to make some adjustments to the selected EA.

> **An Enterprise Architecture (EA):** *A set of business and engineering artifacts, including text and graphical documentation, that describe and guide the operation of an enterprise-wide **system**, including instructions for its life cycle operation, management, evolution, and maintenance. Specific content of these artifacts can include a vision or mission statement, a set of system requirements, a Business Process Architectural View, a Business Systems Architectural View, a Data Architectural View, an Applications Architectural View, and a Technology Architectural View.*

> **An EA Framework:** *An Enterprise Architecture (EA) framework is a business and engineering recipe (i.e., a blueprint, a set of instructions, a specification) for the construction of an Enterprise Architecture (EA) and its system.*

A definition of a *Best EA Framework*: An EA framework that meets the following criteria:

- <u>Institutional</u>: It supports the Institutional mandate of the Enterprise.
- <u>Corporate Culture</u>: It reflects the Corporate Culture of the Enterprise.
- <u>Representation</u>: It provides strong representation and integration capabilities (e.g., text, graphics, traceability, data repository, import/export, and report generation).
- <u>System Requirements</u>: it supports all functional and performance requirements (i.e., *successful delivery* of the EA framework and system)
- <u>Cost Constraints</u>: Projected implementation costs of the EA and its associated system are equal to or less than initial, budgeted, allocated funding.
- <u>Cost Efficiency</u>: Economics of scale in representation and integration efforts are demonstrable.
- <u>Customer Satisfaction</u>: Users of the EA framework and system are professionally satisfied (i.e., delivery of a *successful EA framework* and system)

15.5. Categories of EA Knowledge

Still, even with a set of well-defined criteria, the task of determining which tailoring adjustments need to be made is difficult and challenging. As Figure 10 illustrates, the EA architect and his/her team need to consider architecture and system requirements, funding available, whether the public administration undergoing EA change must operate under the guidelines of a larger EA framework, a mix of old and new business processes, needs and preferences of EA users, and many more.

15.6. EA Selection Methodology

A suggested approach to EA selection and tailoring calls for the following steps, as illustrated on Figure 11:

<u>Step 1:</u> Identify and define the EA Objectives. This is a critical step often overlooked, and it calls for a listing of EA objectives or high-level EA requirements. Here the Vision and Strategy work product (WP) should guide this listing. Are non-functional (i.e., performance) EA requirements significant in the new EA and system? Is the contemplated EA transformation relatively minor (looking at next 4-6 years only), or it is to be substantial (the next 15-20 years)?

<u>Step 2:</u> Identify and define the Institutional Environment. Here the EA planner searching for a best EA framework must become aware of the institutional setting of the organization, whether it is a Federal Agency, State, or private sector institutional setting. The FEAF, for example, is not likely to be an appropriate framework for a banking organization.

<u>Step 3:</u> Identify EA framework candidates. Here the EA planner would want to become familiar with the varios EA frameworks available, their strong and weak points, as we have begun to do in this chapter.

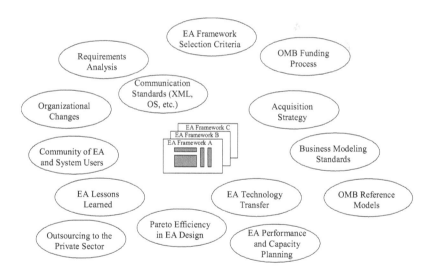

Figure 10. Categories of knowledge that influence EA selection and Tailoring

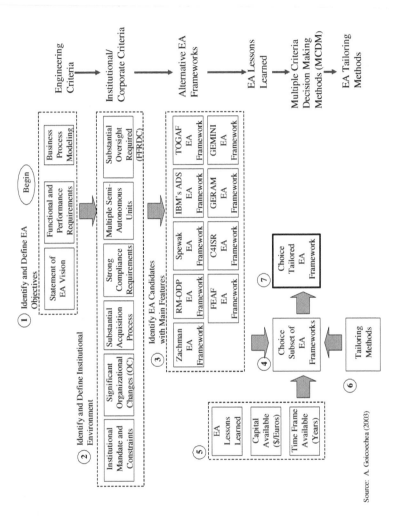

Figure 11. A Methodology for EA Framework Selection and Tailoring

Source: A. Goicoechea (2003)

<u>Step 4:</u> Select a subset of EA frameworks, the Choice Set of EA frameworks. If the organization that is considering modernizing its enterprise architecture is an auto manufacturer (e.g., Ford, Honda, Seat, etc.) then the EA planner may opt for TOGAF, IAF, and GERAM as candidates to consider, for example. From this point on the process concentrates on the pros and cons of this subset of EA frameworks.

<u>Step 5:</u> Selection of the Choice Tailored EA Framework. Inputs to Step 4 can be the experience and lessons learned in the application of EA frameworks in the Choice Set of Frameworks. Capital and time available to carry out an EA program will undoubtedly also be significant factors, so that the Net Present Value (NPV) of a proposed EA can also be included in an economic analysis or business study of an EA. If the EA planner feels that TOGAF reports on earlier EA work appear more readily in the published literature than, say, for earlier work with IAF and GERAM then he may want to select TOGAF as the more appropriate of all EA frameworks (i.e., his best EA framework) to modernize the EA of the auto manufacturer. Multiple Criteria Decision Making (MCDM) methods can assist in this critical step (Goicoechea, Duckstein, and Zionts, 1992; Goicoechea, Hansen, and Duckstein, 1982)

<u>Step 6:</u> Tailoring activities and methods. Tailoring activities generally call for either, cutting off some parts of his choice of a best EA framework (e.g., do away with compliance with interoperability standards as appropriate, only), modifying an EA framework (e.g., reduce the number of work products to 8 only), or introducing a new element (e.g., a new, proprietary information security standard). Today there are no "EA tailoring methods" as such available, instead an EA program relies on experienced EA engineers and architects to recommend tailoring cuts that must be negotiated with EA owners in the interest of balancing cost savings and sound EA design practices.

<u>Step 7:</u> Tailored EA Framework of Choice. Finally, this is the EA framework that has emerged out of this process and that the EA planner now recommends to EA owners as the best EA framework to use to conduct the modernization of an existing architecture.

15.7. Conclussions

- Considerable progress has been made in EA Framework development in the EA community (i.e., DoD and Federal Agencies, also Private Sector).
- Substantial capital has been invested in EA Framework development and implementation in the EA community (i.e., EA modernization projects). Yet, there remains to see published "lessons learned" and lists of costs and benefits associated with the EA programs in this most spectacular development period of 1985-2005 and the next 20 years.
- We are still gathering "lessons learned" in those EA modernization programs, trying to figure out where we are doing things right, where we are not (see Chapter 18, EA Lessons Learned). Need to figure out what these lessons mean in terms of guidelines for tailoring EA frameworks to EA customer needs.
- We know relatively little about which EA Framework "fits" best a particular customer. In order to gain insight here we are going to need to measure and evaluate EA work performed to date. The OMB reference models offer the promise of guiding this EA evaluation effort.
- Should we invest resources to learn how to select a "best EA Framework" from a set of emerging EA Frameworks? We are still trying to figure out how to do this task.
- Should we invest resources to learn how to "tailor" a choice EA Framework to functional, institutional, cost, and timeframe needs of an EA customer? Again, the answer is probably yes, given that this is mainly an ad-hoc process.
- Is there a difference between "a successfully delivered EA framework and system" and a "successful EA framework and system"? Most definitely yes, given that it is over time, after delivery of an EA framework and system, that customer/citizen/user satisfaction will determine success of an EA effort, as the case should be, really.

15.8. Exercises

E15.1 Consider the following multiple criteria decision making (MCDM) method, on Figure E15.1 and comment on its strengths and weaknesses with reference to the EA methodology presented earlier in Section 15.6.

Criteria:	Representation Capabilities of Alternate EA Frameworks				
	EA 1	EA 2	EA 3	•••	EA Z
1. Multiple Views	O O	O	O		O
2. Enterprise Culture	O	O	O O O		O
3. Business Process Modeling	O	O O	O O		
≡					
14. Import/Export Capability	O O O	O	O O		O O

Criteria:	EA Functional Requirement
1. Multiple Views	X X
2. Enterprise Culture	X
3. Business Process Modeling	X X X
≡	
14. Import/Export Capability	X X X

Legend and Weights:

Limited support:	O	Minor Requirement:	X
Good Support:	O O	Strong Requirement:	X X
Strong Support:	O O O	Very Strong Requirement:	X X X

Criteria:	Representation Capabilities of Alternate EA Frameworks				
	EA 1	EA 2	EA 3	•••	EA Z
1. Multiple Views	⊗ ⊗	X ⊗	X ⊗		X ⊗
2. Enterprise Culture	⊗	⊗	O O ⊗		⊗
3. Business Process Modeling	X X ⊗	X ⊗ ⊗	X ⊗ ⊗		X X X
≡					
14. Import/Export Capability	⊗ ⊗ ⊗	X X ⊗	X ⊗ ⊗		X ⊗ ⊗
Total Score	7	5	6		4

Decision Criterion:

EA Framework with largest Total Score is best (e.g., EA-2 has a score of 5 points)

Order EA Frameworks from best to worst score: **Ordering** {EA-1 (best), EA-3, EA-2,…EA-Z (worst)}

Figure E15.1. An Application of a Multiple Criteria Decision Making (MCDM) Method

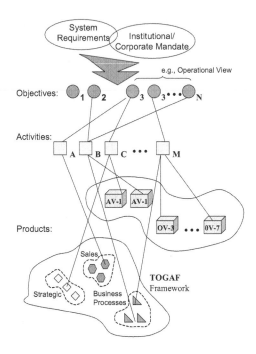

Figure E15.2. An EA Tailoring Approach (*Source*: A. Goikoetxea 2003)

E15.2 Consider the following diagram in Figure E15.2 and set of sub-steps as a candidate "tailoring method" for Step 6 in the EA Methodology of Section 15.6 and propose changes as needed, e.g., place yourself in the role of an EA architect and propose changes and improvements to this tailoring method.

Sub Steps (in Step 6):
1. Convert system requirements and institutional mandate into EA objectives by VIEW or VIEWPOINTS categories (e.g., Operational View, Business View, Technology View, etc.).
2. Identify and define specific EA activities that can support the EA objectives.
3. Map EA activities to subset of "best" architectural view products in candidate EA framework in Choice Subset of EA Frameworks.

4. Repeat steps 1-3 for each candidate EA framework in the Choice Subset.
5. Share findings with recommendations with Customer for a Preferred EA Framework (PEAF).
6. Repeat process as needed.

Chapter 16

Multiple Criteria for Enterprise Architecture (EA) Evaluation and Assessment

16.1. Introduction

While in Chapter 15 we presented a list of prominent EA Frameworks, a list of concepts and a methodology for EA framework selection and tailoring, in this chapter we present a related list of concepts and a methodology for EA evaluation and assessment. That is, in this chapter we ask the questions: Once the EA planner and owner have selected an EA framework and the actual EA work begins, HOW do we know we are going in the right direction as we continue to build the EA, WHY is the EA work to be evaluated (e.g., reporting to GAO, efficiency in project management, other), how is the evolving EA to be evaluated (e.g., questions?, EA indicators? Other?), how often is the EA work evaluated (e.g., every 3 months?, every 6 months? Other?), WHO does the evaluation?, and WHAT is done with the results and findings of this periodic EA evaluation and assessment? These are, then, the main questions that we want to address in this chapter.

16.2. How this Chapter is Organized

A review of the literature on decision models with multiple criteria is presented in Section 16.3. Some uses and benefits of EA indicators are listed in Section 16.4, while OMB's EA indicators are presented in Section 16.5 with special reference to the indicator hierarchy featured in the Performance Reference Model (PRM). Highlights and findings of GAO's five-stage EA maturity model (EAMM) are discussed in Section 16.6, and an extension of this model to cover other two EA dimensions is proposed. Finally a plausible list of market and technology drivers of EA indicators is postulated in Section 16.7

16.3. Literature Review

There is an ample body of literature on the topic of decision making, specifically on decision making using multiple criteria that has appeared in the last 8-10 years. A large variety of Multiple Criteria Decision Making (MCDM) methods have been formulated and applied to problems in problems in engineering and business areas such as transportation, natural resource allocation, financial planning, and business process modeling (Goicoechea (Goikoetxea), Duckstein, and Zionts, 1992). A gamma of MCDM discrete and continuous methods with applications in engineering, business, and government problems have also been published (Goicoechea (Goikoetxea), Hansen, and Duckstein, 1982); MCDM *continuous methods* (Cohon 1978, Steuer 1977; Haimes et al., 1975; Zeleny 1975) are those that make use of decision variables that generally have values in the range $[0, \infty]$, and often use linear programming models to arrive at a *non-dominated solution* (i.e., a vector of values for each one of the decision values in the problem at hand; MCDM discrete methods (are those that make use of decision values that can have only discrete values, such as those in the range $[0, 1, 2, 3, \ldots\infty]$, often use discrete models such as ELECTRE (Duckstein, Bogardi, and Szidarovszki 1979; Roy 1968) and Applied Hierarchical Method (authors of AHP method here! Need to UPDATE this entire list of publications with more recent ones in 2000-2005!) to arrive at a *ranking* of alternative courses of action or designs.

However, only in the last 2-3 years there have been a few publications that address the subject of criteria for the evaluation of enterprise architectures (EA). Hagan (2003) has proposed seven high-level criteria for EA evaluation. It is this latter body of literature that we want to highlight in this chapter.

16.4. The Uses and Benefits of EA Indicators & Metrics in the Enterprise

There are several prominent good reasons for using EA metrics (i.e., EA indicators):

- A starting point for answering fundamental questions and issues being raised by technical and managerial personnel in the EA planning community.
- An awareness of the rearrangement of priorities by EA sponsors in DoD and the Federal Agencies taking place today.
- A list of Lessons Learned in EA representation, design, and assessment that can be leveraged by EA projects in an EA program.
- An elicitation of EA needs, recommendations for mid-course corrections, and views on the role of Federally Funded Research and Development (FFRDC) organizations (e.g., MITRE Corporation, others) in the EA arena – via a survey with multiple choice and commentary.
- A catalyst for Organizational Change (OC) within the enterprise, without which the technological transformation of the Enterprise is not possible.
- A knowledge basis that EA planners can share with EA owners to exchange insight, lessons learned, and views on EA frameworks, design, implementation, and assessment.

16.5. High-Level Criteria for EA Evaluation

Hagan (2003) has proposed seven high-level criteria to apply during the EA creation an use stages, as presented on Table 1.

Although Hagan (2003) does not suggest a *scale of measurement* for these high level criteria, the EA planner and EA owner could apply the *ordinal scale* and use terms such as Poor, *Good, Very Good, and Excellent* to evaluate the EA work products (see Chapter 1 for a list of the various scales of measurement).

Table 1. A Set of High-Level EA Evaluation Criteria
(Source: Adapted from Hagan, 2003)

EA Criteria (Ci)	Description	Comments
C1: Right Target	This criterion asks whether the vision and strategic goals of the EA are being supported as the EA work advances.	The business vision (e.g., implementation of public access to agency data via digital means, quick agency response to citizen's inquiries for data reports, etc.) of the enterprise needs to be reflected accurately in the EA work being carried out.
C2: Well-Engineered	Is the EA being designed to provide desired services to the public in a quick and cost-effective manner?	Some desired qualities include the flexibility to change in response to new drivers, data sharing, security protection, privacy, interoperability, and ability to be upgraded.
C3: Well-Described	Do the EA work products contain the necessary information presented in a useful, readable manner consistent with the chosen framework?	Completeness, consistency, traceability, and readability are important aspects of those products. Additionally, the EA work products should incorporate cross-agency, cross-departmental, state, local, and outsourcing relationships.
C4: Well-Captured	Is the EA captured in such a way that it is available easily, maintainable, can have different elements extracted for selected audiences, and can be analyzed?	The EA should be available electronically, possibly on a web site, and captured with tools such that it can be easily managed and updated. Portions for executive, engineering, contracting, or other audiences should be extractable while conforming to security, privacy, and release concerns.

Table 1. (*Continued*)

EA Criteria (Ci)	Description	Comments
C5: Invest Well	Do the EA work products, including the EA Transition Plan contain enough detail on investments needed to achieve the "To-be" architecture?	To guide investment decisions, the EA must indicate where changes are needed and the dependencies and sequencing among the changes using the Capital Planning and Investment Control Process (CPIC).
C6: Manage Well	Does the EA provide information necessary to manage change, support cost and value assessments, assess the impact of potential changes, and identify risks?	The EA Transition Plan should describe an strategy for addressing project dependencies, field release sequencing, risks and their management. The EA should also support metrics to assess costs and value.
C7: Guide the EA development	Does the EA provide guidance for developers to know what environment they must fit into and the standards they must follow?	The EA, through its standards profile and description of the environment and context into which a new capability must operate, should provide the builder with the necessary 'build to' information.

16.6. OMB's EA Reference Models and EA Indicators

After the last 4-6 years of EA work done in the Private Sector and many of the Federal Agencies, some statistics are beginning to emerge:

- <u>Private Sector</u>: 70% of Global 2000 IT organizations (ITOs) currently have an EA program in place, ranging from EA concept to mature business implementation in an EA solution *(Allega 2003), www.aemes.fi.upm.es*
- <u>Private Sector</u>: Fewer than 5% of ITOs have an EA measurement program in place: *"We are still trying to figure out how to measure the effectiveness of and maturation of the EA process"*

- Federal Agencies: 93 Agencies were surveyed in order to assess progress of EA efforts using multiple criteria distributed over 5 maturation stages (Stage 1 is lowest maturation): *"The average EA management maturity stage for the 96 responses was 1.76 when measured against survey version 1.0 in 2002 of our framework and 1.33 when compared with survey version 1.1 of our framework"* (2003 GAO Report).

The Office of Management and Budget (OMB) has a list of EA attributes to measure, as shown on Figure 1.

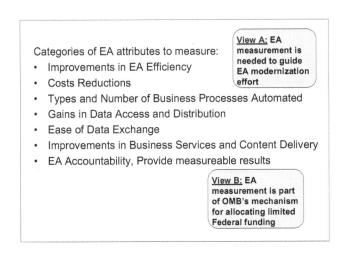

Figure 1. A List of Reasons for Measuring and Assessing Enterprise Architectures

A three-level hierarchy of indicators to measure and assess the various contents of EAs appears prominently in OMB's Performance Reference Model (PRM), as shown on Figure 2. Why EA indicators? One view is that indicators and measurement are needed to assess the level of EA completion and thus guide the EA modernization effort. Another view is that EA measurement is part of OMB's mechanism for allocating limited Federal funding to on-going EA efforts, i.e., get high EA indicator values and get funded for the next phase, otherwise funding for the next phase is not available or it is delayed.

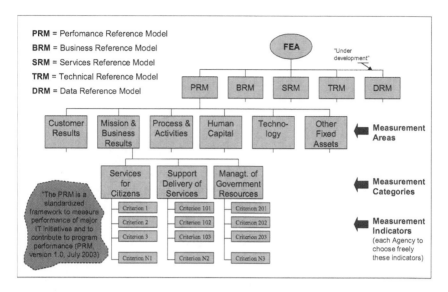

Figure 2. A Hierarchy of EA Indicators (Metrics) proposed by the Office of Management and Budget (OMB)

We use the term *indicator* and *metric* interchangeably to have the same meaning and purpose: *A category, class, or dimension of the enterprise architecture (i.e., work product content) that is to be measured.* Examples of these indicators are shown on Figure 3, e.g., Indicator 2: Average amount of time in months required to review a patent application (for the US Patents Office).

Within this general PRM model, each Agency can choose freely and propose to OMB its own set of indicators and scale of measurement. This approach presents EA project personnel to work with its own Agency operations and executive personnel, as well as OMB personnel, in the identification of EA indicators, their measurement, and assessment towards the achievement of EA goals.

A four-phase EA assessment process has been proposed by OMB, as shown on Figure 4. During Phase I specific areas (e.g., business processes in the Business Processes Architectural View) of the EA are identified and the appropriate indicators are created. During Phase II a gap analysis can be conducted to identify opportunities of EA improvement. It is then during Phase III that actual Ea improvements are implemented and progress towards achieving EA goals is monitored and

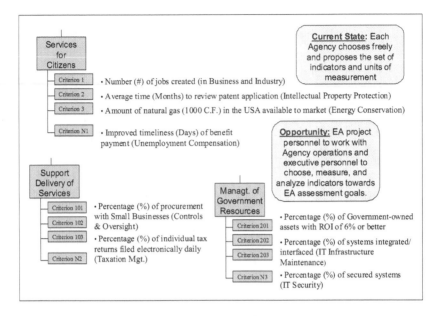

Figure 3. Some Examples of EA Indicators

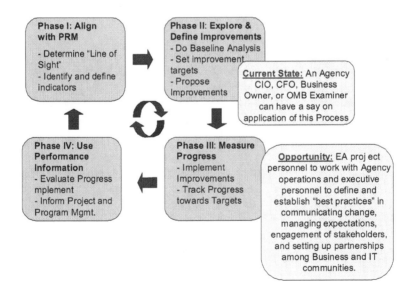

Figure 4. OMB's Proposed Four-Phase High-Level EA Assessment Process (How to use EA Indicators)

documented (i.e., use of indicators before and after implementation of the EA improvements). Finally, during Phase IV the information gathered though the use of indicators is made available to EA management for analysis and decision making.

Money is limited, even in a Federal setting. Accordingly, use of various rationale and funding mechanisms is made by OMB to distribute these limited money resources among competing Federal agencies, as depicted in Figure 5. A rationale can be: *Reward with next level of funding those Agencies that follow guidelines and make progress towards EA compliance, otherwise deny or delay funding.* A resulting policy can the be: Fund EA programs that follow and adhere to EA compliance guidelines. Next, such policy is implemented through the application and use of EA indicators.

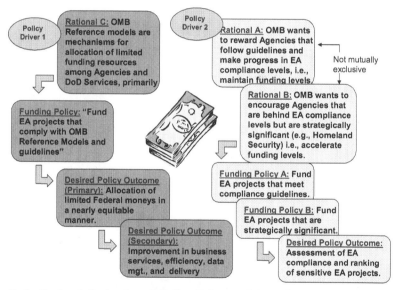

Figure 5. Institutional Rational and Policy Drivers of EA Planning and Funding (WHY EA measurement is needed)

16.7. GAO's EA Maturity Model and Findings

In one of its roles as "watch entity" for the public interest, the General Accounting Office (GAO) conducted in 2003 a survey of some 93

Agencies to ascertain EA progress and practices with three objectives in mind (GAO 2003):

- To determine progress made by Federal Agencies in managing EA maturity.
- To determine effectiveness of its own actions towards promoting EA practices across the Federal Agencies, and
- To Collect information on Agency experiences and practices.

As depicted on Figure 6, a petition was initiated in the US Congress to request GAO to conduct a survey of EA progress and practices across the landscape of Federal Agencies, and eventually a total of 93 of these Agencies participated in this survey.

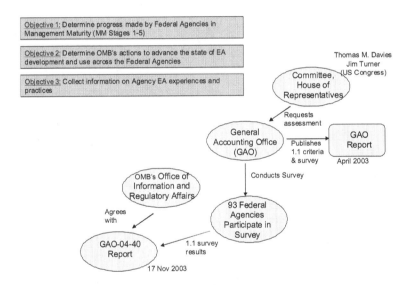

Figure 6. GAO 2003 Report on EA Progress Among Agencies (WHO Drives and Uses EA Metrics/Indicators)

Five stages of EA maturity were envisioned in the GAO model, with Stage 1, Creating EA Awareness, being the stage that represented the most basic EA capabilities and Stage 5, Leveraging the EA for Managing Change, representing the most advanced EA capabilities. Next, within each maturity stage there were 4-6 EA indicators that could be answered with a "Yes" or "No", as depicted in Figure 7. All indicators in one stage had to receive a Yes-response for the EA program in an agency to be considered to have met all EA maturity requirements at that particular stage. In the case of the US Department of Agriculture shown in Figure 7, there were 2 Yes responses and 1 No responses to the indicators in Stage 2; accordingly, this agency did not pass all A criteria for Stage 2 and it is classified as being in Stage 1.

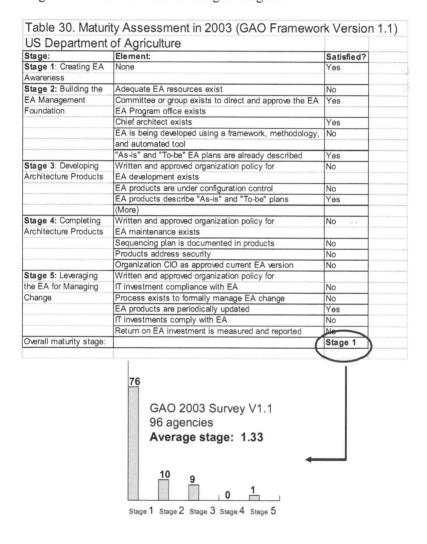

Table 30. Maturity Assessment in 2003 (GAO Framework Version 1.1) US Department of Agriculture		
Stage:	**Element:**	**Satisfied?**
Stage 1: Creating EA Awareness	None	Yes
Stage 2: Building the EA Management Foundation	Adequate EA resources exist	No
	Committee or group exists to direct and approve the EA	Yes
	EA Program office exists	
	Chief architect exists	Yes
	EA is being developed using a framework, methodology, and automated tool	No
	"As-is" and "To-be" EA plans are already described	Yes
Stage 3: Developing Architecture Products	Written and approved organization policy for EA development exists	No
	EA products are under configuration control	No
	EA products describe "As-is" and "To-be" plans	Yes
	(More)	
Stage 4: Completing Architecture Products	Written and approved organization policy for EA maintenance exists	No
	Sequencing plan is documented in products	No
	Products address security	No
	Organization CIO as approved current EA version	No
Stage 5: Leveraging the EA for Managing Change	Written and approved organization policy for	
	IT investment compliance with EA	No
	Process exists to formally manage EA change	No
	EA products are periodically updated	Yes
	IT investments comply with EA	No
	Return on EA investment is measured and reported	No
Overall maturity stage:		Stage 1

76

GAO 2003 Survey V1.1
96 agencies
Average stage: 1.33

10   9   0   1

Stage 1   Stage 2   Stage 3   Stage 4   Stage 5

Figure 7. Findings of GAO EA Maturity Model 2003 Survey

Of the 93 Federal Agencies that participated in this GAO survey 76 agencies were classified as being in Stage 1, 10 agencies as being in Stage 2, 9 agencies as being in Stage 3, none as being in Stage 4, and 5 agencies as being in Stage 5, thus yielding an average stage value of 1.33.

16.8. A Proposed Extension of the GAO EA Maturity Model

It is possible to build an EA that achieves all management maturity (MM) stages, yet it does not work, that is the EA lacks in performance and scalability, for example. Similarly, it is possible to build an EA that achieves all MM stages, yet business excellence is not achieved. Accordingly, it would make sense to extend the current GAO model to one has three dimensions as shown on Figure 8:

- Dimension 1: Management Maturity (Current GAO Model)
- Dimension 2: Performance Engineering and Efficiency (new)
- Dimension 3: Governance, Integration, and Use (new)

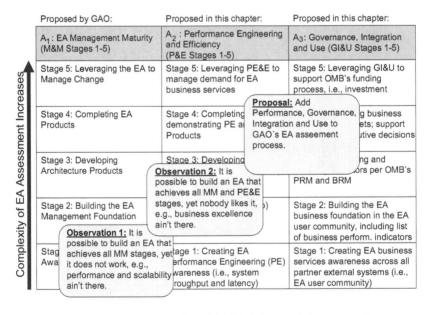

Figure 8. Proposed Extension of GAO's 5-Stage EA Assessment Process

These three dimensions of an EA Program can now be envisioned as shown in Figure 9. Seen this way, we may deduce there is yet a "long road ahead" in the task of completing a thorough and balanced survey of the state-of-the-art of EA work done in the Federal agencies.

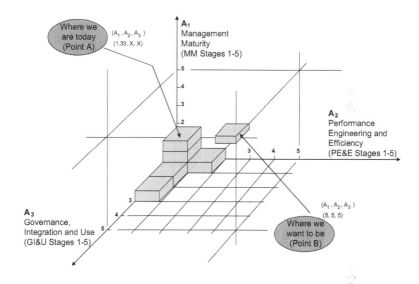

Figure 9. A Proposal for a 3-Dimensional EA Indicator/Metric Space

16.9. Global Market and Technology Drivers of EA Measurement Needs

Our national priorities and perceptions of what is important in EA content may also change over time, as suggested in Figure 10, and the nature of indicators will likely change accordingly, i.e., number and types of EA indicators need to evolve over time.

New paradigms in business services will likely call for new technologies (e.g., Customer Relationship Management, CRM). Agencies are beginning to shift from heavy systems purchase and acquisition to purchasing of business services.

Portions of the customer base (US population) may bypass certain government services and do business with business entities in the Private Sector (e.g., switch from US postal services to private, non-federal express mail services), etc. If so, and based on these business and

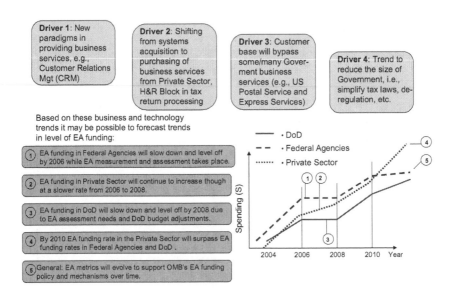

Figure 10. Market and Technology Drivers of EA Planning & Funding (WHY EA Indicator/Metrics are evolving)

technology trends, it may be possible to forecast trends in the level of EA funding to anticipate in the following 4-6 years:

- Funding of Federal Agencies will slow down and level off by 2006-2008 while EA assessment takes place.
- Funding in the Private Sector will continue to increase through 2006-2010.
- By 2010 EA funding in the Private Sector will surpass EA funding in the Federal Agencies, and
- EA metrics will evolve over time in order to support OMB's changes in funding policies.

16.10. An EA Compliance Checklist

The Federal Chief Information Officer Council (CIOC 2001) has issued guidelines to insure that all Federal Agencies comply with the Clinger-Cohen Act (CCA). See Chapter 19, EA Implementation Strategies for an example of an *EA compliance checklist.*

16.11. Conclusions

- The urgency for measurement and assessment of EA efforts in a setting of limited Federal Agenciy (mainly) and DoD spending is now more apparent than ever before.
- The average level of effort in EA management maturity across 96 Federal Agencies is only 1.33, on a scale of 1-to-5 (2003 GAO report).
- OMB's Performance Reference Model (PRM) is a realistic basis and framework for the definition of EA measurement indicators that could support PE&E and GIU metrics.
- EA measurement and assessment is primarily part of an OMB mechanism for allocating funding. OMB's policy is to distribute limited EA funding across Agencies and DoD. Federally Funded Research and Development Center (FFRDC) organizations can become an increasingly important instrument of this policy through internal organizational change (OC) and focused support of EA planning, design, and assessment.
- FFRDC organizations play an increasingly significant role in advising Federal Agencies and DoD on how to leverage EA growth in the Private Sector towards improving efficiency in their own EA efforts.
- Likely, the "lessons learned" in the course of applying EA indicators in the public sector (i.e., Federal, State, and Regional public offices) and the government sector (i.e., Armed Services) will spill out and gain application in EA needs in the private sector (i.e., auto industry, airline industry, banks, hospitals, schools, etc.)
- EA indicators will evolve over time in order to reflect OMB's evolving funding policies and GAO's perception of what is important in EA program content and development in the Federal Agencies.

Chapter 17

e-Business, e-Government, e-Commerce, and Digital Administration

17.1. Introduction

Almost everyone now days is talking, it seems, about e-Government, e-Business, e-Learning, e-Democracy, e-Commerce, ... and the list goes on. Almost every business activity wants to have the letter *e* (for *electronic*) as a prefix to that business activity as if to communicate a new approach to doing business with implied economic and technological advantage. If so, why, where, when to do it, when not to do *e-Something*, what are the business and economic advantages, the costs, what does this paradigm mean about efficiency, how does it relate to the new technologies of information and communication (TICs), how does it relate to enterprise architectures (EA), how does it relate to digital administration (DA), who is doing it, and who is paying for it? These are some of the questions that we will be trying to address in this chapter.

Enterprise Architecture (EA) planning, design, and implementation is about making two things happen: (1) technological change, and (2) organizational change (OC). Technological change in turn is about the use of the technologies of the information and communication (TICs); in this sense, this chapter is about taking a closer look at some of the technologies presented and discussed in earlier chapters. Likewise, the entire book is about digital administration given that a functional enterprise architecture is a requirement for efficient and effective digital administration, be it in the Federal Agencies or in the Private Sector.

17.2. How this Chapter is Organized

A list of benefits and expectations for improved business activity are seen as the drivers of electronic technologies, is noted in Section 17.3. A partial list of the new technologies is presented in Section 17.4, while a list of TIC-supported services is given in Section 17.5. A distribution of TIC-supported transactions in e-Government is shown in Section 17.6, followed by highlights of a Parliament-sponsored study and survey on the use of the new technologies to promote citizen participation and e-Democracy values in Section 17.7. Also, the basic components in a technology architecture for e-Commerce are listed in Section 17.8. Finally, an *Appendix* is included with a brief description of some of the new, electronic technologies.

17.3. Drivers of e-Something

Regardless of the business domain in mind (e.g., commerce, health services, military, government, democratic processes, etc.) there are a number of objectives and expected results that are common to the owners of business establishments, government centers, and citizen organizations (Rajput 2000):

- To Increase the size of its customer base.
- To attain competitive advantage.
- To align with new/improved customer relationship management (CRM) strategies.
- To process more transactions per unit of time (e.g., hour, day, or month).
- To do things faster.
- To provide customers with the means to participate (customer empowerment).
- To do business more efficiently.
- To reduce costs (in Government) or increase the return on the investment (ROI) in business

A provider of health services (e.g., a hospital or clinic) may want to have its own e-Business unit or contract with an e-Business provider to improve processing of patient insurance forms. Patients arriving to a hospital to obtain health services provide data (e.g., name, date of birth, name of insurance company, purpose of visit, etc.), this data is entered into a form directly on the screen of a computer by a trained clerk, information on health services provided are entered into the form, next the form is sent to the insurance company, and shortly thereafter the hospital receives payment for health services provided. The business transaction between the hospital and the insurance company can now completed within a matter of minutes or hours, not days or weeks. In principle this is how e-health is supposed to work, and often it does.

17.4. The New Technologies of Information and Communication (TICs)

In parallel with the advent of the Enterprise Architectures (EAs) over the last 8-10 years we are all witnessing the birth and application of a large number of technologies commonly referred to as the *new communication and information technologies* (CITs) or new technologies of the information and communication (TICs, as are known in Spanish-speaking countries). In this section we present and highlight a list of the more prominent CITs, in alphabetical order (adapted from Rios Insua, 2004 and Rajput 2000):

Content search, formatting, and delivery media:
- Advanced Streaming Format (ASF)
- Channel Definition Format (CDF)
- Cryptography and security
- Dynamic Hypertext Markup Language (DHTML)
- e-mail (electronic mail)
- Extensible Markup Language (XML)
- Extensible Style Language (XSL)
- Graphics Interchange Format (GIF)
- Hypertext Markup Language (HTML)
- Joint Photographic Experts Group (JPEG)
- Local Area Network (LAN)
- Internet
- Interactive digital television (IDTV)
- Moving Pictures Expert Group (MPEG)
- Musical Instrument Digital Interface (MIDI)
- Open Software Description (OSD)
- Quick Time
- Radio
- Resource Description Framework (RDF)

- Search Engines
- Standard Generalized Markup Language (SGML)
- Synchronized Multimedia Integration Language (SMIL)
- Virtual Reality Modeling Language (VRML)
- Waveform Audio File Format (WAVE)
- Wireless Markup Language (WML)
- Wireless Telephone, and
- Wireless Application Protocol (WAP)

Types of content
- Audio files
- Interactive content
- Text in plain files and databases
- Streaming audio files
- Streaming video files
- Stored images in databases, and

For a brief, introductory definition of these technologies please see *Appendix* in this chapter.

17.5. TIC-Supported Services

If we think of the types of services that these technologies can support, then we can include the following areas of TIC-supported services:

e-Commerce Area:
Content Delivery:
- Database applications
- Web hosting
- Webcasting

Content handling:
- Appliance applications
- Terminal emulators
- Internet browsers
- Media players

Semantic Content:
- Area
- area

e-Democracy Area:
- On-line registration of citizens
- Electronic voting
- On-line voting
- Real-time transmission of debates
- Queries to databases
- Posting on documents, other information on the Web
- On-line group decision making
- On-line lobbying
- On-line initiatives presented by citizens
- Electronic surveys
- Forums for citizen participation
- Electronic campaigning

e-Government area:
- Income tax-return filing
- Electronic voting
- Property tax collection
- (more)

See a brief description of each TIC in *Appendix*. For more details it is recommended that the reader simply place a "search" in the internet with the acronym for the TIC of interest, e.g., ASF: Advanced Streaming Format.

17.6. e-Government

Some definitions of e-Government include: "The use of the TICs by the government to modernize the State", and "the of the TICs to facilitate/promote citizen participation in democratic processes and a dialogue between Government and Society".

Some of the published works discuss and document how digital, on-line services are impacting democratic processes, including citizen participation in the legislative processes and decision making (Rios Insua, 2004; Goikoetxea and Lizarralde, 2004). A distribution of types of TIC-assisted transactions conducted in Spain in 2002-2004, for example, is shown on Figure 1.

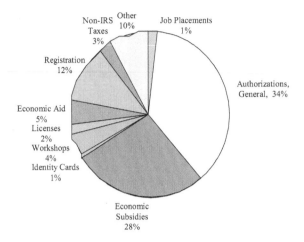

Figure 1. Distribution of Types of TIC-assisted Transactions in e-Government in Spain (*Source*: Adapted from Rios Insua, 2004)

17. 7. e-Democracy

The new Technologies of Information and communications (TICs) offer opportunities today that were unthinkable only a decade ago. These opportunities are now available to individuals and organizations in the Public Sector (e.g., Parliaments, City Halls, Health, Transportation, Public Services, etc.) and the Private Sector (e.g., labor and trade organizations, banks, corporations, small businesses, etc.) to facilitate and expand the dialogue between citizens and their representatives in government, as depicted in Figure 2. Today more than ever before, the TICs (e.g., e-mail, mobil phones, FAX, video, teleconferencing, electronic signature, digital imaging, etc.) can enable citizen-based, non-profit organizations such as invigorate that dialogue to help promote the values and principles of e-Democracy.

In a study sponsored by CALRE, the organization of presidents of Parliaments and Regions with legislative authority in the European Union (EU), and the Basque Government, a team lead by the University of Mondragon (Goikoetxea and Lizarralde 2004, Martinez et al., 2005) identified values and principles of e-Democracy as follows:

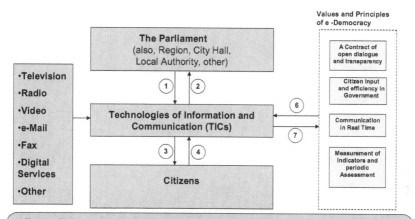

Figure 2. An Interactive e-Democracy Model (*Source*: Martinez et al. 2005)

- e-Democracy is the exercise of democratic processes and activities in the dialogue between a Parliament and its Citizens (I.e., Society) that aspire to a condition of social, economic, and political well-being, a condition that is actively promoted by the application of the Technologies of Information and Communication (TICs) – *Values of e-Democracy*
- e-Democracy aspires to provide the means of information and comunication (TICs), processes of dialogue, norms and stardards of behavior between a Parliament and its Society – *Technologies and processes of communication in real time (RT).*
- e-Democracia is dedicated to the proposition that a Parliament is responsible for its decisions and actions to its own Society, and that this Society wishes and asks for an open, complete, and transparent rendition of all facts and events associated with those decisions and actions, included the use of all resources in that Parliament – *A contract of dialogue and transparency between a Parliament and its Citizens.*
- e-Democracy aspires to the promotion of transparency, the discovery of all financial transactions (i.e., total accountability),

efficiency, and the attainment of maximum impact of resources on proposed solutions, as well as the incorporation of these aspirations as inputs to the decision making process – *Citizen input, efficiency, and maximum impact on the workings of a Parliament (i.e., values of interaction), and*

- e-Democracy is dedicated to the measurement and monitoring of these values of interaction between a Parliament and its Citizens as these values are promoted and amplified by the TICs, as well as the publishing of these statistics of performance within regular time intervals (e.g., every 2 years) – *Measurement and reporting of results on schedule.*

Similarly, objectives of e-Democracy were determined to be as follows:

- To facilitate the access by Citizens of all documents on political debates and initiatives within its Parliament and, whenever possible, all other complementary documents produced during the research, processing, storage, and retrieval of related data (e.g., sources of information) – *Transparency*
- To promote the creation of means of electronic communication to amplify the dialogue between a Parliament and its Citizens, including individuals, groups of individuals, labor and professional organizations – *Citizen participation*

A main objective of the study itself was to create a set of 35-40 indicators of e-Democracy that could measure the impact of the new digital technologies (i.e., digital administration) towards the promotion of the values and objectives of e-Democracy outlined above. Shown on Table 1 is one such indicator in the area of citizen participation.

Families of indicators in this study were as follows:

Family 1. Culture of Participation (Institutional Participation)

Training/Education/Formation: Indicators in this sub-family are intended to capture information on education and training activities offered to citizens by the Institution on the topics of democratic values and the technologies of information and communication (TICS).

Promotion: Indicators in this sub-family are intended to capture information on activities that promote democratic values and practices, as well as the use of the TICs.

Table 1. Indicator 26: Digital Services – Variety of Citizen Participation Activites

NAME	Digital Services – Variety of Citizen Participation Activites
DEFINITION	The objective of this indicator is to assess the variety of citizen participation activities.
OWNER	Team Mondragon Unibersitatea (MU)
SOURCE	Office of Administrative e-Democracy Services
INDICATOR with METHOD OF COMPUTATON (Indicator Format)	Select the option that best describes information feedback from citizens back to the Institution: 1. Currently we have a list of e-mail addresses of legislators and administrative e-Democracy services personnel available to citizens. 2. In addition to a list of e-mail addresses of legislators and administrative e-Democracy services personnel, citizens can subscribe to parliamentarian initiatives of interest. 3. In addition to a list of e-mail addresses of legislators and administrative e-Democracy services personnel and subscription to parliamentarian initiatives of interest, citizens can also ask questions and make recommendations to their representatives in the Institution. 4. In addition to a list of e-mail addresses of legislators and administrative e-Democracy services personnel and subscription to parliamentarian initiatives of interest, asking questions and making recommendations to their representatives in the Institution, citizens also have access to a weekly calendar of Institution/Parliament events. 5. In addition to a list of e-mail addresses of legislators and administrative e-Democracy services personnel and subscription to parliamentarian initiatives of interest, asking questions and making recommendations to their representatives in the Institution, and a weekly calendar of Institution/Parliament events, surveys are conducted by the Institution to assess degree of citizen satisfaction regarding the use of the TICs, variety and quality of information exchanged between the Institution and its citizens.

Table 2. Indicator 14: Organization– Institutional Infrastructure and e-Democracy Digital Services

NOMBRE	Organization – Institutional Infrastructure and e-Democracy Digital Services
DEFINITION	With this indicator it is of interest to determine the extent of the use of digital signature as method of authentication in transactions between an Institution and its citizens.
OWNER	Team Mondragón Unibersitatea (MU)
SOURCE	Chief Information Officer (CIO)
INDICATOR with METHOD OF COMPUTATON (Indicator Format)	Select state of availability of authentication and digital signature in support of the TICs: 1. Digital signature is not available at this Institution. 2. Digital signature is utilized internally, within the Institution, as a means to enable the institution to certify authenticity of internal users. 3. Digital signature is utilized externally to support e-Democracy services, including certification of authenticity of external users (i.e., the user is who he/she says he/she is). 4. Digital signature is utilized internally and externally to support e-Democracy services, including certification of authenticity of users (i.e., the user is who he/she says he/she is).

Family 2. Government Transparency

Accessibility: Indicators in this sub-family are intended to capture information on the accessibility of services made available to citizens, including detail on design of activities, languages, and technologies used to communicate these services.

Organization: Indicators in this sub-family are intended to capture information on changes in the internal organization and administration of an institution, including operating rules and procedures, resulting from the implementation and use of the TICs, as well as training of personnel to bring about these changes.

Proactivity: Indicators in this sub-family are intended to capture information on the nature, quality, and formatting of procedures that citizens can use to access documents within the Institution, including surveys conducted to measure level of citizen satisfaction in the course of accessing those documents.

Family 3. Citizen Participation

> *Services that Promote Citizen Participation:* Indicators in this sub-family are intended to capture information on the various types of activities that promote citizen participation through digital communication means, including the evaluation of frequency of these means, levels of privacy, user authentication and certification.
>
> *Efficiency of Services:* Indicators in this sub-family are intended to capture information on the efficiency of digital services that promote citizen participation and the measures of efficiency utilized.
>
> *Citizen Satisfaction:* Indicators in this sub-family are intended to capture information on the level of satisfaction achieved by citizens in the use of digital services designed and implemented to promote citizen participation.

Next, the indicators are loaded into IT4ALL, a web-based tool created by Robotiker Inc. and funded by *Sociedad para la Promocion y Reconversion Industrial* (SPRI) of the Basque government, depicted in Figures 3 and 4. A total of 74 Parliaments and Regions with legislative capabilities in the European Union (EU) are currently participating in this survey on their use of new technologies to provide digital services to citizens.

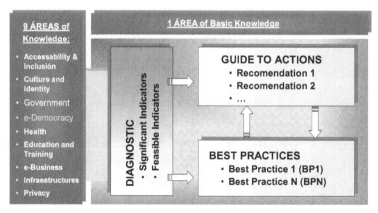

The IT4ALL tool facilitates the Diagnostic Activity

Figure 3. Basic architecture of the Web-based Tool IT4ALL (Courtesy of SPRI, Tecnalia Inc., and Robotiker Inc.)

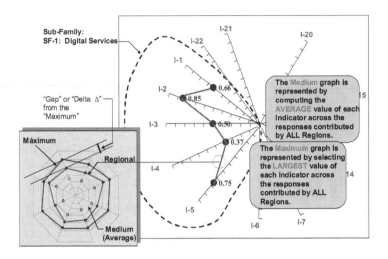

Figure 4. Representation of e-Democracy Indicators in the IT4ALL tool for Auto-Diagnosis by participating Parliaments and Regional Local Authorities

17. 8. A Systems Technology Architecture for e-Commerce

Technology use patterns in the area of e-Commerce are beginning to appear. Rajput (2000) has noted that a systems technology architecture for e-Commerce makes use of four levels of organization, as shown on Figure 5.

A first level, *Enterprise Technology Infrastructure*, houses Web portals, Internet Directory Services (IDS), signature certificates, and payment infrastructure components in order to provide data access services, and transaction processing services. A second level, *Electronic Computing Networks*, is made up of Internet resources, paging network resources, and data communication services; this level, then, provides the transport layer. A third level, *e-Commerce Information Appliances*, is represented by the more recent technologies of hand-held PCs, cell phones, pagers, and web TV; these technologies provide a system-user interface. Finally, a fourth level, *e-Commerce Business Domains*, addresses business partners, customer base, and internal staff; this layer, then, represents people either as customers and consumers of services or engineers and computer personnel working as service providers.

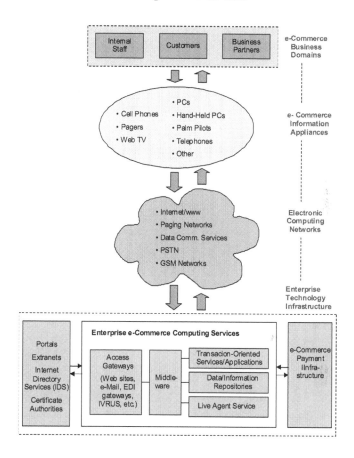

Figure 5. A Systems Technology Architecture for e-Commerce (*Source*: Rajput 2000)

17.9. Who is Paying for the New Technologies

The general public is paying for the new technologies. Federal, State, and Local government organizations are providing web-based services to citizens. Small businesses, medium-size companies, and large corporations are implementing the new technologies of information and communication (TICs) all across their enterprise architectures (small or large) in order to improve business processes and gain a competitive edge. The cost of these technological and organizational improvements are covered by additional taxes collected from citizens, or by added product costs collected from buyers of goods and services. The expectation is that benefits resulting from the use of these new technologies are greater than the costs of implementing these new technologies.

Acknowledgements

The author wishes to thank Juan Mari Atutxa, ex-President of the Basque Parliament, Izascun Bilbao, President of the Basque Parliament, Rut Martinez, Representative for European Affairs, and Jon Goikolea, ex-Chief of Cabinet of the Basque Parliament for giving Mondragon Unibersitatea (MU) the opportunity to provide technical support to their e-Democracy survey and study. From the beginning Rut and Jon provided the vision, the requirements, the institutional detail and structure needed to guide this project sponsored by the Basque Parliament. Very special thanks to all members of the Working Group integrated by representatives from various Parliaments and Regions in the European Union who have contributed most valuable suggestions on the content and form of the indicators throughout Phases 1 and 2. Very important, thanks also to Osane Lizarralde, Urtzi Markiegi, Dr. Silbia Sarasola, Dr. Luxio Ugarte, Dr. Aitor Oyarbide, Unai Elorza, and Itziar Perez, all members of the MU technical team who contributed their expertise and counsel to the development of the indicators in areas of law, citizen participation, organizational change management, security and privacy. Our thanks to Xabier Abaroa, Pablo Ruiz, Virginia Castaños, and Marta Mencia from Tecnalia Technology Corporation for providing comments and encouragement to multiple drafts of the list of indicators, to José Ignacio Zudaire and Juanjo Duque of SPRI and Leandro Ardanza and Josu Ocáriz of CIFAL-Bilbao for allowing the MU to participate in the IT4ALL plan and process. Last but not least, also, thanks to Ignacio Oliveri, Rector of MU, Javier Retegi, Jose Mari Aizega, Mila Belategi, Sabin Fernandez, Txema Perez, and Iñaki Lakarra at MU for their institutional support and encouragement throughout this project and study.

Appendix

Advanced Streaming Format (ASF): This technology is Microsoft's proprietary digital wrapper for "streaming" (high volume processing) of audio and video material. Its format does not require that the audio and video that it is about to process be specified, and instead it requires to know the specification of the material, thus allowing ASF files to be encoded in basically any audio/video format. ASF format is based on objects which can be considered to be byte-sequences that can contain metadata on the artist, title, album and genre for an audio track, or the director of a video track.

Channel Definition Format (CDF): An open specification that permits a Web publisher to offer frequently updated collections of information or channels from any web server for automatic delivery to compatible receiver programs on PCs or other information appliances. Automatic here means that the user need only choose the channel one time and, thereafter, scheduled deliveries of information to that user will occur without further intervention. Standard Web server means that any web server that uses the HTTP 1.0 protocol, o a later one, can broadcast channels. "Compatible" means that any program that implements processing and retrieving content as specified by the CDF format. CDF is actually an application of the Extensible Markup Language (XML) that contains various elements including Channel, Item, UserSchedule, Schedule, Logo, Tracking, and CategoryDef.

Joint Bi-Level Image experts Group (JBIG): This technology is used to compress data, i.e., to store large amounts of data in a relatively small physical area. It is used for the compression of bi-level images. It can also be used for coding greyscale and colour images with limited numbers of bits per pixel. It can be seen as a form of facsimile encoding, similar to Group 3 or Group 4 fax, offering between 20 and 80% improvement in compression over these methods (about 20 to one over the original uncompressed digital bit map). Direction for this technology comes from a group of experts nominated by national standards bodies and major companies to work to produce standards for bi-level image coding. The 'joint' refers to its status as a committee working on both ISO and ITU-T standards. The 'official' title of the committee is ISO/IEC JTC1 SC29 Working Group 1, and is responsible for both JPEG and JBIG standards (see http://www.jpeg.org).

Joint Photographic Experts Group (JPEG): This technology makes possible compressing images (up to 20% plus). The original standard for digital images (IS 10918-1, popularly referred to as JPEG) was developed 15 years ago, and with the major increase in computer technology since them, and lots of research, it was felt to be time for a new standard capable of handling many more aspects than simply making the digital image files as small as possible. JPEG 2000 uses 'wavelet' technology. and as well as being better at compressing images (up to 20 per cent plus), it can allow an image to be retained without any distortion or loss (see http://www.jpeg.org).

Interactive/Digital Television (iDTV): In contrast to analogue television, digital television encodes sound and video in bytes making possible more channels and better picture quality to the user. There are several ways in which digital television can arrive to a home or company, including via satellite, cable, and terrestrial. Government agencies use this TIC to get information out to the general public, but it also allows the general public to interface with those government agencies, thus making this technology "interactive". "For those that don't know Integrated Digital TV's (IDTV's) are TV's that have a built in OnDigital tuner instead (or as well as) the usual analogue terrestrial tuner" (see http://www.bbc.co.uk/digital/questions/idtv.shtml).

Moving Picture Experts Group (MPEG): MPEG (pronounced M-peg), stands for Moving Picture Experts Group, is the name of family of standards used for coding audio-visual information (e.g., movies, video, music) in a digital compressed format. The major advantage of MPEG compared to other video and audio coding formats is that MPEG files are much smaller for the same quality. This technology provides interoperability means among audio/visual content used in the digital media and on the air. Interoperability means that the user can be sure he/she can use the content and not be bugged with incompatible formats, code, metadata, and other paramenters. MPEG is a committee of ISO/IEC that is open to participants from industry and the general public that want to create an interoperable multimedia infrastructure (see http://www.mpeg.org).

The Open Software Description Format (OSD): A primary medium for the distribution of software used to be the magnetic floppy disk. Individuals and companies used "floppies" to transfer software from one computer platform to another. More recently, compact discs (CDs) have become the choice medium to transfer software because of their digital nature and capacity to store large amounts of data. The OSD specification allows the rapid flow of software from a server to other computer platforms making use of metadata in the form of directed graphs that describe software interdependencies. Developed by Marimba and Microsoft, it builds on XML technology to describe, deliver ("push"), and install software components through the Web, as opposed to the user having to download ("pull") the software to his/her platform (see http://www.opensource.org/docs/definition_plain.phprm).

Standard Generalized Markup Language (SGML): This technology was originally designed to enable the sharing of machine-readable documents in large projects in government, legal, and the aerospace industry, which need to remain readable for several decades. It has also been used extensively in the printing and publishing industries, but its complexity has prevented its widespread application for small-scale general-purpose use. Both SGML and XML are "meta" languages because they are used for defining markup languages which have a specific vocabulary (labels for language elements and their attributes) and a declared syntax (grammar defining a hierarchy of language elements). Conceived in the 1970s, the SGML gave birth to XML, published as a W3C Recommendation in 1998 (SGML, ISO 8879: 1986). See http://en.wikipedia.org/wiki/SGML.

Synchronized Multimedia Integration Language (SMIL): SMIL (pronounced smile) stands for Synchronized Multimedia Integration Language. It is a markup language (like HTML) and it is designed to be easy to learn and deploy on Web sites. SMIL was created specifically to solve the problems of coordinating the display of a variety of media (multimedia) on Web sites. By using a single time line for all of the media on a page their display can be properly time coordinated and synchronized. Developed by the World Wide Web Consortium and released on June 15th 1998 (see http://smw.internet.com/smil).

Virtual Reality Modeling Language (VRML). A computer language that can be used to describe 3-D objects in an environment where the user can "interact" and participate. A most common way to display, show, browse, play, or view VRML files, models, or worlds (.wrl file extension) is with a free VRML plugin, also known as a browser, player, viewer, reader, add-on, client, toolkit, program, software, or ActiveX control. The user can download and install a VRML plugin in his/her web browser. VRML is the Virtual Reality Modeling Language, a standard method to display 3D models on the web (http://cic.nist.gov/vrml).

Waveform Audio File Format (WAVE). A format for storing audio data on a computer system. There are many file formats for storing audio files (see http://ccrma.stanford.edu).

Wireless Markup Language (WML). An XML language used to specify content and user interface for WAP devices. WML is supported by almost every mobile phone browser around the world (see http://sbc.webopedia.com/TERM/W/WML.html).

Wireless Application Protocol (WAP). This technology supports development of Web-based applications that run over wireless networks. It is the leading global open standard for applications over wireless networks. WAP provides a uniform technology platform with consistent content formats for delivering Internet and Intranet based information and services to digital mobile phones and other wireless devices.(see devices below for more information) The purpose of WAP is to enable easy, fast delivery of relevant information and services to mobile users (see http://www.webopedia.com/TERM/W/WAP.html).

Chapter 18

Lessons Learned in EA Planning, Design, and Development

18.1. Introduction

After the last 6-8 years of EA planning, design, and development in the Federal Agencies, mostly, there are a number of *lessons learned* across the EA user community, but it is still too early to have a full catalog of all experiences and their distillation into "what to do in EA work" and "what not to do in EA work" recommendations or best practices. Also, the experience of EA planners and designers varies from one EA program to another and, therefore, it is realized that the lessons learned do reflect specific qualities of its own "EA institutional setting" (e.g., Federal Agency, US Air Force, a financial organization in the Private Sector).

18. 2. How this Chapter is Organized

The main feature and contribution of this chapter is a list of EA lessons learned, presented in Section 18.3, EA Lessons Learned. Short and Sweet.

18.3. EA Lessons Learned

As we might have anticipated, there is a large number of things that can go wrong or wry at each stage of EA planning, design, and development. Conversely, we can say, there are many things that can go well if EA planners exercise caution, experience, and do make use of those lessons learned. One collection of lessons learned is shown on Table 1 Kauzlarich 2004).

Table 1. Lessons Learned in EA Planning, Design, and Development
(Source: Kauzlarich 2004)

Lesson Learned	Description	Comment on Potential Causes or Circumstances	EA Phase
1	EA Resources needed to support multiple, parallel activities often are not in place.	EA scope is too broad and complex. Too many parallel projects or activities.	All phases: Planning, Design, Development, Testing, and Release
2	Release strategy did not address pressures from user community to deliver functionality in the field early in the game.	The "chunks" of EA functionality to be delivered are too big and require long periods of development (e.g., 1-3 years). Need to plan to deliver smaller "chunks" of EA functionality, say every 6 months.	Release
3	Lack of integration among EA program components.	One contractor does component A (e.g., project, or activity within a project) and another contractor does component B, but these two contractors are not coordinating their effort well. Result: Deadlines are not met.	Planning and Design
4	PRIME Contractor not playing role of systems integrator.	Lack of clarity about roles of EA Owners and PRIME Contractor. EA Owners needs to be more explicit on the "what to do", vs. PRIME Contractor to address the "how to do." The Systems Engineering (SE) function is not well represented in EA program.	Planning, Design

Table 1. (*Continued*)

Lesson Learned	Description	Comment on Potential Causes or Circumstances	EA Phase
5	EA Owner(s) did not engage 3rd party (FFRDC) effectively.	Role of Federally Funded Research and Development (FFRDC) organization participating in EA program not well defined or understood by EA Owners. FFRDC organization's effectiveness is limited.	
6	Lacking of requirements validation and management process.	"Creeping" of requirements not controlled, and validation of requirements is postponed to later EA phases. Need to baseline requirements early in the EA effort; need to control "creeping, and not let it grow out of hand.	All EA phases.
7	Role of Systems Engineering Office (SEO/EA) not understood by all participants.	The role of the SEO/EA as systems engineering integrator, holder of EA standards, and entity for making final EA decisions may take months to be understood. Meantime, decisions that need to be made do not happen.	Planning
8	Poor management and coordination of 4-8 contractors in EA effort.	EA Program Management Office (EA Owner side) slow in coordinating effort with office of PRIME. Pressure to start EA work effort.	

Table 1. (*Continued*)

Lesson Learned	Description	Comment on Potential Causes or Circumstances	EA Phase
9	Delays in validation of the Applications Architecture (AA) design slows EA effort.	Applications Architecture changes several times, e.g., switch to Object-Oriented applications development and environment in the "middle" of the design. Decision to opt for a rules-based AA "late" in the design phase.	Design
10	Delays in validation of physical infrastructure design.	Change from 2-tier to a 3-tier computer architecture.	Design
11	Contract vehicle: *Cost Plus* contract does not yield project closure.	Type of contract is crucial in EA program success. The perception (by EA Owners) can be that with Cost Plus contract the Contractor will be in "no rush" to complete work, and that Contractor will ask for more money/time than initially agreed.	All phases
12	Lack of control points/gating	Long sequence of EA milestones not adequately planned, monitored, and controlled. Some EA milestones must occur within certain time windows otherwise EA program will experience major delays and not meet expectations of EA Stakeholders.	All phases

Table 1. (*Continued*)

Lesson Learned	Description	Comment on Potential Causes or Circumstances	EA Phase
13	Lack of EA Performance and Capacity Planning can delay delivery of a successful EA.	A perception on the part of some EA Owners and Planners that "EA performance" is something that involves "fine tuning of things" only and can left until the very end of the EA program. A perception on the part of some EA owners that EA performance planning can subtract resources and delay implementation (e.g., software development) of EA functionality.	All EA phases
14	Uncoordinated procurement process (e.g., purchase of software, hardware, other) can delay milestone delivery.	Different projects may opt for the same, common, software product but while management on one project approves purchase, management on the other project hesitates and lengthens process. Worse, yet, management in one project buys equipment without consulting with management in other projects. Budget utilization is poor.	Development, Testing, Implementation, Fielding

Table 1. (*Continued*)

Lesson Learned	Description	Comment on Potential Causes or Circumstances	EA Phase
15	Cost and Schedule slipping can delay EA milestone delivery.	Project scheduling needs to be realistic and reflect "project dependencies". There will be individual project schedules and then there is the need for a "master schedule" across the entire EA effort. Need to manage and control "project dependencies" at the project level and at the EA program level (e.g., SEO).	All phases
16	Need to watch, monitor, and provide for quality of "deliverables".	An EA quality team that looks after the accuracy, completeness, and readability of the content of the various *work product documents* is missing. EA Owners want and appreciate quality in the "deliverables", and will not sign off (i.e., not approve system design baselines) otherwise.	All phases
17	Get buy-in from "above" and buy-in from "below" in the EA Organization.	EA planners need to have friends on all echelons of the EA organization, as well as in the EA user community (i.e., external systems personnel)	All phases

Table 1. (*Continued*)

Lesson Learned	Description	Comment on Potential Causes or Circumstances	EA Phase
18	Balance the EA teams with Business and IT personnel. Also, make use of personnel with deep experience in the EA organiztion (known as Subject Matter Experts os SMEs).	SMEs are a very valuable resource because they know well the business processes of the "As-is" EA and can lend valuable support to the integration of new business processes and technologies.	All phases
19	Plan the institutionalization of the EA program in the EA organization	As soon as possible, create an EA office (EAO), an Enterprise Systems Engineering Board (ESEB), and get appointed a Chief Enterprise Architect within the EA organization and one Chief Enterprise Architect on the PRIME contractor organization.	All phases
20	Concentrate EA effort and resources on the "To-be" EA business processes before attempting to bring in any technologies.	As the GAO has pointed out on repeated occasions (see Chapters 4 and 16), EA efforts go stray when the EA teams underestimate and skip critical definition steps in the Business Processes Architectural View and they jump too quick into buying technology products and services.	All phases

18. 4. Conclusiones

Applying the wisdom and experience of "EA lessons learned" can mean the difference between a successful EA program and one that is bloated with schedule problems, faulty coordination of effort across projects, dissatisfaction in the EA user community, and costly project overruns. Technological transformation of the EA goes hand-in-hand with the organizational change (OC) of the EA. One needs and depends on the other.

Chapter 19

EA Implementation, Compliance, and Governance Strategies: A Road Map to EA Success

19.1. Introduction

After having presented and discussed a large variety of EA concepts, methodologies, standards, institutional issues, and technology challenges in earlier chapters, this chapter is about how to build a successful Enterprise Architecture (EA). It is about "lining up all the ducks" so that the institutional side of the picture, the business side, the engineering side, and the financial side are all addressed as a necessary condition to be met prior to and during the actual construction of the EA.

As discussed in earlier chapters, business, industry, and government organizations have communicated a clear and marked desire to arrive at both business and technical solutions that address the entire enterprise, not just a part of it. In fact, these business process and business systems drive these architecture design efforts today,

19.2. How this Chapter is Organized

This chapter is about "lining up all the ducks" so that all resources that need to be available and in place are so as the EA program is about to get started and, once it gets started it stays in due course. Section 19.3 presents a list of success factors for building EAs, while Section 19.4 is about the engineering side of EA building, including a list of work products to gather and the formation of an Enterprise Systems Engineering Board (ESEB) to guide and coordinate the EA building process. An example of a "checklist" of organizational change (OC) tasks is presented in Section 19.5, while an example of a checklist of EA compliance requirements is presented in Section 19.7. The vital importance of EA Governance and securing support from the EA stakeholder community are highlighted in sections 19.6 and 19.8 respectively.

19.3. Success Factors in Building an EA

As we have seen throughout the earlier chapters, building an enterprise architecture is a complex, lengthy, can-be-costly, and dynamic endeavor requiring a lot of planning and resources. There are five main "success factors" to consider:

- EA Engineering
- Organizational Change (OC)
- Institutional EA Governance
- EA Compliance
- Securing Support from your EA Stakeholders Community

19.4. EA Engineering, How to Do it Right

Generally, an existing enterprise architecture is large and complex, consisting of many sub-systems, often geographically distributed, and requiring many teams of peoples with a large variety of skills and operating procedures. Also, the "To-be", new architecture will generally be large and complex. Accordingly, then, one strategy is to "break down" the "To-be" architecture into several EA projects, say 4-6 EA projects, i.e., "devide and conquer" approach. If so, what rationale do we employ to identify and constitute those EA projects? We begin by grouping business systems by "business affinity" so that eventually each grouping of business systems is constituted into an EA project.

Grouping of Business Systems and Allocation to Projects

Because of the very fact that enterprise architectures are very large and can involve 200-400 business systems, often more, the need exists to "break" an architecture into smaller pieces that are subsequently constituted as "projects" to be built by a community of contractors, as Figure 1 depicts. Although the current state-of-the-art, does make use of experience and sound engineering practices, there is not a well-defined, repeatable, and efficient basis or rationale for architectural decomposition and allocation to projects. A rationale, however, is needed to guide the determination of the number of decomposition levels N1 in an architecture, i.e., should an architecture have 2, 3, 4, or more levels of decomposition?; should "children" business systems have one "parent"

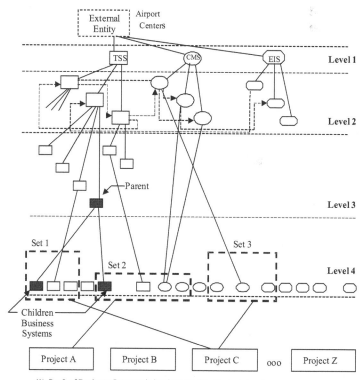

(1) Set 2 of Business Systems is implemented by Project A only.

(2) Set 1 and Set 3 of Business Systems are implemented by Project C only.

(3) At the lowest level (Level 4 in illustration above) business systems to be implemented by a project are not implemented by another project.

(4) However, at the next higher level, Level 3, we can see that a "Parent" business system is implemented in part by Project A and in part by Project C.

Figure 1. Breaking the "To-be" Enterprise Architecture into Multiple EA Projects

business system only (i.e., hierarchical relationship) or more than one parent (i.e., cyclic graph)?; and what criteria to use in breaking an enterprise architecture of business systems into multiple, inter-dependent projects (e.g., do the break up as to end up with the smallest number of interfaces possible, other criteria)? These are some of the questions addressed by EA planners within a central coordinating body often called the Enterprise Architecture Office (EAO) or the Enterprise Systems Engineering Board (ESEB).

Enterprise Systems Engineering Board (ESEB)

With multiple on-going EA projects there is the need for a coordinating body such as an Enterprise Systems Engineering Board (ESEB). Such board has responsibility and authority (derived from the EA Owners) for the following:

- To determine of EA standards (e.g., computer languages, communication protocols, interface types, database types, EA tools, etc.) to be adopted in the EA program.
- To enforce application of EA standards throughout all EA projects, including issuing of "EA standards waivers" when special needs justify such waiver and non-adherence to EA standards on a project-by-project basis.
- To approval or disapprove of sub-system designs proposed by project management.
- To guide the EA program towards the design, development, and documentation, of the "To-be", new Enterprise Architecture.
- To insure that each EA project is guided by the completed new Enterprise Architecture.
- To promote implementation of an Organizational Change (OC) Plan throughout the EA program, and
- To provide for and enforce a Systems Engineering Program that adheres to a Quality Control Plan (QCP) so that coordination among technical teams across the various EA projects takes place observing systems engineering (SE) best practices.

An initial, recommended checklist of EA engineering tasks is shown on Table 1.

Table 1. A suggested Checklist of Engineering Tasks in EA Work

Engineering/ OC Task	Description	EA Phase
1	Set up an Enterprise Systems Engineering Board (ESEB) made up of a representative from each EA project, plus one chair person named by the EA Owners.	All EA Phases: Planning, Design, Development, Testing, and Release
2	Set up an EA Requirements Team (EAT), consisting of 2-4 people, depending of EA resources available.	Planning mainly, but all other phases as well
3	Set up an EA Business Systems Team (EABT)	Planning, and Design
4	Set up an EA Applications Team (EABT)	Planning, and Design
5	Set up an EA Database Team (EADT)	All phases
6	Set up an EA Infrastructure Team (EAIT)	All phases
7	Set up a Release and EA Transition Team (EATT)	Development, Testing, and Release
8	Allocate engineering and management personnel to each EA project	All phases
9	Set up a Calendar of EA Milestones for all EA phases, including completion dates for all EA Work Products	All phases
10	Prepare and approve (by ESEB) list of Work Products to be completed	Planning, Design
11	Prepare and approve (to baseline) EA Requirements work product (document)	All phases
12	Prepare and approve table of contents for the work product: Vision and Strategy Architectural View (interviews of EA owners to be conducted)	Planning, Design
13	Prepare and approve table of contents for the work product: Business Systems Architectural View (interviews of EA owners and management personnel to be conducted to gather information of current business systems)	Planning, Design

Table 1. (*Continued*)

Engineering/ OC Task	Description	EA Phase
14	Prepare and approve table of contents for the work product: Applications Architectural View	Planning, Design
15	Prepare and approve table of contents for the work product: Database Architectural View	Planning, Design
16	Prepare and approve table of contents for the work product: Infrastructure Architectural View	Planning, Design

19.5. Organizational Change (OC)

Anyone who has actually participated in doing EA work realizes the vital importance of Organizational Change (OC) activities in the success of an EA program. Table 2 presents an initial list of OC activities.

Table 2. A suggested Checklist of Organizational Change (OC) Tasks in EA Work

OC Task	Description	EA Phase
1	Set up an Organizational Change (OC) Team (OCT), consisting of 3-4 people	All EA Phases: Planning, Design, Development, Testing, and Release
2	Insure the participation of an OC representative in the Enterprise Systems Engineering Board (ESEB) made up of a representative from each EA project, plus one chair person named by the EA Owners.	All EA Phases
3	Prepare a list of OC activities and gain its approval (and funding) by the ESEB.	Planning mainly, but all other phases as well

Table 2. (*Continued*)

OC Task	Description	EA Phase
4	Assign an OC representative to each EA project, and coordinate OC activities with the ESEB.	All phases
5	Insure all OC activities and milestones are included and documented in the EA work products; OC team to negotiate with the ESEB those sections with OC content in the EA work products.	All phases
6	Prepare OC modules on EA objectives, new engineering and management roles, new operating procedures, new training, etc., and coordinate with ESEB their distribution and use in the projects.	All EA phases
7	Set up EA Certification Program within the EA Program and secure its approval in the ESEB	All EA phases
8	Identify all persons and organizations in the "EA Stakeholders Community" (EASC) and document their use of and interests in the success of the new EA; coordinate all OC activities with the ESEB and the EASC.	All EA phases

19.6 Institutional EA Governance

This EA success factor makes reference to the fact that every Federal Agency must follow the guidance of its own institutional setting, i.e., the Federal Enterprise Architecture Framework (FEAF), as discussed earlier in Chapters 1 and 2. In the case of EA work done outside the Federal Agency sector, as is the case with EA work done in the Private Sector, such institutional setting does not apply and instead guidance under TOGAF (see Chapter 12) and the Object Management Group (OMG) is the appropriate direction to follow.

19.7. EA Compliance

The Federal Chief Information Officer Council (CIO 2001) has issued guidelines to insure that all Federal Agencies comply with the Clinger-Cohen Act (CCA), including:

- Description of the purpose and value of an EA.
- Description of the relationship of an EA to public investment, enterprise engineering, capital planning (CAP), and program management.
- Translation of the Agency's vision-and-strategy document into EA goals, objectives, and strategies.
- Establishment of an Enterprise Architecture Program.
- Management Office (EAPMO) within the Agency.
- Appointment of an EA Chief Architect.
- Identification of EA Compliance Criteria and their satisfaction as a basis for new and future public investment.

An example of a checklist of EA Compliance requirements is presented on Table 3.

19.8. Securing Support from your EA Stakeholders Community

The most successful EA programs are those that engage their own "EA user community" in the planning and building of the EA. As noted above in Section 19.5, Organizational Change (OC), the OC team provides a most essential service in the early identification of the often 10-15 groups of individual users and communities that are either integral components of the EA (e.g., EA centers geographically distributed in cities and States), external EA users (e.g., other Federal Agencies), and EA providers (e.g., software and hardware providers). All these EA users represent the "EA stakeholders Community". Interviews with members of this community are carried out, recommendations for EA requirements are gathered, and EA stakeholders meetings are held regularly (3-4 times a year) to report EA progress and to seek continued comment and feedback from these valuable EA stakeholders.

Table 3. A suggested Checklist of EA Compliance Requirements in doing EA Work

Compliance Rqmt.	Description	Evidence of Compliance	Project Signature	ESEB Signature	BSMO Signature
1	**Does the Project satisfy the EA Business Systems Definition?**				
1.1	**Scope:** Are all relevant EA Business components addressed in this EA Project? • Business Systems Assignments to Projects (as in Chapter 4) • Interface Assignments to Projects Business Direction Model • Business Systems Definitions	Project Management Plan	Signed	Signed	Signed
1.2	**EA Allocated Baseline:** Does the project implement all allocated EA Business and Technical Model requirements? • Process Thread Performance Model • Enterprise Conceptual Data Model • Data Management Framework	EA System Requirements Report Data Conversion Plan			

Table 3. (*Continued*)

Compliance Rqmt.	Description	Evidence of Compliance	Project Signature	ESEB Signature	BSMO Signature
2	**Does the EA System meet Performance Requirements?**				
2.1	**Performance:** Does the Project plan assure all performance requirements allocated to the Project will be maintained over time? • Process Thread Performance Model	Technology Model View - Performance Section Management Plan Systems Acceptance Plan	Signed	Signed	Signed
2.2	**Early performance planning:** Are all non-functional (i.e., performance) requirements built into the design, development, and test plan documents?	Project System Test Plan Coordination with EA Program Test Plan			

Table 3. (*Continued*)

Compliance Rqmt.	Description	Evidence of Compliance	Project Signature	ESEB Signature	BSMO Signature
3	**Does the Project apply EA Standards and Conventions?**				
3.1	Is the project applying EA tools approved by the ESEB? • EA building tools (e.g., Telelogic's System Architect tool) • UML modeling tools (e.g., Sparx Systems Enterprise Architect Tool)	EA Standards and Conventions work product	Signed	Signed	Signed
3.2	Is the EA Project applying interface communication standards? • XML standards • Database CRUD standards • Software Configuration Item (CI) naming standards	EA Data View work product Technology View work product			

Table 3. (*Continued*)

Compliance Rqmt.	Description	Evidence of Compliance	Project Signature	ESEB Signature	BSMO Signature
4	**Does the EA Project meet all Security Requirements?**				
4.1	**Data Security and Privacy**: Does the Project comply with the Security requirements of the EA? • Security & Privacy standards • Taxonomy of Security & Privacy Functions	Security Certification Package - Security Risk Assessment section Security Plan Contingency Planning Document			

Chapter 20

A Mathematical Foundation for Enterprise Architecture Design

20.1. Why a Mathematical Foundation for EA Design?

Up until now there have been no attempts to discover and assemble the theoretical underpinnings of Enterprise Information Architecture (EA) design. There are, however, several reasons for the promotion of a mathematical foundation, in the opinion of this author:

- *Advance the state-of the-art:* A mathematical foundation will enable engineers and practitioners to make use of concepts, methods, and design activities already available in the fields of software engineering, economics, mathematics, and operations research and Multiple Criteria Decision Making (MCDM) (Goicoechea 2000, 2001, 1982) in order to advance the state of design, representation, and assessment of Enterprise Architectures.

- *EA Design:* Through a mathematical foundation of EA it is possible to demonstrate that all architectural views are partial views of the same multi-dimensional design that engineers strive for in the design of an EA; each architectural view may be initiated by a different engineering team, yet all architectural views must eventually converge to support and provide for one and only one final, EA design baseline.

- *EA Performance:* Given a set of system requirements there are multiple architectures that can be built, each one satisfying that original set of requirements. Architecture A, for example, while it meets most requirements it may be limited in terms of scalability.

415

Architecture B, on the other hand, meets all the requirements but makes use of non-modular components that will require costly replacements during its life cycle; the concept of Pareto design frontier can guide the engineer in his/her search for the best possible system performance for a particular combination of technologies.

- *EA Decision making support:* Enterprise architectures generally call for substantial capital outlays over 3-5 year contract periods; owners of the EA need to have the means to assess levels and rates of expenditures required at each step of the design and development process; these assessments are needed in turn as inputs to the institutional decision making process that governs resource allocation and associated expenditures; a mathematical foundation supports the decision making process through the design and application of EA metrics and attribute trade-off analysis.

- *EA Cost Efficiency:* Every dollar invested by EA owners ought to return at least that dollar amount and ideally more in the course of the life cycle of that architecture. Decisions on component selection and final architectural design ought to be made on the basis of both technical and cost considerations so that the ratio of dollar benefit to dollar cost is greater than 1.0 in the EA lifecycle. A mathematical foundation supports cost efficiency through the design and application of attribute trade-off analysis, including cost-benefit trade-off analysis.

Accordingly, this chapter presents a new mathematical framework for the representation and measurement of Enterprise architectures (EA).

20.2. How this Chapter is Organized

This chapter presents a new mathematical framework and foundation for Enterprise Architecture design. Section 20.3 presents the mathematical representation itself with the use of Set Theory to present an 8-tuple capable of storing all essential contents and relationships that can fully characterize an EA. Relationships among multiple views in an EA are represented and explained within an engineering perspective in Section 20.4. The Pareto Optimality Principle and its relevance to EA design is discussed in Sections 20.5 and 20.6 and illustrated with two examples. Finally, Section 20.7 proposes a new EA model for future research.

20.3. EA Mathematical Representation

Parts of an Enterprise Architecture and relationships among these parts can be mathematically represented (i.e., modeled) using concepts and mathematical representations in *Set theory* (Wymore, 1976; Enderton, 1997; Hamburger et al., 1999). It then becomes possible to represent an EA as an 8-tuple consisting of *a set of sets*: a set of requirements, a set of business processes, a set of business systems, a set of data elements, a set of applications, a set of technologies, a set of constraints and business rules, and a set of metrics and their values:

Let: $EA = \{R, B, S, D, A, T, C, M\}$
where:

$R = \{r_1, r_2, r_3, \ldots r_n\}$ is the set of EA requirements

$B = \{b_1, b_2, b_3, \ldots b_n\}$ is the set of business processes in the Business Processes Architectural View.

$S = \{s_1, s_2, s_3, \ldots s_n\}$ is the set of business systems in the Business Systems Architectural View.

$D = \{d_1, d_2, d_3, \ldots d_n\}$ is the set of data elements in the Data Architectural View.

$A = \{a_1, a_2, a_3, \ldots a_n\}$ is the set of software applications in the Applications Architectural View.

$T = \{t_1, t_2, t_3, \ldots t_n\}$ is the set of technologies in the Technology Architectural View.

$C = \{c_1, c_2, c_3, \ldots c_n\}$ is the set of resource constraints, metadata, and design rules.

$M = \{m_1, m_2, m_3, \ldots m_n\}$ is the set of metrics (i.e., indicators) that characterize the Enterprise Architecture.

As shown above, an enterprise architecture (EA) is defined here as a set of eight sets of architectural components. In turn, each set of architectural components needs to be defined in sufficient detail in order to constitute *a recipe* with instructions for the instantiation of the Enterprise Architecture by a business design team and an engineering design team. That is, each and every business process needs to be spelled out in detail with all the activities that make up each business process; each business system needs to be described in terms of services it provides and the business processes these services support; each data table needs to be described in terms of data element content and how it relates to other data tables, and so on. Additionally, the set of constraints document guidelines and rules for the distribution of processing resources across organizational, geographical, business, and marketing boundaries, as well as instructions (i.e., metadata on the composition of the enterprise information architecture) on how to interface the various architectural components. While the set theoretical representation of an EA is fairly straightforward, the volume of detail that needs to be built into each of the eight sets will generally be substantial in the form of *EA work products* (see Chapter 2, Impetus and Motivation for EAs) and other contractor deliverable documents.

The Set of System Requirements, Set R

At the very beginning of the EA planning effort there is a vision of "something in the nature of EAs to be designed", and as this vision takes shape a conceptual design emerges, slowly over a period of weeks, and then specific system capabilities take textual form one by one so that *a set of EA system requirements* emerges. In principle, this is the general trajectory of the emergence, the shaping of requirements after many iterations among the customer (i.e., the EA Owners) and the business and engineering teams. Examples of EA system requirements r_i are as follows:

r_1: System X shall be able to process transactions of type AA, AB, and BB.

r_2: System X shall be able to process 12,000 transactions of type AA over a 24-hour period.

r_3: System X shall be able to process 8,500 queries of type CC to the main database and provide a response to each query in less than 5 seconds 95% of the time.

And so on. Eventually, as many as 200-300 high-level EA requirements may emerge detailing the desires of the EA owner(s) for functionality to be built into the final EA. The requirements management function, in fact, will guide the process of requirements gathering, validation, and finally verification during the testing of the final hardware and software components of a *baseline architecture.*

The Business Process Architectural, View B

Typically, an organization may have hundreds of business processes that are already in place or that it is considering to streamline in the planning phase. Also, each business process will be made up of 5-10 business process activities. Shown on Figure 1 is one such business process, Determine Eligibility of Applicant for Service X1, consisting of four activities: Activity 1.5.1 through Activity 1.5.4.

As the general enterprise information architecture evolves over the first few months in both purpose and content, there will be a recognition of various types of business processes that will be considered basic across all or most enterprise information architectures and that as such will serve as "building blocks" of a portion of the architecture that we will call the Business Process Architectural View.

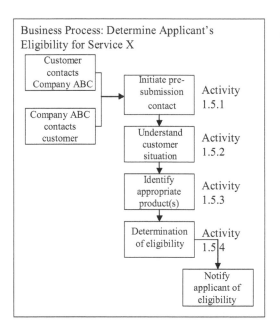

Figure 1. An Example of One Business Process with Four Business Activities

Often an organization has been in operation for a number of years and a decision has been made to streamline its architecture in order to make the organization more efficient in a highly competitive market environment. When this is the case, some existing business processes may end up being modernized and streamlined, other business processes are terminated altogether, while new business processes are created. Examples of business processes are:

b_1: Determine completeness of applicant's personal information

b_2: Determine completeness of applicant's business information

b_3: Format and store account information

b_4: Obtain transcript AA from account in modernized database BADE

b_5: Based on current balance compute interest earned for current billing period.

And so on. This gathering of existing (old) and new business processes (new, modernized) must be carried out early in the design process, sometime after a "vision and strategy" document has been published, and certainly before the creation of business systems is attempted. It is not uncommon for the Business Process Model document to contain 100-200 modernized business processes, with each process decomposed into its own business process activities.

Business Systems Architectural View, Set S

Business systems provide the *services* needed to carry out the activities called for in the business processes activities and, often, one activity will require services from several business systems. The relationship here is then of "one-to-many", i.e., one business activity will require many business systems. Beginning with a list and definition of business processes it is generally not clear how to proceed with the creation of new business systems, replacement or modification of existing business systems, and/or whether these business systems ought to be arranged into 2, 3, or more levels in a *hierarchical business systems tree*, as depicted in Figure 2. Examples of business systems s_i are:

s_1: Registered User Telephone Portal System (parent system)

s_2: Telephone Portal Infrastructure Sub-System (child)

s_3: Telephone Non-Account Services Sub-System (child)

s_4: Telephone Account Services Sub-System (child)

s$_5$: User Internet Portal System (parent system)
    s$_6$: User Internet Portal Infrastructure System (child)
    s$_7$: User Internet Non-Account Services System (child)
    s$_8$: User Secure File Transfer System (child)
s$_9$: Customer Contact Management System (parent system)
    s$_{10}$: Customer Contact Data Management System (child)
    s$_{11}$: Customer Contact Reporting System (child)

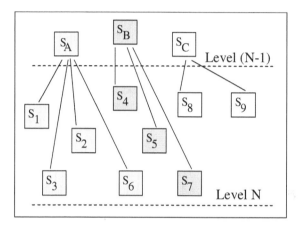

Figure 2. A Hierarchical Tree of Business Systems

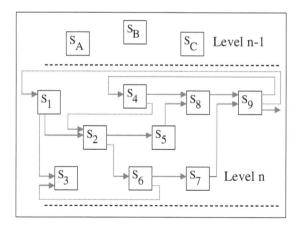

Figure 3. Business Systems Connected by Interfaces

The design process is complicated further by the fact that the number of *interfaces* among systems can grow exponentially with the number of business systems, as depicted in Figure 3. For this reason, the number of business systems proposed ought to be large and varied enough to provide the services needed and not larger as to make possible a manageable set of interfaces.

The creation of a hierarchy of business systems for an enterprise information architecture is often an excruciatingly painful experience at the outset and then slowly over a period of weeks and months it can finally turn into a rewarding design activity, in my opinion. For one, a business team rather than an engineering team ought to create such a business systems hierarchy; this business team would have a set of skills in areas of business process development, customer/owner business interview analysis, and system-database diagram generation (e.g., entity-relationship (E-R) diagrams), with a thorough understanding of the objectives of the enterprise as documented in the vision-and-strategy document. Also, an understanding of the new enterprise organization would prompt the business team to expand the hierarchy both horizontally and vertically (i.e., increase number of levels) as to accommodate the new business organization and its geographical distribution over several cities or regions. The outcome of this activity by the business team would be the listing of business systems, their high-level definition, and their distribution in a hierarchical tree as shown earlier in Chapter 4, The Business Systems Architectural View, Table 1.

Next, an engineering team can come in to define the flow(s) of information from one business system to another, add specific content to the initial set of business system definitions, and begin the task of mapping these data flows to tables and data elements in the main database. This is also a very challenging activity, not devoid of frustrations, that taxes the skills of members of the engineering team as each business systems is given attributes (i.e., functional requirements and business process activities that each business system must support) and data flows from one business system to the next business system are identified and described. The creation of the business systems hierarchy will most likely require 2-4 versions over a six-month time period, each version able to feature more detailed interfaces and data flows than the preceding version.

The Data Architectural View, Set D

Information flows from one business system to another business systems, and some of the information content is stored in the form of data elements in databases, as depicted in Figure 4.

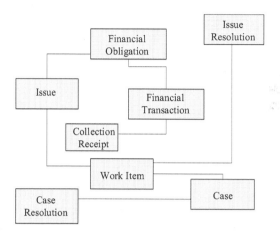

Figure 4. Set of Tables and Relationships in a Data Architectural View

Examples of data elements in set D, the Data Architectural View, are:

Entity (Table): Financial Obligation to Division XYZ
    d_1: Individual account
    d_2: Obligation period
    d_3: Amount due/obligated (dollars)
Entity (Table): Financial Transaction:
    d_4: Amount received (dollars)
    d_5: Date of receipt
Entity (Table): Work Item
    d_6: Payment plan type
    d_7: Delinquency status, and
    d_8: Issue type

Data elements (also called fields or attributes) make up tables, these tables are connected (via foreign keys) in ways specified during the logical data design effort, and the size in bytes of each data element is determined during the physical data design effort. Data flows represented in the Business Systems Architectural View should map to these data elements for purposes of posting data (as in transaction processing and posting of data to the database) or reading data (as in executing queries to the database). This set D would also contain tables that store information other than data element content such as stored procedures for query execution and the data definition language (DDL) that contains the code used to build the physical database itself. Typically 1000-2000 data elements may end up organized into 50-100 tables to constitute the set D, the Data Architectural View.

The Applications Architectural View, Set A

Applications are software implementations of the services (i.e., functionality) provided by the various business systems. Typically, a business system will house several applications. Figure 5 depicts an example of a set of application "layers" that make up an applications architecture. At the "bottom" of this architecture one finds applications that support and make possible a large number of infrastructure services such as e-mail messaging, text formal conversion, data storage, corporate security, and local and wide-area networks; Application Programming Interfaces (APIs) will reside in this layer and serve as connectors to generic and business applications that request any one of those services. The next higher layer will contain specific applications, often Commercial-Off-the-Shelf (COTS) software and hardware products for data storage, database management systems (DBMS), data warehouses, e-mail service, and security directories. Next, a layer of Common Business Applications, will contain an infrastructure of applications that directly support the business functionality of the enterprise such as business rules, business code reference tables, interest computation, payment computation, and balance determination. Finally, at the very "top" of the architecture there will be applications that implement very specific functions with great economy of code (i.e., "thin applications") through the use of APIs that call on a large variety of services already implemented in the lower layers of the architecture. Examples of applications in set A, the Applications Architectural View, are:

a_1: Messaging middleware.
a_2: Local Are Network (LAN) administration.
a_3: Compute return on investment (ROI).
a_4: Corporate budget formation, and
a_5: Division budget formation.

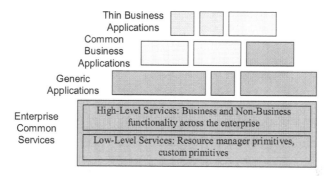

Figure 5. An Applications Architectural View (also, referred to as an "Applications Pyramid Architecture")

Efficient division of business labor computation is intended through such an applications architecture as directed by the Clinger-Cohen Act of 1996 (Public Law 104-106). This Act assigns to the Chief Information Officer (CIO) of each federal government department the responsibility to develop, maintain and facilitate the implementation of an information technology architecture (ITA).

The Technical Reference Model (TRM) is an integral component of an Information Technology Architecture and is required, by the Office of Management and Budget (OMB), as part of a Federal ITA (OMB M-97-16). The purpose of the TRM is to provide a conceptual framework or context to define a common technical vocabulary so that Agencies, Centers, Institutes and Offices that support Federal agencies and/or DoD can better coordinate acquisition, development, and support for information systems, including guidance for the design of efficient applications architectures. Specifically, the TRM is intended to guide the design of the applications architectural view by identifying logical groupings of applications and their interfaces within an enterprise architectural design setting. See Chapter 4 for a discussion on the purpose and contents of the TRM.

Technology Architectural View, Set T

The Technology Architectural View consists of the physical products (i.e., software and hardware) that will house the applications, the database(s), the data warehouse, and service directories, enable transaction processing, direct messages from one platform to another (messaging middleware), enable the flow of information from one business systems to another, and in general enable the day-to-day conduct of businesses throughout the enterprise via portal technology, as depicted in Figure 6.

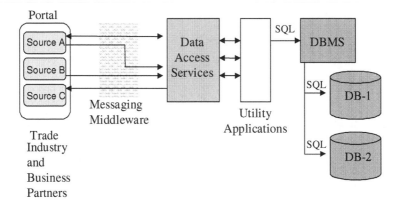

Figure 6. A Portal-based Example of a Technology Architectural View

Examples of components of the set A, the Technology Architectural View, are:

t_1: Registered employee portal
t_2: Third Party employee portal
t_3: Web server
t_4: Applications server
t_5: Sybase database, and
t_6: Database management system (DBMS)

The design, evolution, measurement, and assessment of the Technology Architectural View is discussed in detail in Chapter 8.

Set of Resources, Rules, and Architectural Metadata, Set C

This set contains information on resources needed and available to build the enterprise information architecture, the rules and behavior of the system (i.e., concept of operations), and the various types of data on the organization, storage, updating, and retrieval of data (i.e., metadata). Basically, this set contains information on level of funding available, size and skills of the business and engineering teams, set of assumptions on system operations, team responsibilities, and standards to be observed in the selection and procurement of technologies, as well as detailed instructions for the assembly of those architectural components, including both textual and graphical documentation, i.e. metadata.

Set of Metrics, Set M

This set contains the set of metrics (i.e., indicators) that are used to measure and monitor EA development during the various phases in the life cycle, including system physical design, deployment, and operation. See Chapter 16, EA Evaluation and Assessment, for a discussion on the benefits of metrics to measure and monitor system design and performance throughout the EA life cycle. That chapter reviews the existing body of literature and proposes a new set of metrics for EA measurement.

20.4. Integrated, Multiple Architectural Design Views

Now that we have described the various architectural views that make up an Enterprise Architecture (EA), we can ask several questions. How do these multiple views relate to and support each other, if at all? How do we know the type and amount of detail to build into each view? Who builds these architectural views? Let us begin to answer these questions by saying that initially, during the conceptual design phase, the choice of design variables in the five architectural sets $\{b_1,b_2,b_3,\ldots b_p\}$, $\{s_1,s_2,s_3,\ldots s_q\}$, $\{d_1,d_2,d_3,\ldots d_m\}$, $\{a_1,a_2,a_3,\ldots a_k\}$, and $\{t_1,t_2,\ldots t_w\}$ is very large but lacking in definition, i.e., the design space is very large. Another way of saying this is that the number of possible combinations of business processes, business systems, data elements, applications, and technologies that could be selected and assembled into systems (i.e., EA implementations) that meet some, most, or all the system requirements in R is very large. However, as the design evolves into the logical design phase and the physical design phase thereafter the design space becomes smaller because some poor or expensive design choices are thrown out and by then the design components (i.e., design components) are better defined, as depicted in Figure 7.

> *EA Decision Space:* At each phase of the life cycle, all five architectural views exist (i.e., Business Process Architectural View, Business Systems Architectural View, Data Architectural View, Applications Architectural View, and Technology Architectural

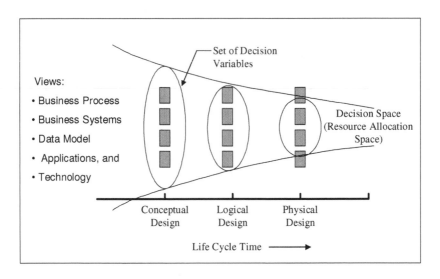

Figure 7. Architectural Views and Decision Space over the System Life Cycle

View), so that each architectural view represents a subset of the decision space itself, as we proceed to show.

For illustrative purposes, consider a design space X made up of only three design variables: X_1, X_2, and X_3; that is the design space is: $\{ \mathbf{X} \in (X_1, X_2, X_3) \}$, as shown on Figure 9. The design space itself is bounded and defined by a set of constraints and relationships among these three design variables that we are calling the *design space boundary*. Next, we can proceed to cut this design space into several architectural slices or planes. *Architectural Plane A*, $(\underline{X}_1^A, X_2^A, X_3^A)$, as noted in Figure 8, is a "cut" of the design space such that this cut is parallel to the $X_2 - X_3$ plane and a distance $\underline{X}_1^A$ from such plane. In this architectural plane the designer is able to choose the values of X_2^A and X_3^A but $\underline{X}_1^A$ must remain constant in value, that is the designer is only concerned with possible values for X_2^A and X_3^A; as such his/her architectural view consists of only X_2^A and X_3^A variables. *Architectural Plane B*, $(X_1^B, X_2^B, \underline{X}_3^B)$ also represents a cut of the design space such that this cut is parallel to the $X_1 - X_2$ plane and a distance $\underline{X}_3^B$ from such plane.

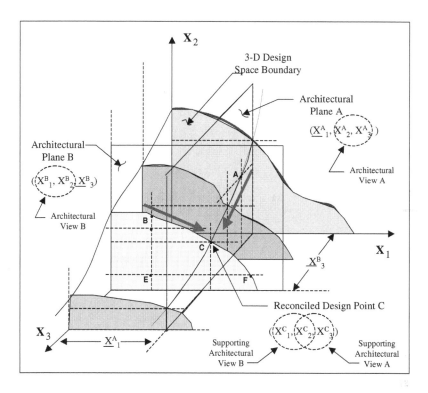

Figure 8. The Design Space and Multiple Architectural Views, 3-Dimensional Case

In engineering terms we would say that *engineering team A* is working with design values in the architectural plane A only, i.e., developing the architectural design view A; similarly, engineering team B is working with design values in the architectural plane B only, i.e., developing the architectural design view B. And so forth.

> *Allocation of EA Architectural Views to the EA Teams:* Each *engineering design team is assigned the task of developing a model view of the system. Initially each of these multiple model views addresses a subset of design variables. As the design advances to the logical design phase and subsequently to the physical design phase, the multiple model views will support each other.*

Next, we let $(X_2^A, X_3^A) \subseteq (\underline{X}_1^A, X_2^A, X_3^A)$, be the *architectural design view A* in the architectural plane A <u>and</u> <u>on</u> the design space boundary itself, and design point B, $(X_1^B, X_2^B) \subseteq (X_1^B, X_2^B, \underline{X}_3^B)$, be the *architectural design view B* in the architectural plane B <u>and</u> <u>on</u> the design space boundary itself. Furthermore, let design point C, $(\underline{X}_1^C, X_2^C, X_3^C)$, at the intersection of architectural plane A, architectural plane B, <u>and</u> the design space boundary; I like to call this point a *reconciled design* because at this design point the architectural design view A and the architectural design view B support each other, i.e. the two architectural views belong to a single point in the design space boundary. This reconciliation of designs is illustrated by the two arrows in Figure 8, representing the migration of a solution along the outer boundary on Plane A and the migration of a solution along the outer boundary on Plane B towards a common design point at the intersection of the two outer boundaries, i.e., design point C.

This reconciliation of designs is illustrated by the two arrows in Figure 8, representing the migration of a solution along the outer boundary on Plane A and the migration of a solution along the outer boundary on Plane B towards a common design point at the intersection of the two outer boundaries, i.e., design point C.

Thus, we have explained here the composition of the various architectural views in terms of basic, core architectural components, and we have shown that each view is a subset of an architectural design point in the design space boundary. Furthermore, these views are said to support each other when they identify subsets of resources of one and only one point in the design space boundary.

Engineering Perspective

During the conceptual phase *Engineering Team A* produces Architectural Design View A (e.g., Business Systems View A) and *Engineering Team B* produces Architectural Design View B (e.g., Data Architectural View B), two distinct points in the design space boundary. Next, as the design progresses and nears the Logical Design Phase, the two architectural design views get closer and closer to each other. Ultimately, as the design progresses and arrives at the Physical Design Phase, the two architectural design views should belong to a one and only one point in the design space boundary, i.e., *the reconciled design C.*

How does engineering team A know about the relevance of its architectural design view to the architectural design view of engineering team B? What are the underlining design principles that guide the engineering teams in the design space? As we see next, one underlining principle include the *Principle of Pareto Optimality* which governs the search for a set of Pareto conditions in the *requirements design space.*

20.5. Pareto Efficient Design Frontier

Traditionally, over the last 50 years, many engineering design problems would consider one criterion only, e.g., design a low-cost car for urban transportation; or design a naval vessel for maximum troops payload over a fixed distance; or design a database to allow very fast query responses, and so forth. Then, over the last 15-20 years a body of research literature has emerged that address design and decision problems characterized by multiple criteria, e.g., initial capital cost of a corporate database, performance (large transaction volume processing, fast query responses, fast server recovery times, etc.), compatibility with legacy systems, training, low maintenance costs, scalability, and so on, also known as multiple-criteria decision making (MCDM) (Goicoechea, 2000; Goicoechea et al., 1990, 1982). However, it has been only in the last 5-10 years that MCDM methods have found application in engineering design and business investment decision making. Central to MCDM theory is the *principle of Pareto optimality*:

> *Principle of Pareto Optimality:* Given a design problem characterized by a set of resources X_i, for $i = 1,2,3,...n$, (i.e., the design space X), and a set of attributes $S = \{(A1, A2, A3,...AJ)\}$ so that each attribute A_j is a function of the X_i, then there is a Pareto solution $S_P \in S$ if and only if an increase in one attribute value is possible only by decreasing one or more of the other attribute values. In our case, the set attributes correspond to the set of system requirements, i.e., Set R in the 8–tuple definition of the EA shown earlier.

20.5.1. Example in Aircraft Design

This principle of Pareto Optimality is illustrated in Figure 9 in an example in aircraft design. System requirements call for an aircraft to be designed that can carry payload P1 over distance D1. As the aircraft design begins, neither the decision space nor the design space are known; it is only after the engineering teams design the various architectural views that the shape and relationship between these two spaces begins to emerge in an iterative fashion. Each 2-dimensional point (p, d) in the decision space maps to one 3-dimensional point (X_1, X_2, X_3) in the design space.

There are three design variables: X_1 wing area, X_2 engine power, and X_3 fuel capacity. For each design

---

Pareto Design

- As the EA design begins, the location of the *Efficient design frontier* is not known.
- As the design begins MORE of both Payload and Distance can be obtained (design points a, d, and e).
- System modeling at discrete life cycle phase points "pushes" the Efficient frontier outwards.
- The Efficient frontier is reached when MORE Payload is only possible at the expense of Distance, i.e., LESS Distance.

---

point (X1, X2, X3) there is a set of requirements (p, d) that is obtained and satisfied in the decision space. Also, for a particular technology (e.g., prop engine technology) the designer is able to choose various combinations of resources X1, X2, and X3 so that each combination (i.e., design) yields a point in the decision space; in this manner the efficient segment EG is obtained. Next, for another technology (e.g., jet engine technology) the designer is able to achieve the efficient design segment DAB, and so on. The aim of the design ought to be to reach the efficient design frontier for the technology(ies) involved where each attribute reaches its fullest potential in harmony with the other attributes. In the efficient design segment DAB, for example, points D and A represent a combinations of payload and range (p_D,d_D) and (p_A,d_A), respectively. If the designer wants to increase the range that the aircraft can travel from d_D to d_A he can only achieve so at the expense of payload, that is by reducing payload from p_D to p_A. Several iterations, in fact, will be required in the course of conducting associated engineering activities (e.g., wing design, configuration management, engine fuel analysis) between the design space and the decision space until a design is finally recommended for approval.

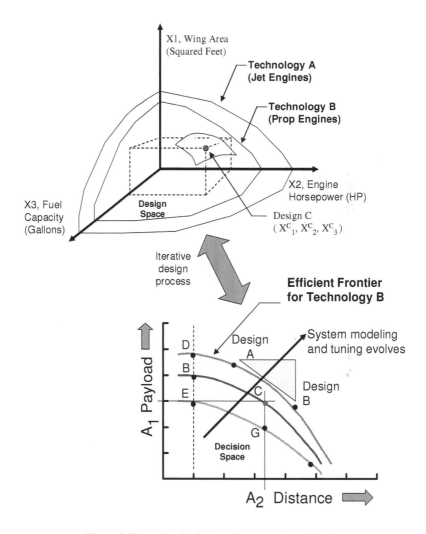

Figure 9. Example of a Design Space in Aircraft Design

20.5.2. Example in Database Design

A second example is shown on Figure 10, this time in database design with design attributes A_1, A_2, and A_3, for query response time (performance), cost, and volume of queries to be processed, respectively.

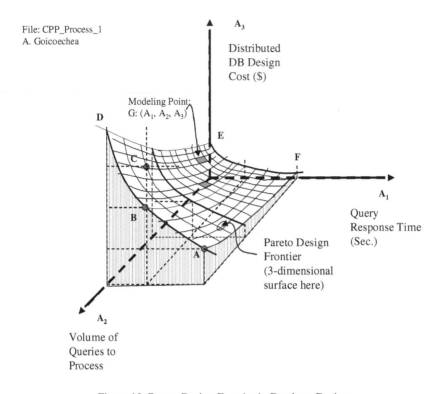

Figure 10. Pareto Design Frontier in Database Design

Initially, engineers strives to arrive at a design that maximizes system performance (small query response times), maximizes volume of queries to be processed (i.e., system throughput), and minimizes design costs in dollars. Let us say that the design process eventually produces solution **C** characterized by the vector (20 seconds, $150K, and 500 queries/day). Additional design effort eventually produces solution **B** with criteria values (20 seconds, $350K, 500 queries/day) which is better than solution **C**. Next, suppose that as the design effort continues within a particular technology (i.e., Sybase data management servers) it becomes apparent that it is no longer possible to produce a design at a cost lower than $350K that would also yield 20 seconds and 500 queries/day. In fact, the only way the engineer is able to obtain a lower design cost is by accepting technical solution **A** with criteria vector (50 seconds, $200K, 500 queries/day). At this point the design effort has reached the Pareto efficient design frontier where designs **A** and **B** are Pareto efficient designs. As the design extends to include volumes of system throughput less than 500 queries/day the Pereto frontier becomes the entire surface ADEF, as shown on Figure 10.

How does EA designer go about reaching the Pareto frontier? How to evolve the design as to be able "to ride" the Pareto design frontier, is a non-trivial matter, understandably so, as depicted in Figure 11.

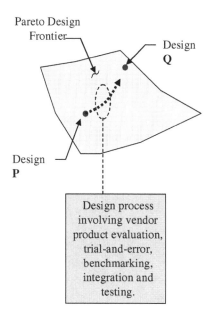

Figure 11. The Design Process on the Pareto Design Frontier

Most often the designer does not know a-priori what the Pareto design frontier looks like, and must rely on benchmarking documentation that a vendor may make available for a specific set of design parameters, that may or may not relate closely to the architecture and set of operating requirements at hand. Consequently, the designer or group of designers must conduct testing of the architecture for a variety of test cases, baseline configurations, and workload scenarios so that each test produces one point in the Pareto frontier of interest, and together these test points eventually characterize and determine the actual Pareto design frontier.

Key in this pursuit is the term *baseline configuration* of architectural components, i.e., resource composition of the architecture. Design point P, for example, entails a particular baseline configuration, while design point Q entails a different baseline configuration. These two configurations must be different in some specific manner, be it in the number of CPUs available for processing, the type of database management system (DBMS) being employed, the choice of transaction monitoring product, or other combination of core architectural components. It is then through the testing of a set of baseline configurations that produces the test results that make possible the determination of the Pareto design frontier. In reality, one is able to say, each baseline configuration is an architecture, and so it is the testing of a set of architectures that produces the Pareto design frontier for a particular set of technologies. See Chapter 9, Distributed Database Design, Section 9.8, Multiple Criteria, for an example and method to reach the Pareto Frontier in a database design problem.

20.6. The Reality of Multiple Design Teams in EA Work

The challenges to reaching the Pareto design frontier by a single EA design team are significant, as we have explored in the earlier sections above. The challenges are compounded when we realize that EA planning and design in most EA programs today require not a single EA design team but multiple EA design teams, each EA design team having 5-10 people, and each EA design team belonging to a different contractor. Thus, we have the task of having to address *multiple design views* and *multiple design teams* in search of a Pareto EA design if we propose to go from a merely academic exercise to a real-world exercise in EA design. The following section proposes how to extend the traditional Pareto optimization problem with a single decision space (requiring a single engineering design team) to an extended Pareto optimization problem with multiple complementary decision spaces (requiring multiple engineering design teams, one team for each decision space).

20.6. Reaching for the EA Pareto Frontier with Multiple Design Teams, New EA Model for Future Research

The formulation of the EA design problem with a single EA design team, as shown on Figure 12, is traditionally treated in today's optimization textbooks (Goicoechea et al. 1982; Fandel and Gal, 1980; Cohon, 1978).

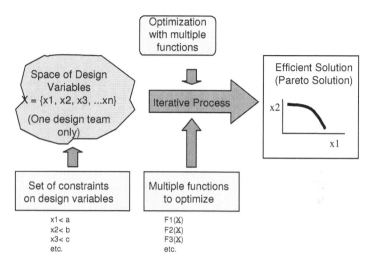

Figure 12. Traditional Pareto Optimization Problem with One Decision Space Only

In this traditional approach all design variables are assigned to one EA design team and the theoretical solution is readily obtained. That is, a single solution is obtained in an iterative fashion.

Unfortunately, this traditional model does not "fit" the reality of EA programs with thousands of design variables, thus requiring not one but several engineering design teams in an EA program.

Proposed new theoretical Pareto model:

> *Consider a design problem characterized by a set of resources Xi, for $I = 1,2,3,...n$, such that $X = \{X1, X2, X3, ...Xn\}$ is the design space, a set of attributes $A = \{A1, A2, A3, ...AJ\}$ such that each attribute Aj is a function of the design variables Xi, and that there exists a Pareto solution S. Next, we consider that this design space is partitioned into m subspaces $Q = \{Q1, Q2, Q3, ...Qm\}$ such that the intersection of any pair of these subspaces is not empty (not null), and that each subspace has its own individual Pareto solution Tm. Question: What is the relationship among these individual Pareto solutions Tm. Question: Given that such relationship is known, is it possible to use these individual solutions to arrive at the global solution S? This situation corresponds to today's design environment where*

there is not a single design space (and a single design team) but instead there are multiple design subspaces and a design team assigned must be assigned to each design subspace.

A graphical representation of this new design problem is shown in Figure 13. A formulation of the new Pareto design problem must be carried out so that the following structure is reflected:

- The original set of functions to optimize ("to satisfy" in the Pareto sense, actually) is now partitioned into *n sub-sets of functions*, the large decision space is now partitioned into *n decision sub-spaces*, and the original variable constraint space is now partitioned into *n constraint sub-spaces*.
- There is now a set of n Pareto optimization problems, each one made up of one sub-space of functions, one decision sub-space, and one constraint sub-space, e.g., $\{POP_i, \text{ for } i = 1,2,3,...n\}$.
- Each Pareto optimization problem is able to produce its own individual Pareto solution, $SPOP_i$
- The *intersection* of any pair of function sub-spaces cannot be *empty* and, instead, at a minimum one function is common in the pair.
- The *intersection* of a pair of decision sub-spaces cannot be *empty* and, instead, at a minimum one decision variable is common in the pair.
- The *intersection* of a pair of constraint sub-spaces cannot be *empty* and, instead, at a minimum one constraint is common in the pair.

Once the n POP problems are represented following the structure outlined above, each problem is assigned to one engineering design team so as to constitute the Business Process Design team, the Business Systems Design team, the Applications Design team, the Database Design Team, and the Architecture Design team. Accordingly, the decision variables in the decision sub-space of the Business Process Design team are variables such as X_A, number of processes of type A, X_B, number of processes of type B, X_C, number of processes of type C, etc., Similarly, decision variable in the Applications Design Team are variables such as Y_A, number of software applications of type A, Y_B, number of software applications of type B, Y_C, number of software

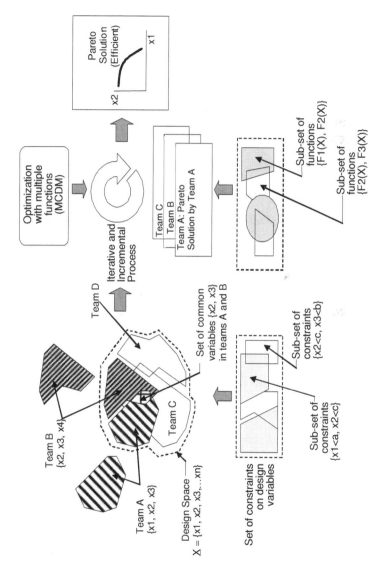

Figure 13. Proposed New Analytical EA Pareto Problem and Iterative Process

applications of type C, etc. Also, the constraint sub-space for each problem POP_J contains pre-set values for the decision variables in the other POP_Q problems where $Q \neq J$. Then, each time a set of individual Pareto solutions $\{SPOPi, \text{ for } i = 1,2,3,...n\}$ is obtained, this set of values is used to replace the pre-set values and a new iteration of individual Pareto values, $\{POPi, \text{ for } i = 1,2,3,...n\}$, is obtained. This *Pareto EA iteration process* is repeated 4-6 times until the value difference between two consecutive SPOPi iterations is smaller than a desired *Pareto threshold value*, $\Delta SPOP$.

The experience of this author is that in the "real world" of EA planning and design, an iterative EA design process similar to the theoretical

Pareto iteration process described above does take place among the contractor teams, and that although it is often chaotic, expensive, and time-consuming eventually *does* produce an Enterprise Architecture design that does meet all the EA requirements, and one that likely is close to an EA Pareto EA design. How close to or far away from a theoretical EA Pareto EA design a real-world EA design is? We may never be able to ascertain the difference, i.e., the *EA gap*. However, the proposed new EA Pareto model and the Pareto EA iteration process described above offer the potential for reducing the EA gap thus producing significant cost savings in EA planning and design, we believe.

20.7. Conclusions

In the course of exploring the mathematical foundations for enterprise information architecture representation, design, and measurement some insight was gained and several issues become apparent:

- It was shown that the each of the five architectural views is really a subset of the same design solution (i.e., the design space). Initially in the design, during the conceptual design phase, each engineering team designs one architectural view and, typically, there is little information on the ability of, say, the Business Systems Architectural View to support the Data Architectural View or any of the other three architectural views. Instead, each architectural view corresponds to a different design point in the Pareto design frontier. As the design process evolves to the

Logical Design Phase and the Physical Design Phase the architectural views become more and more supportive of each other and eventually become truly subsets of the same design point.

- A set theoretical representation offers economy of text and efficiency in communication, as intended by the 8-tuple mathematical formulation of an enterprise information architecture proposed here, we believe.
- Attribute tradeoff analysis requires specific knowledge of the Pareto frontier of an enterprise information architecture. This knowledge can be acquired in several ways, including benchmarking and testing of a set of baseline configurations, as conducted by various engineering teams.
- During "real world" EA planning and design, an iterative EA design process similar to the theoretical Pareto iteration process described above does take place among the contractor teams, and that although it is often chaotic, expensive, and time-consuming eventually often *does* produce an Enterprise Architecture design that does meet all the EA requirements, and one that likely is close to an EA Pareto EA design.
- The proposed new EA Pareto model and the Pareto EA iteration process described above may offer the potential in the near future for reducing the *EA gap* thus producing significant cost savings in EA planning and design in Industry, Government, and the Public Administration sectors.

Glossary

Agent

Software code/routine that resides on a platform and waits for a particular event to happen so that it can perform specified task(s), e.g., an agent on a database management system (DBMS) alerts the database administrator (DBA) when the remaining disk space reaches a programmed low level point.

Application

A software program or collection of software programs that can be activated to produce services needed by the business systems in the enterprise. A software program that automates the execution of a business function.

Applications Architectural View

The set of software applications that are needed to provide the totality of computer-based services in an enterprise architecture, including definition of each application, rules for the design of the applications, an ordering of these applications according to the business systems that they will be supporting, and a plan for the distribution of these applications across physical components of the enterprise architecture. In this manner, an enterprise architecture may consist of 300-400 applications distributed across those physical components.

Application Capacity Model

A model whose purpose is to estimate an application's capacity requirements based on a business-oriented workload description.

Application Performance Model

A model whose purpose is to predict the performance of an application based on a business-oriented workload description.

Attribute

A characteristics or dimension of an entity in a database. An entity will usually have 5-10 attributes, depending on the detail and complexity to be captured during the modeling effort. Attributes are also known as data elements and fields. Examples of attributes in the Aircraft entity are Type (Boeing 747, Douglas D-123, Lockheed 711, Airbus 200, other), Seat Capacity (50, 75, 225, other), Owner (Global Airlines Services, United Airlines, Euskadi Airlines, other), Crew (4, 6, 8 , or more).

Bandwidth

Communications transfer rate associated with LANs, WANs, input/output (I/O) channels, etc. Usually expressed in bits per unit of time, as in Megabits per second (Mbps) or Gigabits per second (Gbps).

Baseline

A product that has been formally reviewed and agreed upon, and that can be changed only through formal change control procedures.

Business Activity

A main activity in an organization necessary for its successful operation and financial well-being. In the case of a banking organization these activities include processing incoming check deposits, posting money amounts to the appropriate individual or corporate accounts, computing interest, managing loans to businesses, and conducting internal balance and control procedures at the end of each business cycle (i.e., daily, weekly, other) to mention a few.

Business Case

Represents an organization's justification for spending money. It takes into consideration the life-cycle costs and benefits, as well as the risks.

Business Process

A grouping of 5-10 business activities that share in business affinity and that are carried out in a pre-determined sequence for purposes of accomplishing a significant business operation or goal.

Business System

A logical representation of functionality to be executed by the enterprise in the course of carrying out a business activity or business process. A business process is made up of several business activities, and several business systems may be needed to carry out a single business activity, i.e., a business system houses services needed to carry out one or more business activities.

Capacity

The amount of work a hardware device is capable of doing. MIPS (for central processing units (CPUs)), Gigabyte (GB) (for memory or disk storage), and Mbps (for LANs and WANs) are common ways of expressing capacity.

Conceptual Data Model (Schema)

A detailed specification of the data entities, a list of attributes that characterize each entity, and a complete set of entity relationships that are technology independent. At this point it is recommended to have this conceptual model, also called schema, in graphical format, and entity-to-function mappings, as well as storing these specifications as metadata in a data dictionary or metadata repository.

Data Architectural View

A framework for the identification, definition, representation, organization, and management of data in the Enterprise Architecture (EA). Data are represented through the use of entities, attributes, and relationships.

EA Decision Space: At each phase of the life cycle, all five architectural views exist (i.e., Business Process Architectural View, Business Systems Architectural View, Data Architectural View, Applications Architectural View, and Technology Architectural View), so that each architectural view represents a subset of the decision space itself, as we proceed to show.

Decision Space

A set of decisions that can be taken in a problem. At each phase of the life cycle, all five architectural views exist (i.e., Business Process Architectural View, Business Systems Architectural View, Data Architectural View, Applications Architectural View, and Technology Architectural View), so that each architectural view represents a subset of the decision space itself.

Design Review

A facilitated review of the design to identify potential performance issues.

Disaster Recovery Planning

The engineering and business function that addresses the types of potential catastrophic and unscheduled events that can result in the loss of business continuity in one or multiple parts of an enterprise architecture and that, accordingly, proceeds to identify and describe points of risk and vulnerability, a set of disaster recovery requirements, a disaster recovery contingency plan, and a disaster recovery plan.

e-Democracy

The exercise of democratic processes and activities in the dialogue between a Parliament and its Citizens (I.e., Society) that aspire to a condition of social, economic, and political well-being, a condition that is actively promoted by the application of the Technologies of Information and Communication (TICs).

Enterprise

An organization supporting a defined business scope and mission. An enterprise is composed of intedependent resources (e.g., people, organizations, capital, and technologies). These resources must coordinate their functions and share information in support of a common mission.

(Source: Adapted from TEAF)

Enterprise Architecture

A set of business and engineering artifacts, including text and graphical documentation, that describes and guide the operation of an enterprise-wide system, including instructions for its life cycle operation, management, evolution, and maintenance.

Specific content of these artifacts can include a vision or mission statement, a set of system requirements, a Business Process Architectural View, a Business Systems Architectural View, a Data Architectural View, an Applications Architectural View, and a Technology Architectural View.

Also:

A strategic information asset base which defines the agency's mission and business activities supporting the mission, the information necessary for agency operations, the technologies needed to support the operations, organizational needs, and transitional strategies to implement business and technology changes. An enterprise architecture is an integrated model or representation.
(Source: Adapted from FEAF version 1.1)

Enterprise Architecture Framework

An Enterprise Architecture (EA) framework is a business and engineering recipe (i.e., a blueprint, a set of instructions, a specification) for the construction of an Enterprise Architecture (EA).

EA Planning

Enterprise Architecture Planning (EAP) is the set of business and engineering methods, procedures, and activities that are applied to an Enterprise Architecture Framework for purposes of translating a "vision and strategy" into a set of system requirements and a set of architectural views leading to the construction, operation, and maintenance of an Enterprise Architecture (EA).

Enterprise Performance Engineering Model

A set of models spanning the enterprise based on a consistent methodology, assumptions, and input data. Collectively, these models will form a coherent, integrated view of the enterprise.

Entity

Any person, organization, sub-system, or event that produces, gathers, uses, or distributes data in the enterprise or the external systems with which it communicates. Entities identified early in the design of the data architectural view generally end up as tables later on during the logical design phase. Examples of entities are Reservation Form, Payment, Payment Plan, Passenger, Cargo, Aircraft, Individual Account, and Accounting.

Framework

A logical structure for classifying and organizing complex information, including a set of guidelines for the construcion of an Enterprise Architecture (EA).
(Source: FEAF version 1.1)

Functional Requirements

Refers to the business functions that the application must satisfy. They are the baseline business requirements from which all lower-level requirements are derived.

Indicator

We use the term indicator and metric interchangeably to have the same meaning and purpose: A category, class, or dimension of the enterprise architecture (i.e., work product content) that is to be measured, e.g., data query response (in seconds).

Interface

Data interchange across a physical media, i.e., pipeline, channel, connector; both business and technical data can be interchanged; and types of interface media include phone line, FAX, message middleware, other.

Life-Cycle

This begins with the Vision & Strategy phase of the ELC and continues through the Operations and Maintenance phase. Life-cycle CP/PE activities cover all time periods of the software application from birth to death of the application.

Logical Design

Details at a high level the architecture associated with the implementation of the specific environments of the project.

Organizational Change (OC) Management

A business activity that anticipates and addresses resistance and anxiety among people within an organization that is experiencing technological change in order to meet new business objectives, and then conducts activities (e.g., OC workshops) to explain change, propose new roles and responsibilities, and to gain consensus to move forward together as a team.

Pareto Frontier

The set of attributes with highest possible values in an architecture. Given a design problem characterized by a set of resources Xi, for i = 1,2,3,...n, (i.e., the design space X), and a set of attributes S = {(A1, A2, A3,...AJ)} so that each attribute Aj is a function of the Xi, then there is a Pareto solution SP ∈ S if and only if an increase in one attribute value is possible only by decreasing one or more of the other attribute values.

Performance

Concerned with the amount of elapsed time to do a unit of work. Transaction rates, job turn-around times, etc. are common performance metrics.

Performance Engineering

Part of the systems engineering process. Pro-activity associated with designing performance into an application. The drivers for this activity are the application's performance requirements. The term performance engineering is often used to include capacity planning.

Performance Requirements

One of the categories of business requirements that drive the design/development of an application where most often the time dimension is of the great importance (e.g., "The system shall be able to process 1.5 million transactions in 24 hours")

Standard

A standard can be : (1) an object or measure of comparison that defines or represents the magnitude of a unit; (2) a characterization that establishes allowable tolerances or constraints for categories of items; and (3) a degree or level or required excellence of attainment [SESC93].

Technical Architecture

A capability, a discipline, and an approach used to define, apply, and maintain the technology environment within the organization. It embodies the life cycle for defining the organization's technical strategy, setting and adopting technical standards, and maintaining the technology environment through changes in both business and technology. It can be thought of as the technical equivalent of the business strategy (i.e., the future shape of business given a current environment).

Technical Reference Model (TRM)

A body of knowledge that identifies and describes the information services used throughout a government agency or organization by specifying set of standards on software and hardware behavior, called the Standards Profile; it guides the grouping and use of services as to produce and promote interoperability and economic efficiency throughout the enterprise.

Technology

A collection of methods and physical means that make use of physical laws to realize a product or service that is deemed valuable by a human being (i.e., a carpenter, shoe maker, a farmer, engineer, computer scientist, an accountant, a musician, etc.). Examples of technologies are data storage devices, local area networks, cable TV, and messaging middleware.

Technology Architectural View

A set of information technologies (i.e., physical means) that are grouped in a manner prescribed by a set of principles (e.g., methods) in order to implement a set of business systems (Business Systems Architectural View), a data model (Data Architectural View), and a set of applications (Applications Architectural View) that will make possible the execution of a set of business processes (Business Process Architectural View). Typically, an enterprise architecture may consist of hundreds and even thousands of technologies.

Transaction

>   *Refers to a unit of work being done, and can be either a unit of work from a user point of view or one from a system point of view, e.g., sending a query to a database and getting a response.*

Walkthrough

>   *As used within this document, means the same as "review" – as in design review and code review.*

Workload

>   *The work that a given application processes.*

Workload Characterization

>   *Quantitative definition of the workload for a particular application. Its dimensions are what, when, how much, and how large.*

Work Product

>   *A document that contains detailed design of a system being built. The set of "deliverables" in an Ea project, e.g., The C4ISR architecture framework is a long set of descriptive documents called architectural "work products".*

Bibliography and Related Links

Bibliography (Chapter 1)

Catalyst, CSC Methodology, 2005,
  http://www.csc.com/solutions/knowledgemanagement/mds/mds122/index.shtml
C4ISR Architecture Framework 2.0, *Coordination Draft*, 19 November 1997, C4ISR
  Architecture Working Group (AWG).
Driscoll, Jr., F.B., Architecture Assessment & Evaluation Criteria, *Working Paper*,
  Software and Engineering Center, Dept. W908, MITRE Corporation, 5 June 2004.
Enterprise Life Cycle (ELC): Quick Reference Guide, Computer Sciences Corporation,
  2002.
Enterprise Architecture, an End-to-End Approach to Re-aligning IT with Business Aims,
  Butler Group United Kingdom, February 2004, www.butlergroup.com
Finneran, T., "Enterprise Architecture: What And Why?" *Data Administration Newsletter*,
  URL: www.tdan.com
General Accounting Office (GAO), Veterans Affairs Sustained Management Attention is
  Key to Achieving Information, 2002.
Goicoechea (Goikoetxea), A., D.R. Hansen, and L. Duckstein, *Multi-objective Decision
  Analysis with Engineering and Business Applications*, John Wiley and Sons Publishers,
  560 pages, New York, 1982.
Goicoechea (Goikoetxea), A., "Requirements Blueprint and Multiple Criteria for
  Distributed Database Design", Proceedings of the International Council on
  Systems Engineering (INCOSE), Mid-Atlantic Regional Conference, Reston,
  Virginia April 6-8, 2000.
Hagan, P., Seven High-Level EA Evaluation Criteria, EA Book, MITRE Corporation,
  2005, http://www.mitre.org/tech/eabok/documents/chapter7.pdf
Hilliard, R., Kurland, M., Litvintchouk, S., Rice, T., Schwarm, S., "Architecture Quality
  Assessment", Working *Paper*, The MITRE Corporation, 1996.
Hilliard, Kurland, Litvintchouk, Rice, Schwarm, "Architecture Quality Assessment",
  Working Paper, 1997, http://citeseer.ist.psu.edu/hilliard97mitres.html.
Lucas, T., and J.F. Mohr, IRS Business Systems Modernization: Case Study,
  http://www.csc.com/industries/government/knowledgelibrary/uploads/967_1.ppt

Perks, C., and T. Beveridge, *Guide to Enterprise IT Architecture*, Springer, New York, 2003.

Spewak, S.H., *Enterprise Architecture Planning: Developing a Blueprint for Data, Applications and Technology*, Wiley Publishers, QED, New York 1992.

Sustained Management Attention is Key to Achieving Information Technology Results, *GAO-02-703 Report*, June 2002.

Zachman, J., "A Framework for Information Systems Architecture", *IBM Systems Journal*, Vol. 26, No. 3, 1987.

Bibliography (Chapter 2)

ArchitecturePlus
   www.itpolicy.gsa.gov/mke/archplus/archhome.htm

Clinger-Cohen Act (Information Technology Management Reform Act), January 3, 1996
   www.itpolicy.gsa.gov/mks/regs-leg/s1124_en.htm

C4ISR Architecture Framework, version 2.0, Department of Defense, Architectures Working Group (AWG), 18 December 1997.

C4ISR Architectures Working Group
   www.c3i.osd.mil/org/cio/i3/AWG_Digital_Library/

Department of Defense Technical Reference Model, version 1.0, November 5, 1999
   www-trm.itsi.disa.mil

Department of the Treasury CIO
   www.treas.gov/cio/

Department of the Treasury Information Technology Strategic Plan 2000-2003, November 17, 1999
   www.treas.gov/cio/itsp.pdf

Finneran, T., "Enterprise Architecture: What And Why?" *Data Administration Newsletter*, URL: www.tdan.com

Federal Agencies Information Architecture Working Group
   www.itpolicy.gsa.gov/mke/archplus/group.htm

Federal Chief Information Officers Council
   www.cio.gov

Federal Enterprise Architecture Framework, version 1, September 1999.
   www.itpolicy.gsa.gov/mke/archplus/fedarch1.pdf

General Accounting Office, Assessing Risks and Returns: A Guide for Evaluating Federal Agencies' IT Investment Decision-making, Version 1, GAO/AIMD-10.1.13, February 1997
   www.gao.gov/policy/itguide/

General Accounting Office, Information Technology Investment Management: A Framework for Assessing and Improving Process Maturity, Exposure Draft,

Version 1, GAO/AIMD-10.1.23, May 2000
www.gao.gov/special.pubs/10_1_23.pdf

General Accounting Office, Measuring Performance and Demonstrating Results of Information Technology Investments, AIMD-98-89, March 1998
www.gao.gov/special.pubs/ai98089.pdf

General Services Administration, Office of Information Technology
www.itpolicy.gsa.gov

Hagan, P., *The OMB Reference Models, EA at a Crossroads*, Powerpoint, MITRE Technical Exchange Meeting (TEM) Series, 16 June 2003.

IEEE 1471, Recommended Practice for Architectural Description, DRAFT

Information Assurance Technical Framework Forum
www.iatf.net

Information Technology Investment Portfolio System (I-TIPS)
www.itips.gov

Joint Technical Architecture (JTA)
http://jta.disa.mil/

Levels of Information System Interoperability (LISI)
http://www.c3i.osd.mil/org/cio/i3/AWG_Digital_Library/pdfdocs/lisi.pdf

OMB Releases Business, Service Component and Technical Reference Models, Executive Office of the President, 12 June 2003
www.feapmo.gov

OMB Circular A-130, Management of Federal Information Resources, Revised, February 8, 1996
www.whitehouse.gov/OMB/circulars/a130/a130.html

OMB Memorandum M-97-16, Information Technology Architectures, June 18, 1997
www.whitehouse.gov/OMB/memoranda/m97-16.html

OMB Memorandum M-00-07, Incorporating and Funding Security in Information Systems Investments, 28 February 2000
www.whitehouse.gov/OMB/memoranda/m00-07.html

OMB, Proposed revision of OMB Circular No. A-130, in Federal Register, Vol. 65, No. 72, April 13, 2000, pages 19933-19939
www.whitehouse.gov/omb/fedreg/rev-a130.pdf

Perks, C., and T. Beveridge, *Guide to Enterprise IT Architecture*, Springer, New York, 2003.

Spewak, S.H., Enterprise Architecture Planning: Developing a Blueprint for Data, Applications and Technology, Wiley Publishers, QED, New York 1992.

TAFIM 94, U.S. Department of Defense. Technical Architecture Framework For Information Management (TAFIM) Volumes 1-8, Version 2.0. Reston, VA: DISA Center for Architecture, 1994, www-library.itsi.disa.mil/tafim/tafim.html

Treasury Enterprise Architecture Framework (TEAF), Department of the Treasury, Chief Information Officer Council, July 2000, version1.
www.treas.gov/cio

The Open Group Architecture Framework (TOGAF) Technical Reference Model, version 5, 1999
    www.opengroup.org/togaf
U.S. Customs Service, Enterprise Architecture Blueprint, October 1999
    www.itpolicy.gsa.gov/mke/archplus/eab.pdf
U.S. Customs Service, Technical Reference Model Introductory Guide, August 1999
    www.itpolicy.gsa.gov/mke/archplus/trm.pdf
Zachman, J., "A Framework for Information Systems Architecture", *IBM Systems Journal*, Vol. 26, No. 3, 1987.
Zachman Institute for Framework Advancement
    www.zifa.com

Bibliography (Chapter 3)

Enterprise Architecture Management System (EAMS), US Department of Agriculture Enterprise Architecture Site, 2002, http://www.ocio.usda.gov/irm/e_arch/
Enterprise Life Cycle (ELC): Quick Reference Guide, Computer Sciences Corporation (CSC), 2002, www.csc.com
Federal Enterprise Architecture: A Practical Guide, Chief Information Officer Council, Version 1.0, February 2001, also U.S. Customs Service, 7681 Boston Boulevard, Springfield, Virginia 22153, USA, rob.c.thomas@customs.treas.gov
Levi, M.H. and M.P. Klapsis, FirstSTEP Process Modeler: a CIMOSA Compliant Modeling Tool, Interfacing Technologies Corporation, Canada, 2002, www.interfacing.com
Use Enabling Technology to Improve GAO's Crosscutting Business Processes, http://www.gao.gov/sp/html/strobj426.html

Bibliography (Chapter 4)

Alexander, I, A., "A Co-Operative Task Modeling Approach to Business Process Understanding", *workshop* on Object-Oriented Business Process Modeling, ECOOP 98, Brussels, Belgium, July 20-24, 1998, also available at http://www.scenarioplus.com/talk/approach_to_task_modelling.html and at http://www.ibissoft.se/oocontr/alexander.htm
Cockburn, A., "Using Goal-Based Use Cases", Journal of Object Oriented Programming, November 1997, also available at http://members.aol.com/acockburn/papers/usecases.htm
Enterprise Architecture Management System (EAMS), US Department of Agriculture Enterprise Architecture Site, http://www.ocio.usda.gov/irm/e_arch/

Federal Enterprise Architecture: A Practical Guide, Chief Information Officer Council, Version 1.0, February 2001; also U.S. Customs Service, 7681 Boston Boulevard, Springfield, Virginia 22153, USA.

Henderson-Sellers, B, Graham, I., The OPEN Modeling Language (OML) Reference Manual, SIGS Books, NY, 1997, available at http://www.csse.swin.edu.au/cotar/OPEN/OPEN.html

IRS Guidance on Economic Analyses in Investment Business Cases, GAO Report GAO-02-234R, http://www.gao.gov/new.items/d02234r.pdf

Lucas, T. and J.F. Mohr, IRS Business Systems Modernization, Case Study, *Working Paper*, http://www.csc.com/industries/government/knowledgelibrary/uploads/967_1.ppt

Martin, J., Odell, J. J.: Object-Oriented Methods: a Foundation. Prentice Hall, Inc. 1998

Technical Architecture Framework For Information Management (TAFIM), U.S. Department Of Defense, Volumes 1-8, Version 2.0. Reston, VA: DISA Center for Architecture, 1994, also at www-library.itsi.disa.mil/tafim/tafim.html

Bibliography (Chapter 5)

Codd, E.F., *A Relational Model of Data for Large Relational Databases*, Communications of the ACM 13, pages 77-89, June 1970.

Codd, E.F., *The Relational Model for Database Management Version 2*, Addison-Wesley, 1990.

Date, C.J., *An Introduction to Database Systems*, Addison-Wesley, 1995.

Enterprise Architecture Management System (EAMS), US Department of Agriculture Enterprise Architecture Site, http://www.ocio.usda.gov/irm/e_arch/, text

Federal Enterprise Architecture: A Practical Guide, Chief Information Officer Council, Version 1.0, February 2001, rob.c.thomas@customs.treas.gov, also U.S. Customs Service, 7681 Boston Boulevard, Springfield, Virginia 22153, USA.

Goicoechea, A., *Requirements Blueprint and Multiple Criteria for Distributed Database Design, Proceedings of the International Council on Systems Engineering* (INCOSE), Reston, Virginia, April 5-8, 2000.

Goikoetxea, A., *Datu-base Banatuak Diseinatzeko Betebeharren Aurreproiektua eta Hainbat Irizpide, EKAIA Journal*, Euskal Herriko Unibertsitateko, University of the Basque Country, No. 14, 2001.

McFadden, F.R., J.A. Hoffer, and M.B. Prescott, *Modern Database Management*, Addison-Wesley, 1999.

Simon, A., *Strategic Database Technology: Management for the Year 2000*, Morgan Kaufman Publishers, 1995.

Viescas, J.L., *Running Microsoft Access 97*, Microsoft Press, ISBN 1-57231-323-4, www.mspress.microsoft.com, 1997.

Bibliography (Chapter 6)

Enterprise Architecture Management System (EAMS), US Department of Agriculture Enterprise Architecture Site, http://www.ocio.usda.gov/irm/e_arch/

Federal Enterprise Architecture: A Practical Guide, Chief Information Officer Council, Version 1.0, February 2001, rob.c.thomas@customs.treas.gov, also U.S. Customs Service, 7681 Boston Boulevard, Springfield, Virginia 22153, USA.

Leavitt, N., *Two Technologies Vie for Recognition in Speech Market,* Computer, pgs. 13-16, IEEE, June 2003, editor Lee Garber, L.garber@computer.org

Moore, J.W., *Software Engineering Standards: A User's Road Map,* IEEE Computer Society, Los Alamitos, California, 1998.

Object Management Group, http://www.omg.org/news/about/liaison.htm

Reynolds, G.W., *Information Systems for Managers,* West Publishing Co., University of Cincinnati, 1995.

Rudolph, P., "Harmonization and Standardization", *Air Traffic Technology International 2001.*

Rumbaugh, J, I. Jacobson, and G. Booch, *The Unified Modeling Language Reference Manual,* 550 pages, Addision-Wesley, 1999.

[SESC93] SESC Long Range Planning Group, *Master Plan for Software Engineering Standards,* Version 1.0, Dec. 1, 1993.

State of the Art in Architecture Frameworks and Tools, Paper, Telematica Institute, 5 August 2002, https://doc.telin.nl/dscgi/ds.py/Get/File-22327

Bibliography (Chapter 7)

Boggs, W. and M. Boggs, UML with Rational Rose 2002, Sybex Editorial, San Francisco, USA, 2002, www.sybex.com

Booch, Jacobson, and Rumbaugh, UML Reference Manual, Addison-Wesley Editorial, California, 1999, www.awl.com

Eriksson, H.E, y M. Penker, UML Toolkit, 395 pgs., Wiley, New York, 1998.

Gomaa, H., Designing Concurrent, Distributed, and Real Time Applications with UML, Addison-Wesley, New York, 2002.

List of UML tools in the market, www.objectsbydesign.com/tools/umltools_byCompany.html

Object Management Group (OMG), www.omg.org

Reed, P.R., Developing Applications with Java and UML, Addison-Wesley, New York, 2002.

Roff, J.T., UML a Beginner's Guide, McGraw-Hill, Madrid, 2003.

Schmuller, J., Teach Yourself UML in 24 Hours, Editorial Sams, Indiana, USA, 2002.

Bibliography (Chapter 8)

King, A., Commercial Off-the-Shelf Software: Benefits and Burdens, *Working Paper*, MITRE Corporation, 2001,
http://www.mitre.org/news/edge_perspectives/march_01/ep_king.html

Leavitt, N., *Two Technologies Vie for Recognition in Speech Market*, Computer, Vol 36, No. 6, June 2003, neal@leavcom.com

Malone, R., "Supply Chain Technology, Where the Supply Chain Meets the Value Chain", *Inbound Logistics*, vol 23, No. 1, January 2003, www.i2.com

Taub, A., COTS Software Licensing accompanied by Trepidation, *Working Paper*, MITRE Corporation, 2001,
http://www.mitre.org/news/edge_perspectives/march_01/ep_king.html

Bibliography (Chapter 9)

Defense Information Infrastructure (DII) Common Operating Environment (COE), Integration and Runtime Specification (I&RTS), Defense Information Systems Agency (DISA), *Report*, Revision 4.0, October 1999.

Goikoetxea, A., "Requirements Blueprint and Multiple Criteria for Distributed Database Design", *Ekaia Journal*, Euskal Herriko Unibersitateko Zientzi eta Teknologi Aldizkaria, University of the Basque Country, Euskadi, No. 14, 2001.

Goicoechea (Goikoetxea), A., L. Duckstein, and S. Zionts (editors), Multiple Criteria Decision Making (MCDM), Applications in Industry, Business, and Government, *Proceedings* of the IX-th International Conference on MCDM, Fairfax, Virginia, August 5-8, 1992.

Goicoechea (Goikoetxea), A., D.R. Hanson, and L. Duckstein, *Multi-objective Decision Analysis with Engineering and Business Applications*, John Wiley and Sons Publishers, 560 pages, New York, 1982.

Ozsu, M.T., and P. Valdiriez, *Principles of Distributed Database Systems*, , Prentice Hall, 1991.

Simon, A.R., *Strategic Database Technology: Management for the Year 2000*, Morgan Kaufmann Publishers, 1995.

Bibliography (Chapter 10)

ARIS Tool, www.ids-scheer.com

HyPerformix Workbench and Strategizer (formerly called SES/workbench)
http://www.hyperformix.com/products/workbench.htm

Mckencie, D., Tools for Capacity Planning, *Working Paper*,
    http://msdn.microsoft.com/library/default.asp?url=/library/en-
    us/dnbda/html/bdadotnetarch081.asp
Mitri, M., Teaching about the impact of transaction volume on system performance and
    capacity planning, *J. of Information Systems Education*, Vol 12, No. 2, 2005,
    http://www.jise.appstate.edu/12/065.pdf
Performance and Capacity Management, Sun Microsystems, *Working Paper*,
    http://www.sun.com/service/enterprise/performanceandcapacity.html
Savvion Process Modeler, http://www.savvion.com/products/
Proforma, http://www.proformacorp.com/provision/intro.asp
Will, R., EA Performance Planning, *Working Paper*, MITRE Corporation, 2004.

Bibliography (Chapter 11)

Energy 2003: When the Lights Went Out
    http://www.canadiangeographic.ca/blackout_2003/default.html
Energy Matters, May/June 2003, Et cetera,
    http://www.canadiangeographic.ca/Magazine/MJ03/Etcetera
Garvey, M.J., and M.K. McGee, "New Priorities", Information Week, Research, Sept 9,
    2002.
Global Transportation Network (GTN) System Capacity and Performance, Report
    USTPC 171-5.1AC, Lockheed Martin Corporation, Manassas, Virginia, 20
    November 1998.
Initiating the Business Continuity Plan, White Paper,
    http://www.vistastor.com/whitepapers/initiating_bcp.pdf
McFadden, F.R., J.A. Hoffer, and M.B. Prescott, Modern Database Management, 5th
    edition, Addison-Wesley, New York, 1999.
OMB Circular A-130, Office of Management and Budget, Revised, Transmittal
    Memorandum No. 4, 2002.
Out of the trash, into the bluebox, May/June 1999, À la carte
    http://www.canadiangeographic.ca/Magazine/MJ99/geomap.asp
Panettieri, J.C., Survival of the Fittest, *Information Week*, January 10, 1994.
Reynolds, G.W., Information Systems for Managers, 3rd. edition, West Publishing
    Company, New York, 1995.
The Open Group Architectural Framework website
    http://www.opengroup.org/togaf/start.htm

Bibliography (Chapter 12)

Perks, C., and T. Beveridge, *Guide to Enterprise IT Architecture*, Springer, New York, 2003.

Goikoetxea, A. (A. Goicoechea), A., D.R. Hansen, and L. Duckstein, *Multi-objective Decision Analysis with Engineering and Business Applications*, John Wiley and Sons Publishers, 560 pages, New York, 1982.

Goikoetxea, A. (A. Goicoechea), G.Z. Stakhiv, and F. Li, "Experimental Evaluation of Multiple Criteria Decision Support Systems (DSS) for Applications to Water Resources Planning", Water Resources Bulletin, Vol. 28, No. 1, February 1992.

DoD Memorandum, DoD Policy Change: Cancellation of the Technical Architecture Framework for Information Management (TAFIM), signed by J.S. Gansler, Under Secretary of Defense (Acquisition, Technology, and Logistics), Arthur L. Money, Assistant Secretary of Defense (Command, Control, Communications, and Intelligence), and J.L. Woodward, Jr. (Lieutenant General, USAF, Director for Command, Control, Communications, and Computer Systems), January 7, 2000.

Saaty, T.L., *Decision Making for Leaders: The Analytic Hierarchy Process for Decisions in a Complex World*, University of Pittsburgh Press, Pittsburgh, PA., 1990.

Spewak, S.H., Enterprise Architecture Planning: Developing a Blueprint for Data, Applications and Technology, Wiley Publishers, QED, New York 1992.

Vincke, P., M. Gassner, and B. Roy, *Multicriteria Decision-Aid*, Wiley and Sons, New York, 1992.

Zachman, J., "A Framework for Information Systems Architecture", IBM Systems Journal, Vol. 26, No. 3, 1987.

Finneran, T., "Enterprise Architecture: What And Why?" Data Administration Newsletter, URL: www.tdan.com

ArchitecturePlus
www.itpolicy.gsa.gov/mke/archplus/archhome.htm

C4ISR Architectures Working Group
www.c3i.osd.mil/org/cio/i3/AWG_Digital_Library/

Clinger-Cohen Act (Information Technology Management Reform Act), January 3, 1996
www.itpolicy.gsa.gov/mks/regs-leg/s1124_en.htm

The Clinton Administration's Policy on Critical Infrastructure Protection: Presidential Decision Directive 63, May 1998
www.ciao.gov/CIAO_Document_Library/paper598.html

Department of Defense Technical Reference Model, version 1.0, November 5, 1999
www-trm.itsi.disa.mil

Department of the Treasury CIO
www.treas.gov/cio/
Joint Technical Architecture (JTA)
http://jta.disa.mil/
Department of the Treasury Information Technology Strategic Plan 2000-2003,
November 17, 1999
www.treas.gov/cio/itsp.pdf
Treasury Enterprise Architecture Framework (TEAF), Department of the Treasury, Chief
Information Officer Council, July 2000, version1.
www.treas.gov/cio
Federal Agencies Information Architecture Working Group
www.itpolicy.gsa.gov/mke/archplus/group.htm
Federal Chief Information Officers Council
www.cio.gov
Federal Enterprise Architecture Framework, version 1, September 1999.
www.itpolicy.gsa.gov/mke/archplus/fedarch1.pdf
General Accounting Office, Assessing Risks and Returns: A Guide for Evaluating
Federal Agencies' IT Investment Decision-making, Version 1, GAO/AIMD-
10.1.13, February 1997
www.gao.gov/policy/itguide/
General Accounting Office, Information Technology Investment Management: A
Framework for Assessing and Improving Process Maturity, Exposure Draft,
Version 1, GAO/AIMD-10.1.23, May 2000
www.gao.gov/special.pubs/10_1_23.pdf
General Accounting Office, Measuring Performance and Demonstrating Results of
Information Technology Investments, AIMD-98-89, March 1998
www.gao.gov/special.pubs/ai98089.pdf
General Services Administration, Office of Information Technology
www.itpolicy.gsa.gov
Information Assurance Technical Framework Forum
www.iatf.net
Information Technology Investment Portfolio System (I-TIPS)
www.itips.gov
C4ISR Architecture Framework, version 2.0, Department of Defense, Architectures
Working Group (AWG), 18 December 1997.
Levels of Information System Interoperability (LISI)
http://www.c3i.osd.mil/org/cio/i3/AWG_Digital_Library/pdfdocs/lisi.pdf
OMB Circular A-130, Management of Federal Information Resources, Revised, February
8, 1996, www.whitehouse.gov/OMB/circulars/a130/a130.html
OMB Memorandum M-97-16, Information Technology Architectures, June 18, 1997
www.whitehouse.gov/OMB/memoranda/m97-16.html

OMB Memorandum M-00-07, Incorporating and Funding Security in Information
Systems Investments, 28 February 2000
www.whitehouse.gov/OMB/memoranda/m00-07.html

OMB, Proposed revision of OMB Circular No. A-130, in Federal Register, Vol. 65, No.
72, April 13, 2000, pages 19933-19939
www.whitehouse.gov/omb/fedreg/rev-a130.pdf

The Open Group Architecture Framework (TOGAF) Technical Reference Model, version
5, 1999, www.opengroup.org/togaf

U.S. Customs Service, Enterprise Architecture Blueprint, October 1999
www.itpolicy.gsa.gov/mke/archplus/eab.pdf

U.S. Customs Service, Technical Reference Model Introductory Guide, August 1999
www.itpolicy.gsa.gov/mke/archplus/trm.pdf

Zachman Institute for Framework Advancement, www.zifa.com

Bibliography (Chapter 13)

DoD Memorandum, *DoD Policy Change: Cancellation of the Technical Architecture Framework for Information Management (TAFIM)*, signed by J.S. Gansler, Under Secretary of Defense (Acquisition, Technology, and Logistics), Arthur L. Money, Assistant Secretary of Defense (Command, Control, Communications, and Intelligence), and J.L. Woodward, Jr. (Lieutenant General, USAF, Director for Command, Control, Communications, and Computer Systems), January 7, 2000.

Finneran, T., "Enterprise Architecture: What And Why?" *Data Administration Newsletter*, URL: www.tdan.com

Sowell, K., Demonstrated Impact of Architectural Analysis: The Value of Architectures and the Value of Uniform Guidance, *Study* conducted in support of the ISB/ISS, October 2004.

Sowell, K., Overview of the C4ISR Architecture Framework, Version 2.0, A Vehicle for Examining System Strategies in the Context of Business Processes and Mission Operations, *Study* for MITRE Corporation, October 1999.

Spewak, S.H., Enterprise Architecture Planning: Developing a Blueprint for Data, Applications and Technology, Wiley Publishers, QED, New York 1992.

Zachman, J., "A Framework for Information Systems Architecture", *IBM Systems Journal*, Vol. 26, No. 3, 1987.

Website References

ArchitecturePlus
www.itpolicy.gsa.gov/mke/archplus/archhome.htm

C4ISR Architecture Framework, Version 2.0: http://www.c3i.osd.mil/doc/index.html
C4ISR Architectures Working Group
   www.c3i.osd.mil/org/cio/i3/AWG_Digital_Library/
Clinger-Cohen Act (Information Technology Management Reform Act), January 3, 1996
   www.itpolicy.gsa.gov/mks/regs-leg/s1124_en.htm
The Clinton Administration's Policy on Critical Infrastructure Protection: Presidential
   Decision Directive 63, May 1998
   www.ciao.gov/CIAO_Document_Library/paper598.html
Department of Defense Technical Reference Model, version 1.0, November 5, 1999
   www-trm.itsi.disa.mil
Department of the Treasury CIO
   www.treas.gov/cio/
Joint Technical Architecture (JTA)
   http://jta.disa.mil/
Department of the Treasury Information Technology Strategic Plan 2000-2003,
   November 17, 1999
   www.treas.gov/cio/itsp.pdf
Treasury Enterprise Architecture Framework (TEAF), Department of the Treasury, Chief
   Information Officer Council, July 2000, version1.
   www.treas.gov/cio
Federal Agencies Information Architecture Working Group
   www.itpolicy.gsa.gov/mke/archplus/group.htm
Federal Chief Information Officers Council
   www.cio.gov
Federal Enterprise Architecture Framework, version 1, September 1999.
   www.itpolicy.gsa.gov/mke/archplus/fedarch1.pdf
General Accounting Office, Assessing Risks and Returns: A Guide for Evaluating
   Federal Agencies' IT Investment Decision-making, Version 1, GAO/AIMD-
   10.1.13, February 1997
   www.gao.gov/policy/itguide/
General Accounting Office, Information Technology Investment Management: A
   Framework for Assessing and Improving Process Maturity, Exposure Draft,
   Version 1, GAO/AIMD-10.1.23, May 2000
   www.gao.gov/special.pubs/10_1_23.pdf
General Accounting Office, Measuring Performance and Demonstrating Results of
   Information Technology Investments, AIMD-98-89, March 1998
   www.gao.gov/special.pubs/ai98089.pdf
General Services Administration, Office of Information Technology
   www.itpolicy.gsa.gov
IEEE 1471, Recommended Practice for Architectural Description, DRAFT
   Information Assurance Technical Framework Forum
   www.iatf.net

Information Technology Investment Portfolio System (I-TIPS)
www.itips.gov

C4ISR Architecture Framework, version 2.0, Department of Defense, Architectures Working Group (AWG), 18 December 1997.

Levels of Information System Interoperability (LISI)
http://www.c3i.osd.mil/org/cio/i3/AWG_Digital_Library/pdfdocs/lisi.pdf

OMB Circular A-130, Management of Federal Information Resources, Revised, February 8, 1996
www.whitehouse.gov/OMB/circulars/a130/a130.html

OMB Memorandum M-97-16, Information Technology Architectures, June 18, 1997
www.whitehouse.gov/OMB/memoranda/m97-16.html

OMB Memorandum M-00-07, Incorporating and Funding Security in Information Systems Investments, 28 February 2000
www.whitehouse.gov/OMB/memoranda/m00-07.html

OMB, Proposed revision of OMB Circular No. A-130, in Federal Register, Vol. 65, No. 72, April 13, 2000, pages 19933-19939
www.whitehouse.gov/omb/fedreg/rev-a130.pdf

The Open Group Architecture Framework (TOGAF) Technical Reference Model, version 5, 1999
www.opengroup.org/togaf

U.S. Customs Service, Enterprise Architecture Blueprint, October 1999
www.itpolicy.gsa.gov/mke/archplus/eab.pdf

U.S. Customs Service, Technical Reference Model Introductory Guide, August 1999
www.itpolicy.gsa.gov/mke/archplus/trm.pdf

Zachman Institute for Framework Advancement
www.zifa.com

Bibliography (Chapter 14)

Del Convenio SENA–MCC (1997) y la Actualidad: Propuesta para la Modernización de la Formación Profesional, 8 pages, 2004.

Proyecto CONIKA de Implantación de un modelo de Gestion de Centros de FP para el SENA, 18 pages, 2004.

Ministério de la Protección Social, decreto de 2003 Por el cual se modifica la estructura interna y las funciones de las dependencias del Servicio Nacional de Aprendizaje SENA, 40 pages, Bogota, 2003.

Visión del SENA al 2006, Powerpoint file, 59 slides. En ejercicio de las facultades que le confiere el numeral 16 del artículo 189 de la Constitución Política y con sujeción a los principios contenidos en el artículo 54 de la ley 489 de 1998.

Goikoetxea, A., "A Mathematical Framework for Enterprise Architecture Representation and Design", J. of Information Technology and Decision Making, World Scientific Press, Volume 3, Number 1, March 2004.

Goikoetxea, A., "Requirements Blueprint and Multiple Criteria for Distributed Database Design", J. EKARIA., Universidad del Pais Vasco, Zenbakia 14, 2001.

Goikoetxea, A., and O. Lizarralde, "Metodologia de Indicadores e-Democracia para una Encuesta en 74 Parlamentos y Regiones Legislativas en la Union Europea", 5th European Conference on e-Learning, e-Business, e-Democracy, e-Government, and e-Cooperation, Bucarest, ROMANIA, October 21-22, 2004.

Vision del SENA al 2006: "SENA: Una Empresa de Conocimiento", 24 pages, Bogota, September 2002.

Bibliography (Chapter 15)

AMICE Consortium, Open System Architecture for CIM, Research Report of ESPRIT Project 688, 1, Springer-Verlag publishers, 1989.

Arbab, F., et al., "State of the Art in Architecture Frameworks and Tools", *Telematica Instituut*, 8 May 2002, www.telin.nl

Bernus, P., and L. Nmes, "A Framework to Define a Generic Enterprise Reference Architecture and Methodology (GERAM architectural framework)", *Report MTM 366*, CSIRO, Preston, Victoria, Australia, Dec 1994.

Blanc, X., Gervais, M-P, and Le Delliou, J., "The Specifications Exchange Service of an RM-ODP Framework", Enterprise Distributed Object Computing (EDOC) Conference *Proceedings*, pages 86-90, 25-28 Sept 2000.

Goicoechea (Goikoetxea), A., D.R. Hansen, and L. Duckstein, *Multi-objective Decision Analysis with Engineering and Business Applications*, John Wiley and Sons Publishers, 560 pages, New York, 1982.

Goicoechea (Goikoetxea), A., E.Z. Stakhiv, and F. Li., "Experimental Evaluation of Multiple Criteria Decision Models", *Water Resources Buletin* Vol. 28., No. 1, 1992.

Gransier, T., and Schonewolf, W. (editors), "Special Issue: Validation of CIMOSA", *Computers in Industry J.*, 27 (2), 95-213, October 1995.

McDavid, D.W., "A Standard for Business Architecture", *IBM Systems Journal*, Volume 38, No. 1, 1999

McGovern, J., S.W. Ambler, M.E. Stevens, J.L. Linn, V. Shran, and E.K. Jo, A Practical Guide to Enterprise Architecture, 306 pages, Prentice Hall, New Jersey, 2004

Perks, C., and T. Beveridge, *Guide to Enterprise IT Architecture*, Springer, New York, 2003.

"Project Herinrichting Informatievooziening Defensie [PHIDEF]", Netherlands Ministry of Defense *Report*, the Netherlands, 1997.

Saha, P., "Analyzing the Open Group Architecture Framework from the GERAM Perspective", *Working Paper*, Institute of Systems Science, National University of Singapore, Singapure, 2005.

Schekkerman, J., *How to Survive in the Jungle of Enterprise Architecture Frameworks, Creating or choosing an Enterprise Architecture Framework*, 2nd Edition, Trafford Publishing, Victoria, Canada, 2004

Spewak, S.H., *Enterprise Architecture Planning: Developing a Blueprint for Data, Applications and Technology*, Wiley Publishers, QED, New York 1992.

Vallecillo, A., RM-ODP: The ISO Reference Model for Open Distributed Processing, Working Paper, ETSI Informatica, Universidad de Malaga, 2005, av@lcc.uma.es

Williams, T.J., "Pera and GERAM, Enterprise Reference Architectures for Enterprise Integration", *Working Paper*, Institute for Interdisciplinary Engineering Studies, Purdue University, Indiana, USA, 2005.

Vernadat, F., "Modelling CIM Enterprise with CIMOSA", in *Proceedings*, Rensselaer's Second International Conference on Computer Integrated Manufacturing, 236-243, May 1990.

Youngs, R., D. Redmond-Pyle, P. Spaas, and E. Kahan, "A Standard for Architecture Description", *IMB Systems Journal*, Volume 38, No. 1, 1999.

Zachman, J., "A Framework for Information Systems Architecture", *IBM Systems Journal*, Vol. 26, No. 3, 1987.

Bibliography (Chapter 16)

Goicoechea (Goikoetxea), A., D.R. Hansen, and L. Duckstein, Multi-objective Decision Analysis with Engineering and Business Applications, John Wiley and Sons Publishers, 560 pages, New York, 1982.

Goicoechea (Goikoetxea), A., E.Z. Stakhiv, and F. Li., "Experimental Evaluation of Multiple Criteria Decision Models", Water *Resources Buletin* Vol. 28., No. 1, 1992.

Hagan, P., "Seven High-Level EA Evaluation Criteria", Working Paper, MITRE Corporation, McLean, Virginia, September 2003.

Goicoechea (Goikoetxea), L. Duckstein, and S. Zionts (editors), *Multiple Criteria Decision Making in Business, Industry, and Government*, Book of Proceedings, IX-th International Conference on MCDM, Fairfax, Virginia, August 5-8, 1992

"A Framework for Assessing and Improving Enterprise Architecture Management (version 1.1)" *GAO Report GAO-03-584G*, US General Accounting Office, April 2003, http://www.gao.gov/

General Accounting Office (GAO), description of GAO's EA Maturity Model with 5 stages, www.gao.gov/

"Enterprise Architecture Use Across the Federal Government can be Improved", *GAO Report GAO-02-6*, General Accounting Office (GAO), description of GAO's EA

Maturity Model with 5 stages and results of a survey of some 93 Federal Agencies and their own EA work in progress, http://www.gao.gov/

Hite, R., "Briefing on GAO´s Enterprise Architecture Maturity Framework (Version 1.1)", e-Government Enterprise Architecture Conference, 12 September 2003, http://www.e-gov.com/events/2003/ea/downloads/

Allega, P., "Making Enterprise Architecture Count: Metrics in Action, Meta Group", *Working Paper*, metagroup.com,
http://www.aemes.fi.upm.es/docum/meta/old/Metrics%20in%20Action.pdf

MacDonald, M., "Delivering Metrics in the Enterprise Architecture", *Working Paper*, Visual Mining Inc., http://chartworks.com/EAConf/EAConf-MMacDonald-VisualMining1.ppt

"Leadership Remains Key to Agencies Making Progress on Enterprise Architecture Efforts", General Accounting Office (GAO) *Report* GAO-04-40, 17 November 2003, www.gao.gov/cgi-bin/getrpt?GAO-4-40, also www.gao.gov/highlights/d0440high.pdf

Goikoetxea, A., D.R. Hansen, and L. Duckstein, *Multi-objective Decision Analysis with Engineering and Business Applications*, Book, John Wiley and Sons Publishers, 560 pages, New York, 1982.

Goikoetxea, A., E.Z. Stakhiv, and F. Li., Experimental Evaluation of Multiple Criteria Decision Models, *Water Resources Bulleting*, Vol. 28., No. 1, 1992.

Perks, C., and T. Beveridge, *Guide to Enterprise IT Architecture*, Springer, New York, 2003.

Spewak, S.H., *Enterprise Architecture Planning: Developing a Blueprint for Data, Applications and Technology*, Wiley Publishers, QED, New York 1992.

Zachman, J., "A Framework for Information Systems Architecture", *IBM Systems Journal*, Vol. 26, No. 3, 1987.

The Performance Reference Model, Version 1.0, Federal Enterprise Architecture Program Management Office (FEAPMO), July 2003.

Bibliography (Chapter 17)

Fountain, A.E., *Building the Virtual State: Information, Technology, and Institutional Change,* Brookings Institution Press, 2001.

Martin Granados, I., *Utopias y Realidades del Gobierno Electronico (e-Government) en España, Mapa Descriptivo,* 1st. Congreso On-Line del Observatorio para la CiberSociedad, http://cibersociedad.rediris.es/congreso

Martinez, R., J. Goikolea, A. Goikoetxea, and O.Lizarralde, "e-Democracy Indicators: A Hierarchy of e-Democracy Indicators and their use in an ICT Survey of 74 Parliaments and Regions with Legislative Capacity in the European Union (EU)", Proceedings, International Association for the Development of the Information Society (IADIS), Qawra, Malta, 27-30 June 2005.

Goikoetxea, A., and O. Lizarralde, "A Methodology for the Development of e-Democracy Indicators: A Three-Phase Approach to a Survey on the Use of the Technologies of Information and Communication (TICs) in 74 Parliaments and Regions in the European Community (EC), Phase 1", Proceedings, 5th European and International Conference on e-Commerce, e-Government, e-Democracy, and e-Business, Bucharest, ROMANIA, October 21-22, 2004.

Rajput, W. E., *e-Commerce Systems Architecture and Applications*, Artech House, London, www.artechhouse.com, 2000

Rios Insua, D., *Mas Allá del Gobieno Electronico: Hacia la Democracia Electronica (e-Democracy)*, Revista datospersonales.org, Madrid, Spain, No. 8, 30 March 2004.

Pesquera, M.A., *e-Logistics: Comercio Electronico y Gestion Logistica*, Novoprint, SA, Barcelona, 2000.

XML W3C Working Draft, http://www.w3.org/pub

JPEG home page, www.jpeg.org

MPEG home page, www.chiariglione.org/mpeg

Nueno, J. L., J. Viscarri, and J. Villanueva., Porqué comercia tan poco el comercio electrónico: Internet y los consumidores Españoles, IDELCO Press, Madrid 2000.

Finneran, T., "Enterprise Architecture: What And Why?" Data Administration Newsletter, URL: www.tdan.com

II Congreso Internacional de Sociedad de la Informacion y el Conocimiento, www.cisic.org/cisic2004

Casacuberta, D., iniciativa de e-Democracia, www.edemocracia.com

Bibliography (Chapter 18)

Board Briefing on IT Governance, It Governance Institute, Information Systems Audit and Control Foundation, ISBN 1-893209-27-X, Rolling Meadows IL 60008, 2001.

Office of Management and Budget, Circular No. A-130, Management of Federal Information Resources, November 30, 2002.

Federal Enterprise Architecture Framework (FEAF) Version 1.1, Federal CIO Council, September 1999.

DoD Architecture Framework Version 1.0 (Draft)

Treasury Enterprise Architecture Framework (TEAF) Version 1, Department of the Treasury Chief Information Officer Council, July 2000.

Enterprise Architecture Development Tool-Kit, V 2.2, National Association of State Chief Information Officers (NASCIO), July 2002 (provides guidance on roles).

The President's Management Agenda, Fiscal Year 2002, Executive Office of the President, Office of Management and Budget.

Using the Business and Performance Reference Models to Help Improve Citizen Services, Norman Lorentz, Federal Enterprise Architecture Program Management Office OMB, October 7-8.

Kauzlarich, V., "Lessons Learned in EA Planning, Design and Deployment", Working Paper, Mitre Corporation, McLean, Virginia, USA, 2004.

The Business Reference Model Version 1.0, FEA PMO, July 2002.

Performance Reference Model Development, FEA PMO, October 29, 2002.

A Framework for Information Systems Architecture, John Zachman, IBM Systems Journal, September 1987.

Zachman, John, personal communication (e-mail) October 18, 2002 on risks associated with slivers.

Based on diagram from Diane Reeves, OCC.

See 18, 19.

Diane Reeves, personal Communication, E-mail, EA Maturity Assessment Model, July 16, 2002.

A Practical Guide to the Federal Enterprise Architecture, Version 1.0, Chief Information Officer Council, February 2001.

Enterprise Architecture Planning, Steven Spewak, 1995.

Enterprise Architecture Use Across the Federal Government Can Be Improved GAO-02-6, United States General Accounting Office, February 2002.

OMB Leadership Critical to Making Needed Enterprise Architecture and E-government Progress GAO-02-389T, United States General Accounting Office, March 2002.

Enterprise Architecture Desk Reference Executive Summary Defining the Role of the Enterprise Architecture, META Group, 2002.

GARTNER GROUP.

Enterprise Architectures Conference Proceedings, META Group and DCI, October 8-10, 2002.

Implementing Enterprise Architecture – Putting Quality information into the hands of Oil and Gas Knowledge Workers, Cox, G.A., Johnston, RM, Palermo, R.M., Society of Petroleum Engineers, SPE 68794.

Evaluation Criteria for Meeting the Department of Commerce Information Technology Architecture Requirements http://www.doc.gov/cio/itmhweb/arch_criteria.html

Questions or Criteria for Evaluating Agency Enterprise Architectures, personal communication email, Gerald Stoopman received August 28, 2002, (believed criteria from OMB).

Treasury Bureau Enterprise Architecture (EA) Status Update, Final Version for FY 2002, May 20, 2002, personal communication email, George Brundage.

USIGS 2005 Architecture Evaluation, Stephen A. Hirsch, MITRE Corporation.

SEI ATAM MATERIALS.

Enterprise Architecture – What Works, What Doesn't, George Brundage, Scott Bernard, Col. Bill Nelson, Lewis Sanford, Briefing Slides, Oct 8, 2002.

Lessons Learned, Notions, Tips, and Tricks, Based on Years of Enterprise Architecture Experience, Michael Tiemann.

Bibliography (Chapter 19)

A Practical Guide to Federal Enterprise Architecture, Chief Information Officer (CIO) Council, Version 1.0, February 2001.

Cook, M.A., *Building Enterprise Information Architectures: Re-Engineering Information Systems,* Prentice Hall, 1996.

Hagan, P., Governance-Related Issues for the Federal Enterprise Architecture Framework (FEAF) Revision Working Group, Working Paper, January 2003.

"Information Technology Investment Evaluation Guide: Assessing Risks and Returns", *GAO Report* GAO/AI-10.1.13, February 1997.

"A guide for Evaluating Federal Agencies' IT Investment Decision Making", *GAO Report* GAO/AI-10.1.13, February 1997.

Rechtin, E., and M.W. Maier, The Art of Systems Architecting, CRC Press, New York, 1997.

Zachman Institute for Framework Advancement, www.zifa.com

References (Chapter 20)

Cohon, J.L., Multiobjective Programming and Planning, Academic Press, New York, 1978.

Enderton, H.B., *Elements of Set Theory*, Academic Press, 1997.

Fandel, G., and T. Gal, *Multiple Criteria Decision Making, Theory and Applications*, Springer-Verlag, New York, 1980.

Hamburger, P. A. Hajnal, and A. Matte, *Set Theory*, Cambridge University Press, 300 pages, 1999.

Goikoetxea, A., "A Mathematical Framework for Enterprise Architecture Representation and Design," *International Journal of Information Technology & Decision Making (ITDM)*, Vol. 3, No. 1, March 2004.

Goicoechea, A. (Goikoetxea, A.), D.R. Hansen, and L. Duckstein, *Multi-objective Decision Analysis with Engineering and Business Applications*, John Wiley and Sons Publishers, 560 pages, New York, 1982.

Spewak, S.H., *Enterprise Architecture Planning: Developing a Blueprint for Data, Applications and Technology*, Wiley Publishers, QED, New York 1992.

Zachman, J., "A Framework for Information Systems Architecture", *IBM Systems Journal*, Vol. 26, No. 3, 1987.

Enterprise Life Cycle (ELC): Quick Reference Guide, Computer Sciences Corporation, CSC publication PRIME-PPMT-C2T1-006, New Carrollton, MD, 2002.

Goicoechea, A., "Requirements Blueprint and Multiple Criteria for Distributed Database Design", Proceedings of the International Council on Systems Engineering (INCOSE), Mid-Atlantic Regional Conference, Reston, Virginia April 6-8, 2000.

Goicoechea, A., "Requirements Blueprint and Multiple Criteria for Distributed Database Design", Ekaia Journal, Euskal Herriko Unibersitateko Zientzi eta Teknologi Aldizkaria, University of the Basque Country, Euskadi, No. 14, 2001.

Defense Information Infrastructure (DII) Common Operating Environment (COE), Integration and Runtime Specification (I&RTS), Defense Information Systems Agency (DISA), Report, Revision 4.0, October 1999.

Principles of Distributed Database Systems, by M.T. Ozsu and P. Valdiriez, Prentice Hall, 1991.

Multiple Criteria Decision Making (MCDM), Applications in Industry, Business, and Government, by A. Goicoechea, L. Duckstein, and S. Zionts (editors), Proceedings of the IX-th International Conference on MCDM, Fairfax, Virginia, August 5-8, 1992.

Multi-objective Decision Analysis with Engineering and Business Applications, by A. Goicoechea, D.R. Hanson, and L. Duckstein, John Wiley and Sons Publishers, 560 pages, New York, 1982.

Strategic Database Technology: Management for the Year 2000, by A.R. Simon, Morgan Kaufmann Publishers, 1995.

Wymore, A.W., Systems Engineering Methodology for Interdisciplinary Teams, Wiley, New York, 1976.

Appendix

Contents and Instructions for Installation of Software CDs

System Architect CD

To install System Architect, get an installation code by visiting: http://www.telelogic.com/eapda/, and fill out a form that will auto-send to you an e-mail with a code. This code allows you to use the software for 30 days.

(1) Install Products

System Architect (SA):	Powerful modelling software designed to provide all the tools necessary for development of successful enterprise systems.
SA Information Web Publisher:	An add-on option to System Architect that enables you to generate complete websites of model information from the SA repository (called Encyclopedia).
SA Compare:	An add-on option to System Architect that enables you to compare two SA encyclopedias.
SA Catalog Manager:	An add-on option to System Architect that enables you to manage and specify role-based access control to shared, enterprise-level encyclopedias.

(2) Browse CD Products   Enables you to browse through all CD
directories, including the Manuals,
which contains these manuals:
- Conversion.pdf
- Extensibility_usrprops.pdf
- Extensibility_VBA.pdf
- Installation Guide.pdf
- Popkin_Process.pdf
- UserGuide.pdf

(3) Contact Us   Mailing addresses, telephone numbers,
Fax, websites, and e-mail addresses of
Telelogic Inc. in the USA and Europe.

Enterprise Architect CD

To install Enterprise Architect simply place the CD in D drive of your
laptop or PC.

(1) Enterprise Architect Trial CD (3 options)

- Installation File for the trial version of Enterprise Architect
  Version 6.5 Build 797

- Installation File for the trial Linux Version of Enterprise
  Architect Version 6.5 Build 797

- Installation File for the read only Version of Enterprise Architect
  Version 6.5 Build 797

(2) MDG Integration for Visual Studio

At the click of a button, Model Driven Generation (MDG) Integration
allows you to reverse engineer and generate .Net code from UML
elements using EA's template driven Code Engineering Framework.

- Installation file for the MDG Integration for Visual Studio 2005.
- Multimedia demonstration of MDG Integration for Visual Studio
  2005.

(3) MDG Link for Visual Studio.NET and Eclipse

MDG Link creates a close coupling between EA and the development environment, MDG Link for Visual Studio.NET to provide a lightweight bridge between EA and Visual Studio.NET 2003, whilst MDG Link for Eclipse is used to bridge between EA and Eclipse

(4) MDG Technologies

The Model Driven Generator (MDG) Technologies allow for a logical collection of resources pertaining to a specific technology to be bundled into one centralized location in Enterprise Architect. With MDG Technologies the user has the option of granular importation of UML Profiles, UML Patterns, Code templates and Language types to be contained in a single, easy to access area contained in the Enterprise Architect Resource View.

(5) UML Resources

- EA User Manual in PDF format (on CD)
- EA User Manual (online)
- UML Tutorials
- UML Patterns, and
- XML Schema Generation

(6) Contact Us

If you would like to purchase Enterprise Architect, please visit our purchase page at www.sparxsystems.com.au/products/ea_purchase.html. For further information, please contact us at sales@sparxsystems.com.au.

Index

Biographical Sketch

Ambrose Goikoetxea, Ph.D.
agoikoetxeal@euskalnet.net
Department of Computer Sciences
Mondragon University, www.mondragon.edu
Euskadi

January 2006

Dr. Ambrose Goikoetxea has over 20 years of experience in the design and application of systems engineering methods and tools to problems in software engineering, business process modeling, Enterprise Architecture (EA) planning, design and assessment, decision support system (DSS) design, database (DB) design, transportation systems modeling, data fusion for object classification, and design of multiple criteria decision support systems (MCDSS).

B.S. in Aeronautical Engineering, M.S. in Mechanical Engineering, and Ph.D. in Systems, Industrial Engineering, and Operations Research from University of Arizona, EE.UU, 1980. Since February 2004 he is a Professor in the Department of Computer Sciences, Mondragon University (MU), Euskadi (Basque Country), where he teaches UML software engineering courses and is co-principal investigator in several EA projects; also, as Director of the e-Democracy Project he leads a multi-discipline team in the creation of indicators to assess the implementation of the information and communication technologies (ICTs) in 74 Parliaments and Regions with legislative authority in the

European Union (EU); application of methodologies of Enterprise Architectures to needs in medium and large corporations to improve productivity and decision making.

In April 1999 he joined the Software Engineering Center (W908) of the MITRE Corporation, Virginia, EE.UU, as a Sr. Information Systems Engineer. In that capacity he supported business systems architecture development in the IRS Modernization Enterprise Architecture, applications test planning and business rules integration in the Customer Account Data Engine (CADE), and performance assessment of messaging middleware (MQSeries). At MITRE he also completed an architecture design to support intra-site and inter-site data backup, failover, and recovery for the Army's Defense Message System (DMS). While at MITRE he co-organized the 2003-2004 workshop series on "The Theory and Practice of Enterprise Architecture Planning, Design, and Assessment", with over 50 presentations contributed by scientists in all 6 MITRE regions. Prior to joining MITRE he was the Performance-and-Capacity lead engineer for the Global Transportation Network (GTN) at Lockheed Martin Corporation, in Manassas, Virginia (1997-1999) where he created the system performance and capacity planning (PCP) group, designed and instituted PCP processes, responsible for setting up a suite of modeling and measurement tools.

Associate Professor in the Systems Engineering Department, George Mason University, Virginia, EE.UU, 1985-1990, teaching engineering courses and conducting research in analytical models for decision making. Technical Director of STATCOM Inc., design of decision support systems (DSS), 1990-1995. President and Technical Director of Integrated Technologies and Research, Inc., from 1995 to 1997, where he designed and developed decision support systems for the U.S. Army Corps of Engineers. In 1985 and 1986 he was NASA-ASEE Research Fellow at the Goddard Space Flight Center, in Greenbelt, Maryland, designing decision support systems for NASA managers to assist with systems engineering and configuration functions of space projects; also, a member of the Man-Machine Interface Design Group. 1979, NASA-ASEE Research Fellow, Jet Propulsion Laboratory of the California Institute of Technology (Cal-Tech); evaluation and selection of projects in the areas of solar-thermo power plants, underground nuclear plant location analysis, and urban public transportation systems. Organizer and General Chairman of the *IX-th International Conference on Multiple Criteria Decision Making (MCDM)*, Fairfax, Virginia, August 5-8, 1990. Dr. Goikoetxea is a recognized speaker at international conferences on system performance modeling, decision analysis, distributed database design, and risk analysis. A member of several engineering professional organizations, and a lecturer in the Department of Engineering Management, Department of Operations Research, and the Department of Management Science of George Washington University, 1990-Present. He is the author of over 20 published papers and 3 technical books taught in engineering, information systems, mathematics, economics, and business universities in over 30 universities in the USA, Latin America, Asia, and Europe.

Technical Chair and co-organizer (with Universidade Aberta of Portugal and other universities in the European Union) of the IADIS (*International Association for the Development of the Information Society*) international conferences on applied computing and web-based communities (www.iadis.org/ac2006, and www.iadis.org/wbc2006) held in San Sebastian, 25-28 February 2006; over 250 professionals from 20-25 countries participated in this event.

37720718R00287

Made in the USA
San Bernardino, CA
24 August 2016